Real Estate
and the Law

Real Estate and the Law

Robert N. Corley
University of Georgia

Peter J. Shedd
University of Georgia

Charles F. Floyd
University of Georgia

RANDOM HOUSE
Business Division  New York

First Edition

9876543

Library of Congress Cataloging in Publication Data

Corley, Robert Neil.
  Real estate and the law.

  Includes index.
  1. Vendors and purchasers—United States. 2. Real property—United States. 3. Land use—Law and legislation—United States. 4. Real estate business—Law and legislation—United States. I. Shedd, Peter J. II. Floyd, Charles F. III. Title.
KF665.C58   346.7304'3   81-20992
ISBN 0-394-32546-X   347.30643   AACR2

Manufactured in the United States of America

Preface

This book is designed to cover the subject matter offered in a traditional real estate law course. In addition, economic and financial topics as they relate to legal issues involving real estate are included. The professor can utilize this book in any number of ways to meet the needs of a pure real estate law course or a course with a broader perspective. This text is not limited to the real estate student interested in a brokerage career. Although we believe that such a student will find this book most useful, other students interested in real estate in general and real estate transactions in particular should find the coverage of this book to be beneficial.

In order to enhance the readability of this book and the organization of any course using this book, we have included numerous section headings that identify the materials discussed. Another learning technique includes review questions and problems at the end of each chapter.

Foremost, *Real Estate and the Law* is an attempt to provide a text that incorporates into textual material actual court decisions as teaching tools. We have emphasized the use of case decisions since they represent a major source of legal principles to which real estate students typically have not been exposed. As present and potential parties to real estate transactions, students likely will encounter legal issues that ultimately may be resolved by the court system. Therefore, throughout this book we have used case decisions in two forms.

First, interspersed in the text of each chapter there are approximately six cases that have been briefed. These briefs reinforce and illustrate the point made in the text immediately preceding the case. This briefed form provides the student with the essential elements of each case and makes the case more easily understood while saving the student valuable time.

Second, at the end of each chapter there are two or three edited court opinions. These cases are footnoted in the text of the chapter. The edited opinions appear as written by the judge. We have omitted citations in order to enhance the readability of the cases. Wherever actual language of the opinion has been deleted, an ellipis appears. Generally the omitted language involves an issue or procedural matter that is irrelevant to the purpose of the case as used to illustrate a point in the text. These edited cases help demonstrate the type of analysis and reasoning used by judges in reaching their conclusions.

We believe that *Real Estate and the Law* is flexible in its approach. In other words, either the briefed or edited cases or both can be assigned without materially altering the coverage of the subject matter.

The first eight chapters of *Real Estate and the Law* set forth the general legal principles related to real estate. After completion of Chapter 1, which describes the subject matter called real estate; Chapter 2, which discusses various ownership interests; and Chapter 3, which continues with easements, licenses, profits, and water rights; the student will have a basic background of the myriad real estate interests that exist. Chapter 4 includes methods of acquiring these ownership interests in real estate. Chapter 5 examines the various deed documents that are so vital to many transfers of real estate interests. Chapters 6 and 7 discuss tools and techniques of private and public controls of land use. Finally, Chapter 8 involves issues of taxation and real estate. These first eight chapters prepare the student to study and understand transactions related to real estate.

Chapters 9 through 16 are concerned with real estate transactions. Chapters 9 and 10 deal with real estate brokerage principles. In Chapter 11 we examine the traditional sales contract and alternative types of contracts. Establishing and protecting title to real estate is the topic of Chapter 12. Chapter 13 discusses closing a real estate sales transaction. Legal aspects of financing the purchase of real estate is the topic of Chapter 14. Chapter 15 describes mechanic's liens and how they relate to real estate transactions. Chapter 16 concludes the book with a look at the vital landlord-tenant relationship.

While preparing this book, we have kept in mind the fundamental differences in the educational needs of business people as opposed to lawyers. We have presented the material in such a way to illustrate legal principles that must be considered in the students' present and future decision-making process. It is our hope that we have met the need to provide a book that combines good examples of case decisions as illustrative teaching tools with readable textual materials.

Finally, we would like to thank our colleagues whose reviews and helpful suggestions were of valuable assistance in the final preparation of this manuscript. We are grateful to:

H.M. Bohlman, Arizona State University
Michael Bottelo, El Camino College
Glenn E. Laughlin, Oklahoma State University
Zach Mason, North Texas State University
Nicholas Ordway, University of Texas at Arlington

ROBERT N. CORLEY
PETER J. SHEDD
CHARLES F. FLOYD

Contents

ix

Table of Cases

Real Estate and the Law

1

Introduction

1. Scope of the Text

The subject matter of this book is the law as it relates to real property. As will be developed later, property is best defined as "the bundle of rights" that a person has in relation to something. The adjective *real* when defining property refers to land. Throughout this book we will be concerned with the law and legal principles as applied to the ownership, possession, and use of land, and with the law as it relates to a variety of transactions involving real property. For example, law impacts the land sales transaction in the area of brokerage, contracts, duties and rights of the participants, financing, and acquisition of good title. In addition to discussing these concepts relating to real property law, this book will also examine the impact of government on the ownership, transfer, and use of real estate.

This first chapter provides background material essential to understanding the more technical material in the chapters that follow. This background information includes the meaning of various terms as well as the distinction between real and personal property. Finally, this chapter discusses the various methods of describing real estate.

Sources of Real Estate Law

2.   Introduction

The law of real property is based on both statutes and the common law. By *statutory law,* we mean that a legislative body has enacted a law, usually called a statute but sometimes called an ordinance. The term *common law* is used to describe the legal principles that are announced originally by courts. The common law is judge-made law.

The constitution of most states incorporates the common law of England as legal principles in this country. Today, courts still decide cases that result in the creation of new legal principles. Case law or common law continues to provide numerous precedents relating to real property issues. Courts also have the important and sometimes difficult task of interpreting statutes or ordinances. Thus, the principles of real property law discussed in this text are based on a combination of legislative actions and court decisions.

3.   Legislation

The United States Constitution is the single most important source of all law, including those affecting real property. The Federal Constitution and the various state constitutions set forth the general guidelines of all legal rights. In particular, the Fifth Amendment to the United States Constitution directly protects property rights when it states:

> No person shall . . . be deprived of life, liberty, or property, without due process of law; nor shall private property be taken for public use, without just compensation.

Specifically, this provision prevents the United States government from depriving persons of their real property without due process and without just compensation. Through the Fourteenth Amendment to the Constitution, state and local governments also are prohibited from denying a person property without due process and without just compensation.

As a result of this constitutional provision, the question frequently arises: Has a "taking" of real estate occurred? In other words, what legislative actions constitute a taking, or when does compensation have to be paid because of an act of a government? These issues are discussed in detail in Chapters 6 and 7. Remember throughout any study of law that the United States Constitution is the supreme law of the land and that any legislation that conflicts with a constitutional provision may be declared to be invalid or unconstitutional by the courts.

Legislation passed by the Congress or a state legislature usually is called a statute. Acts passed by local governments usually are referred to as ordinances. These statutes or ordinances are a major source of real property law. Numerous examples of statutes and ordinances are found throughout the chapters which follow. Although these legislative acts and others do differ among the various states, throughout this book we present the generally accepted principles followed by most states. If the principles are to be applied to a specific factual situation, the law of the state involved should be checked.

Legislation typically is written in broad language so that its application in any given factual situation may not be definite. Indeed, many times legislative bodies will leave gaps in statutes or ordinances. Through their interpretation, courts become the gap-fillers, thereby supplying a vitally important source of real property law. Thus courts create precedent and affect real property law by judicial interpretation of legislation.

4. Court Decisions and Judicial Remedies

Court decisions are so crucial to the development and understanding of real estate law that we use examples of these decisions throughout this book. In each chapter appellate court decisions are presented in a briefed form. At the end of each chapter, several edited decisions also are included.[1]

Historically, the judicial system was divided into courts of law and courts of equity. As a result, the remedies available to litigants have been described as either legal or equitable. The legal remedy is dollar damages, and in suits filed in a court of law the plaintiff usually is seeking a money judgment. This legal remedy is used when a monetary award will place the aggrieved party in as good a position as if the legal wrong had not been committed.

[1]For the student who is not familiar with the process of litigation or with some of the terms that are used in these cases, it is helpful to trace a lawsuit from beginning to end. See page 22 for the steps in a typical lawsuit.

A typical use of the legal remedy of dollar damages is to recover for a *trespass.* A trespass occurs anytime an uninvited party comes onto the owner's land. An uninvited person trespasses by entering another's land even though the act is unintentional. For example, a person who innocently takes a walk through a wooded area likely could trespass on several people's real estate. This concept of trespassing is discussed several places in this book with regard to the duty the landowner owes to a trespasser and to the liability of the trespasser to the landowner. In these latter cases at law, the landowner usually is seeking money damages.

In certain situations courts will conclude that money is insufficient to make all parties "whole" again. In these cases the relief sought is said to be equitable. Typical equitable remedies include the granting of an injunction, specific performance, or rescission of an agreement. An *injunction,* in essence, is a court order to stop or enjoin some activity that is damaging someone. A typical use for an injunction is to stop the existence of a nuisance. A *nuisance* may result when the land of one owner is used in a way that unreasonably or unlawfully interferes with neighboring owners' use of their land. An industrial plant emitting noxious odors near a residential area may create a nuisance. Using this nuisance theory as a method of controlling use of land is discussed in detail in Chapter 7.

Case 1.1

Norval Hillmer operated a trailer-court business on land that he owned. Within one-half mile of this land, the McConnell Brothers operated a rabbit-processing plant. At this plant, dead rabbits were butchered; the meat was frozen; the hides were cured and stored; and the carcasses were transported to a dump. Norval Hillmer filed suit seeking to enjoin the McConnell Brothers' processing plant as a nuisance. Hillmer relied on a state statute which prohibited the depositing of a carcass of any dead animal from any slaughterhouse within one-half mile of any inhabited dwelling where the same may become an annoyance to any person.

Issue: Is this process plant a nuisance that the court may enjoin?

Decision: Yes. An injunction is granted.

Reasons: The evidence produced at the trial of the case showed that the noxious odors from the McConnell Brothers' plant was annoying and was within one-half of a mile from Hillmer's trailer-court business. Having found that these facts are within the meaning of the applicable statute, a judgment and order to close this plant was entered.

Hillmer v. McConnell Brothers, 414 P.2d 972 (Wyo. 1966).

Specific performance is a court order that a promised act be completed as promised. Courts often will grant specific performance of a contract for the sale of an unique item. For example, since no two pieces of real estate are exactly alike, courts can order that a seller in breach of a contract specifically perform the contract by deeding the property to the buyer. This remedy places the parties in the position they would have been in if the agreement had been completed. Most courts agree that the right to seek specific performance does not deprive the aggrieved party of the right to seek money damages too.

Case 1.2

Bacmo entered into a contract to purchase real estate from Strange. Strange refused to convey the title, and Bacmo brought this action, claiming he should be entitled to specific performance and damages incident to Strange's refusal to perform under the contract.

Issue: Is a claimant who is entitled to specific performance also entitled to money damages?

Decision: Yes. A claim for specific performance does not preclude a claim for damages.

Reasons: The overwhelming weight of authority is to the effect that the disappointed purchaser may be awarded money damages for the seller's delay in making the conveyance, in addition to being granted specific performance. If Strange had conveyed on time, Bacmo could have renovated the property for $7,000 less than at the time of the trial and could have made a profit of $12,200 by renting the property during this period. He should be entitled to recoup his damages as well as be entitled to the conveyance.

Bacmo Associates v. Strange, 338 A.2d 487 (D.C. App. 1978).

Another example of an equitable remedy is *rescission* of a contract. For instance, if one party is induced to enter into a contract by fraud or misrepresentation, courts will allow the innocent party to withdraw from the agreement. Rescission allows a party legally to withhold performance of an obligation. In essence, this equitable remedy places the parties in the same position they were in prior to any contractual agreement.

The Subject Matter

5. Introduction

Frequently the legal terms *real estate* and *real property* are used interchangeably. However, there is a distinction between these terms. The term "real estate" technically refers to the physical land surface, the space above that surface, and the area beneath it. On the other hand, "real property" consists of all the legal rights that a person can have in land and things permanently attached to it.

Real property must be distinguished from personal property. Personal property includes all of the legal rights of ownership or possession in relation to things that do not qualify as real property. The term "personal property" also is used to represent physical items or things that are not real estate. Examples of personal property include cars, clothing, and other personal belongings. Personal property also describes rights in intangibles such as trade names and patents.

6. Real vs. Personal Property

For a number of reasons it is important to know whether an item of property is classified as real or personal. This distinction may be important in determining (1) the application of conflicts-of-law principles, (2) the right of inheritance, (3) the method of transfer, and (4) the application of the statute of frauds.

Conflicts-of-law principles are used to determine the applicable substantive law when a case or issue involves more than one jurisdiction. For example, assume that land in Indiana becomes the subject of a lawsuit in Kentucky. Which state's substantive, as opposed to procedural, law would be used to decide the controversy? Generally, in cases involving real property interests, the law of the land's location will control. Therefore, Indiana substantive law would be used by the Kentucky court to resolve this dispute. However, suppose that Bill, a California resident, is the owner of a tractor in Arizona. If Bill borrows money using the tractor as collateral and fails to pay the debt, a court in Arizona or California handling the lawsuit that involves this debt and tractor likely would apply California law because rights to personal property are usually determined by the law of the owner's domicile.

Many states distinguish between real and personal property in matters of inheritance. If someone dies without leaving a valid will, in some states the deceased's real property may pass according to one formula and the personal property according to another. For example, a state may give a surviving spouse with children one-third of the real property and one-half of the personal property. Thus this distinction may determine a survivor's rights to a deceased person's property.

The formality and requirements of a personal property transfer are much less than those for the transfer of real property. Personal property is exchanged or sold informally, and a bill of sale may or may not be given to conclude the transaction. Title to real property is transferred by a formal legal document called a deed. All deeds must be properly signed, witnessed, acknowledged, and delivered before title to land is actually transferred. Chapters 5 and 12 cover these matters with respect to real property interests.

A statute, known as the statute of frauds, prohibits lawsuits to enforce some contractual agreements unless there is written evidence of the agreement signed by the defendant. The statute of frauds for real property is different from that for personal property. In the latter, there are several means for satisfying the statute, such as part payment and delivery of the goods. Because real property is so important and usually involves a large financial commitment, contracts involving real estate are subject to certain requirements, and complete written evidence of the terms of the contract is usually required. Sales contracts are the subject matter of Chapter 11, and the statute of frauds is discussed in further detail there.

7. Fixtures

Whether a particular item of property is considered real or personal often changes from time to time. For example, an item such as a furnace that is clearly movable personal property at the time it is sold becomes so attached to land when incorporated as part of a building that it is then treated as part of the real estate. This type of item is called a *fixture*. Since fixtures are incorporated as part of the real property, the rights in relation to them are the same as the rights to the land to which they are attached. Determining whether an item is a fixture or not is important for determining:

1. The value of real property for tax purposes.
2. Whether a sale of the real estate includes the item.[2]
3. Whether the item is part of the security given to a creditor.
4. Whether the item goes to the landlord or can be removed by the tenant upon the termination of a lease.

Typical examples of indoor items that were once personal property but are likely to become fixtures are built-in kitchen appliances, such as dishwashers and ranges, central heating and air-conditioning systems, electrical wiring, and attached lighting devices. A fence or an irrigation system are examples of outdoor fixtures.

Courts and state legislatures have devised several tests that generally will aid in the factual determination of fixture status. The most crucial test for determining if something is a fixture to be treated as real property is the parties' *intent*. For example, if the landlord and tenant agreed that the wall-to-wall carpeting installed by the tenant would remain after the lease terminated, the carpet is a fixture and the landlord retains title to it as part of the real property. Unfortunately, parties to a lease or sales contract do not always express their intent; therefore, other fixture tests have become very important.

If an item of personal property becomes attached or annexed to the real estate it will likely be considered a fixture. The damage to the land or building that would be caused by removal becomes crucial to this *annexation test*. This test alone fails to be satisfactory, since an air-conditioner compressor may be readily removed even though it was attached. For example, this fixture may be temporarily removed to be repaired. These factors do not destroy an item's fixture status if the parties intend the item to remain a fixture.

The *adaptation test* asks, in essence, whether the item was added to increase the value of the real property. This test states that if the item increased the real property's value, that item is a fixture. However, seldom are items added to land or a residence to decrease the real property's total value. Once again, the overriding test is the parties' intent along with the annexation and adaptation tests. In other words,

---

[2] **Paul v. First National Bank of Cincinnati,** page 24.

these latter tests are useful because they help determine the crucial issue of whether something was intended to become a fixture.

The law of fixtures does not always provide clear-cut distinctions between real and personal property. In order to prevent potential dispute, the parties involved should clearly state their intent as to each fixture. By contractual agreement, they can decide whether an item is to be treated as real or personal property. Although a written agreement usually is best, the parties' intent can be expressed orally.

Case 1.3

The Lee-Moore Oil Company, installed gasoline pumps and storage tanks under an oral agreement with the owner and operator of "Marley's Store" that this equipment would remain on the premises so long as the operator purchased gasoline solely from Lee-Moore. Cleary subsequently purchased the property and elected to purchase gasoline from another source. The previous owner had testified to having informed Cleary orally prior to the sale that the equipment was property of Lee-Moore. Lee-Moore offered to remove the equipment or sell it to Cleary at the market value. Cleary refused, claiming the equipment at the time of purchase was "firmly affixed" and was a part of the real property.

Issue: Is an oral agreement sufficient to maintain status of property as "personal" even after it has become firmly affixed to the real property?

Decision: Yes

Reasons: As a general rule, property once firmly attached to real property becomes a part of the property. This rule, however, must be dependent on the circumstances surrounding the action. Property placed on the land of another with the owner's permission may by agreement remain personal property even in the absence of any written agreement. Such an agreement, whether express or implied, becomes binding on subsequent owners of the property who have some notice of the agreement.

Lee-Moore Oil Company v. Cleary, 245 S.E.2d 720 (N.C. 1978).

There are special categories of fixtures for which the law makes an exception to the general treatment given to fixtures. These include trade, agricultural, and domestic fixtures. A tenant who leases a factory or warehouse building is allowed to attach trade fixtures such as machinery, office equipment, and counters to the building without losing the right to remove these items promptly on the lease's termination. These items do not become a part of the real estate. Likewise, agricultural fixtures belonging to a tenant might include chicken houses or hog pens. Domestic features such as a window air conditioner may be added by the tenant to make the premises more comfortable. Upon removal of these special trade, agricultural, or domestic fixtures, the tenant is responsible for returning to the landlord's possession the real estate in the same condition in which it was originally when the lease began. However, the tenant does have the right to remove them. Failure to remove such fixtures before the lease expires or within a reasonable time thereafter might result in a court's conclusion that the tenant has abandoned or lost all interests in these items. In the alternative, the tenant has the right to sell the trade fixtures when the lease terminates.

8.   Surface, Mineral, and Air Rights

This book is about the law as it relates to the actual real estate (the land itself) and to the legal rights (real property) connected with the land. It must be kept in mind that real estate is not limited to just the surface of the earth. Indeed, the real estate includes the air above the earth's surface and the space below it. Originally, a landowner's real property interests were conceptualized to be pie-shaped, beginning at the earth's center and extending through the surface boundaries indefinitely into outer space until it reached the heavens. Thus, an owner of real estate has mineral rights and air rights.

Mineral rights and air rights may be owned by a person other than the owner of the surface. For example, it is common for a surface owner to sell to a third party the rights to any oil, gas, coal, and other minerals that may be located below the surface. Likewise, the air rights may be transferred and used by persons other than the owner of the surface. For example, office buildings have been constructed over the tracks of railroads, with the owner of the building owning only the air rights.

Today, ownership of air space is usually limited to a reasonable distance above the surface. Obviously, a jet airplane flying over land at an altitude of several thousand feet rarely interferes with the owner's enjoyment of the land. However, when aircraft or other interference is so low that a reasonable use of the land is prevented, the owner can recover for trespass.[3] A developing area of law concerns a landowner's

[3]**United States v. Causby,** page 26.

right to sunlight. This right has become especially important to those who are dependent on solar energy. Questions have arisen and will continue to arise about whether it is legal to build a tall structure on a lot if that building will partially or totally block the adjoining landowner's use of sunlight. Future court decisions and legislative enactments are needed to determine whether to use a system of permits or some other alternative basis of allocation of sunlight.

In addition to this broad concept of real estate, you should also understand how it is described legally. This topic is examined in the following sections.

Legal Descriptions of Real Estate

9. Introduction

A description of the property involved is essential in listing agreements, contracts, deeds, and other documents that affect title to real estate. The description in listing agreements and contracts must be adequate to give the parties the general idea of the property being listed or sold. Often informal means of description are used for these purposes. For example, the street address for residential or commercial locations or the phrase "John Harris' farm in Macon County" may be sufficient to let the parties know what properties are involved.

However, when it comes to actually transferring title to real estate through a deed, a more precise legal description is necessary. The exact boundaries of the land being conveyed is essential for a proper transfer. In the United States, real estate is generally described by use of the Metes and Bounds system, the Rectangular Survey system, and by references to recorded surveys, generally known as *plats*.

10. Metes and Bounds

The original way to achieve a formal legal description of the boundaries of any piece of land was to use the metes-and-bounds method. *Metes* are the distances used in a description, and *bounds* are the directions of the actual boundaries that enclose a piece of land. A metes-and-bounds description starts at a designated point of beginning or monument, and through specific distances, courses, directions, and reference points locates the outlying boundaries of the land. It is clear that reference points are very crucial to the metes-and-bounds descriptions. Before subdivision developers began using iron pins to mark these points, natural monuments were often used. Such monuments might be "the large oak tree," "the spring-fed stream," or "the old Indian rock mound." Although reference to such natural objects could cause some confusion, since these items are subject to change over time, they are still used today to describe some rural land. When these natural monuments have been changed or destroyed over time, difficult questions arise as to the precise boundaries. Today, particularly in residential subdivisions, these reference points are commonly iron stakes or pins which were driven into the ground at each corner of the lot.

A typical modern metes-and-bounds description would start in a manner similar to the following: "Beginning at an iron pin on the Western side of Wesley Oaks Street 95 feet South from the Southwestern corner of the intersection of Sixth Avenue and Wesley Oaks Street, as measured along the Western side of Wesley Oaks Street." This quoted language simply describes the beginning point of an accurate metes-and-bounds description. From the starting point, each boundary is detailed in its length, the direction it runs, and the point where it begins and ends. It is vitally important that this description actually enclose the property involved. In other words, each boundary must begin at the preceding boundary's end and end at the next boundary's beginning. The description of the last side must always conclude at the point of beginning.

What happens when there is a conflict within a legal description? Courts generally will follow a precise metes-and-bounds description before relying on general statements in legal documents. In establishing an exact boundary, courts will refer first to any natural monuments in the description. Second, they look for references to artificial monuments. Third, they examine the property's adjacent boundaries. Fourth, they will rely on the directions and distances of the boundries as described. Finally, a general statement as to how much land is involved is least important in describing the land's boundaries.

Case 1.4

Roy Parr conveyed to defendant Worley a tract of land described as "lying to the east" of the public highway, "containing 25 acres, more or less." Subsequent to the transaction, Parr purported to convey to a third party the mineral interest in all the land within the highway right of way. Parr brought this action to quiet title to the mineral interest. From the survey prepared for the court, the piece of land deeded to Worley contained 25.80 acres when measured from the edge of the right of way, and 31.57 acres when measured from the highway's centerline. Parr contends the quantity of acreage cited in his deed to Worley makes clear his intent to retain the land under the highway.

Issue: Was the land lying within the highway right of way excluded from the conveyance to Worley through the phrase "lying to the east of" the public highway?

Decision: No. The conveyance included all interest to the highway centerline.

Reasons: It is a generally accepted rule that a conveyance of land abutting on a road, highway, or other way is presumed to convey ownership to the centerline of the way, absent express words of exclusion in the instrument. Parr's contention that it is the quantity of acreage cited in the description that controls is in direct conflict with the established hierarchy whereby location of boundaries resorts in order to: natural monuments or landmarks; artificial monuments; adjacent boundaries; courses and distances; and lastly the intention of the parties, in which case the doubt will be resolved in favor of the grantee.

Parr v. Worley, 559 P.2d 382 (N.M. 1979).

11. Rectangular Survey

Shortly after the end of the Revolutionary War, when the westward movement from the original states began, a method of describing wilderness land was required. The United States Congress approved a description method based on the rectangular survey system. In essence, new undeveloped land was divided into tracts, called *quadrangles* or *checks,* that consisted of twenty-four-mile squares. These quadrangles were subdivided into areas six miles square called *townships.* Every township was again subdivided into thirty-six equal *sections* containing one square mile or 640 acres of land.

This rectangular survey system is based first on *principal meridians* running north and south and *base lines* running east and west. Placement of these meridians and base lines generally coincided with an established landmark, such as the mouth of the Ohio River. The principal meridian was drawn north-south through the river's mouth, and the base line was drawn east-west to intersect the merdian at the landmark. A surveyor would then mark off twenty-four miles from the principal meridian and the base line in each direction. Because the earth is round, parallel lines running north and south begin to converge as they proceed northward. To counteract this convergence, *guide meridians* were drawn every twenty-four miles east and west of the principal meridians. To get accurate rectangular quadrangles, *correction lines* were drawn every twenty-four miles north and south of the base lines. Exhibit 1.1 shows the survey of quadrangles.

These quadrangles, which were twenty-four miles square in area, produced sixteen townships. To identify each individual township, reference is made to the intersection of the principal meridian and the base line. Each series of townships east and west of the principal meridian is called a *range*. A cross reference to the township and the range designates the location of specific land. See Exhibit 1.2 for a depiction of quadrangles divided into townships.

EXHIBIT 1.1   TWENTY-FOUR-MILE QUADRANGLES

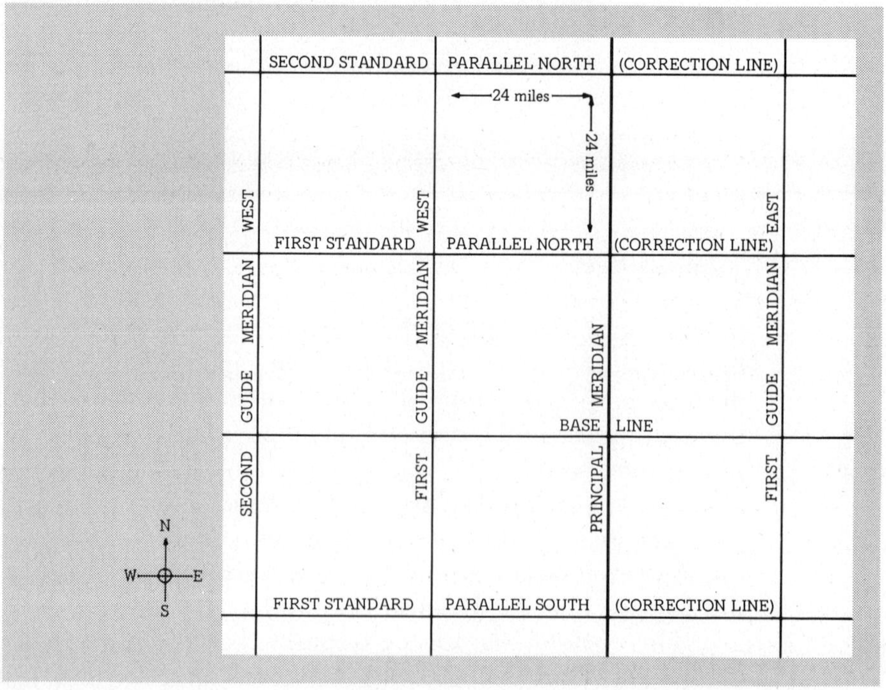

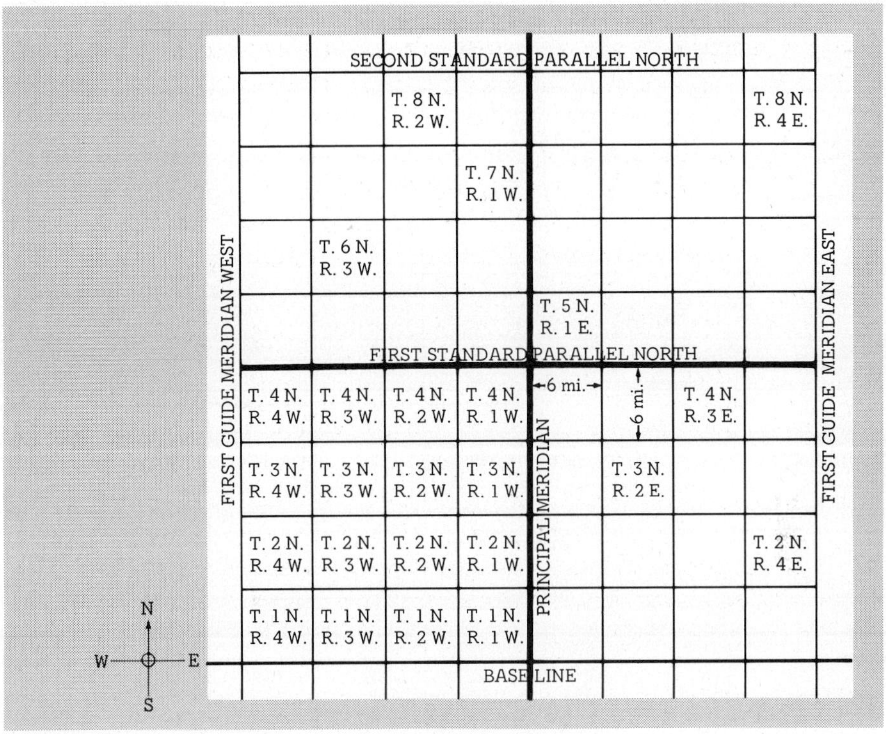

SECOND STANDARD PARALLEL NORTH

T. 8 N.
R. 2 W.

T. 8 N.
R. 4 E.

T. 7 N.
R. 1 W.

FIRST GUIDE MERIDIAN WEST

T. 6 N.
R. 3 W.

FIRST GUIDE MERIDIAN EAST

T. 5 N.
R. 1 E.

FIRST STANDARD PARALLEL NORTH

←6 mi.→   ↕6 mi.

T. 4 N.
R. 4 W. | T. 4 N.
R. 3 W. | T. 4 N.
R. 2 W. | T. 4 N.
R. 1 W. | T. 4 N.
R. 3 E.

T. 3 N.
R. 4 W. | T. 3 N.
R. 3 W. | T. 3 N.
R. 2 W. | T. 3 N.
R. 1 W. | T. 3 N.
R. 2 E.

PRINCIPAL MERIDIAN

T. 2 N.
R. 4 W. | T. 2 N.
R. 3 W. | T. 2 N.
R. 2 W. | T. 2 N.
R. 1 W. | T. 2 N.
R. 4 E.

N
W ⊕ E
S

T. 1 N.
R. 4 W. | T. 1 N.
R. 3 W. | T. 1 N.
R. 2 W. | T. 1 N.
R. 1 W.

BASE LINE

EXHIBIT 1.2   QUADRANGLES INTO TOWNSHIPS

The rectangular survey required that each township be divided into thirty-six equal sections. Within any given township, sections were numbered beginning in the northeast corner, moving westerly, then southerly one section, and back easterly. This process continued until all sections were numbered. Exhibit 1.3 demonstrates this numbering process. Each one of these sections consists of one square mile or approximately 640 acres.

The rectangular survey system is the principal method of land description in all states north of the Ohio River and west of the Mississippi River except Texas. This system is also vital to legal descriptions in Mississippi, Alabama, and Florida. These states' rural areas generally are sold in patchwork pieces. Of course, farms in these states may be less than the sectional size of 640 acres. For example, a buyer may purchase the Northwest one-fourth of the Southeast one-fourth of the Northeast one-fourth of Section 14 of Township 2 North, Range 4 West of the Third Principal Meridian. How many acres does the above

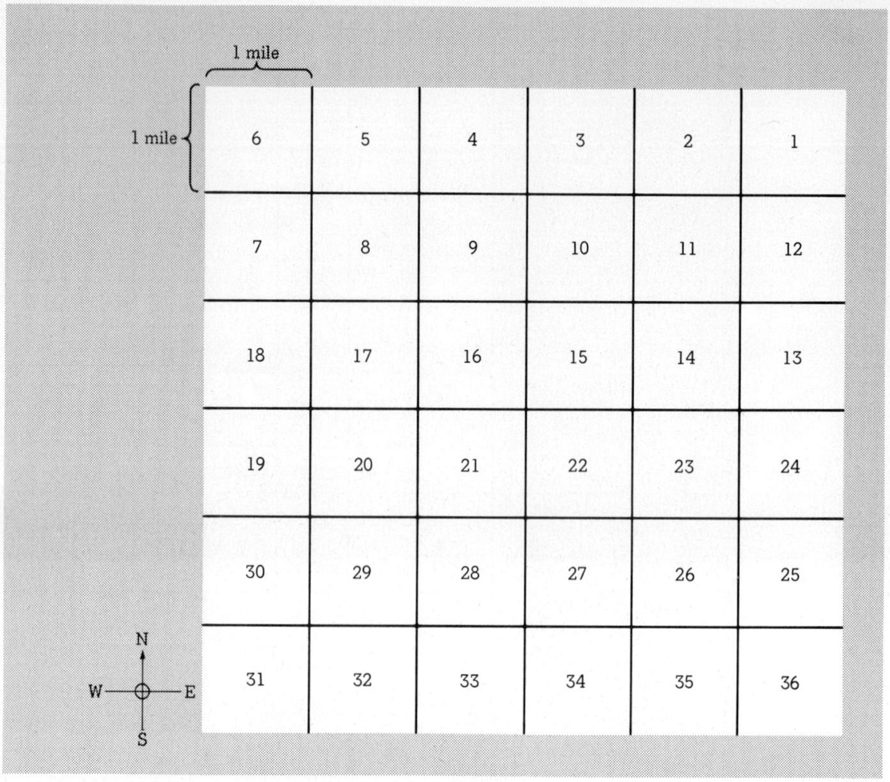

EXHIBIT 1.3   TOWNSHIPS INTO SECTIONS

describe? The answer is ten acres. To help clarify this point, look at the subdivision of a section in Exhibit 1.4.

12.   Combined Use of Metes-and-Bounds Description and Rectangular Survey

The rectangular survey system is very well suited for describing the large acreage involved in farmland. However, the system becomes difficult to use when describing the small subdivision lots found in most communities. To keep subdividing a section of 640 acres into one-half-acre or smaller lots becomes quite onerous. Therefore, metes-and-bounds descriptions become vital to clear legal descriptions.

It is just as important to have a precise legal description of a one-half-acre lot as of a large farm for a deed passing title. This follow-

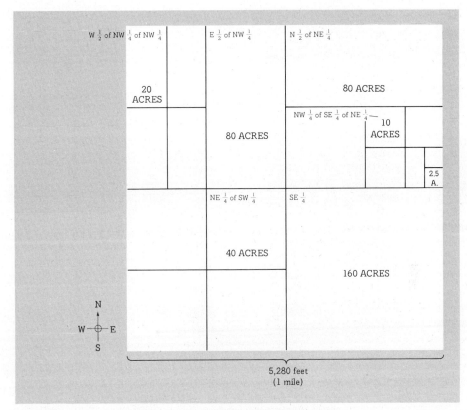

EXHIBIT 1.4   SUBDIVISION OF A SECTION (640 ACRES)

ing description is an example of how the rectangular survey method and the metes-and-bounds description can be used together to produce an appropriate description.

Part of the S.W. ¼ of the S.E. ¼ of Section 15, T. 57 N., R. 35 W., of the 5th P.M., Buchanan County, State of Missouri, beginning at a point being 202 feet east of the S.W. corner of the S.E. ¼ of said Section 15, running thence north 82 degrees east 200 feet to an iron pin; running thence east 104 degrees 100 feet to an iron pin; running thence south 82 degrees west 200 feet to an iron pin; running thence west 104 degrees 100 feet to the point of the beginning.

Assuming that Exhibit 1.5 is the southwestern quarter of the southeastern quarter of section 15 in township 57 north, range 35 west of the fifth principal meridian, this lot would appear as shown.

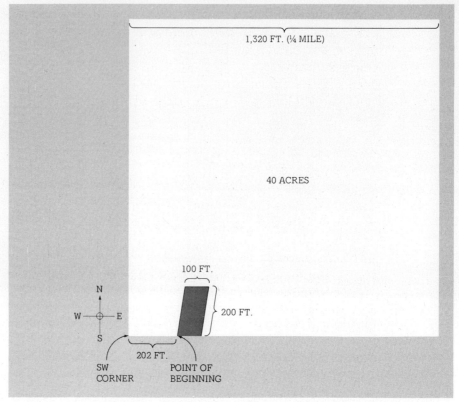

EXHIBIT 1.5   SW ¼ OF THE SE ¼ of SECTION 14 OF T. 57 N., R. 35 W. OF THE
5th P. M.

13.   Reference to Plats and Other Documents

A common alternative to the above-discussed methods of legally describing real estate is the reference to recorded surveys, often called
plats. Plats or similar documents include the streets, blocks, and lots as
they actually exist. Land can be described by simply referring to the
appropriate plat while stating the lot number, the block, and the subdivision. For example, a listing agreement or a sales contract could include a description as "Lot 3, Block G of the Green Acres Estate as
recorded in Plat Book 8, page 37, in the Clerk's Office at the Buchanan
County Circuit Courthouse." Although use of plats is an accurate legal
description by itself, the plat is based on either a metes-and-bounds or
a rectangular-survey description.

In Chapter 12, we will discuss title searches which involve a study
of deeds held by previous owners of a piece of real estate. Accurate legal

descriptions contained in prior deeds are often referred to in writing a new description. At the end of the lengthy legal description it would not be uncommon to find a phrase something like: "This property being the same as that conveyed to Phil and Diane Watkins by deed from Charles Edwards on March 28, 1964, as recorded in Deed Book 134, page 823, in the Clerk's Office of Jonesboro County, New Hampshire."

14.   Condominiums Described

The use of plats is especially important in describing an owner's share in a condominium complex. A *condominium* usually is a complex of housing units, each of which is individually owned. The common areas, such as sidewalks, yards, entrances, pools, tennis courts, and recreational buildings, are owned jointly by all the unit owners. Typically, these common areas are managed and maintained by an association of the condominium owners. These ownership interests in a condominium complex are considered to be real property, whereas an owner of an interest in a cooperative owns only personal property.

A *cooperative,* which consists of a nonprofit corporation and its shareholders, is another way to own and operate a residential development. Although in physical appearance a cooperative housing complex may not differ from a condominium, the ownership is quite different. The corporation owns the entire housing complex, and the individual shareholders own an interest in the corporation. Most frequently, a shareholder will have the rights of a tenant with the corporation acting as the landlord.

In addition to the distinction between the ownership of real and personal property, other differences must be kept in mind when discussing condominiums and cooperatives. A condominium involves multiple taxpayers, while the corporation owning a cooperative is treated as a single taxpayer. Next, each individual owner has a personal mortgage liability under a condominium arrangement, whereas in the case of cooperatives, the corporation usually mortgages the entire complex in a single transaction.

Finally, because it is an interest in real estate, a condominium unit must be accurately and legally described whenever it is transferred by an owner. Normally, the entire condominium complex is platted, and that plat is placed in the public records. Then owners deeding their unit to another person can simply describe their interests by making reference to the recorded plat while specifying the particular unit involved. An interest in a cooperative complex is transferred by selling the stock in the controlling corporation. In other words, this latter transfer is much less formal than the transfer of a condominium unit.

15. Preparation of the Legal Description

Since recorded documents that contain precise legal descriptions affect title to real estate, these descriptions should be prepared only by a licensed attorney. Real estate brokers or salespeople who attempt to draft legal descriptions may be creating potential risks for themselves and for those they serve. First, an improperly worded description in a contract may obligate the seller or buyer to sell or buy property not intended. Even if the contract can be reformed to reflect the correct description, the real estate agent could lose all or part of his commission. In addition, the agent who improperly described the land may be liable for any damages suffered by an injured party.

If these reasons are not enough to discourage brokers and salespeople from drafting descriptions, the threat of being charged with the unauthorized practice of law provides another strong reason. Requiring legal counsel to prepare the legal description is even more important in deeds, mortgages, and other instruments directly affecting title to land. The technical aspects of legal descriptions presented above should help emphasize the need for good accurate descriptions of real estate drafted by persons with legal training.

Introductory Cases

Summary of a Lawsuit

A lawsuit usually begins in the trial court with a plaintiff filing a legal document called a *complaint*. This complaint sets forth allegations of the plaintiff and the relief sought. The complaint, along with a *summons*, is delivered or served on the *defendant*. The defendant responds to the court by admitting or denying each allegation of the complaint. This response by the defendant is called an *answer*. The complaint and answer, which are called the *pleadings*, form the issues to be tried in the lawsuit.

Prior to the trial, both parties can learn about information pertinent to the case through a process known as *discovery*. For example, a party's lawyer may ask the other party oral questions that must be answered under oath. This exchange is called taking a *deposition.*

The parties also may make motions to the trial judge that help clarify the issues or that may terminate the case. For example, if the defendant fails to file an answer on time, the plaintiff may move for a *default judgment.* If this motion is granted, the plaintiff is awarded the relief to which he or she is entitled. Other motions that might terminate the litigation without a trial are a motion for a judgment on the pleadings or a motion for a summary judgment. If a trial judge looking at the pleadings finds that one of the parties is entitled to a decision in his or her favor, that party's motion for a *judgment on the pleadings* may be granted. When a judge examines other documents, including affidavits of the parties, in addition to the pleadings and decides one party is entitled to a decision, a motion for *summary judgment* may be granted. Either the plaintiff or the defendant can make these two motions.

Assume that the parties to a lawsuit complete these pre-trial stages and the case is ready to be tried. If a jury is used, it is the finder of the facts. The trial judge determines legal issues by rulings throughout the trial. Such rulings could include what evidence is admissible and what instructions on the law are given to the jury.

Evidence is presented through the direct and cross examination of witnesses. At the conclusion of the plaintiff's evidence, the defendant can move for *directed verdict.* This motion, if granted, is the judge's determination that, as a matter of law, the plaintiff is not entitled to a verdict. The motion for a directed verdict, if granted, terminates the case.

Assuming the defendant's motion for a directed verdict is denied, the defendant presents its evidence. At the close of the defendant's case, both parties can move for a directed verdict in their favor. If these motions are denied, the lawyers for both parties will argue to the jury (or the judge, if a jury is not used) why the case should be decided in favor of their respective clients. After the closing argument, the judge instructs the jury on the legal principles to be applied to the facts as the jury finds them. The jury then deliberates the case and hopefully returns a *verdict* on which the court enters a *judgment.*

At this point the losing party can move for a *judgment notwithstanding the verdict (j.n.o.v.).* Such a motion asserts that the trial judge should rule that the jury could not legally reach the verdict it did. If this motion is granted, the outcome of the case is switched, and the party losing according to the jury verdict actually wins. Finally, the losing party can make a motion for a new trial. If granted, the judge has determined that during the trial some mistake was made that denied the losing party a fair trial.

As the result of any ruling by the trial judge on a legal issue, the losing party may appeal the case to a reviewing court. The federal judicial system and most state systems involve two levels of appellate review. The losing party at the trial level has a right to appeal to the appropriate reviewing court. The party that appeals from a trial judge's judgment is called the *appellant;* the other party is the *appellee.* At the conclusion of the first review, the losing party may request a second review before the highest court in the judicial system. The petition for permission to bring a case before this highest court usually is known technically as a *petition for a writ of certiorari.* The party who files a petition for a writ of certiorari is referred to as the *petitioner;* the other party is the *respondent.*

Reviewing courts normally will review only the trial judge's legal rulings. Very seldom will an appellate court review the factual findings in a case. The facts as determined at the trial level are accepted. In reviewing the trial or appellate judges' rulings on legal issues, courts of review may find no significant errors. In that case, the lower court's decision will be *affirmed.* If significant errors exist, the decision below will be *reversed* and the case sent back to the lower court for further proceedings. This is known as a *remand.*

Paul v. First National Bank of Cincinnati
369 N.E.2d 488 (Ohio Com. Pleas. Ct. 1976).

Black, J.

As the purchaser for $575,000 of an elegant residence known as Long Acres, located in Indian Hill, Hamilton County, plaintiff Lawrence M. Paul sues the defendants for removing and converting from the buildings and grounds certain items of property, ... [including four handmade lighting fixtures around swimming pool, lighting fixture in living quarters of apartment over stable, two lighting fixtures removed from chapel, three metal cranes, and four garden statues].

["Long Acres" is a picturesque estate that covers ninety-seven acres and includes a seventeen room house furnished with unique items such as marbled archways and a pipe organ. The purchase contract entered into by the parties contained a metes and bounds description and included the following paragraph.]

"II. Together with all of *electrical,* plumbing, heating and bathroom fixtures, all window and door shades, venetian blinds, awnings, curtain rods, window and door screens, storm windows and storm doors, affixed wall mirrors, drapery rods, attached linoleum, wall to wall carpeting, stair carpeting, *built-in ranges and ovens,* built-in refrigerators and dishwashers, landscaping, shrubbery, attached television aerials and *all fixtures relating to said real estate, . . .*"

On October 14, 1971, this transaction was closed by payment of the purchase price in exchange for deed to the property. Possession was not delivered until January 15, 1972, under the terms of the contract, . . .

When possession was delivered to plaintiff on January 15, 1972, he noticed that a number of items were missing that had been on the property both before and after the date of the purchase contract. The defendants admit that these items had been removed by the individual defendants before surrendering possession. . . .

. . . [T]he [Ohio] Supreme Court designated six "facts" to be considered in determining whether an item is a fixture:

(1) The nature of the property;
(2) The manner in which the property is annexed to the realty;
(3) The purpose for which the annexation is made;
(4) The intention of the annexing party to make the property a part of the realty;
(5) The degree of difficulty and extent of any loss involved in removing the property from the realty; and
(6) The damage to the severed property which such removal would cause. . . .

Using the Supreme Court's considerations, the light "fixtures" (there is no other available word) from the swimming pool, the stable apartment and the chapel are clearly fixtures in contemplation of law. . . . They are of a type universally recognized as fixtures. This is true even though the pool "fixtures" were hung on brackets and could be unplugged and simply lifted off the brackets. But they were designed and produced solely and only for the swimming pool, from the same design as was used for the light fixture in the porte cochere (which was not removed). Further, the poles from which they were taken are barren and incomplete without them.

The three metal cranes and the four garden statues also meet five of the six criteria, in the judgment of the court. The "nature" of these items is that they were a part of the total elegance of Long Acres. They are not the type of fixture which would be commonly found on other lawns or in other gardens in Hamilton County, but they are an integral part of this sumptuous country estate. The cranes were "annexed" by being bolted or screwed into concrete foundations in a manner similar to the annexation of the marble table in the Great Hall, an item clearly admitted by all defendants to be a fixture passing with the real estate. The four garden statues (busts?) were not simply placed on top of their columns, but were held in place by a six-inch pipe protruding from the columns into the bases of the statues. The purpose of fixing these into position was to ensure their presence and preservation as part and parcel of the landscape and approach to Long Acres. These cranes and statues were not items moved about at the whim of the owner or according to the seasons: they were permanent implacements, intended to be part of the continuing visual effect of the estate. While no great difficulty was encountered in removing any of them, their absence is a source of loss. The cranes were prominent in the approach to the front door, and that approach is damaged without them. They were shown in several photographs attached to the appraisal which was prepared by the Cincinnati Real Estate Board and considered by plaintiff before entering into the purchase contract. The removal of the statues leaves the columns on which they stood barren and incomplete; the columns appear to have been vandalized. . . .

[The court then holds that these defendants are liable for the removal of these fixtures, for punitive damages, and for attorneys' fees under Ohio law.]
Judgment accordingly.

United States v. Causby
328 U.S. 256 (1946).

Douglas, J.

This is a case of first impression. The problem presented is whether respondents' [Causby's] property was taken within the meaning of the Fifth Amendment by frequent and regular flights of army and navy aircraft over respondents' land at low altitudes. The Court of Claims held that there was a taking and entered judgment for respondent. . . .

Respondents own 2.8 acres near an airport outside of Greensboro, North Carolina. It has on it a dwelling house, and also various outbuildings which were mainly used for raising chickens. The end of the airport's northwest-southeast runway is 2,220 feet from respondents' barn and 2,275 feet from their house. The path of glide to this runway passes directly over the property—which is 100 feet wide and 1,200 feet long. The thirty to one safe glide angle approved by the Civil Aeronautics Authority passes over this property at eight-three feet, which is sixty-seven feet above the house, sixty-three feet above the barn and 18 feet above the highest tree. . . .

Since the United States began operations in May, 1942, its four-motored heavy bombers, other planes of the heavier type, and its fighter planes have frequently passed over respondents' land and buildings in considerable numbers and rather close together. They come close enough at times to appear barely to miss the tops of the trees and at times so close to the tops of the trees as to blow the old leaves off. The noise is startling. As a result of the noise, respondents had to give up their chicken business. As many as six to ten of their chickens were killed in one day by flying into the walls from fright. The total chickens lost in that manner was about 150. Production also fell off. The result was the destruction of the use of the property as a commercial chicken farm. Respondents are frequently deprived of their sleep and the family has become nervous and frightened. . . . These are the essential facts found by the Court of Claims. On the basis of these facts, it found that respondents' property had depreciated in value. It held that the United States had taken an easement over the property on June 1, 1942, and that the value of the property destroyed and the easement taken was $2,000.

It is ancient doctrine that at common law ownership of the land extended to the periphery of the universe. . . . But that doctrine has no place in the modern world. The air is a public highway, as Congress has declared. Were that not true, every transcontinental flight would subject the operator to countless trespass suits. Common sense revolts at the idea. To recognize such private claims to the airspace would clog these highways, seriously interfere with their control and development in the public interest, and transfer into private ownership that to which only the public has a just claim.

But that general principle does not control the present case. For the United States conceded in oral argument that if the flights over respondents' property rendered it uninhabitable, there would be a taking compensable under the Fifth Amendment. It is the owner's loss, not the taker's gain, which is the measure of the value of the property taken.... Market value fairly determined is the normal measure of the recovery. And that value may reflect the use to which the land could readily be converted, as well as the existing use.... If, by reason of the frequency and altitude of the flights, respondents could not use this land for any purpose, their loss would be complete. It would be as complete as if the United States had entered upon the surface of the land and taken exclusive possession of it.

We agree that in those circumstances there would be a taking.... The owner's right to possess and exploit the land—that is to say, his beneficial ownership of it—would be destroyed....

... The path of glide for airplanes might reduce a valuable factory site to grazing land, an orchard to a vegetable patch, a residential section to a wheat field. Some value would remain. But the use of the airspace immediately above the land would limit the utility of the land and cause a diminution in its value....

We have said that the airspace is a public highway. Yet it is obvious that if the landowner is to have full enjoyment of the land, he must have exclusive control of the immediate reaches of the enveloping atmosphere. Otherwise buildings could not be erected, trees could not be planted, and even fences could not be run. The principle is recognized when the law gives a remedy in case overhanging structures are erected on adjoining land. The landowner owns at least as much of the space above the ground as he can occupy or use in connection with the land. . . . The fact that he does not occupy it in a physical sense—by the erection of buildings and the like—is not material. As we have said, the flight of airplanes, which skim the surface but do not touch it, is as much an appropriation of the use of the land as a more conventional entry upon it. We would not doubt that if the United States erected an elevated railway over respondents' land at the precise altitude where its planes now fly, there would be a partial taking, even though none of the supports of the structure rested on the land. The reason is that there would be an intrusion so immediate and direct as to subtract from the owner's full enjoyment of the property and to limit his exploitation of it. While the owner does not in any physical manner occupy that stratum of airspace or make use of it in the conventional sense, he does use it in somewhat the same sense that space left between buildings for the purpose of light and air is used. The superadjacent airspace at this low altitude is so close to the land that continuous invasions of it affect the use of the surface of the land itself. We think that the landowner, as an incident to his ownership, has a claim to it and that invasions of it are in the same category as invasions of the surface....

The airplane is part of the modern environment of life, and the inconveniences which it causes are normally not compensable under the Fifth Amendment. The airspace, apart from the immediate reaches above the land, is part of the public domain. We need not determine at this time what those precise limits are. Flights over private land are not a taking, unless they are so low and so frequent as to be a direct and immediate interference with the enjoyment and use of the land. We need not speculate on that phase of the present case. For the findings of the Court of Claims plainly established that there was a diminution in value of the property and that the frequent, low-level flights were the direct and immediate cause. We agree with the Court of Claims that a servitude has been imposed upon the land. . . .

[The Court then decided that the easement taken by these overflights had not been adequately described.]

Since on this record it is not clear whether the easement taken is a permanent or a temporary one, it would be premature for us to consider whether the amount of the award made by the Court of Claims was proper.

The judgment is reversed and the cause is remanded to the Court of Claims so that it may make the necessary findings in conformity with this opinion.

Reversed.

REVIEW QUESTIONS

1. What are the principal sources of laws affecting real estate?
2. Define and distinguish the judicial actions called *trespass* and *nuisance*.
3. What are four reasons why it is important to distinguish between real property and personal property?
4. Bob Acquire signed a contract to purchase a large home from Sally Solder. When Bob took possession of the property, he noticed that several lighting fixtures, numerous outdoor statues, and an oven-range appliance had been removed by Sally. If the contract was silent as to who was entitled to these items, who would win if Bob sued for their return? Why?
5. How were an owner's real property interests originally conceptualized? Is this concept still pertinent today?
6. What are the basic methods of legally describing real estate?
7. Define each of the following terms:
   Check   Section   Base line
   Township   Principal meridian
8. Assume that the box below is one section. Shade in the W ½ of the NE ¼ of the SW ¼ of that section. How many acres are shaded?

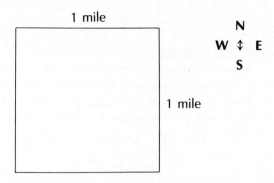

1 mile

1 mile

N
W ↕ E
S

2

Ownership Interests in Land

1. Introduction

Ownership of land takes many forms. Ownership or legal title is not absolute. As we will see throughout this book, two people may claim to own a piece of real estate. One person's title will be superior to the other, but even the person with superior title can lose the interest to someone else with an even better claim of ownership. Ownership should be considered as a collection or bundle of rights to possess, use, and transfer the land. Possession is the physical control of land that can be exercised by a person. Use is the utilization of the land for a material benefit. Transfer of an ownership interest may include a sale or gift of all or only a portion of the entire bundle of rights. An owner of land may have all or only some of these rights. For example, a landlord may have title to an apartment building, but the tenants enjoy the right of possession to the individual units. The purpose of this chapter is to discuss some of the more common types of ownership interests of real property. The next chapter will discuss other interests and rights in land, such as easements, licenses, profits à prendre, and water rights.

2. *Estates in Land: The Historical Background*

Ownership interests in real property often are described as estates in land. Such estates may be absolute, or they may be qualified by some condition. As you study the various estates in land, remember the bundle-of-rights concept of ownership. This bundle-of-rights may be held entirely by one person, or it may be divided into several interests held by two or more persons.

Although persons involved in the real estate industry may not encounter all of these estates in land, it is necessary to understand the various interests which are possible and the limitations associated with them. For example, a typical buyer of real property insists on receiving what is known as a fee simple absolute title. The basic characteristics of a fee simple title therefore are quite significant. The various estates in land discussed in the chapter are also quite important in proper estate planning. For example, a man's will may provide that the family house should go to his wife for as long as she lives, and when she dies the house is to pass to their children. The interests of the wife and the children are not fee simple estates. A thorough understanding of estates in land, including their historical development, is needed to understand these common transactions involving real estate.

The present-day system of estates in land has as its roots the ownership of land during England's feudal system. In A.D. 1066, William the Conqueror gained control of England after the Battle of Hastings. Upon his capture of England, William seized all the land as his own. Only the King owned real property; however, since he could not use or manage all this land, parcels were distributed to lords or barons. In return for the right to hold this land, the barons promised to provide services to the King. Since the barons could not manage all the land they held, they subdivided their share among their loyal knights. Likewise knights distributed their holdings among servants, who would actually manage or farm the land.

The downward distribution of land in feudal England concerned only the right to possess the property. All ownership interests were vested solely in the King. This right to hold land was compensated by the upward flow of services, such as servants acting as soldiers and sharing the crops that were grown. In addition, each tier of landholder promised the next higher tier loyalty, dilligence, and good faith.

Approximately 100 years after William the Conqueror's establishment of the feudal system, it began to crumble. Individuals started to assert their right to personal freedoms, including ownership of land.

During this same period, knights began to sell their landholdings to servants in return for money, rather than services. Furthermore, payment of taxes was substituted for the services formerly provided. The lack of services flowing up the pyramid to the King weakened his ability to maintain power. The imposition of taxes was not well received by individuals, many of whom led revolts. Finally, on June 15, 1215, at the signing of the Magna Carta, the right of individuals to own real property was established. The King's power to control land use under the feudal system has given rise to modern governments' power to tax real property and to regulate the use of land through its inherent powers. These land-use controls are discussed in Chapters 6 and 7.

The decline of the feudal system and the establishment of the individual's right to own real property resulted in the creation of estates in land by which ownership interests could be divided among several individuals. The estates were classified either as *freehold,* which means the interest lasts for an indeterminable time period, or as *nonfreehold,* which is an interest that lasts for a definite and determinable period or is terminable at will. The chart which follows classifies and summarizes all of the estates in land currently in use. The number in parentheses to the right of each heading represents the section in which each estate is discussed.

EXHIBIT 2.1   ESTATES IN LAND

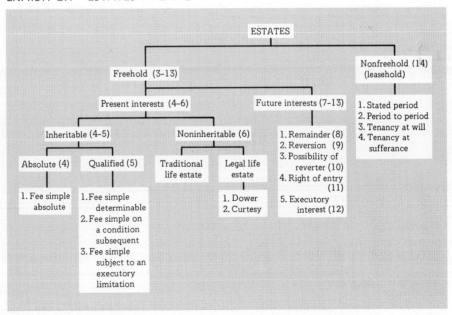

Freehold Estates: Present Interests

3. Introduction

The freehold estates are separated into those interests that are presently possessed and those that may become possessory in the future. These latter estates are called future interests. Present possessory interest are also either inheritable (the owner can pass his interest at his death) or noninheritable (the interest ends with death).

Inheritable freehold estates also can be subdivided into absolute and qualified interests. An absolute ownership interest signifies that the owner's rights are unlimited insofar as the ability to transfer the property is concerned. The owner of a qualified estate is limited in the ability to transfer the property because of some stated conditions. In discussing these estates, the terms *grantor* and *grantee* are often used. The grantor is the party who transfers (by sale or gift) a real property interest; the grantee is the party who receives the interest.

The language used to create an estate is of vital importance in determining the nature of ownership interest and the rights of the owner. The language used will determine if a present or a future interest is created. It also will determine if the interest is inheritable or not.

4. The Fee Simple Absolute

As 1-2

The *fee simple absolute* is the fullest and most complete estate in land. A buyer in the typical residential real estate transaction normally requires that the seller convey or transfer a fee simple absolute interest. Assuming that Aaron is the grantee, the language used to create a fee simple absolute may be any of the following, although the last example is considered most complete and therefore best:

> "To Aaron"
> "To Aaron and his heirs"
> "To Aaron, his heirs, and assigns"

The grantee receives an unlimited fee simple absolute interest. This means that the grantee can transfer the land or any interest therein during that grantee's life or at death. Legally stated, we can say the grantee's interest is alienable, devisable, and descendible. *Alienable* means the grantee can transfer the interest owned while living. *Devisable* means the interest can be tranferred by will. *Descendible* means the interest passes to the nearest living relative if the grantee dies intestate (without a valid will). Whether an owner has a fee simple absolute interest may determine that person's ability, as a grantor, to transfer a fee simple absolute to another person.

Case 2.1

Mable T. Wayburn agreed to sell some real estate to James M. Smith. After they had signed a contract, Mr. Smith refused to purchase this land. He claimed that Mrs. Wayburn did not have fee simple title to this property and, therefore, could not transfer good fee simple title to him. Mr. Smith's claim was based on defects that existed in Mrs. Wayburn's chain of title. The land now being sold to Mr. Smith originally belonged to W. J. Wooten, who deeded title to Allie Walker, who transferred ownership to Mrs. Wayburn. The original owner, Mr. Wooten, deeded this land to Mrs. Walker by using the following language:

" . . . I, W. J. Wooten of Blythewood, S. C. desire to convey to Allie Walker this tract of land (100 acres) to have and to hold her natural life, at her death it is to revert to heirs of her body."

Also in the deed the following language appeared:

"To Have and To Hold all and singular the premises before mentioned unto the said Allie Walker her Heirs and Assigns forever."

Issue: Did Allie Walker receive a fee simple absolute or a life estate interest from W. J. Wooten? Having answered this first question, is James Smith bound to purchase this land?

Decision: Allie Walker received a fee simple absolute interest which she passed on to Mable T. Wayburn. Since Mrs. Wayburn had a fee simple absolute title to this land, her contract to sell it to Mr. Smith was binding to both parties.

Reasons: In determining the intentions of a grantor, the deed must be construed as a whole. Although the language first quoted above seems to have created a life estate, the overall intention of Mr. W. J. Wooten was to convey a fee simple absolute to Allie Walker. This intent was indicated by the use of the words to "Allie Walker, her Heirs and Assigns forever." The holder of a fee simple absolute may pass title to another. Mrs. Wayburn had received fee simple absolute title from Mrs. Walker; therefore,

> Mr. Smith's claim that Mrs. Wayburn lacked good title was incorrect. Being without an excuse for his nonperformance, Mrs. Wayburn is entitled to a judgment against Mr. Smith for breach of contract.
>
> **Wayburn v. Smith,** 239 S.E.2d 890 (S.C. 1977).

In addition to the unrestricted transferability of a fee simple absolute, the grantee also has unlimited use and even abuse of the land. The grantee can sever or divide the total ownership interest in any way desired. Of course, this grantee cannot use the unrestricted interst to create a nuisance which would destroy neighbors' ability to enjoy their land.

5. The Qualified Estates

Since the fee simple absolute is the only unlimited ownership interest, all the other inheritable present freehold estates are qualified in some way. Technically these limited interests are called *defeasible estates,* which means these interests can be defeased or defeated in the future by the happening of an event or a stated condition. There are three types of defeasible estates: fee simple determinable, fee simple on a condition subsequent, and fee simple subject to an executory limitation.

A *fee simple determinable* estate is conditioned on something that will terminate the grantee's ownership interest automatically. Examples of the language that would create a *fee simple determinable* are as follows:

"To First Church so long as this land is used as a church site."
"To Al until these premises are used to serve alcoholic beverages."

This language makes it clear that the grantee's right to the real estate is limited. Nevertheless, subject to the stated limitation, the grantee's fee simple determinable estate is alienable, devisable, and descendible.

Because the grantee's interest is not absolute, the rest of the full ownership must be held by someone. In order to satisfy this requirement, the grantor of a fee simple determinable retains a future interest called a possiblity of reverter. Thus, if a fee simple determinable interest is terminated by the stated event, the ownership interest automatically reverts to the grantor or the grantor's estate. The grantor's ownership interest in this possibility of reverter is a future interest, which is discussed later in this chapter.

A *fee simple on a condition subsequent* estate is similar to a fee simple determinable in that some event may terminate this interest. The unique characteristic about the fee simple on a condition subsequent is that the estate does not end automatically upon the occurrence or nonoccurrence of the stated condition. The grantor explicitly reserves the right of entry upon the real estate. Only when the grantor exercises this right of entry does the grantee's estate actually end.

The following are simplistic examples of a fee simple on a condition subsequent:

> "To the Park Society, provided that the land is used as a public park, and if not, grantor has the right of entry."

> "To Al, but if the land is ever developed for a commercial purpose, grantor has the right of entry."

The phrase "right of entry" is the key element required for the grantor to retain this future interest. Failure to reserve clearly and expressly the right of entry will prohibit the grantor from regaining possession and title. If the right of entry interest is not expressly reserved, most courts will allow the grantor at least to sue for damages due to the breached condition even though the grantor cannot regain possession. This right of entry, the future interest which follows a properly worded fee simple on a condition subsequent interest, is discussed in more detail in section 11. The grantee's rights under a fee simple on a condition subsequent interest are, of course, limited somewhat. Understanding that the limitation continues, the grantee's interest is alienable, devisable, and descendible.

Like other qualified inheritable estates, the ownership interest in a *fee simple subject to an executory limitation* may be terminated upon the occurrence or nonoccurrence of a stated event. However, this estate is different because at the termination of the grantee's interest, the residual estate passes immediately to a person other than the grantor. This third person has a future interest which is called an executory interest.

In order to create a fee simple subject to an executory limitation, the following language is appropriate:

> "To the School Board, but if the land ceases to be used as an educational facility, then to Bob."

> "To Al, provided that he marries before he is twenty-five years old, if not, then to Bob."

Under either of the above, the grantee, Al, has a limited interest that is alienable, devisable, and descendible. Understandably, the grantor retains no interest since all future interests have been given to a third person, Bob. This third party has an executory interest which could become an estate in fee simple absolute if the stated limitation occurs.

Case 2.2

William Eskridge died leaving a will which gave all his property to his wife Bessie in "fee simple." In addition to that provision, the will also stated:

> "Upon the death of my wife, it is my desire that any of the real, personal, or mixed property which I bequeathed to her and which she has not disposed of at the time of her death shall be divided between my closest relatives and her closest relatives, share and share alike, in fee simple."

Bessie Eskridge did die without a will and without disposing of the property that she had received from her husband. Bessie was survived by one of her sisters, her husband's brother, and her deceased sister's children. A dispute arose among these survivors as to who should take the property. If Bessie had a fee simple absolute in her husband's property, all of these survivors would take an interest. If she had a qualified estate, only her surviving sister and brother-in-law would take, since they were the "closest relatives."

Issue: What type of interest did Bessie Eskridge receive pursuant to the terms of her husband's will? Who takes the property involved?

Decision: Bessie had a fee simple subject to an executory limitation; therefore, her sister and brother-in-law now own the property.

Reasons: The original language in William Eskridge's will appeared to create a fee simple absolute in favor of Bessie. However, the court had to determine what William Eskridge's intent was by using the language quoted above. The court reasoned that William intended to give his wife a qualified fee simple estate subject to her failure to dispose of this property during her lifetime. Furthermore, William intended any property not disposed of to go to third parties—their closest relatives. In other words, these relatives had executory interests. By giving this meaning to William Eskridge's will, Bessie held property under a fee simple subject to an executory limitation. Since the stated condition occurred (Bessie failed to dispose of this property), the closest relatives' executory interests became fee simple absolute interests. Closest relatives are determined by degrees of relationships, and brothers and sisters are closer relatives than are nephews and nieces. Therefore, since they were not the "closest relatives," the children of Bessie Eskridge's deceased sister have no interest in the property.

Bradley v. Eskridge, 361 So.2d 100 (Ala. 1978).

---

6. Noninheritable Freehold Estates

A₃ (·7

Essentially a noninheritable freehold estate is an ownership interest of indeterminable length that ends when the holder dies. Traditionally, these interests are called *life estates.* A life estate may be measured by the grantee's life, by marriage, or by some other stated condition. These interests may be created by deed, will, or operation of law.

The typical life estate allows the grantee to possess an ownership interest for as long as the grantee lives. The simple phrase "To Allen for life" creates a life estate with Allen as a life tenant. The life estate has become very useful in estate-tax planning. The grantee, also called the life tenant, has the right to transfer the life estate; however, that transfer is still subject to termination on the grantee's death. For example, suppose Allen receives property to use as long as he lives, and Allen transfers his interest to Barbara. Barbara now owns this property only until Allen's death.

Since the grantee's interest in a life estate ends at the grantee's or another person's death, the grantor might retain a reversionary interest, which is alienable, devisable, and descendible at all times. In the alternative, a grantor may appoint a third party to receive the ownership interest at the life tenant's death. This third person is called a remainderman, and he has a future interest, which also is freely alienable, devisable, and descendible.

A life estate does not have to be based on the grantee's life. Indeed, a grantor can create a life estate in favor of one person that is based on the life of another person. This latter interest is most accurately called an estate *pur autre vie* (for the life of another). In addition, the grantor can condition the duration of the grantee's estate upon any number of conditions. For example, assume that the family residence was owned solely by the husband. If he so desired, he could provide in his will that his wife has the use of the family home for as long as she remains unmarried. This woman's interest would terminate either on her death or on her remarriage, whichever occurred first.

Obviously, a person who has a life estate does not and should not have the freedom to use the land as an owner of a fee simple absolute interest. This life tenant's interest is not permanent, since it is conditioned on a person's life or some event. Nevertheless, the life tenant must pay the real property taxes and any mortgage payments when they become due. Furthermore, a life tenant has the responsibility to maintain improvements on the real estate. In essence, due to the temporary nature of life estates, the law generally requires the life tenant to use the land in a reasonable manner so that the land's value is not diminished or destroyed. In other words, during the period of the life estate's existence, the life tenant cannot waste the land or its resources. A person who has a life estate interest in timber- or oil-producing land cannot unreasonably increase the production of these natural resources. Because they have a future financial interest in the land subject to a present life estate, the grantor or the remainderman may sue to enjoin a life tenant's destruction or waste of that land's value.

Case 2.3

W. L. McClure owned a life estate in a tract of timberland, with the remainder interest being in his children in fee simple absolute. Although this timber had never been cut for commercial uses, McClure began removing timber from the land for profit motives. It was not necessary that the timber be cut in order to properly preserve or protect the property. The remaindermen interfered with McClure's timber-cutting efforts, and McClure commenced this action to enjoin them from interfering.

Issue: Was McClure entitled to cut timber from land in which he possessed a life estate?

Decision: No. McClure was unable to prevent interference by the remaindermen.

Reasons: A life tenant may cut timber only in order to properly preserve and protect the property. McClure's motive was profit, not preservation or protection of the property. He therefore had no right to cut the timber or keep the remaindermen from interfering with him

McClure v. Chastain, 128 S.E.2d 721 (Ga. 1962).

If this timberland had been used to make profits from cutting timber, then the life tenant would have been allowed to continue the cutting operation. Even under this assumption, the life tenant must refrain from increasing the tree cutting which may cause detriment to the land's value.

Most states have created ownership interest to protect surviving spouses from their deceased husband's creditors. These states have enacted statutes that provide for dower and curtesy, which are forms of life estates created by law. *Dower* provides that a wife has some inchoate interest (usually one-third) in all the real property her husband owned during their marriage. The word *inchoate* means incomplete or unfinished. As applied to dower, an inchoate interest indicates that the wife's ownership will become possessory only if she survives her husband.

In its strictest application, once the inchoate dower interest existed in real estate, it could not be removed without the wife's approval. For example, if Mr. Miller owned a piece of real estate, a farm, during his marriage, Mrs. Miller's inchoate dower interest in this farm would attach. Suppose Mr. Miller sold the farm to Mr. Nuckolls, and only his signature appeared on the deed as grantor. When Mr. Miller died, his wife could still claim for as long as she lived one-third interest in the farm Mr. Nuckolls bought. From this example, it is clear that purchasers of land, in states that recognize full dower interests, should always have the grantor and his wife sign the deed. The wife's signature would abolish her dower interest in this real property.

To avoid the potential charge of unconstitutional sexual discrimination against men, some state legislatures created *curtesy* interests or made dower applicable to both sexes. Curtesy, in its historical form, provides the husband with an inchoate interest in the land his wife owned during their marriage. The husband's interest does not become possessory until his wife's death. Like dower, the husband's curtesy interests are only for his life. At the surviving spouse's death, dower and curtesy cease. These legal life estates are taken free from any judgment liens or other creditor's claim except for the purchase-money mortgage (debt incurred to buy the real estate). Some states have required that a minor child be living when the wife dies before the husband's curtesy interests exist. If that state does not have a similar condition on the wife's dower interest, this conditional aspect of curtesy is probably unconstitutional as discriminatory. Modern dower and curtesy vary from state to state; indeed, some states have abolished these interests altogether. Recently, unmarried couples who lived together have asked courts to divide the property they acquired during their cohabitation. This could develop a new area of the law related to the rights of unmarried cohabitants based on contract, rather than property, law.

Freehold Estates: Future Interests

7. Introduction

Because the fee simple absolute interest is the only estate whereby the grantee receives complete ownership rights, all the other inheritable and noninheritable qualified estates are followed by a *future interest.* Since the entire bundle of ownership interests must always be held by someone, the law has to provide where the ownership interest goes upon the happening of those events that terminate the original grantee's interest. Future interests serve this purpose. Basically five types of future interest exist, including

- Remainders
- Reversions
- Possibilities of reverter
- Rights of entry
- Executory interests

8. Remainders

As 1-8

In a general sense, any interest that potentially may survive the original estate is the remainder of that complete ownership interest. However, the law has developed in such a way that the word *remainder* is not applicable to the interest following any fee simple estate. Therefore, remainders are simply those interests given to a third party after a life estate or other interest that is not a fee simple. Third parties may be absolutely certain that they will receive this remainder after the life estate ends, or they may be uncertain due to some condition that must be satisfied.

Parties who are sure they will have present ownership interest when a life estate ends possess a *vested* remainder. For example, if the grantor deeds real property to Alex for life, then to Bill and his heirs, Bill has a vested remainder in fee simple absolute. In other words, regardless of the events that occur, Bill knows his interest will become possessory when Alex dies. This vested remainder has some value; it can be sold or otherwise transferred during the remainderman's life; or it can be conveyed to whomever Bill names in a will. A vested remainder is freely alienable, devisable, and descendible even during the life estate's existence.

Perhaps it is not clear whether a remainderman's interest will definitely become possessory. Some stated condition can make the remainder uncertain. For instance, a grantor could leave land to Angela for life, then if at Angela's death Barbara is twenty-five years old, remainder to Barbara and her heirs. Assuming that Barbara is under the age of twenty-five, she has a *contingent remainder.* Due to the contingency based on Barbara's age, this remainder may never vest. Nevertheless, this contingent remainder is alienable, devisable, and descendible. Of course, if Barbara becomes twenty-five years old during Angela's lifetime, the stated condition is satisfied, resulting in the automatic creation of a vested remainder.

As previously discussed, remaindermen have the right to make sure that the holder of a life estate does not destroy or waste the land's valuable resources. In essence, the grantor who creates a life estate with a remainder intends the life tenant to use the land temporarily and the remaindermen to enjoy the land permanently. Furthermore, if there is more than one person who has a remainder interest, they must all agree how to use the land's resources during the existence of a life estate. Only after the land has been divided or partitioned among the various remaindermen do these individuals have the right to use the land as they please.

Case 2.4

Mittie Threatt owned a life estate in certain timberland as well as a one-fourth undivided interest in the remainder. The other three-fourths remainder interests were owned by her children. Mittie decided to "improve" the timberland by harvesting the mature trees. The children opposed her decision and brought this action to enjoin Mittie from harvesting the timber. Mittie contended that: (1) as life tenant, she could harvest timber; and (2) as owner of a one-fourth undivided interest, she could harvest one-fourth of the total timber without consulting the other owners and without sharing the proceeds with them.

Issue: Does a life tenant of timberland have the right to cut timber? In the alternative, does the owner of a one-fourth remainder interest have the right to harvest one-fourth of the timber without her fellow remaindermen's permission?

Decision: The answer to both questions is no! Mittie was enjoined from cutting timber.

Reasons: A life tenant may not lessen the value of the remainder interests. Mittie's plans were of great magnitude and not merely for the purpose of improving or maintaining the estate. If she were allowed to proceed with her timber-cutting plans, waste would have resulted and the remainder interests of her children would have been diminished. In addition, Mittie as owner of an undivided interest could not sever timber from the land without the consent of the other owners; to allow a co-remainderman to act unilaterally would promote chaos.

Threatt v. Rushing, 361 So.2d 329 (Miss. 1978).

9.   Reversions

Like a remainder, a *reversion* can follow only life estates and other interests which are not a fee simple. The principal distinguishing feature of a reversion is that it is an interest retained by the grantor. If a grantor of a life estate fails to specify where the ownership interest vests at the life estate's conclusion, that grantor retains a reversion. Under these circumstances, the ownership interest would return or revert to the grantor upon the life tenant's death. By necessity a reversionary interest also follows a contingent remainder, since that interest may never be possessed by the remainderman. In a preceding example, if Barbara's remainder is conditioned on her reaching the age of twenty-five before the life estate ends and Barbara does not turn twenty-five before the life tenant dies, the grantor's reversionary interest defeats this contingent remainder. Normally a reversion that follows a contingent remainder is of less value than one that directly follows a life estate, since the latter interest is certain to become possessory. Nevertheless, at all times the grantor's reversion is alienable, devisable, and descendible.

10.   Possibilities of Reverter

As 1-5
PoR - pg 34
FSD - pg 34

The *possibility of reverter* follows a fee simple determinable estate. This future interest held by the grantor operates automatically to return the possessory interest to the grantor upon the occurrence of the stated condition. Examples of a fee simple determinable include "To Adam so long as the land is used for church purposes." If Adam allowed a food franchise to establish a business on this land, Adam's loss of his interest would result in the grantor once again having the preexisting ownership interest. This future interest cannot be called a reversion, because the grantor's interest following a fee simple determinable may never become possessory. There is only a possibility that the interest will revert to the grantor. Despite the uncertainty surrounding the vesting of the possibility of reverter, this future interest is generally considered to be alienable, devisable, and descendible.

Case 2.5

In 1919, Stephens owned certain land which he conveyed to a railroad as a right of way, but only so long as the land was used as a right of way. The deed further stated that if the railroad ceased using the land as a right of way, the land would revert to Stephens and his heirs. In 1937, Stephens conveyed the land to the parents of Tolke, the defendant. This conveyance was subject to the railroad's right of way on the land. Tolke acquired the land in 1956 from his parents. The railroad ceased to use the property as a right of way in 1974, and its rights in the land were conveyed to Tolke in August, 1975. In September, 1975, the State of Oregon obtained a deed to this land from the heirs of Stephens. The State then brought this action for trespass, contending that the conveyance from Stephens to the railroad in 1919 conveyed a fee simple determinable with a possibility of reverter in Stephens and his heirs, and Stephens' heirs became owners of the property in 1974 when the railroad ceased using it as a right of way.

Issue: Did the original deed convey a fee simple determinable, and, if so, did Stephens have the power to convey the possibility of reverter to Tolke's parents in 1937?

Decision: Yes. The 1919 deed conveyed a fee simple determinable, and the possibility of reverter in the grantor's heirs was conveyed to Tolke's parents by Stephens in 1937. Accordingly, the State owned no interest in the land, and the trespass action against Tolke could not be maintained.

Reasons: The deed from Stephens to the railroad used the magic words "so long as," which have consistently been held to create a fee simple determinable. In the 1937 deed to Tolke's parents, Stephens intended to convey his possibility of reverter. This Oregon court decided that a grantor has the power to convey a possibility of reverter to another person. The court reasoned that no policy existed that should prevent a possibility of reverter from being alienable. Therefore, Tolke's parents acquired the possibility of reverter in 1937, and the State acquired nothing from Stephens' heirs in 1975.

State v. Tolke, 586 P.2d 791 (Ore. App. 1978).

A few states (including Connecticut, Florida, Illinois, Iowa, Kentucky, Maine, Maryland, Massachusetts, Michigan, Minnesota, Nebraska, New York, Ohio, and Rhode Island) have statutes that place a limitation of between twenty to forty years on the life of the possibilities of reverter. Thus if the condition stated in the fee simple determinable does not occur within the statutory period from the time the grant was made, the possibility of reverter ceases to exist and the grantee's interest becomes permanent. If the above case has occurred in one of the states that limits the life of possibilities of reverter, the railroad's right of way could not have been defeated. These states limit the life of this future interest so that the uncertainty surrounding an owner's fee simple determinable title will not last indefinitely.

11. Rights of Entry

By using clear language, the grantor can reserve a *right of entry* following a fee simple on a condition subsequent estate. For example, a grantor might convey real property upon the following condition: "To Alicia provided that this land is used as a public park, but if not, the grantor has the right of entry." This right of entry does not automatically terminate Alicia's interest; if the land is not used as a public park, the grantor can take steps to reclaim the full preexisting ownership interest. Until the right of entry is exercised, Alicia will continue to hold the land. Due to its nature, the right of entry commonly is referred to as a power of termination. This future interest can be distributed by will or intestate succession; however, some states do not allow the transfer of the right of entry to another person during the grantor's life. The logic for restricting the alienability of this interest is that it is personal to the grantor. The reasons for exercising or failing to exercise the right of entry may not be the same for the grantor and someone who receives the interest by transfer. Furthermore, a few states have limited the duration of a right of entry in much the same way they have limited the time period of a possibility of reverter.

12. Executory Interests

The possibility of reverter and the right of entry are often called reversionary interests since they originally are retained by the grantor. The *executory interest* more closely resembles a remainder, since it is held by a third party. The present freehold estate called a fee simple subject to an executory limitation actually takes its name from this future interest. For example, land is deeded "to Albert provided that no alcoholic beverages are sold on this property, and if any such beverages are sold, then to Burt and his heirs." Burt has an executory interest that will automatically become possessory if Albert fails to satisfy continuously the condition placed on his present estate. Executory interests generally are alienable, devisable, and descendible. As with the possibility of reverter and the right of entry, some states place a twenty-to-forty-year limit on executory interests. In other words, if the grantee holds a fee simple subject to an executory limitation estate for the statutory period, that interest will be upgraded to a fee simple absolute estate. At that time the executory interest ceases to exist.

13. Special Rules Related to Future Interests

Centuries ago the English courts developed special rules concerning the future interests just discussed. For a more complete understanding of these interests and estates in land, three of these rules are considered.

A. RULE IN SHELLEY'S CASE

This rule applies when a grantor creates a life estate in favor of a grantee and leaves the remainder to the heirs of the grantee. The language of this type of grant might be: "To Donald for life, remainder to Donald's heirs." The life estate and the remainder must be established at the same time in the same conveyance. When a grantee has a life estate and that grantee's heirs have a remainder established by the same conveyance and their interests are both legal or equitable, the grantee has both the possessory estate and the remainder.

In other words, the Rule in Shelley's Case upgrades the grantee's life estate to an inheritable freehold interest, most commonly a fee simple absolute. Today in the United States, most states have abolished this rule by legislation. In these states, under the language quoted in the previous paragraph, the grantee would receive only a life estate. The grantee's heirs would have a type of contingent remainder, since the total number of heirs cannot be ascertained until the grantee's death.

B.   Doctrine of Worthier Title

Grantors may wish to provide a life estate in favor of a grantee but retain a remainder for their own heirs. The language of this grant may be: "To Jonathan for life, then the remainder to the heirs of the *grantor.*" Under the English common law and in most states today, the Doctrine of Worthier Title abolishes the grantor's heirs' remainder and provides that the grantor retains a reversion. Where this doctrine applies, the grantor has the power to transfer this reversionary interest while alive or at death by will or intestacy. During the life estate it is the grantor, not the heirs, who has a cause of action against the life tenant for waste. In the states which have abolished the Doctrine of Worthier Title, the grantor's heirs will have a remainder. Under those laws, the grantor would not have any interest at all.

C.   Rule Against Perpetuities

As has been previously emphasized, the law prefers that ownership of land be definite and held by an ascertainable person. Some future interests, particularly remainders and executory interests, leave the issue of ownership open. For example, suppose that a landowner left a will providing that the family farm should go "to my wife for life, then to my only son's children that reach thirty years old; however, if my son has no children to reach thirty years old, then to the local community government of Fitzgerald." The grantor's grandchildren have a contingent remainder, and the Fitzgerald community has an alternative contingent remainder. There is uncertainty as to who will own this farm after the life estate ends. The law does not allow this uncertainty to last forever. Indeed, the rule against perpetutities provides that all interests must vest, if at all, within a life or lives in being plus twenty-one years from the time the interest in created.

This complex-sounding rule simply limits how long a contingent remainder or executory interest can exist before it becomes void. In the example above, assume all these facts:

1. When the grantor died, his only son had no children.
2. The grantor's wife, the life tenant, died before her son died.
3. The grantor's son died when his only children were two and six years old.

Is there any way these two grandchildren can reach the age of thirty within twenty-one years after their father died? No! Therefore, as long as there were no grandchildren alive when the grantor died, this grant violates the rule against perpetuities whether the grantor's wife and son died as stated or not.

Future interests (including remainders, executory interests, and contractual options[1]) are void if they will not vest within the time period provided by the rule against perpetuities. However, this rule generally does not apply to charitable gifts. When the future interest is void, the grantor is deemed to have retained a reversion. Thus, in the family-farm example above, the land would go to whomever the grantor designated in his will to take any residual interests not otherwise given away in his will.

14. Nonfreehold Estates

A nonfreehold estate is a possessory interest created by the establish-ment of a landlord-tenant relationship. Typically these estates are called leasehold interests, and they may last for a definite time period or for as long as the parties are willing to continue their relationship. For the duration of a lease, the tenant possesses or occupies the land with the understanding that the landlord retains full ownership of the real property. Leases can be divided into the following four categories:

Intro - pg 31

- Tenancy for stated period
- Tenancy from period to period
- Tenancy at will
- Tenancy at sufferance

A lease for a stated period of time occurs when a landlord and a tenant enter into an agreement for a specified term. The stated period may be forty years, five years, one month, or any other agreed-upon time. Some states interpret a lease for ninety-nine years or longer as actually conveying a fee simple absolute interest. Often when the stated period exceeds one year, the lease is referred to as a term of years. In most states the statute of frauds requires that all leases be in writing and

[1]Thomas v. Murrow, page 54.

signed by the parties if the lease period will exceed one year. The tenancy for a stated period terminates automatically at the end of the period. Unless otherwise provided, this lease is not terminated by either the destruction of the premises or the death of the tenant or the landlord.

The tenancy from period to period is created when the landlord and tenant agree to continue their relationship from year to year or month to month. For example, the agreement may establish an original term of one year, with the provision that the lease is to continue from year to year unless terminated by either party upon proper notice. The method of giving proper notice should be set forth in the lease agreement. Notice of termination thirty to sixty days prior to the expiration of a period seems most common.

If a lease term is not specified, the parties likely have entered into a tenancy at will. As the name implies, this lease lasts as long as both the tenant and landlord desire. The tenancy at will can be treated as a lease from month to month. The required termination notice is provided by state statute. A thirty-day notice is most typical for the tenant; however, some states require that the landlords give sixty days advance notice of termination. Although the tenancy at will might last more than one year, the original agreement does not have to be in writing, since the possibility of its ending within one year always exists.

A tenancy at sufferance occurs when a tenant refuses to leave the premises at the termination of the lease. The landlord must decide either to evict this holdover tenant or to negotiate a new lease aggreement. A tenancy at sufferance also might occur when a homeowner has the existing mortgage foreclosed and sold at a public auction. Until the original mortgagor moves out, a tenancy at sufferance is established with the purchaser at the foreclosure sale being treated like a landlord.

The lease transaction and the landlord-tenant relationship is discussed in more detail in Chapter 16.

Concurrent Estates

15. Introduction

The preceding discussion of property interests has been based on the assumption that only one person owns each interest. These interests are known as estates in severalty. However, all real and personal property may be owned by more than one person at the same time. The most widely used forms of concurrent ownership are the

- Tenancy in common
- Joint tenancy
- Tenancy by the entirety
- Community property

The word "tenancy" as used in this section should not be confused with the same word used in the landlord-tenant relationship.

16. Tenancy in Common

As 1- 9a The traditional form of multiple ownership is the *tenancy in common.* Each owner who is a tenant in common owns an undivided proportional interest of the entire property; however, the shares do not have to be equal. For example, suppose a landowner, who has a fee simple absolute interest, dies without a valid will and is survived by two children, Alice and Bill. These survivors would become tenants in common of their parent's land. Furthermore, suppose Alice sells one-fifth of her interest to Carla. Now Alice, Bill, and Carla are tenants in common owning 40 percent, 50 percent, and 10 percent, respectively. This example shows that the interests owned by tenants in common generally are freely alienable, devisable, and descendible.

Tenants in common are fiduciaries for each other. This means that each owner is in a position of trust and confidence with respect to all the other cotenants. For instance, if one of the cotenants is responsible for managing the mutually-owned land, the cotenant must exercise good-faith judgment. Upon incurring reasonable expenses in maintaining or repairing the real property, the managing owner can expect to recover the pro rata share of the expenditures from the other cotenants. Also with respect to their mutual-fiduciaries duties, possession by one or more of the cotenants is held to be for the benefit of all cotenants. Therefore, one cotenant generally cannot gain exclusive ownership of real estate by having sole possession over a long time period. An ouster of fellow cotenants must occur before one cotenant's claim can be considered adverse to the other's ownership interests.

Case 2.6

Upon the death of Thomas Jones and his wife in 1936, their real property passed to their six children as tenants in common. Since that time, one son, Hardie, has been in sole possession of this land. Hardie has farmed, pastured, and collected rents on the land. Hardie now files suit against his brothers and sisters, and he asks the court to declare him the sole owner of the land formerly held by these parties as tenants in common.

Issue: Can one cotenant, who has exclusive possession of the real estate, become the sole owner and defeat the other cotenants' ownership interest?

Decision: No, not as long as the cotenant in possession recognizes the other cotenants' rights.

Reasons: The possession of one tenant in common is presumed to be possession of all cotenants. The mere use of the land, the payment of taxes, and the collection of rents by one cotenant does not necessarily demonstrate that party's adverse interest. Indeed, the intent to hold land as the exclusive owner to defeat cotenants' interests must be proven. It also must be proven that the other cotenants were aware of this adverse possession. In this case, Hardie failed to show that his intent and his actions were adverse to his brothers' and sisters' interests. Therefore, his possession of this land was deemed to be possession for all the tenants in common. In other words, title to this land remained in all these children's names as tenants in common.

Jones v. Ball, 320 So.2d 665 (Ala. 1975).

---

17. Joint Tenancy

A₃ 1-9b   A more specialized type of multiple ownership is the *joint tenancy with right of survivorship.* This right of survivorship means that upon a cotenant's death the surviving fellow owners will automatically divide the share that the deceased person owned. Courts generally do not favor this right of survivorship; therefore, the creation of a joint tenancy must be very specific. The following language often is used:

> "To Alex and Betty, not as tenants in common, but as joint tenants with right of survivorship."

If Alex and Betty remain joint tenants and Betty predeceases Alex, Alex will become the sole owner of the property.

In order to establish a valid joint tenancy, the four unities of time, title, interest, and possession must be present. The unity of time requires that the joint tenants' ownership be created in the same convey-ance. To have the unity of title, each owner must have the same estate, such as a fee simple absolute, a remainder, or any other estate, which is created by the same conveyance. The unity of interest means each owner has the same percentage interest subject to the owners' interest. For example, two joint tenants must each own 50 percent of the undi-vided property, three own 33.3 percent each, four own 25 percent each, and so forth. Finally, unity of possession is present only if each joint tenant has the right to possess all of the real estate subject to the owners' rights of possession.

Originally, due to the unity-of-time requirement, a grantor who was the sole owner of a piece of land could not create a joint tenancy with right of survivorship between himself and a grantee. To get around this problem, the grantor had to deed the property to a friendly third party, known as a straw man, who would then transfer that property to the grantor and friend as joint tenants. Some states have abolished the need to use a straw man in the above situation. In other words, these states have relaxed the unity of time requirement under these particular circumstances.

The right of survivorship prevents a joint tenant from passing his interest by will or intestate succession. Nevertheless, joint tenants may agree to terminate their respective rights of survivorship,[2] or these interests may be freely transferred by one of the joint tenants during his or her life. This latter power is called the *right of severance.* It is very important to realize that a transfer of any of the joint tenants' interests results in a termination of the joint tenancy and the right of survivor-ship. Suppose a landowner passes ownership to his children, Alfred and Beatrice, as joint tenants with right of survivorship and not as tenants in common. There is no doubt that Alfred and Beatrice own this prop-erty fifty-fifty. Assume Alfred sells one-fifth of his interest to Charles. Now Alfred owns 40 percent, Beatrice owns 50 percent, and Charles owns 10 percent as *tenants in common.* The joint tenancy was destroyed or severed by Alfred's conveyance.

However, assume that Alfred, Beatrice, and Charles own a piece of real estate as joint tenants with rights of survivorship. They would each own the entire parcel subject to the rights of the other joint tenants. The unity of interest requirement of a joint tenancy means that these parties each own a thirty-three percent undivided interest in the prop-erty. What would be the result if Charles transferred his interest to

[2]Estate of Gebert v. Gebert, page 55.

David? How would Alfred, Beatrice, and David now concurrently own this property? To answer these questions, Alfred and Beatrice must be viewed as one owner and David as another. As to their combined interest, Alfred and Beatrice are still joint tenants. Together they own this property as tenants in common with David. Thus, if Alfred predeceases Beatrice, she acquires his thirty-three percent interest by right of survivorship. Then Beatrice and David are tenants in common owning two-thirds and one-third interests, respectively.

18.   Tenancy by the Entirety

A tenancy by the entirety is a specialized type of joint tenancy. The distinguishing characteristic of the tenancy by the entirety is that it can be created only between husbands and wives. As in the joint tenancy, the right of survivorship is present in a tenancy by the entirety. Moreover, this right of survivorship generally is assured. Indeed, the interests held by each of these cotenants, as individuals, are not alienable, devisable, or descendible. Once a tenancy by the entirety is created, the right of survivorship is destroyed only by the couple voluntarily and jointly conveying their combined interests or by a court partitioning or dividing the couple's interests. A divorce suit involving a couple owning real property as tenants by the entirety is a common example of when a court would partition the joint interests, thereby terminating the right of survivorship. Until the tenancy by the entirety is terminated, a creditor of one spouse cannot make a claim against real estate owned by a couple jointly in the entirety.

The four unities discussed above must be present to create a valid tenancy by the entirety. However, some states relax the unity of time in order for a spouse, who is the sole owner, to create a tenancy by the entirety with the other spouse without the use of a straw man. If the language of creation does not clearly specify a tenancy by the entirety, most courts will interpret the concurrent estate to be a tenancy in common. Most courts' general preference for a tenancy in common indicates that the existence of the right of survivorship will be narrowly construed. Whereas some states have abolished the tenancy by the entirety altogether, other states rely on this form of joint ownership as the most important method for spouses to own property together.

Some people have proposed that use of the right of survivorship is a way to avoid the need for a will and probate proceedings. Such advice is very short-sighted. The use of rights of survivorship may aid in efficient estate planning. However, joint tenancies with right of survivorship also may cause substantial estate- and gift-tax liability. Whether a joint tenancy or a tenancy by the entirety is preferable to a tenancy in common cannot be universally answered for all situations. Consultation with an attorney experienced in real property law and estate planning is the best practice when deciding how real estate should be owned by more than one party.

19. Community Property

Eight states (Arizona, California, Idaho, Louisiana, Nevada, New Mexico, Texas, and Washington) recognize a system of property rights between husbands and wives called community property. In these states, all the property acquired during the marriage, whether real or personal, may be considered property of the marital community. In other words, ownership of this property is divided fifty-fifty between the husband and the wife. This division disregards the financial contribution each spouse actually made to the property's acquisition. Community property laws have typically permitted the husband to manage the community property. Although he may be able to transfer personal community property without his wife's consent, he cannot dispose of her real property without her prior approval. Therefore a purchaser of real community property must obtain the husband's and wife's signatures on the sales contract and the deed. A modern trend is to let the wife alone enter into contract with respect to personal property; however, both spouses must be involved in real property transactions.

It is possible for married couples in one of these community property states to acquire property that is not subject to a spouse's interest. Examples of this separate property might include property owned prior to the marriage or property received by one of the spouses as a gift, bequest, or devise. Also any income derived from a spouse's separate property continues to be separate property.

A husband's and wife's interest in their community property is not automatically subject to the right of survivorship. In other words, each spouse's one-half interest can be transferred to anyone by a valid will. If a spouse dies without a will, that interest passes either to the surviving spouse or to surviving descendents, depending on the applicable law of the various states. The states that follow this community property framework do allow married couples to own property as cotenants using one of the concurrent ownership interests discussed above.

Therefore, if a couple owned property as joint tenants or as tenants by the entirety, the right of survivorship would exist.

Cases on Ownership Interests in Land

Thomas v. Murrow
262 S.E.2d 802 (Ga. 1980).

Bowles, J.:

On February 21, 1959, J. A. Thomas, father of appellant C. H. Thomas, conveyed by warranty deed to the appellees, Charles H. Murrow and Joe D. Murrow, a 1.66 acre lot upon which stood a cotton gin. On the same date the Murrows and J. A. Thomas executed a contract which granted J. A. Thomas an option to repurchase the land should the operation of the cotton gin ever cease. After describing the land which the Murrows had just purchased, the option contract stated in pertinent part:

"That said purchase includes other property, but it is distinctly agreed and understood that the consideration recited in the warranty deed this day made by said Thomas to the undersigned, includes the option of said J. A. Thomas to repurchase the above described land from the undersigned or their heirs or assigns, at any time within a five year peiod after the undersigned or their heirs or assigns cease to operate a gin on said lot, and that said J. A. Thomas, his heirs or assigns, shall pay the sum of ONE DOLLAR consideration for said described land, at the time this option is exercised."

In 1975, J. A. Thomas died and the appellant, C. H. Thomas, became the owner of the option which he attempted to exercise in 1977. After the Murrows denied having ceased operation of the cotton gin, Thomas brought suit for specific performance. During the course of the pretrial proceedings the Murrows raised the issue of the rule against perpetuities and so Thomas amended his complaint to seek alternatively rescission, reformation, damages, and/or construction of the warranty deed and the option as the grant of a defeasible or conditional fee. The Murrows counterclaimed seeking to have fee simple title declared to be in them and the option cancelled as a cloud on their title.

The case was tried before a jury on the issue of whether or not the Murrows had ceased operating the cotton gin. At the close of the evidence, the trial court directed a verdict in favor of the Murrows finding that the option violated the rule against perpetuities. Thomas appeals the granting of the directed verdict.

1. The repurchase agreement entered into between the parties was an option in its legal sense. The instrument referred to itself as an option and it contained common place phrases depicting such a document. As Thomas states in his brief: "An option gives the Grantee the right to purchase land at a stated price within a definite time limit." This is what Thomas had. The property did not automatically revert to him when the cotton gin ceased operations. He had to pay one dollar within five years to regain title to the land. The fact that the amount to be paid was one dollar does not change the legal effect of the option. One dollar is not the only sum involved. The original purchase price was $27,000 and the option agreement specifically stated that the sum included the value of the op-

tion. The warranty deed conveyed fee simple title and the option agreement gave an option to repurchase. Construed together the same result obtains.

2. Thomas next contends that if the agreement is, in fact, an option, then the trial court should have granted reformation to reflect the intention of the parties. No evidence was submitted at trial which indicated that the agreement did not reflect the intention of the parties. The question is whether or not the manner in which the parties reflected that intention violates the rule against perpetuities.

3. The option in this case does violate the rule against perpetuities . . . because the cotton gin conceivably may not cease operations until after the twenty-one year period. "The owner of realty may legally sell it to another at an agreed price, and at the same time reserve the right to repurchase the land within a specified time. However, the clause in the present deed, which authorized the grantor to purchase the land at a stated price, without fixing any time limit during which the property should be so used or within which the option should be exercised, was void as violative of the rule against perpetuities." . . .

Judgment affirmed.

Estate of Gebert v. Gebert
157 Cal. Rptr. 46 (Cal. App. Ct. 1979).

After nearly thirty years of marriage Edward and Rosemary Gebert separated, and she filed for divorce. During their marriage, these parties owned a 53-acre ranch as joint tenants. Pending the divorce proceedings, Edward and Rosemary agreed that their ranch should be sold with each of them to receive one-half of the proceeds. This personal agreement was reduced to an informal writing which each party signed on July 22, 1975.

Exactly one week later, Edward died of a heart attack. After his death, it was discovered that Edward had executed a will on June 21, 1975, leaving his entire estate to his nephew and his nephew's wife. This nephew and his wife sued Rosemary and claimed the one-half interest that Edward had owned in the ranch because the contract terminated the joint tenancy. Rosemary argued that the informal agreement signed on July 22, 1975, was only a record of the parties "thoughts." She asserted that any agreement between Edward and herself was not to be effective until a formal agreement was drafted by their lawyers.

Jefferson, J.:

. . . The trial court . . . found that . . . "the parties intended to divide and separate their interests in the Glory Ranch . . . and agreed to do so, as evidenced by the course of dealing between the parties prior to July 22, 1975, and the agreement of July 22, 1975, itself. . . . " Thus the agreement was found to be valid and enforceable.

. . . "The Agreement of July 22, 1975, to sell and divide the proceeds of the Glory Ranch was wholly inconsistent with and interfered with the rights of survivorship, and negated any intention of the survivor to succeed to the other's interest in said prop erty.... The legal effect of the aforesaid interference with the right of survivorship was to sever the joint tenancy ownership...."

Thus, the court concluded that Edward and Rosemary had, before Edward's death, become tenants in common with respect to their interests in the subject property, and, as a result, Edward's share passed by his will to petitioners Joseph and Roni Gebert, rather than to Rosemary by operation of law if she had been a surviving joint tenant of joint tenancy property....

It is generally recognized that a joint tenancy consists of an estate owned jointly in undivided equal shares by two or more persons. At common law, four "unities" were essential to the creation of a joint tenancy—the unities of interest, title, time and possession. "Although California law still requires these same four unities, [they] have been modified substantially from the original common-law concepts." ...

The principal characteristic of joint-tenancy property ownership is the right of survivorship which accrues to a surviving joint tenant; the surviving joint tenant succeeds to the interest of the deceased joint tenant by operation of law. A termination of the joint tenancy, prior to the death of one joint tenant, by converting title to another form such as tenancy in common, destroys this right of survivorship.

The decisional law has recognized various ways in which a joint tenancy may be terminated with the consequent destruction of the right of survivorship. Our review of the decisional law concerning joint tenancy severance supports the conclusion that a major distinction is made between cases in which a joint tenant acts unilaterally with respect to the subject property (short of conveying away his interest), often without the knowledge of the other, and

cases in which the action with respect to the subject joint tenancy property involves both or all the joint tenants. In the first situation, the unilateral action (short of conveying away his interest) does not sever the joint tenancy ordinarily, while in the second situation, the combined action of the joint tenants may have that effect.

The issue before us involves the question of what joint action by joint tenants is deemed sufficient to terminate joint tenancy ownership.... One such action to convert a joint tenancy into a tenancy in common is by "written mutual agreement."

When does a written mutual agreement between joint tenants evince an unequivocal intent to terminate the joint tenancy? ... [I]t was held that a written contract between joint tenants for the sale by one and purchase by the other of the seller's interest terminates the joint tenancy even though the contract is not performed prior to the death of one of the joint tenants. The sale and purchase contract [acts] ... as a conversion of a joint tenancy into a tenancy in common by "written mutual agreement."

In the case at bench, the written agreement between joint tenants is for the sale of the property to a third person—not to one of the joint tenants. Rosemary contends that an agreement between joint tenants to sell the property to a third person is not an act which is "clearly indicative of an intent to terminate" the joint tenancy ...

... Rosemary emphasizes that the actual language of the agreement contemplates a future sale of the ranch ... which, she argues, is inconsistent with an intention to sever the joint tenancy upon execution of the informal settlement agreement. It is our view in the case before us, that whether the agreement is framed in the present or future tense is not of substantial materiality. What is of more importance is the context in which the agreement was made, the surrounding circumstances at the time, and the bargaining by equals with respect to the dissolution of their material status. . . .

. . . The evidence before the trial court was clearly sufficient to support the trial court's concept of the agreement—that it represented the expressed intention of Rosemary and Edward to settle their property differences. It is inconceivable that they were bargaining with a view toward retaining their rights of survivorship until the property was sold and the proceeds received and divided equally between them. On the contrary, it is clear that, by their agreement to sell the ranch, they intended then and there, unequivocally, to terminate the joint tenancy and right of survivorship. We conclude, therefore, that the trial court correctly found that the execution of the agreement itself effected a change from joint tenancy to tenancy in common. . . . The trial court's judgment properly awarded a one-half interest in the subject properites to petitioners.

Affirmed.

REVIEW QUESTIONS

1. Define and distinguish between the following terms:
   a. Freehold estates and nonfreehold estates
   b. Present interests and future interests
   c. Inheritable interests and noninheritable interests
   d. Absolute interests and qualified interests
2. When Scott sold his land to Bailey, the deed stated, "To Bailey, his heirs, and assigns." Who is the grantor? Who is the grantee? What ownership interest was conveyed?
3. Define what it means to say property interests are:
   a. alienable.
   b. devisable.
   c. descendible.
4. Identify the type of estate each person mentioned has in "Blackacre."
   a. Olivia conveys "Blackacre" to Albert so long as Albert remains a bachelor.
   b. Olivia conveys "Blackacre" to Albert and his heirs, but upon the express condition that if the property is used for nonresidential purposes, Olivia may enter and terminate the estate hereby conveyed.
   c. Olivia conveys "Blackacre" to Albert, but if the land is used to serve alcoholic beverages to the public, then to Bob and his heirs.
   d. Olivia conveys "Blackacre" to Albert for life, then to Bob and his heirs, only if Bob reaches the age of twenty-one. (Assume Bob is not twenty-one years old at the time of this conveyance.)
   e. Olivia conveys "Blackacre" to Albert for life, then to Bob and his heirs, but only if Bob reaches the age of twenty-one, if not then to Carla and her heirs. (Again assume Bob is not twenty-one years old at the time of this conveyance.)

5. Rasch agreed to sell real estate to Berg, who paid a $5000 deposit to Rasch at the signing of the contract. At that time Rasch was married, but his wife did not sign the contract. When Berg discovered the land could not be developed as desired, he sought to rescind the contract. Assuming this transaction occurred in a state that recognized dower interests, how could Berg justify his rescission?

6. John Elder, in his will, left some real property to his daughter for life, then to his grandchildren for life, and then to his great grandchildren when they reach the age of twenty-one. Do any of these devises violate the rule against perpetuities? Discuss.

7. Thomas agreed to rent a two-bedroom house from Louise for a five-year period. Typically the lease must be in writing to be enforceable. Why? What type of lease, or nonfreehold estate, is involved in this transaction?

8. In a will, Frances left real estate to "Mary and Henry for life with survivor taking in fee simple." Henry sold his interest in this property to Ted. Henry then died before Mary. Who has superior title to this property—Mary or Ted? Why?

9. Peter and Paul were business partners who owned real estate as joint tenants and not as tenants in common. At the time of Peter's death, a dispute arose between Peter's heirs and Paul as to who owned Peter's one-half interest in the property. Who is entitled to the property interest that Peter had? Explain.

10. Hugh and Winnie, as husband and wife, owned a home in Arizona that qualified as community property. After a dispute, Hugh sold this house. The buyer received a deed signed only by Hugh. Did this buyer receive good title to the real estate? Explain.

3

Other Interests and Rights in Land

1. Introduction

A person may have interests or rights in land other than those estates in land discussed in the previous chapter. Without actually shifting title to real property, certain interests allow a person to use the owner's land. Examples of these types of interests include: easements, licenses, and *profits à prendre*. Further, owners whose land touches a body of water have certain rights and duties with respect to using the water. These water rights also are discussed in this chapter.

Easements

2. Types

Easements are both a nonpossessory property interest held by one party and a restriction on the ownership interest of another party. Basically an *easement* is a right given to one person by a landowner to use that owner's land in a specified manner. For example, a landowner might grant to the local utility company the right to bury electrical cables under part of the owner's land. Traditionally, an easement is either affirmative or negative in nature. An affirmative easement consists of the right to use land not owned. An example of a negative easement might occur when a landowner is restricted from building a structure over a certain height (say five stories) on the land owned.

An easement usually is characterized as either an easement appurtenant or an easement in gross. An *easement appurtenant* exists when an owner of real estate has the right to use a part of another owner's land. A dominant and a servient estate must be present in order to have an easement appurtenant. A *dominant estate* is the land that is being served or benefited by the existence of an easement on some other land. A *servient estate* is the land on which the easement actually exists. Generally, this servient estate is referred to as the burdened land.

Suppose that Chris Hilsman and Fred Bridges were neighbors and each wanted to have a paved driveway. In order to save in many respects, suppose the Hilsmans and the Bridges decided to share the building costs of one driveway, which was to be located on both sides of their boundary line. Before either neighbor would be willing to pay half of the driveway's expenses, they would need assurances of their right to use it. This could be accomplished by Chris granting Fred and Fred granting Chris an easement appurtenent for the purpose of using the portion of the driveway on each other's land. Both of these lots would be the burdened or servient estate as well as the benefited or dominant estate. In essence, the easement appurtenant relates to each party's land and is not merely a personal right or obligation. In other words, any future owners of these lots would have the use of this driveway, and these future owners would be obligated to share the driveway with one another.

In an *easement in gross* no dominant estate exists. In other words, an individual, whether an owner of real property or not, possesses the right to use another's land. A landowner's permission granted to the city for a sewer right of way or a grant to a utility company to run wires across the land are examples of easements in gross. The servient estate is the land on which the easement exists; however, the benefit of the easement is not associated with a specific piece of real estate.

The owner of an easement (whether appurtenant or in gross) has the primary responsibility for maintaining that part of the servient estate that is affected by the easement and consequently has the right to come onto the servient estate for the purpose of maintenance. The owner of the servient estate should not block or inhibit the easement's use. However, if the easement is obstructed it may be terminated as discussed in Section 7, below.

3. Easements Created by Grant or Reservation

Both easements appurtenant and easements in gross may be established in a number of ways. The most common methods of creation are by express grant or reservation, implication, or prescription.

Easements represent ownership interests in land as well as restrictions on the freehold owner's title. Since interests in land ownership are involved, easements should be created by express written legal documents, commonly called *grants*. These grants must designate the parties; must accurately describe the property being burdened (the servient estate) in all cases, and the benefited land (the dominant estate) if an easement appurtenant is created; and must be signed by all the parties. The grant should specifically state the permissive use conveyed. A very common easement is for ingress and egress over the servient estate to the dominant land. For example, suppose Samuel owned rural property that fronted on a public highway to the north. Linda owned the land directly south of Samuel's, and her best access to the highway was over Samuel's land. Samuel could expressly grant Linda the right to use the fifteen feet along his eastern boundary. This easement appurtenant is represented in Exhibit 3.1. In this example, Samuel's land is the burdened or servient estate, while Linda's land is the benefited or dominant estate.

An easement may also be established by an *express reservation*. Now assume that if Samuel sold the northern half of his land to Bob, the remainder of Samuel's property would be landlocked. In the deed transferring ownership of the frontage land to Bob, Samuel could reserve a right of passageway along the eastern boundary of Bob's newly-acquired land. By this express reservation in the sale of land, an easement appurtenant has been created. Exhibit 3.2 depicts this easement. Prior to looking at this figure, can you determine whose land is the dominant and who owns the servient estate?

The issue has been raised whether a seller of land can reserve an easement over the land being sold when that easement is in favor of a third person. The following case addresses this question.

Center Company was the owner of certain real estate. In 1970, it sold a portion of this land to Sedgwick House. Two years later, Center Company conveyed the remainder of its land to Brademas. In the deed delivered to Brademas, Center Company reserved an easement across Brademas' land allowing the Sedgwick House to discharge its surface and drainage water onto Brademas' land. These transactions can be depicted as follows:

Lot "A"
Owned by Center Co.

Sedgwick House   Center Company

Sedgwick House   Brademas
                        - - - - - - - - - - -
                        ↑
                        Drainage easement
                        granted to Sedgwick
                        House by Center Co.
                        at time lot sold to Brademas.

Brademas filed suit against Center Company and Sedgwick House, seeking to have this easement declared nonexistent.

Issue: Can one party (Center Company) transfer land to a second party (Brademas) and reserve an easement across this land in favor of a third party (Sedgwick House)?

Decision: Yes. This reserved easement is valid.

Reasons: It was clearly the intent of Center Company to create an easement in favor of Sedgwick House at the time the land was sold to Brademas. There is no question that Center Company, as the grantor, could have reserved this specific easement for itself. Having reserved a particular interest from the operation of the grant, the grantor may transfer the reserved easement to whomever it chooses. There is no justifiable reason why the grantor should be prevented from doing in one step that which it can do in two.

Brademas v. Hartwig, 369 N.E.2d 954 (Ind. App. 1977).

EXHIBIT 3.1   EASEMENT CREATED BY EXPRESS GRANT

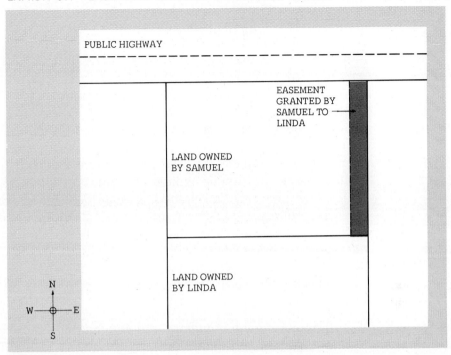

EXHIBIT 3.2   EASEMENT CREATED BY EXPRESS RESERVATION

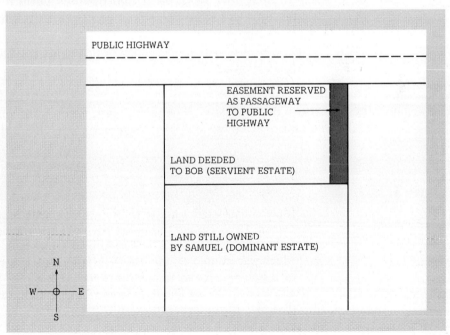

4. Easements Created by Implication

Sometimes when easements are not expressly created, the right of permissive use may be implied from the factual circumstances. A landowner might use part of the land to benefit another party. If the landowner then transfers one part and retains the other, it is best that all easements be expressly stated. However, in cases such as the preceding examples concerning access to landlocked property, often no mention of an easement will be made in a sales transaction. If in Figure 3.1 Samuel sold the portion designated to Linda and allowed her to use the road on the property he retained, an easement by *implied grant* likely would be established. Likewise in Exhibit 3.2, Samuel's continued use of the passageway over the land granted to Bob would create an easement by *implied reservation.* In both these situations, the implied easement is called an *easement by necessity.*

Typically, an easement created by implication must be accompanied by these factors:

- The title to the dominant and servient land must have been in one person and then a portion granted to another.
- The previous use of one tract of land for the benefit of another portion must have been clear and obvious upon inspection.
- The previous use must have been continuous before the owner divided the interests.
- The easement must be necessary in order for the benefited land to retain its value.

The crucial issue in determining whether an easement is implied is the question of necessity. The following case is an example of a grantee claiming that an implied easement exists on the grantor's land.

Case 3.2

Joule constructed a house on the western part of a tract that he owned. He occupied the house for fifteen years, until he sold it to Haines. The house was served by a septic-tank system, all of which was located on the tract sold to Haines except for ten feet of a line which ran under property retained by Joule. Lackey acquired the house and tract from Haines without any knowledge that part of the septic-tank system ran under land retained by Joule. Joule informed Lackey that if Lackey did not remove that portion of the system that ran under Joule's land, Joule himself would dig it up and remove it. Lackey brought this action seeking to enjoin Joule from severing the line.

Issue: Did Lackey acquire an easement by implication to operate a septic-tank line under Joule's land?

Decision: Yes. Joule was enjoined from interfering with the operation of Lackey's septic-tank line.

Reasons: The court outlined the four requirements of an easement by implication as: (1) unity of title followed by separation of title; (2) obvious benefit to the dominant estate and burden to the servient estate at the time of separation of title; (3) use of the premises by the common owner in their altered condition long enough before separation of title and under such circumstances as to show that the change was intended to be permanent; and (4) reasonable necessity for the easement. There was clearly a unity of title followed by separation, since Joule at one time owned both tracts. Thus the first requirement was satisfied. There was obvious benefit to the dominant estate Joule sold and a burden to the estate which he retained which existed at the time the ownership of the land was separated. Accordingly, the second requirement was also satisfied. The use by Joule of the system during the fifteen years that he occupied the house was sufficient to show that the change was intended to be permanent, satisfying the third requirement. The fourth requirement of reasonable necessity for the easement was satisfied by the testimony of sewage-system experts that the existing system was the only one that would work.

Lackey v. Joule, 556 S.W.2d 114 (Mo. App. 1978).

Some courts have indicated that an easement by implication is not as likely to be found benefiting the grantor and burdening the grantee. This result seems appropriate, since the grantor can expressly reserve any easement he might wish to have. In other words, the grantor's intent to reserve an easement must be clearly established.[1]

5. Easements Created by Prescription

Obtaining a prescriptive easement is similar to securing ownership by adverse possession. The servient estate must be actually used by some-

[1]Sierra Screw Products v. Azusa Greens Inc., page 78.

one other than the owner, openly, hostilely, and continuously for the statutory time period.[2] To use land openly means that the user comes on the land and acts entitled to be there. Such a user does not use the land secretly as if to hide the use. Hostile use means the user treats the land as if, and represents to other that, he is the true owner of an easement. If the landowner has given permission for the use of land, hostility does not exist. The hostile user does not readily admit the lack of an easement's existence. To be continuous, the use must be uninterrupted for the time period provided by the applicable statute. The statutory period for acquiring an easement by prescription varies between seven and twenty years, depending on the pertinent states' law. These elements of prescription are very similar to those required for gaining title by adverse possession, which are discussed in detail in Chapter 4.

The major distinction between a person acquiring title by adverse possession and one seeking an easement by prescription is that the latter does not have to claim to be the landowner. In addition, some states provide for a shorter statutory period of use for the creation of a prescriptive easement than for the acquisition of title by adverse possession.

6. Nature of Easements

Whether an easement is temporary or permanent depends on whether it is personal or touches and concerns the land. An easement in gross usually benefits only one person or a group of people. Seldom will this benefited individual be allowed to transfer the rights under the easement. This limited transferability of the easement's benefit is due to the personal nature of the use granted. Courts are hesitant to allow the assignment of such personal easements, because they do not want to increase the possible burden on the servient estate. Despite these general rules of property law, the original parties to a personal easement may provide for the contractual assignment of these rights without prior approval. Parties to a contract may create whatever agreement they desire, as long as it is legal.

When an owner grants the local utility company an easement to use the land for its electrical wires, the company normally could pass on this

[2]Adshead v. Sprung, page 79.

right to another organization, as long as the burden on the servient estate is not increased. For example, this utility company could permit a cable television company to run its cable alongside those of the utility. This right is known as a *commercial easement in gross.* Today, as a practical matter, most easements in gross are of this commercial nature. Many easements in gross that are intended to benefit an individual may be interpreted to be a license. (See Section 8, below.)

When the burdens of an easement in gross directly touch and concern the land, the easement will pass from the landowner to the successor in title. If the owner of the servient estate sold the lot to another, this transfer probably would not destroy the dominant party's right to use the land. Therefore, the easement is just as viable under the grantee's ownership as it was under the original owner's.

Under an easement appurtenant, both the benefits to the dominant estate and the burdens on the servient estate are directly related to the land rather than merely to the landowner. The owners represented in Figures 3.1 and 3.2 own their respective lots subject to an easement of passageway over the northern land. If ownership of these lots were to change, the easement should still exist, since the passageway is still necessary for the southern landowner to have access to the highway.

To be sure that easements will run with the land, they should be written and filed on the public record. Then any prospective buyer can determine whether the land being purchased is benefited or burdened or both with one or several easements. Although recording of easements is the best method of giving the public notice, an easement which is obvious upon inspection of the land may pass benefits and burdens respectively to successive owners. Easements created by implication are examples of unrecorded easements that should pass from owner to owner.

7. Termination of Easements

Easements generally are permanent and pass to successor owners. However, the rights and restrictions of an easement may be terminated by agreement, abandonment, or merger.

Parties affected by the easement's existence may always expressly agree to terminate their respective rights in the easement. This agreement should be written and recorded so that notice is given to all those interested that a prior easement no longer exists. Suppose an easement was created by an express grant or reservation which specified it would last only for a limited term. Upon the expiration of that time period, the easement automatically would terminate.

One individual, a group, or a business will possess the benefits of an easement in gross. The landowner of the dominant estate will be benefited by an easement appurtenant. If these benefited parties do not exercise their rights to use the servient estate over a period of time, the easements might be extinguished by abandonment. There is no general rule applicable to when an easement is abandoned. Time periods of permissible nonuse differ from state to state and from case to case. In addition to the nonuse of the easements, states generally require some act to block the easement's use before an abandonment is possible.

Case 3.3

In 1873, the owner of a gristmill acquired an express easement from a neighbor to use the neighboring land for a millrace (a canal through which water flows in order to drive the mill). The servient estate was purchased by John Ruffalo, who was aware of the easement's existence. Later, in 1949, the Walters acquired the dominant estate, and the deed they received expressly referred to the millrace easement. The gristmill had been torn down in 1948. The Walters did not use the millrace from 1949 until 1972, when they decided to reconstruct the historic gristmill. When they attempted to begin using the millrace easement, Ruffalo objected and sought to have the court declare that this easement had been terminated by abandonment.

Issue: By their failure to use the millrace for an extended time period, did the Walters lose their easement?

Decision: Yes. This millrace easement had been abandoned.

Reasons: In addition to a showing that the owner of the dominant estate intended to abandon the easement, there must be evidence of either (1) adverse possession by the owner of the servient estate, (2) actions by the easement owner that render the easement's use impossible, or (3) obstruction of the easement by the owner of the easement that is inconsistent with its future enjoyment. Having found an intent to abandon this millrace easement by the

Walters, in addition to the facts that the gristmill had been torn down and that no water had flowed through the millrace for nearly thirty years, the court ruled that this easement was terminated by abandonment.

Ruffalo v. Walters, 348 A.2d 740 (Pa. Sup. Ct. 1975).

A third situation in which an easement appurtenant is terminated occurs when title of both the dominant and servient estate is vested (or merged) in one owner. If the party who possessed the benefits of an easement in gross acquired the burdened land, this type of easement would no longer exist. Extinguishment of easements in this manner is called *merger,* since the burdens and the benefits are joined in one owner, and the reasons for the easement no longer exist.

In Figure 3.1, Samuel owned land north of Linda, who was landlocked. In that example, Linda received an easement appurtenant allowing her family to cross Samuel's land. Assume that Samuel sold his house and lot to Gilbert. Further assuming that Gilbert had actual knowledge or constructive notice of the easement encumbering this purchased land, this restriction to Gilbert's full ownership would still exist. If Gilbert were to buy Linda's property instead of Samuel's, he would receive the benefits of this previously-created easement appurtenant. However, suppose Gilbert purchased both Samuel's and Linda's real estate. Title of the dominant estate (Linda's land) and the servient estate (Samuel's land) would now be held by one person, the benefits and burdens of the easement to use the passageway being merged. Since Gilbert would own the land where the passageway is located, he would not need permission to use it. Acquisition of these dominant and servient estates does not have to occur simultaneously.

What would happen if, after obtaining both lots, Gilbert sold the land previously owned by Samuel to Phyllis? Would Gilbert still have access to the passageway on Phyllis' land? In other words, is the easement which was terminated by merger revived by selling either the dominant or servient estate while retaining ownership of the other? The answer is *no!* Assuming Gilbert did not expressly reserve the right to use the passageway, his rights under the prior easement do not survive this transfer. (A *new* easement probably would be created by implication, since Gilbert must necessarily cross Phyllis' land to reach the road.)

Other Interests

8. *Licenses*

A landowner who gives another person permission to use land may create a *license* rather than an easement. A license does not transfer an interest in real property to the licensee, but it does restrict the licensor's title. Whereas easements are created by express grants or reservation, by implication, or by prescription, licenses are established by either written or verbal permission of the landowner. Whether an easement or a license has been created often depends on the intent of the parties. Their intentions are usually determined from express statements or conduct.

Unlike easements, licenses are of a personal, nonpermanent nature. Licenses typically are not considered as touching, concerning, and running with the land; therefore, the benefits under a license and the burdens to the licensor's land generally do not pass to successive owners. In other words, the licensee cannot assign the rights under a license to a third party, and when the licensor sells the property, that land is no longer burdened.

Since they are of a nonpermanent nature, licenses are considered revocable. The licensor generally can terminate the licensee's right to use the land. For example, a landowner might orally permit neighborhood children to cut through the yard on their way to and from school. Interpreting this permissive use as a license, the landowner (licensor) could stop these neighborhood children from walking through the yard at any time.

There are three exceptions to the general rule that all licenses are revocable. First, when a license is *coupled with an interest,* the licensor cannot deny the licensee's right to enter upon the land. An example of this type of irrevocable license occurs when an owner of personal property must go onto another person's land in order to take possession of the personal property. If you park your car in a lot, the owner of that lot cannot deny you the right to reenter the lot to retrieve your car within a reasonable time.

The second situation that results in an irrevocable license involves a licensee who expends money or time or both on improving the permitted use. Assume that the Wilsons, who lived next door to the Stones, agreed to let the Stones dig a small ditch across their backyard as a temporary solution to a drainage problem. Since all parties agreed this drainage ditch was not permanent, the Wilsons have granted a license to the Stones. If with the Wilson's knowledge the Stones put drainage tile on the walls and bottom of this ditch, some states would hold that the license has become irrevocable. This conclusion is based on one of the following theories:

1. By the licensor's failure to object, the license has actually become a *grant* of a permanent interest.
2. By failing to object, the licensor is *estopped* from denying the existence of a permanent right.

Finally, the third instance in which a license becomes irrevocable occurs when the licensee pays some valuable consideration to the licensor in return for the right to use the licensor's land. A common example of valuable consideration is money. Whether a license which is irrevocable is treated similarly to an easement in that it becomes permanent and runs with the land depends on the law of the state where the land is located. Frequently, courts will not let the licensee under an irrevocable license transfer the existing rights. However, courts have held that a purchaser of the licensor's land cannot terminate an irrevocable license that the purchaser has notice of when the land is purchased. Of course, these irrevocable licenses are like easements in that they may be terminated by agreement, abandonment, or merger.

9.　Profits À Prendre

Another restriction on a landowner's title that creates a property interest in the possessor is the *profit à prendre.* Rather than merely the right to use another's land granted by an easement or license, a profit allows the actual removal of the land or resources. Profits are similar to leases for the removal of oil and other minerals, gravel, sand, or water from the landlord's property, except that a lease usually contains a royalty payment whereas a profit does not. These profits should be created in writing and recorded by the profit holder to secure his rights. Although the burden of a profit on real estate usually passes from landowner to landowner, the profit itself is personal and cannot be assigned without the landowner's approval. Generally profits may be abolished in manners similar to the termination of easements—by agreement, abandonment, or merger.

Case 3.4

All the land involved in this case was owned by Elijah Pocknett at one time. This land is pictured as follows:

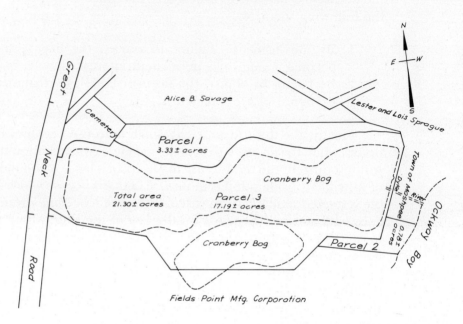

In 1885, when Pocknett sold Parcel 3 he granted "the privilege to take sand from my land adjoining to sand the swamp for a Cranberry Bog, ..." Through a series of transactions, Carol Konner became the owner in 1971 of Parcels 1, 2, and 3. Alice B. Savage had previously purchased the land directly north of Parcel 1. In all the transactions, the language quoted above was included in the deeds. From 1944 until the date of this decision (October 3, 1977), no one has taken steps to remove sand from the Savage property for bogging purposes on Parcel 3. When Alice Savage died, her executors sought to have their rights as well as Konner's rights declared. The cranberry bog was not in a usable shape; the dikes and water flumes were in disrepair; and Konner had built a pond on part of Parcel 3. Savage's executors argued that any interest Konner had in the Savage property had terminated.

Issue: What type of interest, if any, did Konner possess with regard to the Savage property? Was this interest, if any, terminated by abandonment?

Decision: Konner possessed a *profit à prendre* in that she could remove sand from the Savage property. No, this *profit à prendre* was not terminated by abandonment.

Reasons: From the language of Pocknett's grant in 1885, a profit was clearly established. This grant was more than allowing a mere use of land; it allowed the actual removal of sand from the grantor's land. It was the clear intent of the grantor that this interest be appurtenant both to the dominant and servient estates. Thus, when this same clear language was used in all the deeds related to transfers of these parcels of land, the profit's benefits and burdens were also transferred. As to the issue of the profit's termination, it is true that a *profit à prendre* can be abandoned in much the same way that an easement can. However, continual nonuse must be accompanied by an intent to abandon. The failure to maintain the cranberry bog in a usable form throughout the years does not mean that Konner could not reestablish the bog. Furthermore, the pond she built on Parcel 3 was only one acre in size, a fraction of the entire bog. The use of Parcel 3 as a cranberry bog is not now impossible. Therefore, Konner's right to remove sand from the Savage property for use on Parcel 3 as a bog is not terminated.

The First National Bank of Boston v. Konner, 367 N.E.2d 1174 (Mass. Sup. Judicial Ct. 1977).

Water Rights

10. Introduction

Water has been divided into four principal classes: (1) navigable water, (2) nonnavigable water on the land's surface, (3) subterranean water, and (4) surface water. The rights of any landowner depend on what type of water the land touches and where the land is located.

The owner whose land touches a navigable body of water, such as an ocean, a sea, or a river, generally owns the land to the high-water mark. The owners of such land are called *littoral* proprietors. The government usually owns the water and the land underneath it. Disputes over a landowner removing water from these navigable waterways seldom occur, because there is usually a sufficient amount of water to be shared by all owners whose land touches the water. The principal issue involving navigable waters has been pollution. Laws regulating the pollution of these waters exist at both the federal and state levels.

11. Riparian Rights Theory

The rights of a landowner to use water from a nonnavigable lake or stream are much more complex. Generally land that touches a nonnavigable body of water is called *riparian* land, and the landowner's right to use the water is determined by *riparian* rights. Assume that a small stream runs a course from its source (springs, for example) in the hills to a lake several miles away. Over this course, several owners whose land touches the stream might have the opportunity to use this fresh water. Do the landowners who live closest to the stream's source have a greater right to withdraw or divert the water than the owners down the hill? This issue often arises in terms of whether the upper riparian or lower riparian owners have equal or superior rights to the water.

The laws that answer this question have developed in a way that reflects the abundance or scarcity of water within the geographical area. For example, two theories with regard to an owner's rights to nonnavigable bodies of water have been used. In the Eastern United States, the dominant theory is that of the *riparian rights doctrine.* Under this theory, all owners whose land borders the water have equal rights to the water. However, due to the inherent conflict between upper and lower raparian owners, states have adopted one of two theories within the framework of the riparian rights doctrine.

Originally, the colonies adopted the English rule that no riparian owner could affect the *natural flow* of the water. Thus, each upper riparian owner could use as much water as was needed as long as the stream or lake was not diminished as it reached the next riparian owner. In the eastern states, sources of water have been plentiful in the past. Therefore, diminishing the flow of a stream or the level of a lake may not adversely affect another riparian owner. In this situation there is no justifiable reason to apply the natural-flow theory strictly. This is especially true if this theory would prevent an owner from using water on the land for a beneficial industrial use such as a factory or a utility plant. Thus, no state in the United States follows this theory absolutely.

The states east of the Mississippi River generally rely on the *reasonable use* theory. This concept allows all riparian landowners to use all the water they need as long as the use is not unreasonable. These uses are allowed even though the flow of the water may be diminished or prohibited from reaching a lower riparian owner. Courts generally have examined the type of use to determine reasonableness. For example, every riparian owner has the right to use water for domestic purposes before any of them can begin using the water for industrial or commercial purposes. Ultimately, this issue of reasonableness is a factual question that must be resolved by the jury or other fact finder.

Case 3.5

Pendergrast and Aiken owned adjoining tracts of land through which flowed a creek. Aiken owned the downstream tract, which he wished to develop. He began having fill dirt dumped on his land and ran a thirty-six inch pipe under the dirt for the creek. During periods of rain, the creek began backing up on Pendergrast's tract and flooded his basement to varying depths of between thirteen inches and five feet. The thirty-six inch pipe was completely inadequate to handle the flow. Pendergrast brought this action for damages, alleging that Aiken had created a nuisance.

Issue: Was Pendergrast entitled to damages for the injury done to his property by surface waters?

Decision: Yes, if Aiken's actions were unreasonable.

Reasons: The court adopted the "reasonable use" rule in order to decide the case. This rule allows each landowner to make reasonable use of his land even though, by doing so, he alters in some way the flow of surface water, thereby harming other landowners. Liability is incurred only when this harmful interference is found to be unreasonable. The "reasonable use" rule recognizes that when people are forced by social and demographic pressures to live in close proximity with each other and with commercial and industrial development, there will be, of necessity, increased conflict over the proper utilization of land. The case was remanded to the trial court for a jury determination of whether Aiken's use of his land was reasonable.

Pendergrast v. Aiken, 236 S.E.2d 787 (N.C. 1977).

---

12.   Prior Appropriation Theory

Due to the arid conditions that exist west of the Mississippi, many states have rejected these riparian-rights theories and have adopted the *prior appropriation doctrine.* Colorado was the first state to establish that the first person to use a body of water for some beneficial economic pur-

pose had a superior right to use all the water needed. This right exists
even though other landowners may be denied sufficient water for their
needs. This concept is based on the premise that there is not a sufficient
supply of water to satisfy everyone's needs; therefore, one or more
owners should be allowed to use all the water for some worthwhile
purpose. As with riparian owners, a prior appropriator has the right to
use the water rather than having title or ownership to the water. Indeed,
prior appropriation states usually establish a permit system whereby a
governing authority can maintain control of the water's use.

13. Underground Water

Through scientific advances we now know that water exists beneath the
land's surface, either in defined channels or in pockets that are not
clearly located. This first type of underground water is referred to as
an *underground* or *subterranean stream,* while the latter type is called *percolating* water. Frequently, these types of underground water sources are
called merely ground waters. Issues involving underground streams
usually are resolved by applying the same principles that would be used
if the body of water existed on the earth's surface. Colorado, which
allows unlimited use of water from above ground streams, limits use of
underground water to a reasonable amount. Once again, the permit
system is of vital importance to the use of this water.[3]

With respect to use of percolating waters, states generally apply a
reasonable-use test. A landowner may use the water beneath the land
for industrial, agricultural, or other purposes that are necessary to the
beneficial use of the land. This type of test is necessary because a well
drilled on one owner's land may be supplying water that was under a
neighbor's land previously.[4]

Case 3.6

The City of Jacksonville purchased several small parcels of land
and constructed five water wells on them. The water was pumped
approximately five miles to the city, to supplement its water sup-

[3]Colorado Ground Water Commission v. Dreiling, page 80.

[4]California applies a correlative-rights theory to percolating water. This theory
permits a landowner to use only his or her share of the water below. Due to difficult
issues of proving what each owner's share is, this theory is not used outside California.

ply for sale to its customers. Adjacent landowners in the same watershed depended on the same subterranean water for their water supply. They commenced this action, asserting that the removal of water by the city would deplete the quantity and quality of the existing water supply.

Issue: Was the city entitled to remove subterranean water?

Decision: Yes, but only to the extent that other riparian owners would not be damaged.

Reasons: Each riparian owner is entitled to a reasonable use of its subterranean water rights. The law seeks to promote the greatest beneficial use of the water as well as the greatest beneficial use by each owner with a minimum of harm to others. It is therefore permissible for a riparian owner to remove subterranean waters and use them away from the lands from which it was pumped if it does not injure the common supply of other owners. The city should accordingly be precluded from removing water from the wells in question to the extent that it would damage other riparian owners.

Lingo v. City of Jacksonville, 522 S.W.2d 403 (Ark. 1975).

14. Surface Water

The term *surface water* is used to represent that water which exists on the land's surface but is not within a defined bed or stream. Rainfall or melting ice are common examples of surface water. The principal issue that arises with respect to surface water is what owners may do to discharge this water from their land. States have adopted one or two theories. The *common-enemy* theory allows owners to construct a channel or ditch to aid in removing surface water even though this discharge may be concentrated on adjoining land. The *natural-flow* theory states that no landowner may divert surface water from its natural paths of drainage if that change would damage neighboring land. For example, in a natural-flow state, a developer of a subdivision cannot build a drainage system that would concentrate the discharge of rainfall so as to cause flooding or erosion of a neighbor's land. At any time a landowner can grant to the developer an easement appurtenant that would allow water to be dumped on the servient estate. With a properly granted easement, discharging surface water outside its natural flow should not create any liability for the developer.

Cases on Other Interests and Rights in Land

Sierra Screw Products v. Azusa Greens, Inc.
151 Cal. Rptr. 799 (Cal. App. 1979).

The defendant, Azusa Greens, Inc., operated a golf course in the City of Azusa, California. In 1969, Sierra Screw Products purchased from defendants approximately twenty-three acres of undeveloped land adjacent to the third and fourth fairways of the golf course. By 1971, Sierra had constructed a building on the property next to the golf course. Shortly thereafter, Sierra received reports of golf balls striking employees' automobiles parked on the premises, as well as the employees themselves.

Sierra filed suit against Azusa Greens, Inc., and claimed the design of the third and fourth fairways created a nuisance which should be enjoined. The trial court found that a private nuisance did exist, and it ordered the defendants to redesign the fairways involved to eliminate the invasion of golf balls onto plaintiff's property.

The defendants appeal, claiming they have an implied easement which allows the operation of the golf course and permits golf balls to land on plaintiff's property.

Jefferson, J.:

Defendants argue that, since plaintiff Sierra, at the time of negotiations for the purchase of the property adjacent to the golf course, observed and knew that golf balls from the golf course landed on the property being purchased, an implied easement against Sierra's property arose in favor of the golf course—an easement for the intrusion of golf balls onto plaintiff Sierra's property.

. . . "The law does not favor the implication of easements. . . . Whether an easement arises by implication on a conveyance of real estate depends on the intent of the parties, which must *clearly* appear in order to sustain an easement by implication."

(Emphasis added.) Furthermore, "in view of the rule that a conveyance is to be construed against the grantor, the court will imply an easement in favor of the grantee more easily than it will imply an easement in favor of a grantor." The principle is well established that "[t]he purpose of the doctrine of implied easements is to give effect to the *actual intent* of the parties as shown by all the facts and circumstances." . . .

Defendants assert that all the elements necessary for an implied easement in favor of defendants' golf course to have golf balls go upon the land of plaintiffs are present here: (1) a unity of ownership before sale of part of the property to plaintiff Sierra; (2) the dominant parcel—the golf course—was used for such a long and continuous time as a golf course to establish it was meant to be permanent; and (3) the easement is reasonably necessary to the beneficial enjoyment of defendants' land as a golf course. . . .

[T]he evidence introduced in the instant case was not such as to require the trial judge to find, as a matter of law, that there existed in favor of defendants an implied easement for golf balls to land on the property sold to plaintiff Sierra, arising from the circumstances of the sale from defendants to plaintiff Sierra. The provisions in the contract relating to fencing are sufficient to negate a required finding that the parties had a clear intent for defendants to have an easement for their golf balls to fall on the land of plaintiffs. . . .

Judgment affirmed.

Adshead v. Sprung
375 A.2d 83 (Pa. Super. Ct. 1977).

Jacobs, J.:

This appeal, involving a familiar type of dispute between neighboring landowners, is taken from a final decree in equity holding that Beatrice R. Adshead, appellee, has acquired a prescriptive easement over a portion of land owned by Johann and Madga Sprung, appellants, and permanently enjoining appellants from maintaing a fence that interferes with the easement. For the reasons that follow, we agree with the chancellor that plaintiff met her burden of proving the existence of prescriptive rights, and that appellants failed to show either permissiveness of the use or abandonment of the easement.

Appellee has resided at 7418 Lawndale Avenue in Philadelphia since October 13, 1949, when she and her husband took title to the property. . . .

Appellants reside at 7420 Lawndale Avenue, adjacent to appellee's property, and own the property by virtue of a deed dated June 11, 1962. Separate driveways on each of the properties run side by side for most of the length of the properties and lead to separate garages. . . .

From October, 1949, until June 19, 1975, appellee indiscriminately drove over the common driveway area to and from the garage at the rear of her property. On about June 19, 1975, appellants erected a chain link fence along the boundary line between the two properties. The fence effectively narrows the driveway area so as to completely impede appellee's access to her garage.

After a letter sent by appellee's attorney to appellants was unsuccessful in obtaining removal of the fence, appellee instituted this action in equity to enjoin obstruction of her alleged easement over the driveway area. The chancellor found that appellee had acquired a prescriptive easement in the common driveway area, and enjoined appellant's obstruction of the easement by the fence. . . .

The narrow issue for our determination is whether the chancellor erred in finding that appellee had acquired a prescriptive easement in the driveway area. This finding, if supported by adequate evidence in the record, will not be disturbed on appeal. . . .

An easement by prescription is created by adverse, open, continuous, notorious and uninterrupted use of the land for twenty-one years. To acquire an easement by prescription, the evidence and proof thereof must be clear and positive. . . . Appellee's use of the driveway area was open and notorious in light of the fact that the driveway was located immediately adjacent to appellant's property. We are also persuaded that the use was open and notorious by Plaintiff's Exhibit 2, a photograph showing tire tracks leading from the paved area of appellant's property toward appellee's garage. Appellants do not apparently challenge these facts. They allege, however, that the use was not continuous and uninterrupted for twenty-one years. In support of this allegation, appellants point out that during periods of marital separation between appellee and her ex-husband, appellee did not use the common drive because she was without a car. They therefore conclude that the continuity essential to satisfy the prescriptive period was lacking. There was direct testimony, however, that during these periods of separation, the driveway area was openly used by appellee's friends, parents, and former husband on the occasions when he came to visit the children. We agree with the chancellor that the requisite continuity was not lacking simply because appellee's use of the driveway area diminished during periods of separation between her and her husband. Appellee proved that she used the driveway when needed from 1949 until erection of the fence in 1975, and that her use was more than sporadic. We will not hold that day-to-day use was required to satisfy the continuity element essential to the creation of prescriptive rights.

Appellants also contend that adversity was lacking in the use of the common driveway area. . . .

. . . There is no such evidence of permission in the present case. To the contrary, appellee testified that she never asked or received permission from appellants or their predecessors to use the driveway; her testimony was clear that she used the land in question as she pleased, without permission. The legal principle thus applicable to the present case is that

> "[W]here one uses an easement whenever he sees fit, without asking leave, and without objection, it is adverse, and an uninterrupted adverse enjoyment for twenty-one years is a title which cannot be afterwards disputed. . . ."

Finally, appellants attempted to prove permission by the fact that when they paved their portion of the driveway area in May, 1975, they told appellee she could not use the driveway that night, and she complied by parking along the street. This occurrence does not prove permission, but rather indicates that appellee pursued the prudent course of not driving her car on fresh cement. . . .

For the foregoing reasons, we conclude that the elements required for the creation of prescriptive rights in appellee have been proved by clear and positive evidence. We also conclude that appellants failed to prove license or permission to rebut the evidence of adversity. . . .

Decree affirmed.

Colorado Ground Water Commission v. Dreiling
606 P.2d 836 (Colo. 1979).

Erickson, J.:

The Colorado Ground Water Commission (the Commission) and Hobart Hallock (Hallock), plaintiffs in the trial court, have appealed a judgment denying their claims to enjoin the operation of two wells located in the North High Plains Designated Ground Water Basin, and denying

Hallock's claim for damages resulting from the operation of the wells. The wells are presently owned by defendant William Joseph Leiker (Leiker) and were formerly owned by defendant A. F. Dreiling (Dreiling). We reverse and remand for further proceedings in accordance with the directions contained in this opinion.

On January 11, 1968, Hallock received Commission approval for an irrigation well with an annual appropriation of 320 acre feet, which was subsequently increased to 800 acre feet. Two weeks later, January 25, 1968, Dreiling received approval from the Commission to place two wells on land adjacent to Hallock's. The permits specified that neither of the wells was to be located within one-half mile of Hallock's well.

On April 8, 1969, the Commission notified Dreiling by certified mail that one of his wells had been located and drilled within 1,500 feet of the Hallock well, in violation of a condition imposed by the well permits. The Commission conducted a hearing and found that the well was not drilled in compliance with the permit, because it was situated less than one-half mile from the Hallock well. The commission ordered the well plugged and abandoned. (Hereafter referred to as the "illegal well.") Dreiling did not appear at the hearing and did not appeal the Commission's order.

In response to the Commission's order, Dreiling removed the pump from the illegal well but did not plug it as required by the order. With the exception of one brief period, however, he discontinued further pumping from the illegal well.

In the spring of 1974, defendant Leiker purchased Dreiling's land containing the two wells, and commenced irrigation of the farm with both wells. Before he acquired the land, Leiker had retained an attorney to inquire into the status of Dreiling's wells. The attorney contacted the Division of Water Resources but mistakenly described the location of the wells as being in Township 30 rather than Township 20. That mistake apparently caused a Division representative to look to the priority list, which included the two wells, rather than the Commission files. The priority list did not reflect the plug and abandon order and, consequently, the Division representative informed Leiker's attorney that both wells were on the priority list and appeared to be in good standing.

Upon taking possession of Dreiling's land, but prior to completing its purchase, Leiker replaced the pump on the illegal well and began pumping operations. Immediately thereafter, Hallock notified Leiker that the well had been ordered plugged and abandoned, and requested that Leiker stop using that well. After consultation with counsel, Leiker declined and continued to irrigate with both wells. Hallock subsequently made a complaint to the Commission.

The Commission filed suit against Dreiling, requesting that the trial court enjoin the use of the illegal well. Because Leiker was in the process of purchasing Dreiling's land he intervened as a co-defendant. Hallock subsequently joined the action as a co-plaintiff and requested damages. Prior to trial, the complaint was amended to include a request for an injunction on the use of Leiker's legal well as well as the illegal well.

[The trial held for the defendants on the three grounds. First, the Commission was estopped or prevented from enjoining the use of the well since it misinformed Leiker that the well was in good standing. Second, Hallock was barred from seeking an injunction since he had not acted promptly. This is known as being barred by the doctrine of laches. Finally, there was no showing that Leiker's wells had diminished the amount of water available to Hallock.]

[The Supreme Court found that Leiker could not justify reliance on the Commission's approval of using the well since Leiker's attorney had provided the wrong information as to the well's location. Next, the court determined that Hallock had acted promptly in protecting his rights. Finally, as to the issue whether Leiker's use of water affected Hallock's supply, the court wrote as follows:]

"The General Assembly rejected the pure appropriation doctrine as to ground water. It declared that while the appropriation doctrine should be recognized, it must be modified to permit the 'full economic development of the designated ground water resources.'"

Under the appropriation doctrine as applied to waters of a natural stream, a person is entitled to appropriate water so long as there is any water in the stream. . . . When applied to designated [under] ground waters, however, that doctrine is modified to allow only appropriation to the point of reasonable depletion as set forth by the Commission.

. . .The Colorado Ground Water Commission empowered:

"To supervise and control the exercise and administration of all rights acquired to the use of designated ground water. In the exercise of this power it may, by summary order, prohibit or limit withdrawal of water from any well during any period that it determines that such withdrawal of water from said well would cause unreasonable injury to prior appropriators; except that nothing in this article shall be construed as entitling any prior designated ground water appropriator to the maintenance of the historic water level or any other level below which water still can be economically extracted when the total economic pattern of the particular designated ground water basin is considered; . . ."

Prior to this case, we have not specifically held that the modified doctrine of prior appropriation permits junior rights in a designated ground water basin to be enjoined when they interfere with the senior appropriation rights. Because the trial court made no finding on this question, we decline to do so now. Instead, we remand this case for further proceedings to determine whether the modified doctrine of prior appropriation should be applied to determine whether the operation of Leiker's legal well has unlawfully interfered with Hallock's senior right to his allotted share of water in the designated ground water basin.

Reversed and remanded.

REVIEW QUESTIONS

1. Define and distinguish the following terms:
   a. Easement and license
   b. Affirmative easement and negative easement
   c. Easement appurtenant and easement in gross
   d. Dominant estate and servient estate
2. What four requirements must be met in order to establish an easement by implication?
3. A residential developer owned property that fronts Lake Michigan and property just across the street. All this property was developed except for one lake-front lot that was advertised as a means of access to the lake for property

owners across the street. The developer sold this "access" lot, and the new owner sought to develop it. The subdivision sued, claiming it had an implied easement of access to the lake over this lot. Who should win? Why?

4. In 1971, Steve Owens purchased a store and land from Raymond, who had owned that property for twenty-five years. Throughout his ownership, Raymond had used a gravel driveway as a means of ingress and egress to his store. This driveway was located on land owned by a neighbor. No mention of the driveway was made in the deed Steve Owens received. When Steve continued to use the driveway after his purchase, the neighbor sued to enjoin his trespassing. Steve claimed he was entitled to use the driveway because a prescriptive easement existed. What requirements must Steve prove in order to win?

5. Name and explain at least three methods used to terminate the existence of an easement.

6. Copeland, a real estate owner, orally gave the Gas Company permission to bury a natural-gas pipeline across his property. After Copeland sold this land to M. O. Carlin, Carlin requested that the pipeline be removed from his land. When the Gas Company refused to remove its pipeline, Carlin sued to quiet title. Should the Gas Company's right to run this pipeline be treated as a license or as an easement? Is the permission to run the pipeline revocable by Carlin?

7. Define the term *"profit à prendre."* How is a profit distinguished from an easement?

8. In the text, four general types of water were discussed. List and describe these categories.

9. The phrase "riparian land" has been used to describe all land located adjacent to nonnavigable bodies of water. Actually, the riparian-rights doctrine must be distinguished from the prior-appropriation theory. What is the difference?

10. Schmidt owned real estate that was adjacent to Eger's land. Schmidt built a drainage ditch across his property in order to facilitate runoff of surface water. As a result of his ditch, surface water was deposited on Eger's land at one concentrated spot, causing erosion of the soil. To stop this concentrated flow, Eger stopped up Schmidt's ditch. Assuming the land is located in a jurisdiction applying the natural-flow theory, what would be the result if Schmidt sought to enjoin Eger's blockage of this ditch?

4

Methods of Acquiring Title to Real Estate

1. Introduction

Title to real property represents the legal ownership of such property. The several methods of acquiring title to real property are usually classified and described as acquisition by transfer from the previous owner or by operation of law. Passage of ownership voluntarily may be by sale, by gift, or by will. Two very important examples of ownership transferring by operation of law are adverse possession and accretion. These topics are the subject matter of this chapter.

Title to real estate obtained by transfer from the previous owner is usually vested by delivery of a document known as a deed. The various types of deeds and the essential characteristics and legal requirements of each are discussed in the next chapter. The other methods of acquiring title are discussed in this chapter.

Transfer of ownership by one person to another most often occurs when the property is sold. Since a sale is the most common form of transfer of ownership, contracts for the sale of real estate are the subject of a separate chapter—Chapter 11. The actual closing of the sale and the transfer of title are so important that a thorough treatment of these subjects is presented in Chapter 13.

A transfer may also be made by gift during the owner's lifetime, or it may occur on the owner's death. If the owner dies leaving a will, the transfer is established by the fact of death, proof of the validity of the will, and the probate proceedings that establish the rights of the parties named in it. If the owner dies without leaving a will, the transfer of title and the identity of the new owner are established by the death of the owner, the applicable statutes, and the probate proceedings. Parties who obtain title to real property upon the death of the previous owner do not necessarily receive a deed. Their title can come from the law and legal proceedings proving the transfer.

2. Transfer by Living Gift

A gift of real estate is a transaction between the *donor,* who makes the gift, and the *donee,* who receives it. A living gift must be distinguished from a gift on death, commonly referred to as a testamentary gift. Living gifts are often referred to as *inter vivos* transfers in order to contrast them with testamentary ones.

A promise to make a gift is not legally enforceable. Courts will not require a donor to complete a gift that is incomplete or that has been only partially completed. However, an *inter vivos* gift that is completed cannot be revoked. A donor cannot recover the subject matter of a completed gift. Therefore, it is often important to determine if a gift is in fact complete.

In order for a gift to be valid, each of the following elements must be established:

1. The donor must have intended to make a living gift (donative intent).
2. The subject matter of the gift must have been delivered (delivery).
3. The donee must accept the gift (acceptance).

As a practical matter, acceptance is usually presumed. There are few situations in which delivery could be rejected. Thus, if the donee refuses to accept the gift, this can be treated as an ineffective delivery by the donor. Therefore, the primary issues in gift cases involve questions of donative intent and delivery. These issues are raised in tax cases as well as in cases involving the title to property. In tax cases, the issue may be when the gift is complete, because at that moment a taxable event is established.

Issues of donative intent frequently arise because documents are not always what they appear to be on their face. For example, assume that a minister decides to purchase a local tavern. In order to keep his ownership a secret, he directs that title to the land be deeded to a friend. Later this friend claims the land as his own. Did the minister intend to make a gift of the land to his friend? If the minister did not have donative intent, there would be no gift and he could reclaim his land.

There must be an intent to make a present gift, and not merely a gift in the future. In addition, a gift must be completed during the lifetime of the donor. A gift to take effect on or after the donor's death must satisfy the law as a valid will. For example, assume that Otis signed a deed conveying property to Dan and delivered the deed to Earl. Earl was told to hold the deed until Otis died and then to give it to Dan. There would be no gift because of lack of donative intent, and the deed could not be used as a will because it would not meet the legal requirements of a will.

To satisfy the requirement of delivery, the donor must relinquish all control over the deed instrument, either to the donee or to some third person commonly known as an escrow agent. The third person must be someone beyond the absolute control of the donor so that it is clear that the donor has parted with possession of the deed with the intent to transfer the title. Third persons may be used when the actual donee is unavailable and the donor desires to make an immediate gift. Whether or not the the delivery to a third person is valid depends on the factual situation. For example, handing the deed to a secretary for later delivery to the donee usually would not suffice. The intent for a present delivery is required. Among the important factors to be considered are the donor's ability to destroy the deed and the other aspects of control retained by the donor.

In the following case, the court was concerned with the issues of intent and delivery.

Case 4.1

Gus Bloom signed a warranty deed in 1958 naming Edgar Bloom, a nephew, as a grantee of 360 acres. After Gus died in 1975, the deed was found in a sealed envelope in his safe deposit box. "To be delivered to Edgar Bloom upon my death" was written on the envelope. The deed was not recorded until after Gus' death. The First National Bank was appointed administrator of Gus' estate. It claimed title to the land, contending that there was no delivery of the deed to Edgar, who therefore had no interest in the land.

Issue:　　Was the deed a valid transfer of title to Edgar?

Decision:　　No.

Reasons:　　Gus retained possession of the deed in his safety deposit box, retained the keys, and paid taxes on the land until he died. These factors are inconsistent with an intent to make a present conveyance of the land to Edgar. Gus' statements were also inconsistent with a present gift; he had told Edgar that the land would be his "after I'm gone," or "when I go," or "if something should happen to me." All these comments indicate that he did not relinquish fee ownership of the land. The fact that Edgar did not know of the deed until years after it was executed also serves to demonstrate that Gus did not intend a present conveyance and that there was no valid delivery.

First Nat'l Bank in Minot v. Bloom 264 N.W.2d 208 (N.D. 1978).

Transfers on Death

3. Introduction

The transfer of ownership on death is either by will or by laws which establish the identity of the new owners when the deceased did not leave a will. In effect, the state has made a will for those who do not make one for themselves. A person who dies leaving a will is said to die testate, and the deceased is called the *testator.* A person who dies without a will dies *intestate,* and title to property passes according to the state's statute on intestate succession.

The settlement of estates requires that some person or corporate entity step into the shoes of the deceased and handle the affairs. A testator may select the person or persons to do this by nominating them in the will. These persons are called *executors.* When there is no will, the law specifies those persons entitled to perform this function in order of priority. For example, a spouse would usually have priority over a child, and a child would have priority over a grandchild. The personal representative of a person who dies intestate is called an *administrator* and is appointed to this position by the probate court.

In the event that a valid will fails to name an executor or the executor refuses or is unable to perform the duties, the court appoints a personal representative who is usually called an *administrator with the will annexed.*

The function of the personal representative is to gather up the assets, pay all debts including death taxes, and distribute the property to those named in the will or the appropriate statute on intestacy. When a will purports to pass real property, the will provision is known as a *devise,* and those receiving the property are called *devisees.* If the property is personal property, the gift is a *legacy* or *bequest,* and the recipients are *legatees.* If a person dies intestate, the parties inheriting the real property are called *heirs at law.*

The law varies from state to state as to what happens on death to the "bundle of rights" associated with land. In most states, the title to real estate passes to the personal representative and remains there until the probate proceedings are complete. If it becomes necessary to sell the land to pay debts and taxes, it is sold and the devisees or heirs at law never obtain any interest in the land. In a few states, title to real estate passes immediately to the devisees or heirs at law, subject to divestiture if necessary to pay debts. In these states, only the title to personal property passes to the executor or administrator.

A will serves several functions. First of all, it disposes of the property of the testator by identifying those persons to receive it. Secondly, a will usually designates the personal representative (executor) to settle the estate. Third, a will may be used to reduce the cost of administering estates by directing the court to waive requirements such as obtaining a surety contract, the official bond of the executor, or court orders to sell assets. Fourth, a will may designate persons to serve as guardian of the estate and as guardian of the deceased's minor children.

Finally, a will is a tax-planning device to reduce both income and death taxes. It should always be kept in mind that a properly drawn will has the potential to reduce taxes significantly in substantial estates.

Sometimes two people attempt to execute one document as a joint will. The law requires proper execution by both. However, it should be recognized that joint wills should *not* be used. In addition to tax problems caused by joint wills, there are frequent questions as to the revocability of the will after the death of one party. Rather than a joint will, married persons should consider mutual wills—ones which are more in pursuance of a common plan. Such wills are usually reciprocal, in that they contain gifts to the other spouse and then a common plan on the death of both.

The sections which follow will discuss some of the legal requirements for a valid will. These will be followed by a discussion of the laws on intestacy.

4. Testamentary Capacity

In order to make a valid will, the testator must be of legal age in the state of domicile and possess testamentary capacity. The legal age in some states is as low as fourteen, but eighteen is the usual minimum age for making a will. Testamentary capacity is significantly different from mental capacity for many purposes. It is not based on the testator's freedom from a mental illness which may have required treatment or commitment. Testamentary capacity is much less than that required for entering into contracts. A person need not be able to understand a business transaction in order to make a will. However, it should be recognized that a person with sufficient mental capacity to transact ordinary business and to act naturally in the ordinary affairs of life has capacity to make a will, because the standard for capacity to execute a will is less than the standard for contractual capacity.

All that testamentary capacity requires is that the testator have the capacity to (1) know the nature and general extent of his property, (2) know the natural objects of his bounty, and (3) make a plan or scheme of distribution. A testator must have the capacity to know these things; actual knowledge of them is not necessary. In other words, a person suffering from a serious illness, such as alcoholism or drug addition, may still have sufficient testamentary capacity.[1]

5. Formalities of Execution

The law requires certain formalities upon the execution of the will. Some states also expedite probate proceedings when additional formalities are observed. The usual formalities are described as *attestation* by attending witnesses.

The execution of a will requires that the testator or some person in his presence and at his direction sign the will. A signature may be by mark or with the assistance of another person. A person may be unable to write and still desire to execute a will. Therefore, the law allows someone else to sign the testator's name to the document. Consequently, proof that the signature is not in the testator's handwriting

[1] *In re Kraft's Estate,* page 103.

does not automatically invalidate a will. Wills are usually signed at the end, although in many states a signature any place on the document may suffice if it is the testator's intent by affixing the signature to make the instrument a will. Some states have passed statutes that require the testator's signature to be at the end of the will. In addition to signatures at the end, most wills are signed or initialed on each page in order to prevent someone from withdrawing a page and inserting another in its place.

The testator often signs in the presence of the witnesses, but this usually is not required. It is legally sufficient if the testator acknowledges that his or her signature is on the document or that the signature was affixed by some other person in the presence and at the direction of the testator. This occurs if all of the witnesses are not physically together for attestation of the will.

To be valid, a will must be attested to by witnesses as well as signed by the testator. Most states require only two witnesses, but some require three. Attestation is the opposite of what most laymen understand about the term. It is the process by which the testator watches the witnesses sign the will; it is not the witnesses watching the testator sign. The purposes of attestation are several. First and foremost, attestation is to protect the testator and to provide assurances that the witnesses have signed the document that is to serve as the will. After death a testator will not be available to challenge the document. It is therefore essential that the testator be absolutely sure that no other will has been substituted.

Attestation also serves to establish that the will was in fact executed by the testator, and that the witnesses believed that the testator possessed testamentary capacity at the time of execution. Attestation also establishes that the witnesses did sign in the presence of the testator. A typical attestation clause provides:

> "We, the undersigned witnesses, hereby certify that the foregoing instrument was, on the day of the date thereof, signed, sealed, published and declared by the Testator, as and for his Last Will and Testament, in our presence and hearing, who, at his request, and in his presence, and in the presence of each of us, have subscribed our names hereto as witnesses of the execution thereof, believing said Testator at the time of so signing said Last Will and Testament, as aforesaid, to be of sound and disposing mind and memory and under no constraint or improper influence."

Today in many states, the attestation clause is executed in the presence of a notary public who acknowledges the signatures of attesting witnesses. When the attestation clause is notarized, the will can be admitted to probate by the court without requiring testimony of the witnesses. Since the notary took the oath of the witnesses, their court-room testimony is dispensed with. Of course, this does not mean that interested persons cannot challenge the validity of the will. It simply means that unless someone objects, a notarized attestation clause is all that is required to prove the validity of the will in the first instance in those states that have adopted this procedure.

The law in most states requires attestation by credible witnesses. "Credible" means competent to testify according to common law rules of evidence. Since parties interested in the case's outcome usually were not competent at common law, beneficiaries of the will are not competent credible witnesses. However, beneficiaries who acted as witnesses can be made competent by taking away their gifts under the will. In most states, if witnesses who are beneficiaries under a will are required to testify to validate the will, they will not receive any more of the estate than they would have received had the deceased died without a will. Therefore, the better practice is to prohibit any named beneficiary from signing the will as an attesting witness.

6. Revocation, Republication, and Revival

A will is a revocable document and is said to be arbitrary during a person's lifetime. The testator can terminate the validity of the will at any time. Typically, a will is revoked when a new will is executed. This may be by express terms of the new will or because the second is inconsistent with the first. A will's effectiveness also is terminated when the document is destroyed or mutilated. Destruction can occur when the will is burned, torn, thrown away, or lost. Mutilation might involve partially tearing, cutting, burning, erasing, or otherwise altering an essential provision of the document.

A will is also revoked in whole or in part by marriage and divorce. In most states, marriage revokes a will because it is presumed that the testator would want to make provisions for the new spouse. Divorce usually revokes a will, at least to the extent of gifts to the former spouse.

Most states do not allow partial revocation or changes by deletion or interlineation. These are not allowed because the question usually arises: Who made the changes—the testator or someone else? However, attempted deletions and changes may be evidence of an attempt or intent to revoke the whole will. In such cases, the court must deter-

92   **Real Estate and the Law**

mine the testator's intent. Was revocation of the whole will intended? If not, the will stands as originally written.

It should be understood that once a will is revoked it does not become effective again until expressly reexecuted by the testator. For example, assume that Thelma executes a will on July 14, 1976, and a subsequent will, signed on February 13, 1980, expressly revokes all former wills. If the second will (signed on February 13, 1980) is destroyed by Thelma, the previous will is not revived. The only way that it could be revived is by reexecution. Therefore, if this testator dies after destroying her will and before executing a new one, she dies without leaving a valid will.

7.   Lapsed Devises and Ademption

Since time of death is one of the great uncertainties of life, it is not unusual for a devisee or legatee to predecease the testator. Most states have provided by statute for the contingency of the death of a beneficiary prior to the death of the testator. The usual plan provides that if the devise is to a descendant of the testator, the property will pass to the lineal descendants of the deceased devisee unless the will provides to the contrary. For example, assume that the son of the testator predeceased the testator, leaving grandchildren. The grandchildren would inherit the property that had been devised to their father unless the will provided for a different distribution.

When the devise is not to a descendant of the testator, the law in most states provides that the gift *lapses* or fails. The property then passes with any of the residual gifts under the will. A residual gift is simply a statement in the will that all of the residue and remainder shall pass to a named person. If there is no residuary clause, the lapsed devise or legacy will pass as intestate property just as if there had been no will.

A problem similar to a beneficiary predeceasing the testator arises when the property which is the subject of a devise is disposed of by the testator during his lifetime. When the property of a specific devise or specific legacy is not included among the testator's property at the time of death, the devise or legacy is said to be *adeemed* or to fail. When ademption has occurred, the language of the will pertaining to that property becomes a nullity, and it is ignored.

Case 4.2

William B. Taylor executed a will on February 29, 1968, which left an undivided interest in land in Hartford Township, Ohio, to Dorothy Caldwell. Taylor died on June 16, 1969. When Mrs.

Caldwell claimed she was entitled to this specific devise, it was discovered that Taylor owned a mortgage covering this land in Ohio. At his death, Taylor did not have a specific ownership interest in the Ohio land.

Issue: Did Dorothy Caldwell have any rights to the specific devise?

Decision: No, this devise was adeemed.

Reasons: A specific devise is adeemed if the testator, at death, owns no interest in the described real property. The mortgage held by Taylor, at his death, was not an interest in land; therefore, this devise had been adeemed. Generally, once the devise is adeemed, the devisee has no rights to the proceeds of the sale or to the property received in an exchange. Pennsylvania follows this majority rule. Thus, Caldwell receives nothing under Mr. Taylor's will.

Estate of Taylor, 391 A.2d 991 (Pa. Sup. Ct. 1978).

Sometimes difficult problems arise when a testator has made a specific devise in his will and later enters into a contract for the sale of real estate which has been signed but not fully performed at the testator's death. Since the testator still has legal title to the property because the contract of sale has not yet been performed, is the devise adeemed? In such cases there is still an ademption, because the law treats the contract as being completed and equitably converts the testator's interest in real estate into the proceeds of the sale. The devisee of such property will not receive the proceeds, because such proceeds pass to the beneficiary of the personal property under the will. The same result occurs if the property is taken by some governmental body pursuant to the power of eminent domain.

8.   Intestate Succession

When a person dies intestate, the property passes to the heirs at law or the next of kin according to the law of the appropriate state. (The heirs at law and next of kin are usually the same persons.) For real estate, the appropriate statute of intestacy is that of the state in which the land is located. For personal property, it is usually the law of the deceased's domicile. Therefore, the intestate laws of two or more states may be used in settling the estate of a person who dies without a will.

The intestate statutes provide a schedule that is believed to follow the way a reasonable person would want property distributed among the surviving members of the family. While the laws of intestate succession vary from state to state, a typical scheme of distribution would be as follows:

1. T leaves a spouse and no children: all property to the spouse.
2. T leaves a spouse and children: spouse and each child receive an equal share, with each child's share passing *per stirpes.* (Many states provide that a spouse's interest is a minimum of one-third or one-sixth or some other figure. Thus a spouse with many children is guaranteed the stated share.)
3. No spouse but children: children share equally *per stirpes.*
4. No spouse, no children or lineal descendants: to parents, and brothers and sisters *per stirpes* (surviving parent often receives a double share).
5. No spouse, no children or lineal descendant, no parents, no brothers or sisters: to the closest blood relatives computed by tracing relationship back to a common ancestor.
6. No relatives: to the state.

The foregoing intestacy scheme uses the term *per stirpes,* which must be distinguished from *per capita.* The term *per stirpes* means "by the root." This means that a group of descendants must share the percentage that their parent would have taken had that parent survived the intestate. The term *per capita* means "by the head." In other words, the entire group being considered takes as equals rather than as representatives of their parent's share. Assume the following family.

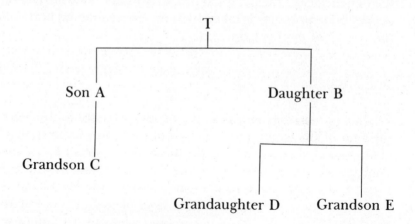

Assume that A and B both predecease T. In this event, the distribution is *per stirpes* or by the root and not *per capita* or by the head. Therefore, C takes one-half of the estate, and D and E each take one-quarter of the estate. If the law distributed the estate *per capita,* each would have taken one-third.

In the foregoing example, if B had survived T and A had not, C would receive one-half of the estate and B one-half. If A had survived T and B had not, A would have received one-half of the estate and D and E each one-quarter.

Of course, the use of *per stirpes* and *per capita* is not limited to intestate succession. These terms often are drafted into the terms of a will. Such use of *per stirpes* and *per capita* is entirely permissible, since a testator can determine how his property is to be disposed of according to his will.

In addition to statutes on intestacy, most states have similar statutes for the disposition of property upon the renunciation of a will by a surviving spouse. The law in most states, in order to protect spouses, grants them the right to elect to take a statutory share in lieu of the provisions of the will. This statutory share is usually at least as much as would have been received under the laws of intestacy. In some cases it is more. This right to renounce a will may be waived by a valid contract. Usually it exists only for spouses and not for children or other heirs. However, if a testator fails to mention a specific child or to provide for any children born after the will is made, statutes in most states allow these children to claim a share of their parent's assets equal to the share they would have received if the testator had died intestate.

9. *Determining Blood Relationships*

It sometimes becomes necessary to determine the closest blood relationship. (See part 5 of the foregoing intestacy scheme.) This is accomplished by tracing each person back to a common ancestor; then those persons with the lowest number of generations take the property *per capita.* The chart below shows family relationships and incidentally can be used to determine the relationship of one relative to another. For example:

A and B are first cousins, and they would share equally.

B and C are first cousins once removed, and B would take before C would.

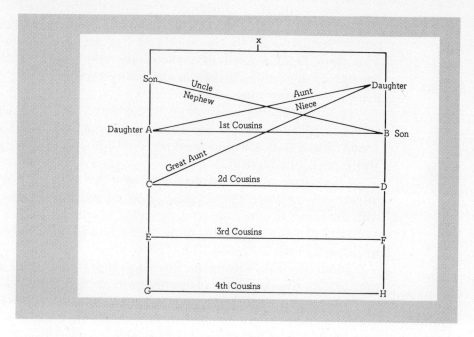

B and E are first cousins twice removed, and B would take before E would.

C and D are second cousins and they would share equally.

D and E are second cousins once removed, and D would take before E would.

D and G are second cousins twice removed, and D would take before G would.

10. Uniform Probate Code

Within the past thirty to forty years, there has been a movement to increase the uniformity of the laws applicable in different states. The National Conference of Commissioners on Uniform State Laws has prepared the *Uniform Probate Code* (UPC). The purpose of the UPC is to clarify, simplify, and make uniform laws that should provide an efficient system of liquidating a deceased person's estate, paying debts, and distributing assets to the proper parties. The deceased person often is referred to as the *decedent*.

The UPC establishes the requirements for a will and for the administration of a decedent's estate. It also describes who can elect to take a share that is not provided in the will, and under what circumstances this election may occur. This Code also provides a scheme of intestate succession in case a person dies without a valid will. For example, a surviving spouse will receive at least one-half of the intestate estate, and an even larger interest if there are no surviving descendents or parents of the decedent.

The UPC abolishes the distinction between real and personal property, all property being treated the same under its provision. Dower and curtesy interests are also abolished, and the UPC substitutes the surviving spouse's intestate share or power to elect against the will. In lieu of an executor managing a testator's estate and an administrator handling an intestate estate, the UPC adopts the concept of a *personal representative* who assists in the gathering and distribution of a decedent's estate.

By 1982, the UPC had been adopted in at least thirteen states (including Alaska, Arizona, Colorado, Idaho, Maine, Michigan, Minnesota, Montana, Nebraska, New Jersey, New Mexico, North Dakota, and Utah). In our increasingly mobile society, there are clear advantages in having uniform laws throughout the country on the descent and distribution of decendents' property. Because these benefits of uniformity exceed the need of each state to have its own peculiar laws, the UPC will likely be more widely adopted in the near future.

Other Transfers by Operation of Law

11. Introduction

We have just seen how intestate succession is one way in which property is transferred from one owner to another by operation of the law. Other methods provided by law in which property ownership can be changed include rights of survivorship, judicial sales, adverse possession, and accretion.

12. Rights of Survivorship

As discussed in the previous chapter, joint tenancies and tenancies by the entirety involve the automatic right of survivorship. As long as this method of ownership is not terminated, the title held by each owner transfers to the surviving owners upon death. This transfer is an example of acquiring title by the operation of law.

13. Judicial Sales

Real estate frequently is a person's most valuable asset. Therefore, when a creditor seeks to collect an overdue debt, real estate may be sold in judicial proceedings to satisfy such a claim. If a creditor has a security interest in the real estate, the property also may be sold by order of the court. Sales of real property pursuant to judicial authority may involve judgments, mortgages, mechanics' liens, or tax-lien foreclosures. Examples of these resulting in a transfer of title are discussed further in subsequent chapters.

14. Adverse Possession—General Requirements

Ownership and possession are not always vested in the same person. Generally the possessor of real estate does not have a right to claim ownership. However, under certain circumstances title to real estate can be acquired by what is called *adverse possession.* In order to be adverse, the possession must be "actual and exclusive, open and notorious, hostile and under a claim of right, and continuous" for the statutory time period. Some states further require that the possessor hold the land "under color of title" during the statutory period. This required statutory period ranges from seven to twenty years, depending upon the state law. All these elements are essential if title is to be obtained by adverse possession as is illustrated by the following case.

Case 4.3

Rosson acquired a tract of land in 1942 and thereafter began cutting firewood and obtaining water from a spring located on an adjacent tract. He erected a fence around his land which also enclosed some of the adjoining tract. Record title to this adjacent land was in Walton. Rosson regularly grazed cattle on the parcel, maintained an outdoor toilet on it, created a junk pile on it, and bush hogged and burned a part of it. When Walton protested, Rosson ordered him off the land. Rosson never sought permission to use the parcel.

Issue: Did Rosson acquire the parcel by adverse possession?

Decision: Yes.

Reasons: Adverse possession must be actual, hostile, open and notorious, accompanied by a bona fide claim of title, and it must continue for the statutory period. It was conceded that Rosson's possession had been continuous for the statutory period. His possession was, of course, actual, and Walton was put on notice that it was open, hostile, and notorious when Rosson ordered him from the land. A claim of right need not be express; it is sufficient that the acts of the adverse claimant indicate a claim of ownership. Rosson's use of the parcel, driving Walton from the land, and the fact that Rosson never asked for permission to use the parcel indicated that the requisite claim of right existed.

Walton v. Rosson, 222 S.E.2d 553 (Va. 1976).

The requirement of actual and exclusive possession does not mean that the adverse possessor must be physically on the land at all times. Certainly improving the land with a residence would be actual possession. However, clearing the land, building a fence along the boundaries, or farming the land indicates that possession does exist. If the possessor allowed other people to use the land without his permission, the possession would not be exclusive. In essence, the adverse possessor must maintain possession as would a reasonable owner.

The phrase "open and notorious" means that the possession must be obvious from appearances upon examination of the land. In other words, the adverse possessor must not try to cover up his or her presence. Indeed, the possessor must freely acknowledge, either verbally or by acts, a claim to the land. The adverse possessor has to exercise control over the land as would the true owner.

The possession must also be hostile. Hostile possession indicates that the possessor does not readily admit or acknowledge any other person's ownership. Similarly, possession under a claim of right means that the possessor believes he or she is the owner and is properly possessing the land. Since the adverse possessor treats the land as if owned, that possessor should consider all uninvited guests as trespassers. If the true record owner seeks to assert a claim of ownership, the adverse possessor must deny the legality of such claims. "Hostile" does not require the possessor to be mean or vicious; it simply means the possessor refused to acknowledge any other person's ownership interest.

A claim of right may arise under several circumstances. The original belief that possession is proper may be based on mistake, payment of taxes, an oral conveyance, or permission of the owner. Most courts will consider the payment of real estate taxes as one factor in determining whether possession is under a claim of right. The failure of the possessor to pay these annual taxes will not, by itself, destroy the adverse possessor's claim to having acquired title. Some states have laws creating a presumption that the mere payment of taxes on unimproved and wild land for a statutory period satisfies the adverse possession requirements. Under these laws it becomes important to know what is unimproved and wild land.[2]

A possessor's use of the land with permission of the owner cannot lead to adverse possession. Regardless of how long a sole possessor may maintain his presence, the possession is not hostile and under a claim of right as long as it is recognized as a permissive use.

Often a last but equally important prerequisite for adverse possession is that the possession be under color of title. This means that the adverse possessor must have a written basis for believing that he is the owner of the real estate claimed. Obviously, a tenant who took possession of the premises while acknowledging the landlord's ownership could not adversely possess the leased property. However, if the possessor's claim of right is formed because of a written document such as a defective deed, the claim is based on color of title.

Some states require the possessor to have color of title in order to possess land adversely. Others simply reduce the number of years required for continuous possession if this written color of title is present. Still others do not require that the possessor's claim of ownership be based on a written color of title at all. These latter states would allow an oral conveyance as the first step in adverse possession.

15. The Statutory Holding Period

To be adverse, the possession must be continuous but not necessarily constant. For example, if a farmer planted and harvested the same land for the required period, his possession has been continuous. Likewise, a person's periodic use of a rustic mountain cabin for hunting, fishing, or vacation trips over the years probably would satisfy this requirement of continuous use. However, failure to possess and use the real estate on a regular basis would not amount to continuous possession. Regardless of whether the statutory period for adverse possession is seven

[2]Schuman v. Martin, page 105.

years, twenty years, or some period in between, all the essential elements must be satisfied for that span of time.

At times it may be hard to imagine how anyone could be confused about what land is owned unless there were a mistake in the deed's property description. Today, adverse possession is much more common with regard to boundary disputes than to possession of entire tracts. The boundary-dispute cases involving adverse possession are of particular importance in residential areas. However, people today are very mobile, especially in these urban areas. Therefore, the following question often arises: Does the same individual have to retain possession for the entire statutory period in order to establish adverse possession? No, the law does not necessarily prevent adverse possession when more than one person possesses the land for the statutory period. Combining the time of possession of one individual with the predecessor's period is called *tacking*.

In order to tack time of possession, the successive possessors must claim under the same claim of right or chain of title. For example, a buyer may be able to tack to the seller's period of possession, or an heir may tack to an ancestor's prior possession. An example of tacking is presented in the following case.

Case 4.4

Dorey owned a large tract of farmland. In 1937, he conveyed part of it to Ozanne. Shortly thereafter, Ozanne erected a fence around her tract but failed to include within the fence a small parcel. Lindl acquired the remainder of Dorey's land in 1972, and his deed from Dorey specifically excluded the land acquired by Ozanne in 1937. The small parcel Ozanne failed to fence was cultivated for over twenty continuous years prior to trial by Dorey and then by Lindl. Lindl was ignorant of the discrepancy between the fence and the true boundary line and regarded the fence as the boundary. Lindl brought this action when he learned that Ozanne claimed the property. Lindl contended that while he had not used the land during the entire twenty-year statutory period for adverse possession, he should be able to tack Dorey's use of the small parcel to his own period of use and thus satisfy the twenty-year requirement.

Issue: Could Lindl tack the possession of his grantor, Dorey, against Ozanne. who also acquired the land from Dorey?

Decision: Yes. Lindl acquired the small parcel through adverse possession.

Reasons: There is a presumption against a grantor's adverse possession of
                land conveyed to his grantee, which can be overcome only by
                open and notorious possession by the grantor. Thus unless Lindl
                could demonstrate that Dorey's possession of the small parcel
                conveyed by Dorey to Ozanne was open and notorious, Dorey
                would have no period of adverse possession which Lindl could
                add onto his own period. The presumption against Dorey's ad-
                verse possession was overcome by the inclosure and cultivation
                of the land. Since Ozanne erected a fence, she had continual
                notice of the open and notorious possession of the small parcel
                by Dorey.

                Lindl v. Ozanne, 270 N.W.2d 249 (Wis. App. 1978).

Adverse possession is grounded on the doctrine of *estoppel.* If the
true record owner of a piece of real estate does not attempt to remove
the adverse possessor during the statutory period, that owner is prevented or estopped from thereafter asserting his title rights. The concept of tacking is entirely logical and justified, because it should not
matter whether the true owner remains silent concerning his property
rights during the possession of one or more persons. Allowing title to
pass to an adverse possessor facilitates achieving the full use of the land.
The concepts of estoppel and tacking help accomplish this purpose of
using the land rather than letting it remain neglected.

16.   Title by Accretion

Accretion literally means the act of growing or adding to something. In
real estate law, it generally is applied to the gradual accumulation of
land by natural causes. Most frequently this build-up of land is created
by water, such as the ocean or a river. This process is called *alluvion.*
When new land forms due to accretion or alluvion, the issue of ownership often arises. Oftentimes the law of accretion and the law of adverse
possession will be intertwined, as this next case demonstrates.

Case 4.5

Mrs. Allison and Mr. Shepherd owned adjoining lots, each having
river frontage. The course of the river changed over the years,
exposing more land, none of which was included in Allison's or

Shepherd's original surveys. Shepherd began logging in the new area, despite Allison's claim that the property was hers. Allison brought this action, contending that she owned the property by adverse possession. Shepherd asserted that Allison lacked color of title to the property, since her deed described her lot as extending only to where the river used to be.

Issue: Did Allison have color of title by virtue of her deed?

Decision: Yes. Allison acquired title to the property by adverse possession.

Reasons: While Allison's deed described her property as running along the meander line of the river, this line can only mean the actual meander line, because such a line is not a permanent visible boundary. Accordingly, land that is bounded by a body of water has as its true boundary the actual body of water, even if there if fact exists a strip of land between the meander line and the actual shore. Allison's deed was therefore sufficient to give her color of title to the disputed area.

Allison v. Shepherd, 591 P.2d 735 (Ore. 1979).

Typically, when the build-up is gradual, the owner of the land that is added to gets to keep the additional land. This same principle applies when land is exposed because the body of water withdraws, decreases in volume, or changes course. When this event is gradual, *reliction* or *dereliction* has occurred.

The sudden removal of soil from one area and its deposit in another area is called *avulsion.* This event usually is caused by a storm or some other unusual occurrence. When the removal and deposit of soil is sudden, the original owners generally are allowed to reclaim it if they act promptly.

Cases on Methods of Acquiring Real Estate

In Re Kraft's Estate
374 P.2d 413 (Alaska 1962).

Dimond, J.:

Albert Kraft died on December 30, 1960, from alcoholism and cancer. A will purportedly executed by him the same day was offered for probate by the named executor, Emil Kraft, brother of decedent and appellee on this appeal. One third of decedent's property was left to his wife, and the residue to a daughter by a previous marriage. The wife, Faye Kraft, filed a petition contesting the will. After a hearing, the court found she had failed to establish any grounds for contest, and ordered that the will be admitted to probate. Faye Kraft has appealed. [She presents for this court's determination the issue of whether decedent possessed testamentary capacity at the time the will was executed.]

. . .

Appellant argues that because of Kraft's extreme illness and the sedation and whiskey which had been given to him on the day of his death, he did not have the physical capacity nor the mental apprehension to make a valid will.

Disease, great weakness, the use of alcohol and drugs, and approaching death do not alone render a testator incompetent to make a will. The question is always whether, in spite of these things, he had sufficient mental capacity to understand the nature and extent of his property, the natural or proper objects of his bounty, and the nature of his testamentary act. In discussing earlier in this opinion . . . we held there was evidence enough to support a finding that he was aware of the fact he was executing his will and that Bennett and Shannon were witnessing that act. If he had this much mental capacity, then since the will had been read to him and he appeared to understand it, it was reasonable for the court to conclude that he also had an awareness of the fact that he was making a final disposition of all his property, and that he was dividing it between his wife and daughter who were the natural objects of his bounty.

Appellant made an effort to establish lack of testamentary capacity by calling as witnesses two physicians who had attended Kraft during his illness. But neither was able to give a definite opinion on this issue one way or the other. Dr. Johnson was asked whether decedent would be competent, in the afternoon of this death, to make a decision how he wanted to dispose of his property. The doctor's answer was: "I wish I could give you a straightforward answer on that question, I honestly don't know." Dr. Keers was asked if he had an opinion as to whether decedent was of sufficient mind and memory to understand the nature and extent of his property, the proper objects of his bounty, and the nature of his testamentary act. The doctor's reply was:

"Yes, I have an opinion, I—I'd say it might be—the answer might be either he had or he hadn't—it would be—it would be difficult to say with any degree of assurance whether or not the man was able to understand."

Appellant also testified in her own behalf. She said that when she visited her husband in the hospital on the day prior to his death, he was being given oxygen because of difficulty in breathing, was unconscious, and was not lucid or rational. On the other hand, the witnesses Shannon and Bennett saw Kraft the following day when the will was signed, and their testimony was that he was conscious and knew what he was doing.

A decision of the issue as to testamentary capacity depended largely, if not entirely, on oral testimony given by witnesses seen and heard by the trial judge. It was his province to judge their credibility, and we may not reverse his decision unless we find it to be clearly erroneous. We cannot make such a finding on the record of this case.

Judgment affirmed.

Schuman v. Martin
531 S.W.2d 26 (Ark. 1975).

Arkansas has a statute that allows a person who pays the property taxes on unimproved and unenclosed land for seven successive years to acquire title to that land. Mrs. Martin and her heirs gained title to some land by possessing it from 1945 until 1955, when the house burned down. After 1955, the land was leveled and the grass was mowed.

Beginning in 1949, the property taxes on the land occupied by the Martins were paid by Florence Schuman. She paid these taxes annually until 1972, except for the year 1964. Since Ms. Schuman had paid these taxes for seven successive years, she obtained a tax deed and claimed title to the land.

The Martins sued Florence Schuman and asked the court to establish who was the actual owner of the land involved. The trial court held for the Martins, and Ms. Schuman appealed.

Smith, J.:

... That the appellees originally acquired title by adverse possession is shown by the weight of the evidence. Their mother bought the property in 1945 or 1946 and occupied a small house upon it until her death in 1947. Possession was continued either by some of the plaintiffs themselves or by tenants until the house burned in 1955. Hence there was continuous possession for more than seven years, which of course ripened into title.

The appellants, however, paid the taxes annually from 1949 to 1972, with the exception of the year 1964, when the appellees paid them. It is now insisted that, after the house burned, the appellants acquired title by the payment of taxes, under color of title, upon unimproved and unenclosed land for seven successive years....

The appellants are mistaken in their understanding of what constitutes "unimproved and unenclosed" land. Those words are used in Section 37–102, which requires payment of taxes for seven years under color of title. The companion statute, Section 37–103, requires payment of taxes for fifteen years without color of title and refers to "wild and unimproved" land. We have repeatedly held that the two statutes refer to the same conditions, "unimproved and unenclosed" being used interchangeably with "wild and unimproved.". . . It is also settled that lands which have been improved cannot be said to be "wild and unimproved" until they have been allowed to revert to the wild state that existed before the improvements were made. . . .

Here the two city lots in question did not revert to their original wild state. After the house burned the appellees paid someone to level off the lots. Thereafter a relative who lived next door to the property looked after it, keeping the grass mowed. There is no proof that the property was allowed to return to its natural state. Consequently the appellants cannot prevail upon the theory that they were paying taxes upon unimproved and unenclosed land, as that phrase has been interpreted through the years.

Affirmed.

REVIEW QUESTIONS

1. Define and distinguish the following:
   a. Inter vivos gift and testamentary gift
   b. Testate and intestate
   c. Executor and administrator
   d. Devise, bequest, and legacy
2. What are the three essential elements of a valid inter vivos gift?
3. Fannie had her attorney prepare a deed giving title to her real estate to her son, Ken. Fannie signed the deed and had it recorded without Ken's knowledge. When he discovered this transaction, Ken informed his mother that he wanted no part of the property. Before the recorded deed could be retracted, Ken died. Is Fannie correct in claiming that her conveyance to Ken was void? Discuss.
4. Majorie and Charles were husband and wife. In 1974, Marjorie transferred real estate she owned to Charles. Prior to this transaction, but during their marriage, Charles had severely beaten and threatened to kill Marjorie. After this transfer of real estate, Marjorie sought to rescind the gift, claiming that she had been fearful Charles would kill her if she did not convey the land as he demanded. Should Marjorie recover title to the land involved? Explain.
5. With respect to wills, what does attestation mean and what is its purpose?
6. William Bennet was to receive a $5,000 legacy under the terms of his friend's will. William signed this friend's will as one of the required witnesses. Does signing as a witness affect the legacy given to William?
7. Lloyd Nielson formally executed a will leaving charitable gifts to the Salvation Army, an association for retarded children, and a club for the blind. At his death, Mr. Nielson's will was found with several changes. The donees of the charitable gifts were scratched through, and in handwriting the Shrine Hospital of Crippled Children and the SPCA were substituted. What affect do these informal changes have on this will? Why?
8. Define and distinguish the following terms?
   a. Lapsed and adeemed testamentary gifts
   b. Per stirpes and per capita
9. List the five requirements essential for acquiring title to real estate by adverse possession. Explain what is meant by each requirement.
10. In 1961, Sullivan ran a fence that was hidden from view due to dense growth. This fence enclosed a seven-acre tract owned by the Realty Corporation. Sullivan occassionally pastured his cows on this land, and he once cut timber from it in 1969. In 1965, Sullivan offered to buy this land from the Realty Corporation. In 1974, Sullivan sought title by adverse possession. If the statutory period applicable to adverse possession is ten years, who should win? Explain.

5

Deeds

1. Introduction

As previously stated, title to real property signifies the legal right of ownership. Title to real property is often transferred from one owner to another by use of a document called a deed. Deeds were a natural outgrowth of the early English system of transfer by which the owner symbolically transferred ownership by handing the new owner a clod of dirt. We have replaced the clod of dirt with a piece of paper. Several elements are necessary to form a valid deed. A deed must be in writing and must:

- Designate the parties to the instrument
- Recite the consideration given for the conveyed interest
- Contain words of conveyance
- Describe thc property conveyed
- Indicate the interest conveyed
- Be signed by the grantor

In addition, the deed must be delivered in the lifetime of the grantor and accepted by or on behalf of the grantee.

Deeds begin by identifying the parties involved in the transfer of title. The owner who is transferring his title is called the *grantor*, while the party receiving the title and becoming the new owner is referred to as the *grantee.* Both these parties must be legally competent in order for the transaction to be binding. Legal competency is discussed in detail in Chapter 11 on sales contracts.

Usually the grantee must give up some benefit or suffer some detriment in return for the ownership interest being conveyed. In other words, the grantor's conveyance must be supported by the grantee's consideration. (See Chapter 11 for the details on the concept of consideration.) In the typical sales transaction, the purchase price serves as consideration for the transfer of ownership. However, in some states, instead of reciting the actual purchase price, a nominal amount (say $10.00) often is mentioned in the deed as the consideration paid to the grantor. This tends to keep the actual purchase price a secret known only to the parties. Some states require that the full and actual consideration involved be recited in the deed.

A valid deed contains language stating that the grantor conveys the real estate to the grantee. These words of conveyance are known as the *granting clause.* Frequently this clause appears immediately after the consideration is mentioned. For example, a typical deed might contain the following language:

> Grantor, in consideration the sum of ten dollars ($10.00), receipt whereof is hereby acknowledged, does grant, sell, and convey unto Grantee, his heirs and assigns, all that tract and parcel of land with improvements thereon described as follows:

The next element of a deed is that of legal description. The property being transferred should be described as accurately as possible so that the precise boundaries can be determined. A mere street address is an undesirable description in the deed, because the address does not establish the exact property boundaries. To describe the real property's precise location, the metes-and-bounds system, the rectangular survey, or the reference plats should be used. At times a combination of these methods is most beneficial, as discussed in Chapter 1.

The legal description is followed by the words that explain what interest is being conveyed. These words form the *habendum clause,* which is sometimes referred to as the "to have and to hold" clause. A typical habendum clause might appear as follows: "TO HAVE AND TO HOLD the premises hereby granted to Grantee, his heirs and assigns in fee simple absolute." Recall from Chapter 2 that ownership interests in real property can include fee simple absolute or lesser estates. The language of the habendum clause should make it clear what type of ownership interest is conveyed.

2. Execution and Delivery of Deeds

It is essential that the grantor sign the deed or have someone else sign as his agent. An agent's authority to sign a deed must be expressed in a written document, often called a *power of attorney,* executed with the same formality as a deed. The deed that satisfies all the foregoing requirements will successfully pass title to the grantee as long as it is delivered to and accepted by the grantee. However, a major concern of the grantee should be the protection of his newly-acquired title to real estate from potential claimants. The principal method of providing this protection is to have the deed recorded in the appropriate government office. A full discussion of the means, effect, and importance of this recording process is developed in Chapter 12.

Most states have laws that require something more than the grantor's signature on the deed in order to have the deed recorded. Typically, these laws require either that the grantor acknowledge his signature before a notary public or that the grantor sign the deed in the presence of a witness who also signs the document. Since some states require two witnesses, it is common practice to have the deed signed by two witnesses as well as before a notary public. Once the deed is properly signed by the grantor and acknowledged or witnessed, it has been fully executed. Some states require that the witnesses' signatures be present in order for the deed to be valid as a conveyance, rather than merely for recording purposes.[1]

Finally, the deed must be delivered to the grantee or to some third person to hold for the grantee until some specified event has occurred. Title to the property does not actually pass from the grantor to the grantee until delivery has been completed. Of course, it is assumed for the purposes of this discussion that the grantee accepts the deed. Refusal to accept the deed really results in an ineffective delivery. The issues of delivery and acceptance of a deed in a sales transaction are the same as those discussed under the section on transfers by gift.

As stated, recording the deed is not necessary for the transfer of title from the grantor to the grantee. However, it is always recom-

---

[1] *Walker v. City of Jacksonville,* page 123.

mended that the grantee record the new deed in the county's record or deed office so that the grantee will be protected against third parties' claims that the original grantor transferred title after the date of the original transfer. This recording of the deed may also protect the grantee from the claims of previous grantees who did not file their deeds. These advantages of the recording system are discussed fully in Chapter 12.

Types of Deeds

3. Introduction

There are many different kinds of deeds used in various states, each having its own special characteristics and legal implications. Some of the more common types are the warranty deed, the grant deed, the bargain-and-sale deed, and the quitclaim deed. There are also special types of deeds named for the legal position of the grantor at the time of conveyance. These special types include the executor's deed, the administrator's deed, the guardian's deed, the sheriff's deed, and the referee's deed in foreclosure.

The essential elements discussed above are the only ones required to have a valid deed. However, some of the common types of deeds include additional elements called covenants and warranties. Covenants are promises and warranties are guarantees that the statements made are true. Traditionally there are five covenants, and whether all, some, or none of them are included in a deed depends on the type of deed required to be given by the grantor and the law of the state authorizing the type of deed. In addition to these covenants, a deed may contain restrictions on the use of the property conveyed. These restrictions are a major subject matter of Chapter 6.

4. General Warranty Deed

The general warranty deed is the broadest and most desirable type (from the point of view of the grantee) of all deeds. In this deed, the grantor makes five traditional covenants, which include:

- Covenant against encumbrances
- Covenant of seizin or ownership

- Covenant of quiet enjoyment
- Covenant of further assurances
- Covenant of warranty forever

By the "covenant against encumbrances," the grantor assures the grantee that no liens or other encumbrances exist against the title to the real property except as noted. Normally, the grantor will exempt from this covenant those encumbrances and restrictions that exist. It is very common to see a deed that excepts from its coverage all encumbrances and restrictions of record. If, through a title search of recorded documents (see Chapter 12), the grantee learns of an existing encumbrance that is not expected, the grantor has breached the covenant against encumbrances and has liability for it. Examples of these encumbrances can include licenses, profits, mortgage liens, tax liens, mechanic's liens, and claims by third parties.

Likewise, if a neighbor has obtained an unrecorded easement by implication or prescription over the land being transferred, the grantee who received a general warranty deed can successfully sue the grantor for the value by which this encumbrance has diminished the property. A grantor who fails to except a present encumbrance from the application of this covenant is liable for its breach. This result should occur whether the grantee had knowledge of or was ignorant of the encumbrance's presence.

Case 5.1

During 1974, Brewer acquired land from Peatross by warranty deed. In early 1974, the city in which the tract was located decided to make improvements to certain areas, to be financed by special assessments of property taxes against land located in the area being improved. A Special Assessment District was established in April 1974. Brewer acquired Peatross' land which was in this district in October 1974, when the improvements in the District were in varying stages of completion but before any actual assessment had been made. In October 1974, there was no record filing of the district in the county records. At the time of the conveyance, Peatross had actual notice of the existence and purpose of the district and knew that the costs being incurred for the improvements were to be assessed against the land he conveyed to Brewer. Brewer brought this action contending that Peatross breached the covenant against encumbrances, as a warranty deed has the effect of guaranteeing that the title conveyed is free of encumbrances.

Issue: Did Peatross breach the covenant against encumbrances?

Decision: Yes. Brewer was entitled to damages.

Reasons: While the mere existence of a special assessment district does not necessarily constitute an encumbrance, it may constitute an encumbrance if there is some burden on the property discoverable in the county records or if the circumstances are such that the grantor either had or should have had knowledge that there was such a burden. Since Peatross had actual knowledge of the burden and was aware of the improvements, the existence of the Special Assessment District was an encumbrance.

Brewer v. Peatross, 595 P.2d 866 (Utah 1979).

The word *seizin* (also spelled *seisin*) means to possess land as the owner of a freehold estate. When a grantor gives a "covenant of seizin" in a general warranty deed, the grantee receives an assurance that the grantor actually owns and has the right to convey the estate described in the deed. The ownership interest involved may be a fee simple absolute, a lesser fee, a life estate, a remainder, or any of the other estates described in Chapter 2. A breach of the covenant of seizin occurs if the grantor's title is inferior to that of a third party.

The "covenant of quiet enjoyment" is the grantor's promise that the grantee shall enjoy possessing the land conveyed without disturbances from people claiming to have title to the same property. In essence, this covenant is further protection for the grantee in the event the grantor's title was defective. Breach of the covenant of quiet enjoyment, like all these covenants, results in the grantor being directly liable to the grantee. A grantor will breach this covenant if someone claims to have an interest in the land that was not excluded from the grantor's promises in the deed. A holder of a lease interest may be just one example of such a claim.

By the "covenant of further assurances" the grantor undertakes to perform all acts that may be required in the future to perfect the title conveyed. For example, if the deed delivered to the grantee is defective for any reason, the grantor has promised to sign and deliver a new deed free from all defects. A common defect in the original deed may be an inadequate property description or improper execution in that the deed was not acknowledged or witnessed, as required for recordation.

In essence, the "covenant of warranty" is a culmination of the protection provided by the general warranty deed. This covenant is the assurance given by the grantor that the grantee will enjoy ownership and possession of the estate conveyed because no one has superior title. Implicit in this warranty, the grantor has the right to convey title and the grantor will assist the grantee in defending this title against any potential claimants who base their claim on events during the time the grantor was the owner. In other words, this covenant of warranty will not make the grantor liable if land is adversely possessed during the time the grantee holds record title. Sometimes this covenant is referred to as the warranty forever.

Exhibit 5.1 is presented to allow the reader to become familiar with the provisions of a typical warranty deed. The normal deed is not divided into the numbered sections shown here. These Roman numerals are used simply to facilitate the following explanation. Section I identifies the parties as "Grantors" and "Grantees." Section II recites the consideration paid in return for the deed, states that the property is being conveyed, and describes the property's boundaries. Section III, which is the habendum clause, actually indicates that the grantees now hold the property in fee simple absolute. These first three paragraphs plus the grantors' signatures satisfy the necessary requirements of a deed.

EXHIBIT 5.1   GENERAL WARRANTY DEED*

I

THIS DEED, made this 20th day of July, 1982, between Donald and Elizabeth Wilson of St. Joseph, Missouri, hereinafter referred to as "Grantors," and Christopher and Margaret Cook of St. Joseph, Missouri, hereinafter referred to as "Grantees."

II

WITNESSETH, that Grantors, in consideration of the sum of ten dollars ($10.00), receipt whereof is hereby acknowledged, do grant, sell, and convey unto Grantees, their heirs, and assigns, all that tract or parcel of land with improvements thereon located in Buchanan County, Missouri, described as follows:

Part of the S.W. ¼ of the S.E. ¼ of Section 14 T. 57 N., R. 35 W., of the 5th P.M., Buchanan County, State of Missouri, beginning at a point being 202 feet east of the S.W. corner of the S.E. ¼ of said Section 14, running

---

*This form is intended for instructional purposes only and should not be relied on in practice, since it may not satisfy all the existing circumstances.

thence north 82 degrees east 200 feet to an iron pin; running thence east 104 degrees 100 feet to an iron pin; running thence south 82 degrees west 200 feet to an iron pin; running thence west 104 degrees 100 feet to the point of beginning. This property is that described as Lot 3, Block G of the Harris Billups Estate as recorded in Plat Book 8, page 37, in the Clerk's Office at the Buchanan County Circuit Courthouse.

III

TO HAVE AND TO HOLD the premises hereby granted to Grantees, their heirs and assigns in fee simple forever.

IV

The Grantors warrant that the premises are free from all encumbrances except for the following:

(a) The underground gas line easement running along the eastern boundary within five feet thereof.

(b) All other restrictions of record.

V

The Grantors, having a fee simple interest and the right to convey such interest, warrant that Grantees, their heirs, and assigns shall enjoy quietly and peaceably possession of the premises.

VI

It is further warranted that Grantors shall procure and execute any further assurances of the title to the premises and that Grantors will forever defend the title to the premises against all claims.

IN WITNESS WHEREOF, Grantors have set their signatures and seals, the day and year first written above.

_____(seal)
Donald Wilson

_____(seal)
Elizabeth Wilson

Signed, sealed and delivered
in the presence of:

_____

_____
Notary Public, Buchanan County
Missouri

Since the document in Exhibit 5.1 is a general warranty deed, the remaining paragraphs contain all the covenants and warranties previously discussed. For example, Section IV provides the grantors' promise that there are no unrecorded encumbrances other than those clearly stated (covenant against encumbrances). Section V includes the grantors' statement that they have a fee simple interest and the right to convey this interest to another person (Covenant of seizin). This provision also contains the covenant of quiet enjoyment. Section VI includes the covenant of further assurances and the covenant of warranty.

5.   Special Warranty Deed

Sometimes a grantor may be hesitant to promise that his or her title is the only claim to ownership. In other words, the grantor does not want to make all five of the covenants and warranties found in a general warranty deed. Perhaps because of confusion in the property's title prior to this grantor's taking possession, the grantor may wish to limit any covenants of title given to the grantee. In such situations, the grantor may execute a special warranty deed instead of a general one. By a special deed, the grantor is guaranteeing only that the grantee is protected against claims arising from the grantor, heirs, assigns, or anyone else claiming title through the grantor. Missing from the deed are all assurances, given in the general warranty deed, that the grantee will have quiet enjoyment, that the grantor will do whatever becomes necessary in order to assure the grantee's newly-acquired title, and that the grantor will forever defend the title given. Basically, the grantor in a special warranty deed has merely promised that he or she has legal ownership and that the real property has not been encumbered by or through him except as stated in the deed. By substituting the language in Exhibit 5.2 for Sections IV through VI in Exhibit 5.1, a special warranty deed would be created.

6.   Grant Deed

In several western states, particularly California, the grant deed is more common than the general warranty deed. In a grant deed, the grantor covenants that while the real estate was owned no interest in this land has been granted to another party, that the property has not been encumbered, and that any title to the property the grantor might re-

EXHIBIT 5.2   LANGUAGE OF A SPECIAL WARRANTY DEED

> Grantors hereby covenant with Grantees, their heirs and assigns that Grantors are lawfully seized in fee simple title to the above described property. Grantors covenant that they have a good right to convey and that the premises have not been encumbered *by or through grantors* except as stated elsewhere in this deed. Grantors also covenant that Grantors and all persons acquiring any interest in the property granted, *through or for Grantors,* will, on demand of Grantees, heirs or assigns, execute any instrument necessary for the further assurance of the title to the premises that may be reasonably required. Finally, Grantors and their heirs will forever warrant and defend all of the property granted to Grantees, their heirs and assigns, against every person lawfully claiming the property or any part thereof *by, through, or under Grantors.*

EXHIBIT 5.3   LANGUAGE OF A GRANT DEED

> Grantors covenant with Grantees, their heirs and assigns that Grantors have not encumbered the property described above except as stated herein; that Grantors have not previously granted any interest in these premises to anyone; and that any interests acquired by the grantors in the premises granted will be conveyed by the proper execution of required documents.

ceive in the future will be transferred to the grantee. A grantor under a grant deed limits personal liability to those encumbrances or claims that arose while the property was owned. The grant deed does not protect the grantee against encumbrances that may have arisen prior to this grantor taking title. In this way, like the special warranty deed, the grant deed is much narrower than the general warranty deed in the responsibility owed to the grantee. Exhibit 5.3 is an example of language used to create a grant deed.

7. Bargain-and-Sale Deed

A deed that implies the grantor has title to the property and the right to convey but does not contain any express covenants as to the title's validity is called a bargain-and-sale deed. This deed is also called a warranty deed without covenants. In essence, the bargain-and-sale deed simply specifies that the grantor "does hereby grant, sell, and convey" some interest in real property to the grantee. If the sales contract fails to specify what type of deed must be delivered, the bargain-and-sale deed may be the only one required. Before a deed that contains covenants can be demanded by the grantee, the sales contract must reflect that a specific type of deed was sought by the grantee.

Whenever a grantee receives only a bargain-and-sale deed, the grantee should get title insurance to protect against potential adverse claims against this newly-acquired title. Title insurance also is recommended for grantees who take title through a special warranty or grant deed. Title insurance is not as vital when title is transferred by a general warranty deed, since the grantee has a cause of action against the grantor for any defects in the title. Of course, title insurance protects a grantee when the grantor is financially insolvent. The concept of title insurance and the protection it provides is discussed in detail in Chapter 12.

8.   Quitclaim Deed

A quitclaim deed transfers any interest that the grantor may have in the property, but it does not give any promises that the grantor has some valid interest. In essence, as the name implies, the grantor simply relinquishes any rights he or she might have had to claim the real estate. The quitclaim deed is used, most commonly, to clear defects in the title to property. For example, suppose Bob wished to sell land he allegedly owned, but Clare, his sister, claimed to own one-fourth interest in the land. Before David, a prospective buyer, would be willing to purchase the land involved, he would want a quitclaim deed from Clare. That deed would indicate Clare had relinquished her rights to one-fourth interest; however, she would not be liable for any defects in the title to this property. In order to get full clear title to this land, David typically would insist on receiving a general warranty deed from Bob as well as the quitclaim deed from Clare.

The grantee who takes property under a quitclaim deed must understand that he may be receiving nothing at all.[2] A person could give a quitclaim deed describing a neighbor's land and not really be giving anything at all. Remember, pursuant to a quitclaim deed the grantor conveys all the interests possessed without assurances that any rights

[2]Miami Holding Corp. v. Matthews, page 125.

EXHIBIT 5.4   LANGUAGE OF A QUITCLAIM DEED

The Grantors, their heirs and assigns convey all the interests they might have in the premises hereby granted to Grantees, their heirs and assigns in fee simple forever. The Grantors, their heirs and assigns shall not hereafter claim or demand any right or title to the aforesaid premises or any part thereof, but they and every one of them shall be excluded and forever barred.

---

of ownership exist. To transfer all a person's rights in someone else's land is to transfer nothing. A sample of the language used in a quitclaim deed is in Exhibit 5.4. This language would be substituted for Sections III through VI of Exhibit 5.1.

With regard to these more common types of deeds, the most important lesson to learn is how much protection each deed gives to the grantee. The order in which these types of deeds were discussed is also the order of the amount of protection provided. The general warranty deed contains the greatest assurances by the grantor that the grantee will have security for nearly all potential claims. The special warranty deed limits the grantor's liability to claims which arise out of the grantor's chain of title. The grant deed, in essence, protects the grantee from encumbrances placed on the land's title by the immediate grantor. The bargain-and-sale deed simply states that the grantor has the right to convey the title involved, but all other assurances are missing. Finally, the grantor who gives a quitclaim deed does not even promise that he or she has any rights in the land at all.

9.   Deeds for Special Uses

There are several other kinds of deeds that have specific purposes. These include the executor's deed, the administrator's deed, the guardian's deed, and the referee's deed in foreclosure. Each of these special deeds is named for the signer, and the warranties given, if any, depend on that signer's capacity. For example, seldom will an executor of an estate be willing to promise that the title being transferred is free from all defects. Therefore, that representative of a deceased person covenants only that the deceased's title is conveyed and that no encumbrance was placed on the property by the executor. The referee's deed in foreclosure contains only the promise that the foreclosure proceedings were legally conducted. There is no assurance that full and unencumbered title is transferred. A grantee taking property under one of these specialized deeds must be aware that the grantor's warranties are very limited or nonexistent. Such a grantee might want to consider supplementing protection against a defective title by purchasing a title insurance policy.

Other Legal Issues Involving Deeds

10. Deed Preparation

In the past, most courts have been hesitant to permit nonlawyers to draft deeds. Currently there are several court cases involving whether title insurance companies can complete form deeds. Lawyers have charged that title insurance companies which draft deeds and handle closings are engaged in the unauthorized practice of law. Similar cases have also involved real estate brokers and salespeople. Title companies and brokers argue that they can fill in the blank deed form as well as any lawyer.

Colorado, Idaho, Michigan, Missouri, New Jersey, New Mexico, Texas, and Wisconsin are the only states with court decisions on record that have allowed nonlawyers to complete form deeds in transactions in which they are not involved as a buyer or seller. Until the United States Supreme Court sets a national standard on the permissible functions of nonlawyers in completing real estate documents, real estate brokers, title insurance companies, and other nonlawyers should find out the current rule in their respective states and should not be involved in the preparation of deeds unless it is clear that it is legal to do so.

11. Construing Ambiguities

Unfortunately, use of the English language often leads to ambiguities. While it is obvious that the best remedy for these uncertainties is the use of clear, precise phrases, a written deed may well contain ambiguous language. When ambiguities do occur, the parties involved normally turn to the courts for an unbiased interpretation.

In general, courts try to determine what the parties intended by the language used. Courts have formulated some rules to aid in construing ambiguous language. For example, if the defective wording is patently (or obviously) unclear, courts will allow oral testimony as to what the parties' intended. When the deed contains a latent (or hidden) ambiguity, courts usually will not permit oral testimony. In other words, if the language used in the deed does not appear to be confusing, it will be interpreted as it appears.[3]

However, if a court discovers that a party's intent is not represented by the language used, these rules of construction will be subordinated so that the true intent is fulfilled. For example, some courts have held that conflicting clauses within a deed must be construed together if at all possible in order to find the parties' intentions. If two clauses cannot be reconciled, usually the one that appears first is given more emphasis. Therefore, a clause that clearly contradicts a previous clause within the deed is ignored as long as this does not destroy the parties' intent.

Case 5.2

In 1955, Robert Camp and his mother, Tincy Camp, purchased a house and lot together. The deed conveyed title to Robert and Tincy as "tenants in common with the right of survivorship." This deed was properly executed, witnessed, acknowledged, and recorded. In 1956, Robert married Hilda Camp, and they had six children by 1966. In that year Robert died. He was survived by his wife, his children, and his mother. Thereafter a dispute arose over the ownership of the house purchased in 1955. Tincy Camp claimed to be the sole fee simple owner by right of survivorship. Hilda and the children of Robert claimed a one-half interest in the property, since Robert and his mother were merely tenants in common.

Issue: What ownership interest do grantees have when they take as "tenants in common with the right of survivorship?"

Decision: Each owner is merely a tenant in common; no right of survivorship exists.

[3]Financial Investment Corporation v. Tukabatchee Area Council, Inc. Boy Scouts of America, page 126.

Reasons: A court's principal function in construing the language of a deed is to search for the intent of the parties. If the language is uncertain and ambiguous, oral testimony by the parties involved can be heard. Furthermore, if two clauses are irreconcilably repugnant in a deed, the first clause prevails over the latter one. By the evidence introduced at the trial court, the parties' intent cannot be clearly determined. Therefore, the rule of construction dictating that a latter contradictory clause be ignored results in the conclusion that these parties were tenants in common with *no* right of survivorship.

Camp v. Camp, 260 S.E.2d 243 (Va. 1979).

12. Rescission of Deeds

Rescission or cancellation a deed's effect is an equitable remedy given to prevent one party from taking unfair advantage of another. Generally, the judicial relief of rescission is allowed to combat misrepresentation, fraud, undue influence, duress, and mutual mistake.

Misrepresentation occurs when a person falsely states a material fact which a second person justifiably relies on and is damaged. When misrepresentation is compounded with an intent to mislead, it is known as fraud. Suppose a buyer of a commercial building asks the seller if the building has ever been burned. If the seller, who knows that a fire has occurred, answers in the negative, the buyer could have the transaction rescinded and recover any money already paid.

A person who has a relationship of confidence and trust with another must take precautions to prevent being charged with exercising undue influence, which means to prevent one from exerting free choice. Often there is no absolute proof that undue influence occurred; therefore, even circumstances that could lead to an adverse conclusion should be avoided. This next case illustrates the court's suspicions about this subject of undue influence.

Case 5.3

Beryl McArthur died in 1973 at the age of seventy-eight. During the last years of her life, she made numerous transfers of property to Danny Yacte, a thirty-two-year-old man who befriended her in those last years. Gmeiner, Beryl's sister, brought these actions, contending that the transfers were gifts made under the undue influence of Yacte. At the time of her death, Beryl's health was failing badly; her sudden transfer of substantially all her assets to Yacte was said to be out of character with her lifelong reputation as a frugal school teacher. Yacte had moved in with her and isolated her from all contact with her relatives. Yacte argued that the transfers were not gifts at all but were in consideration for his one-half interest in a partnership, he was, however, unable to document the supposed partnership in any way.

Issue: Were the transfers from Beryl to Yacte gifts made under undue influence?

Decision: Yes. The gifts were made under undue influence.

Reasons: As is generally the case, there was no direct evidence that Yacte exerted undue influence on Beryl. The legal test of undue influence must therefore be dependent on an analysis of all the surrounding facts and circumstances. In assessing these circumstances, four factors assume primary importance: (1) a result which appears to be the effect of undue influence; (2) susceptibility to undue influence; (3) opportunity to exert undue influence; and (4) disposition to exert undue influence. The first factor was present because the gifts were out of character. The second factor was evidenced by Beryl's deterioration shortly before the transfer. The third factor is normally the easiest to establish, because frequently the beneficiary of the gift lives with the grantor, as was the case here. Finally, the fourth factor was satisfied because Yacte had apparently been responsible for alienating the grantor from the members of her family and had isolated her from all contact with family and disinterested third parties.

Gmeiner v. Yacte, 592 P.2d 57 (Idaho 1979).

Similar to undue influence, duress is another situation for which courts grant rescission as a remedy. Duress may be present when a person's freedom of choice is limited because of an existing threat. In a recent case, a woman deeded some real property to her estranged husband. Later she successfully sought to have her deed rescinded on the grounds that her husband, who had previously beaten her, threatened to kill her if the land was not given to him. This is a classic, albeit sad, case of duress.

A final justification for having a deed rescinded occurs when the parties to the document both misunderstood what was written in the deed. Mutual mistake perhaps arises most frequently in the area of legal descriptions. Whether a court allows rescission depends on whether it finds that both parties really were mistaken.

Case 5.4

Bartlett conveyed to the State Road Commission land described as a parcel of 10.63 acres. It was subsequently discovered that the parcel conveyed actually encompassed 13.13 acres. Bartlett brought this action to rescind the sale on the grounds of mutual mistake and to require the Commission to pay rent on the property it used.

Issue: Was Bartlett entitled to rescind?

Decision: No. The Commission was allowed to retain the land but was required to pay Bartlett the value of the additional acreage at the time of the conveyance.

Reasons: In order to be entitled to rescission, it must appear that the mistake was such that if the true facts had been known the deed would not have been executed. It was apparent in this case that the parties intended a sale of a specific parcel and not a sale of a specific amount of acreage. As both parties mistakenly believed that the desired parcel contained only 10.63 acres, there was a mistake only in computing the purchase price. The mistake did not go to the essence of the agreement but involved only a computational error which was not material and could be adjusted by court order.

Bartlett v. Department of Transportation, 338 A.2d 930 (Md. App. 1978).

Cases on Deeds

Walker v. City of Jacksonville
360 So.2d 52 (Fla. App. 1978).

Boyer, J.:

Appellants (Walkers) appeal from an order determining that appellee Glover is the fee simple owner of a certain parcel of land in Duval County and that Walkers have no interest therein.

This case emanates from an eminent domain proceeding by the City of Jacksonville in which Walker and Glover were made parties defendant. . . .

The record reveals that Glover, an undertaker in Jacksonville, is a step-uncle of the Walkers. The Walkers live in Washington, D.C. In 1971 the Walkers signed and mailed to Glover an instrument entitled "Warranty Deed" which was regular in form, acknowledged by a notary public, but not witnessed. Across the spaces provided for witness signatures appears the word "Blub." The instrument was never recorded, but Glover was made a party defendant in the eminent domain proceeding because the record revealed that he had paid taxes on the property for the years 1970 through 1974. The Walkers filed an answer, in customary form, demanding "full and just compensation to be set by a jury" and attorney's fees. Glover, too, filed an answer, in customary form, but specifically denying that Walkers had any interest in the property and affirmatively alleging sole ownership in Glover. The City of Jacksonville, being only interested in obtaining good title via eminent domain, expressed no interest in the dispute between Walkers and Glover and has taken no part in this appeal.

. . . Glover admitted possession of the subject "deed" and admitted that it had not been recorded. . . . Testifying at the hearing, Glover asserted possession of the property since 1971, which he has been using as a parking lot in connection with his funeral home. He further testified that the Walkers wanted to give him the property but that he paid "$1,000.00 for it anyway." His testimony did not explain the reason for the alleged desire to make a gift by the Walkers. The Walkers, on the other hand,. . . . admitted that $1,000.00 was advanced by Glover, claiming that a portion of that sum was delivered back to Glover to apply on the costs of the funeral of one Mamie Walker, a relative of the Walkers and Glover.

The order of the trial judge here appealed states:

"The Court determines that Ulysses C. Glover was the fee simple owner of the land described as Parcel 49-3 at the time the order of taking was entered herein, and that the Defendants M. Lucius Walker and Inez Walker, his wife, have no valid claim or interest in the land described as Parcel 49-3 or any awarding to be made, therefore."

[A state statute] requires that an interest in land be conveyed "by instrument in writing, signed in the presence of two subscribing witnesses by the party . . . conveying. . . ." The statute specifically provides that a conveyance may not be accomplished "in any other manner."

. . .[I]t is clear that the purported deed is not signed by two subscribing witnesses. Glover urges that, the record being silent on the point, Blub may well be a witness. That is true but Blub cannot be two witnesses. . . .

Glover further urges that since the instrument is acknowledged before a notary public the notary may be considered a witness. . . . Certainly there is nothing to prevent a notary from also being a witness. However, it is not necessary to the validity of an acknowledgement that the acknowledged instrument be signed in the presence of the notary: It is only necessary that the person whose execution is acknowledged be known by the notary to be the person claimed to be and that such person acknowledge to and before the notary the execution of the instrument. . . .

It necessarily follows, and we so hold, that the instrument executed by Walkers was insufficient under Florida law to convey title to Glover.

Glover, however, is not entirely without remedy. The Walkers themselves, in their brief, urged that the defective "deed" may be construed as a mortgage securing the sum which the evidence reveals was "advanced" by Glover to Walkers, viz: $1,-000.00. Although the evidence is scanty in that regard, it is sufficient, particularly in view of Walkers' own admission and argument in its brief. There is ample authority for the proposition that a warranty deed, even when properly executed, may be construed as a mortgage if it was intended by the parties at the time of execution and delivery that it not convey title but rather secure an indebtedness. . . .

Reversed and remanded.

Miami Holding Corp. v. Matthews
311 So.2d 802 (Fla. App. 1975).

Per Curiam.

Defendant-appellant appeals a final summary judgment quieting title to the subject realty in plaintiff-appellees.

On March 18, 1947, J. G. Head's Farms, Inc., conveyed by deed Lot 12, Block 8 of J. G. Head Farms, Unit "A" to Lottie Morrison, a single woman. That deed was not recorded at the time of delivery and subsequently was lost. Thereafter, one Alto Adams, as trustee, entered into a contract to acquire all of the stock and assets of J. G. Head's Farms, Inc. In accordance with the terms thereof, J. G. Head's Farms, Inc., by warranty deed conveyed all the lots it owned at the time by specific lot and block including Block 8 of Unit A. The deed as to Block 8 of Unit A enumerated twenty-two lots by specific number but did not include the lot in question, Lot 12. Thereupon a J. G. Head's Farms, Inc., was dissolved and George Patterson, et al. became trustees for the dissolved corporation.

In 1959, defendant-appellant purchased the properties acquired by Alto Adams from J. G. Head's Farms, Inc. The purchase agreement covered the properties including Unit "A" by specific lot and block. This agreement also required that Alto Adams obtain from J. G. Head's Farms, Inc., a quitclaim deed conveying to defendant any rights, title and interest that J. G. Head's Farms, Inc., may own in the subject properties including Plat of J. G. Head Farms, Unit "A". J. G. Head's Farms, Inc. conveyed such a deed to the defendant and it was recorded on January 8, 1960.

On February 27, 1963, J. G. Head's Farms, Inc., dissolved, through its trustees, executed and conveyed a quitclaim deed on Lot 12, Block 8 of J. G. Head's Farms, Unit "A" to Lottie Morrison who recorded the same on March 4, 1963. This deed recited that it is given as the substitute for previously "apparently lost" deed from J. G. Head's Farms, Inc. to the grantee therein. On May 7, 1970 Lottie Morrison conveyed the subject realty to the plaintiffs, Frank and Patricia Matthews. That deed was recorded on May 15, 1970. Thereafter, plaintiffs filed the instant action against defendant Miami Holding Corporation to quiet title to Lot 12, Block 8 of J. G. Head Farms, Unit "A". Defendant answered and counterclaimed to quiet title thereto in itself based upon the 1960 quitclaim deed from J. G. Head Farms, Inc., to the defendant. Subsequently, both parties moved for summary judgment and after a hearing on these motions, the chancellor entered final summary judgment quieting title to the property in the plaintiffs as against the claims of the defendant. This appeal followed.

Appellant first contends that the court erred in quieting title in the plaintiffs holding that an alleged prior unrecorded warranty deed is effective as to a subsequent innocent purchaser of real property who takes title to such lands by quitclaim deed without notice of the alleged prior unrecorded warranty deed. We cannot agree.

Generally, it is an accepted principle of law that the delivery of a complete deed executed by a grantor who had title to the land invests the grantee with title and in the absence of statutory requirements producing a different result, the grantee is not divested of his title by loss of the deed. . . . Further, where a deed has been lost and its contents are established, it will be presumed that it was executed in conformity with all the requirements of the law. . . . Thus, it is clear that plaintiffs having introduced sufficient competent evidence to establish the contents of the 1947 deed from J. G. Head's Farms, Inc., to Lottie Morrison, the loss of this deed did not divest the grantee, Ms. Morrison, of her title.

Having made the above determination, we turn our consideration to the defendant's claim to the subject property by virtue of the 1960 quitclaim deed from J. G. Head's Farms, Inc. It is well established that the execution of a quitclaim deed, without more, does not necessarily import

that the grantor possesses any interest at all and if the grantor has no interest in the land described at the time of conveyance, the quitclaim conveys nothing to the grantee. . . .

Title to Lot 12, Block 8 of J. G. Head Farms, Unit "A" being vested in Lottie Morrison at the time J. G. Head's Farms, Inc. executed the 1960 quitclaim deed to the defendant . . ., J. G. Head's Farms, Inc. had no interest in Lot 12, Block 8 thereof and, therefore, the quitclaim conveyed nothing therein to the defendant, Miami Holding Corporation. Furthermore, the record clearly reflects that J. G. Head's Farms, Inc. never represented to the defendant that it had any interest in Lot 12, Block 8 of Unit "A" as this lot was not included in the warranty deed to Alto Adams nor in the option to purchase agreement between Adams and the defendant. It is apparent that the quitclaim deed was to operate only as to the properties in which J. G. Head's Farms, Inc. had an interest.

Accordingly, the summary final judgment herein appealed is
Affirmed.

Financial Investment Corporation v. Tukabatchee Area Council, Inc., Boy Scouts of America
353 So.2d 1389 (Ala. 1977).

Bloodworth, J.:

Defendants, Financial Investment Corporation and W. Clyde Jennings, appeal from a judgment for plaintiff, Tukabatchee Area Council, Inc., Boy Scouts of America, holding that plaintiff owns legal title to certain disputed property. We reverse . . .

In February 1964, John and Mabel Haardt conveyed to defendant, Jennings, certain real property, described as follows:

"All that part of the following described real estate lying northwest of Genetta ditch

which bisects the said following described real estate commencing at its western boundary and running thence NE to its eastern boundary, to-wit: All that part of the NE ¼ of Section 26, Tp. 16, R. 17, lying West of the right-of-way of the Atlantic Coast Line Railroad Company containing 146.9 acres, more or less. *Also, all that part of the SW ¼ of the NW ¼ of Section 25, Tp. 16, R. 17, lying on the West side of the Coast Line Railroad, containing 2 acres, more or less.*" [Emphasis supplied.]

In September 1967, the Haardts deeded the italicized portion of the property to plaintiff. When plaintiff learned that defendant, Financial Investment Corporation, was claiming title to the disputed property as successor in the title to defendant, Jennings, plaintiff filed this declaratory judgment action, seeking to quiet title to the property in itself.

A hearing was held . . . at which time extraneous evidence of the acts and declarations of the parties was admitted in evidence, and a final judgment was entered in favor of plaintiff, holding, . . . that it was the intention of the Haardts, which intent was understood by defendant Jennings, to convey to Jennings only that part of the property "lying northwest of Genetta ditch which bisects the said property commencing at its western boundary and running thence northeast to its eastern boundary . . ."; that Haardt retained title to the italicized portion of the property; and, that the Haardts subsequently conveyed legal title to the italicized portion to plaintiff, which is now the sole owner and holder of legal title to said property.

Defendants [contend] . . . that the trial court erred . . . in admitting extrinsic evidence of the parties' intentions because the language of the deed in question was unambiguous. . . .

It is, of course, a fundamental rule of construction that the real inquiry in construing the terms of a deed is to ascertain the intention of the parties, especially that of the grantor, and if that intention can be ascertained from the entire instrument, resort to arbitrary rules of construction is not required. . . .

The courts, in construing convey-ances, must ascertain and give effect to the intention and meaning of the parties, "to be collected from the entire instrument.". . .

Plaintiff argues the trial court was correct in admitting extrinsic evidence of the parties' intentions because, it contends, the italicized language in the deed is ambiguous. It is, of course, true that where a deed is of doubtful meaning, or where the language of a deed is ambiguous, the intent of the parties to the deed as to what property is conveyed may be ascertained by reference to facts existing when the instrument was made, to which the parties may be presumed to have had reference. . . .

However, if the language is plain and certain, acts and declarations of the parties cannot be resorted to, to aid construction. . . .

We have carefully examined the language of the description in the deed, and we conclude that the language contained therein is not, on its face, ambiguous. In fact, the plain meaning of the language of the italicized portion, its punctuation and juxtaposition to the other portion, admit of but one conclusion, that the Haardts intended to convey to defendant, Jennings, the italicized portion of the description.

In ascertaining the intention of the parties, the plain and clear meaning of the deed's terms must be given effect, and parties must be legally presumed to have intended *what is plainly and clearly set out.* . . .

For this reason, this cause is . . . *Reversed.*

REVIEW QUESTIONS
1. What are the essential elements of a valid deed?
2. A deed described the property being conveyed as follows:

"All that parcel of land at Cape Hatteras, known as Fulcher's homestead and described as follows: Beginning at D. W. Fulcher's North corner line, and running from thence along W. J. William's heirs' line Northwesterly to the Sound; from thence to A. C. Guildly's heirs' line to the place of beginning."

In your opinion, is the above an adequate legal description such that the deed which contains it will not be void? Explain.

3. Although delivery of a valid deed to the grantee normally transfers title between the grantor and grantee, the deed should be recorded in order to protect the grantee's newly-acquired title. In addition to the grantor's signature, what do some states require in order to have the deed recorded?

4. List and explain the five covenants that are found in a general warranty deed.

5. Barkett received a general warranty deed from Muscare as a means of transferring property that was subject to a preexisting contract of sale between Muscare and Tropicana. When Barkett discovered this fact, she sued Muscare for breach of the general warranty deed. Did Muscare violate the general warranty deed delivered? If so, how? Explain.

6. Distinguish among the following:
   a. General warranty deed
   b. Special warranty deed
   c. Grant deed
   d. Bargain-and-sale deed
   e. Quitclaim deed

7. In any case involving the construction of language used in a deed, what is the most important thing that courts try to accomplish?

8. Joseph deeded his farm to his nephew, Hubert. At Joseph's death, his two children who had lived with their mother since their parents' divorce sued to have the deed rescinded. Their claim was based on the fact that Hubert had an undue influence on Joseph's decision to transfer ownership of the farm. Joseph and Hubert lived across from one another, farmed together, and shared the profits. When Joseph became ill, Hubert cared for him. Does the relationship of uncle-nephew together with these facts lead to the conclusion that undue influence was exerted? Should the deed be rescinded?

6

Introduction to Land-Use Controls

1. Introduction

Throughout this book we have discussed various ownership interests in real estate and methods for acquiring such interests. The discussion would be incomplete if we did not mention the land-use controls that may restrict a landowner's rights. These controls are categorized as either private or public in nature. Private land-use controls are those restrictions placed on an ownership interest by an individual, company, or other nongovernmental entity. A typical example of private controls is a restrictive covenant.

Public controls that limit an owner's use of land are placed on real estate by governmental bodies at the federal, state, and local levels. In general, these public controls are based on the power of eminent domain and the exercise of the police powers. Specifically, these powers are used to enact zoning ordinances and subdivision or developmental regulations. This chapter serves as an introduction to general private and public land-use controls. The next chapter includes a more in-depth examination of public land-use controls with a special emphasis on zoning.

Restrictive Covenants

2.   In General

Generally, a covenant is a promise made by one person to another. As applied to the law of real estate, covenants often are used by private entities to control the land owned by them or others. These covenants can be either affirmative or negative in nature. For example, promising to maintain a white picket fence around the front yard of a residential lot is a type of *affirmative covenant.* The landowner has promised to take a positive or affirmative action. On the other hand, a *negative covenant* requires the landowner to refrain from some action. For instance, promising not to bring a mobile home onto the property is an example of a negative covenant. In both cases, these kinds of covenants restrict, in some manner, the way in which the property can be used. Therefore, promises that control land use are called *restrictive covenants.*

The principle behind privately imposed restrictive covenants is that burdens placed on one owner's land will benefit the surrounding real estate or its owners. Thus, in the creation, enforceability, and termination of these covenants the respective burdens and benefits must be considered. Covenants that unreasonably burden an owner's interest in using the land should not be created or enforced. At the same time, covenants cannot be terminated if the loss of the benefit to surrounding owners is too great. These issues and others are developed in the following sections.

3.   Creation

Restrictive covenants are created by agreement between two or more parties having an interest in the benefited or burdened real estate. Typically, such parties may be a buyer, seller, landlord, or tenant of real estate. This agreement must meet all the essential requirements of a valid contract, including that it be in writing, since it involves real estate. Typically, covenants will be formed upon the transfer of a real property interest. Therefore, it is most common to have the covenants incorporated into a deed to a single tract of land or to have them made a part of a general development plan. For example, a subdivision developer may file with the appropriate official a master plat that contains a list of restrictive covenants that apply to every lot within the subdivision.

By referring to this master plat in any deed used to transfer land in the subdivision, notice is given that covenants do exist.

4. Enforceability

A restrictive covenant must be reasonable to be binding. If it creates unreasonable or unlawful limitations on an owner's use of land, the covenant will not be enforced. For example, restrictions preventing owners from selling their property to a person of a particular ethnic or racial group are clearly unenforceable because they violate the laws and Constitution of the United States.

Developers of residential subdivisions sometimes use restrictive covenants to create an aesthetically pleasing neighborhood that will increase the value of all owners' land. As long as these covenants are reasonable, they generally are enforceable. Some typical covenants that are reasonable include a limitation of use; the number of feet a house must be set back from the road; a minimum number of square feet in a house; a maximum building height; requirements relating to garages and carports; and a prohibition of temporary buildings or mobile homes. The more specifically the restriction is described, the more likely that covenant will be enforceable. The following case is an example of a covenant written in such general language that its application was questioned.

Case 6.1

Ross and Anne Parker purchased two lots in a subdivision. Although aware that covenants restricted them from bringing a "trailer" onto the lots, the Parkers nevertheless moved a double-width mobile home onto the lots. They had the wheels, axles, and running gear removed, and the home placed on a concrete-and-stone foundation. A water well was drilled, a septic tank was installed, and both were connected to the Parkers' home. After these events transpired, twelve other lot owners filed suit to enforce the covenant by having the Parkers' "mobile home" removed.

Issue: Can the covenant restricting trailers be enforced so that a firmly attached mobile home must be removed?

Decision: No. The covenant's restriction is not applicable to this situation.

Reasons: Restrictive covenants should be construed to allow the greatest freedom in land use. A covenant must be considered reasonably, though strictly; an illogical, unnatural, or strained construction must be avoided. The purpose of this type of covenant restricting trailers is to preserve the residential nature of a neighborhood by preventing temporary structures from being used as homes. The Parkers' mobile home includes three bedrooms, two baths, and a total of 1,400 square feet. In addition, they have added a patio, a two-car garage, and a conventional shingle roof. These characteristics make this "mobile home" appear very similar to other residences in the neighborhood. The prohibition on trailers is not applicable to the Parkers' home.

Heath v. Parker, 604 P.2d 818 (N.M. 1980).

Restrictive covenants may apply to transactions other than those involving buyers and sellers of real estate. Chapter 16 includes a discussion and some examples of covenants enforceable between landlords and tenants. A reading of Section 4 of Chapter 16 is recommended at this time.

Failure to abide by applicable restrictive covenants results in a breach of those contractual promises. Typically, a landowner or tenant who breaches a covenant may become liable for money damages or may be enjoined from continuing to violate the covenant. A party who breaches an enforceable restrictive covenant will not lose title to or possession of the property. This effect of a breach is a major distinction between covenants and conditions that restrict an ownership interest.

Covenants generally are narrowly construed to prevent overly harsh restrictions. For instance, a covenant that prohibits the establishment of a business on certain land would not necessarily prohibit the building of an apartment complex. Although apartments should produce income for the landlord, their principal purpose is for residential use, which is not within the uses prohibited by the covenant. The issue of whether a covenant will be enforced if it conflicts with applicable zoning regulations has arisen frequently. For example, assume that a covenant restricts land use to residential purposes, but the zoning allows commercial uses. Is the use limited to residences only? The answer is yes. Courts tend to enforce the more restrictive of covenants and zoning regulations when they are in conflict.[1]

[1]Lidke v. Martin, page 150.

5. Who May Enforce

Since a restrictive covenant is a type of contractual agreement, the nonbreaching party to the original agreement may enforce it. In order to recover damages or obtain an injunction, the nonbreaching party must be able to show that some damage has been suffered. In other words, to be justified in enforcing a covenant, the party must be able to show how the intended benefit has been denied.

Who may enforce a covenant is not a difficult question when the original contracting parties are the only ones involved. However, the analysis becomes more complicated when a third party becomes involved, which can occur through the purchase, assignment, or sublease of the benefited or the burdened land. Whether a person who receives the burdened land is subject to the covenant or the person who receives the benefited land can enforce the covenant depends on whether the covenant is personal or whether it runs with the land. In order for a covenant to run with the land, the burden or benefit must be intended to be directly associated with the land, and the subsequent third party must receive notice that the covenant exists.

Suppose a developer, Dixon, sells a lot to Charles, who promises in the sales contract that he will maintain a wooden fence around his back yard. Further assume that Dixon now sells all the other lots in the subdivision, with each contract containing a similar clause with respect to the maintenance of a back-yard fence. Under traditional analysis, the benefit of the promises to every other landowner can be enforced by the original purchasers. In other words, each initial purchaser is allowed to stand in the place of Dixon, the developer. In addition, each of these purchasers had notice of the covenant through the sales contract. What would happen if Charles sold his lot to Gladys? Would she be liable for the continued maintenance or initial construction of the fence if she was unaware of the covenant? The most likely conclusion should be that Gladys is not bound by a covenant previously made by her grantor, because she had no notice of its existence. Therefore, her fellow subdivision residents cannot force her to abide by this preexisting covenant.

A different result would occur if this covenant to build and maintain a fence had been recorded in the deed to Charles from Dixon. Likewise, Gladys would have received notice of her obligation if the master plat had contained the covenant to build a fence and previous deeds had referred to the master plat. Even though a third party to a covenant may not actually learn of a covenant's existence, if it is properly recorded all parties are said to receive constructive notice through the available legal documents.

Another way notice may be constructively given is through a common appearance of a subdivision. It is not hard to imagine how notice of a promise to build a back yard fence can be construed from a common design. However, if the original covenant, found only in an unrecorded sales contract, had been to pay an annual $150 fee for the maintenance of a subdivision pool, no constructive or actual notice would have been received by Gladys. Thus, she would not be burdened by the promise made by Charles, since it would be personal to him. In other words, under these latter facts those neighbors who may have been able to enforce Charles' promise to pay a pool fee would not be able to enforce this preexisting covenant as to Gladys.

6. Termination

Restrictive covenants that are personal to the landowner are terminated simply upon the sale of the affected property. Covenants that run with the land are not terminated as easily. Nevertheless, the enforcement of these more permanent covenants can be terminated in any number of ways, including (1) by agreement of the parties, (2) by merger, (3) by release, (4) by waiver, (5) by changed circumstances, or (6) by eminent domain.

The parties who originally created a restrictive covenent can also agree that it is no longer enforceable. This type of agreement should be in writing. A common form of termination by agreement exists when the legal document creating the covenants states that they will last for a specific time period. When a developer places restrictive covenants on all the lots within a subdivision, all the landowners who are benefited and burdened by these covenants may agree collectively that the covenants will not be enforceable. Indeed, sometimes the developer will provide that a covenant is no longer binding when a majority of the landowners decide it is not to be enforced. This decision to terminate the covenant's enforcement becomes effective on those owners in the minority who did not agree to it.

The concept of merger has been discussed in Chapter 3 as a means of terminating easements, licenses, and profits. *Merger* also is one method to terminate a restrictive covenant's application. For example, if the owner of the benefited land acquires title to the burdened land, there would be no justification for the covenant to exist. The conveyance of either parcel of land does not reestablish the prior existing restrictive covenants; however, new covenants can be imposed at any time, as long as they are reasonable.

The benefited party may give up the right to enforce a restrictive covenant through a formal release. A *release* is a contractual promise that a right is being given up now and in the future. Since it is contractual in nature, a release must meet the essential elements of a binding contract, including that there be some consideration and that it be in writing. An agreement to release the right to enforce a covenant essentially terminates the covenant's effectiveness.

Similar to, but not to be confused with, a release is the concept of waiver. A *waiver* is a voluntary relinquishment of a right. A party who does not enforce a restrictive covenant when the right to do so is present can be said to have waived that right. In other words, the benefited party who waives the enforcement of a covenant abandons such right, and the restrictive covenant is thereby terminated. A waiver may occur when one party acquiesces to a violation of a covenant over a long period of time. Whether or not a waiver has occurred is a factual issue that must be determined on a case-by-case basis.

Case 6.2

In 1961, Henry Yeager placed restrictive covenants on land he owned and was subdividing. One covenant stated, "that no swine, poultry, goats, or livestock shall be permitted on the premises." Since 1966, when extensive subdividing of Yeager's land began, horses have been continuously present in the subdivision. Specifically, the Lovejoys have had horses on their land since 1966, the Millers since 1968, and the Cricks since 1973. In 1975, John and Nicki Kelly purchased a house a short distance from where the Lovejoys maintained their horses. Shortly thereafter a dispute arose which was centered around the Kellys' dog barking at the Lovejoys' horses. The Kellys brought suit to enforce the covenant prohibiting livestock from this land.

Issue: Can this covenant be enforced in light of the long-term acquiescence by landowners to the presence of horses?

Decision: No. The right to enforce this covenant had been waived and abandoned by the Kellys and others.

Reasons: Waiver generally is a voluntary and intentional relinquishment of a known right, claim, or privilege. Evidence in this case showed that the Kellys were aware of the covenant and were aware that horses were present on the burdened land before they purchased their home. The Kellys voluntarily waived the right to enforce the covenant by acquiescing in the Lovejoys' right to have horses on the land. In view of this waiver, the Kellys are estopped or prevented from enforcing the covenant. A waiver may be proved by express statement or by actions which must be examined under each case's peculiar circumstances. Here the evidence is sufficiently clear to find that the Kellys had waived their right to enforce the covenant.

Kelly v. Lovejoy, 565 P.2d 321 (Mont. 1977).

A change in the circumstances or the surroundings of real estate burdened by a restrictive covenant can lead to its termination. Courts can refuse to enforce the burdens of covenants if the conditions that give rise to them have changed. For example, a developer of vacant land may have desired that only residences be built on the land. Assume that a covenant limiting this land to residential purposes is present. Over a number of years, the land surrounding the development may become used for commercial purposes. A landowner within the development may decide to use the house as an office. As long as the zoning ordinance permits this use, the restrictive covenant likely will not prevent it due to the changing circumstances of the neighborhood. Termination of a covenant's enforceability based on changed circumstances will be made on a case-by-case basis. Courts will examine the original purpose of the covenants, the degree of change in the surrounding area, and the benefits to be gained from the land as restricted as opposed to unrestricted.

Finally, restrictive covenants may be terminated by exercise of the power of eminent domain. The government's taking of land burdened by a restrictive covenant removes the stated restriction from the land's use. The termination of the covenant's restriction is necessary to allow the government to use the land for the intended public purpose. An interesting question concerning whether owners of land that was benefited by a covenant's existence can seek just compensation when a covenant is voided by the exercise of eminent domain powers is reserved until Section 10 below.

Eminent Domain

7. Introduction

A fundamental interest of individuals is the right to own private property. The Fifth Amendment to the United States Constitution states that property shall not be taken from any person for public use without just compensation. Although this provision applies specifically to the federal government, court decisions have clearly held that it applies to state and local governments as well. These decisions are based on an interpretation of the Fourteenth Amendment's due process clause.

The power of any governmental body to take private property, without the owner's consent, for public use is known as *eminent domain.* This power of eminent domain is exercised through a legal procedure called a *condemnation proceeding.* To be valid, condemnation proceedings must be within the constitutional limitation of the eminent domain powers. Notice and hearing are the fundamental requirements necessary to afford a landowner the required due process of law. In essence, the landowner must be notified that his or her land is being taken and must be given an opportunity to have a hearing. At the hearing, the basic issues will be whether the land is taken for public use and whether the owner receives just compensation.

8. Public Use

The government's intended use for land taken by eminent domain is vitally important, because land can be taken only when it will be used by or for the public. There are two points of view as to the meaning of "public use." Originally, the narrower view was that the land taken must actually be used by the public, as, for example, for the construction of highways, schools, hospitals, and parks on the land.

Today a broader view of "public use" justifies the taking of private land when it will be used for the public's benefit or interest without actually being used by the public. This viewpoint justifies a regulated utility company condemning an owner's land in order to build a power plant at the best location or to run wires over or under the land. Although the public is not physically using the land in these examples, it certainly does benefit from having utilities supplied in a reliable manner at a reasonable cost. This broader logic has been used to justify acquisitions in urban-renewal projects, as the following case demonstrates.

Case 6.3

The City of Chicago commenced condemnation proceedings to acquire title to the Sherman House Hotel, a dilapidated building, and the land it occupied. This exercise of the eminent domain power was to clear the land of a blighted commercial area and to put it to a more productive use. The City planned to sell the land to the Illinois Capital Development Board so that a new State of Illinois Building could be built on the location. The tenants of the hotel building objected to the proceedings; they argued that the City of Chicago could not condemn the building because the City had no intended public use planned. The tenants claimed that the City's intention to sell the land to the State would not satisfy the requirement that the proceedings be based on a public need.

Issue: Can a city condemn land for the purpose of clearing blighted areas, even though the ultimate use may not be by the condemning governmental body?

Decision: Yes. The condemnation proceeding is appropriate.

Reasons: When the primary purpose of a condemnation proceeding is for a public use, it is immaterial that a private enterprise or another governmental body gains a benefit. The taking of a slum and blighted areas in an urban-renewal program is itself a taking for public use, regardless of the subsequent use of the land. In other words, an acquisition that allows clearance and redevelopment justifies the exercise of eminent domain powers.

City of Chicago v. Gorham, 400 N.E.2d 42 (Ill. App. 1980).

If the government cannot justify its need for the condemned land on the basis of public use, the land cannot be taken without the owner's consent. Of course, at all times an owner can agree to sell private property to anyone, including a governmental body that does not plan to use the land in a public manner.

9. *Just Compensation*

Although landowners can claim that the government is acting beyond its authority and is maliciously taking the land when it is not needed for the public use, this argument is seldom successful in condemnation proceedings because of the broad interpretation given to the term "public use." The major issue in most condemnation proceedings is just compensation. Remember, before the government can constitutionally take an owner's land, it must be willing to pay just compensation. Owners can argue in court that the government has not offered just compensation for the use of their land.

Typically, the phrase "just compensation" means the fair market value of the property when it is sold on the open market without artificial restraints. Although some states do not require that a jury determine just compensation, juries often are asked to determine what the government must pay the landowner. Very often, because the jury's sympathy is with the defendant whose land is being condemned, an award of just compensation appears to exceed what is believed to be the land's fair market value. As long as the final award is within the boundaries of the evidence produced during the proceedings, the award will be upheld on appeal.

In order to determine what is just compensation for a piece of property, the government and the owner will have experts testify as to the fair market value. Normally these experts are appraisers who evaluate the land's value by using one of several appraisal methods, which can include the market or sales approach, the income approach, the cost-of-replacement approach, or a combination of these methods.

The requirement of just compensation does not necessarily mean full compensation for all the damages suffered by an owner whose land is taken. Usually, the owner is not reimbursed for the attorney's fees or the fees paid to the expert witnesses. Nor are costs of relocating to a new residence or a new business site included in the meaning of just compensation. Furthermore, a business forced to move cannot collect for the loss of good will that it had established in its previous location. Some laws have been passed in recent years to help displaced persons with these costs that are not included within interpretation of just compensation. This legislation is examined in detail in Section 13 below.

10. Condemning Less Than a Fee Interest

In addition to the basic issues of a public use and just compensation that are present in all eminent domain cases, particular situations may give rise to other issues. Some of the questions that might arise include what happens when the government does not condemn an owner's entire interest, when it condemns more land than is actually needed for the public's benefit, or when it begins using the land prior to completion of the condemnation proceedings. These three issues are the topics of this and the next two sections.

In order to accomplish its purpose, the government may not need to take an owner's entire interest in land. Indeed, a mere easement allowing access to or from some land may be sufficient, or a negative easement restricting the landowner's use of the land may satisfy the government's needs. Consider VORTAC stations, from which radio signals are sent to overhead airplanes so that their positions can be tracked. Although such stations physically take up only a portion of an acre, the area around the station for a radius of approximately one-half mile must not contain any object over six feet high. In other words, the government has no need for the actual land surrounding VORTAC stations; it only needs assurances of open air. In this situation, the government would condemn both the title to the station's physical location and an open-air easement surrounding the building. Thus, the landowner could continue to use the land for farming or similar purposes right up to the VORTAC building. Of course, the owner is entitled to just compensation for the negative easement imposed as well as for the land that was completely taken.

Because an easement is considered a property interest, a holder of an easement is entitled to just compensation if the easement is lost due to a valid condemnation proceeding. The next case illustrates this right of an easement holder.

Case 6.4

The Shell Pipe Line Corporation obtained an easement to maintain a pipeline under some land which the fee owner dedicated for road and street purposes. Shell's easement could be justifiably disturbed only if the cause was for road and street maintenance. The local Flood Control District required Shell to lower its pipeline so that a drainage ditch could be enlarged. Whereas Shell's pipeline ran parallel to the road, the drainage ditch ran perpendicular to and just below the road. Shell seeks compensation for the partial taking of its right to an undisturbed easement.

Issue: Is Shell entitled to just compensation due to the action of the Flood Control District?

Decision: Yes.

Reasons: Shell's pipeline easement is an interest in land, and just compensation is required if it is taken or damaged. The local Flood Control District is a governmental body that does not have as its purpose the maintenance of roads and streets. Therefore, its enlargement of the drainage ditch did not come within the exception to Shell's easement. Having interfered with the easement property right, the Flood Control District must compensate Shell for the cost of lowering the pipeline.

Harris County Flood Control District v. Shell Pipe Line Corporation, 591 S.W.2d 798 (Tex. Sup. 1979).

The existence of restrictive covenants on condemned land can create a similar situation as far as the benefited landowners are concerned. In other words, are owners whose land is not taken but who lose the benefits of a preexisting covenant entitled to be compensated for that loss? Courts are not unanimous in their answers to this question. The majority of the decisions have resulted in conclusions holding that the benefits gained from restrictive covenants are property interests. Therefore, the owners are compensated for the loss of the covenant's effectiveness on neighboring land. Courts in a few states have reached just the opposite result, stating that no compensation is due when covenants' benefits are lost through condemnation. The states that have followed this latter view include Arkansas, Colorado, Florida, Georgia, Louisiana, and Ohio.

A tenant who has the right to possess real estate through a leasehold interest loses less than fee interest when the landlord's land is condemned. These situations create questions about whether the landlord or tenant or both are entitled to just compensation. In Chapter 2, we noted that leasehold interests are property; therefore, the government cannot take a tenant's right to possession without paying just compensation. When the landlord's entire freehold interest is taken, the tenant's nonfreehold interest also is necessarily taken. The fair market value of both parties' interest must be determined. The value of the tenant's possessory rights are dependent on the length of the lease period and the appraised value of that possession. Because the landlord is entitled to full possession at the lease's termination, the value of this reversionary interest also must be calculated. Often the question of just compensation for both parties is the major issue in such condemnation proceedings.

Normally, the tenant's obligation to pay rent and the landlord's obligation to provide possession terminate when the land is taken pursuant to eminent domain powers. However, if the government desires only possession and not fee simple title to the land, only the tenant's interest will be condemned. Upon this occurrence, the tenant will be the only party entitled to just compensation; however, the tenant will remain liable to the landlord for rent owed.

To avoid this situation and other possible complications, the landlord and tenant can agree that the lease expires upon the filing of condemnation proceedings involving the leased land. By this provision, the tenants' interest ceases to exist, and the landlord is the only party to receive just compensation. A similar result occurs if the leasehold interest is a tenancy at will which can be terminated when notice is given by the landlord to the tenant.

11. Excessive Condemnation

Under certain circumstances governmental bodies are allowed, if not required, to take more land than is actually needed for the intended public use. For example, an excessive condemnation might occur if the landowner is left with a parcel of such a small or peculiar size that it loses substantially all its value.

Suppose a public utility is condemning a two-hundred-foot-wide easement to run electrical wires over or under the land. This easement would prevent any building in the area condemned. If this easement begins fifty feet from one of the owner's boundaries and is parallel to it, the owner loses the use of this fifty-foot strip for all practical purposes; it is unlikely that any useful structure could be built on it. Therefore, the utility company should take and pay just compensation for an easement that extends to the land's actual boundaries. This same analysis applies when a fee interest is being condemned.

A taking of an excessive amount of land also can occur in order to protect the private landowner from an adjacent or future public use. For example, a municipality must acquire a sufficient amount of land surrounding a new airport so that landowners will not have their property "taken" due to the noise of jets taking off and landing. The government's failure to condemn enough land may result in owners filing inverse condemnation actions, wherein they seek monetary damages for the loss of their property. Inverse condemnation is discussed in Section 16, below.

12. *Quick-Take Process*

A substantial number of states (including Alaska, Arkansas, Arizona, California, Colorado, Connecticut, Delaware, Florida, Georgia, Hawaii, Illinois, Indiana, Iowa, Kentucky, Louisiana, Maryland, Missouri, New York, North Carolina, Oklahoma, Pennsylvania, South Carolina, South Dakota, Tennessee, Texas, Utah, and Washington) allow the government to take title and possession of land and to use it prior to the completion of a condemnation proceeding. By filing a *declaration of taking* and depositing with the appropriate court an amount in excess of the estimated value of the property condemned, the public's use of this land will not be impeded. The declaration of taking is in addition to, and a not a substitute for, the full condemnation proceedings.

Compliance with the required statutory steps permits the government's full and immediate use of the condemned land while protecting the owner's due process rights to notice and a full hearing.[2] In other words, when an owner's land is taken pursuant to this quick-take procedure, the owner does not lose any rights to challenge the condemnation as illegal or the compensation as insufficient. The court must make a prompt ruling as to the necessity of taking the land for a public use. Further, the owner can argue that the money deposited with the court is insufficient because of the government's bad faith. Again, the judge must make a preliminary ruling as to the adequacy of the funds deposited. If the judge finds that the necessity of public use has not been established or that the estimated amount deposited is too low, the judge can refuse to grant possession and title of the land to the government or require an increase in the amount on deposit. In the alternative, the judge can set a future date for the transfer of title and possession to the government. If possession of the condemned land is not awarded to the government, the owner can continue to use the land in any ordinary manner as long as the property value is not seriously diminished.

[2]Kelso Corporation v. Mayor and City Council of Baltimore, page 151.

The federal government also can exercise its power of eminent domain through a quick-take process. Pursuant to the Federal Declaration of Taking Act, the United States government and its agencies can acquire title and possession to land prior to the final adjudication of the condemnation proceedings. This federal law covers the same issues and affords similar safeguards for owners' rights as do state proceedings.

13.   Legislation and Proposed Laws

A condemnation proceeding gives rise to many questions that do not directly concern the validity of the government's exercise of its eminent domain power. Some of the issues are the method of determining just compensation, the cost to society of relocating displaced owners or tenants, the economic loss suffered by these displaced parties, and other similar policy issues. In an attempt to address some of these questions, Congress adopted the Uniform Relocation Assistance and Real Property Acquisition Policies Act in 1970.

This law is divided into two major subparts. The first concerns the need for a uniform policy of assistance to those people who are displaced by any project of the federal government or one supported by federal financial assistance. The goal of this uniform relocation assistance policy is to make sure that no individuals suffer a disproportionate injury because of a project designed to benefit the public.

This first portion of the law provides that the government shall pay a displaced person's moving expenses, costs for searching for a replacement business or farm, increased interest costs related to financing a replacement dwelling, and reasonable closing costs. A person displaced by a federally-funded project who did not own a home but who rented the condemned building is entitled to an amount that makes it possible either to rent or to make a down payment on a safe, decent, and clean dwelling. Any governmental agency that receives federal funds and is taking property pursuant to its eminent domain powers must provide a relocation assistance advisory service to all those persons being displaced from their homes or businesses.

The second part of this federal law, called the uniform real property acquisition policy, attempts to establish a policy whereby the heads of federal agencies can acquire title to real estate through negotiation instead of litigation. The law requires that the agency have an appraisal of the desired property made. Then the agency's head must make the landowner a good-faith offer that is not less than the appraised value of the property. In addition, the development project must be scheduled, if possible, so that the landowner is given notice at least ninety-days before the property actually is condemned. If negotiations fail to result in an agreement, the agency will commence formal condemnation proceedings. No landowner should be forced to file an inverse condemnation action—a suit for money damages—when the property is being taken.

The federal agency must pay just compensation for any building or other improvement on the land being acquired when the agency requires that these improvements be removed. Furthermore, the landowner must be reimbursed for the payment of recording fees, transfer taxes, penalty costs for prepayment of a recorded mortgage, and other similar costs incident to the transfer of title to the United States. An agency that either abandons its condemnation proceedings or is unsuccessful in acquiring the property condemned must pay the landowner's reasonable expenses, including attorney, appraisal, engineering, and similar fees.

This Uniform Relocation Assistance and Real Property Acquisition Policies Act does not grant any powers to condemn property. The power of eminent domain is founded in the United States Constitution. The provisions of this law in no way affect the all important requirement to provide just compensation. The sole purpose of this federal legislation is to increase uniformity in the ways in which real estate is taken and the displaced people are assisted.

By its terms, the federal law just discussed applies only to federal and state agencies that acquire land with the use of federal funds. Therefore, these provisions do not apply to state agencies which do not use federal funds. In order to make similar acquisition and relocation-assistance policies applicable to the states, the National Conference of Commissioners on Uniform State Laws has recommended that all states adopt the Uniform Eminent Domain Code. This proposed uniform law would remove the discrepancies that exist among the various states in their exercise of eminent-domain powers. Like the federal law, the Uniform Eminent Domain Code does not confer on government the power to condemn property for public uses. This proposed code bascially would make uniform the ways in which acquisitions are to be negotiated, then litigated if necessary; the procedures of the condemnation proceedings; and the calculation of just compensation. To date, no state has adopted the Uniform Eminent Domain Code.

Police Powers

14. Introduction

In addition to the power of eminent domain, governments can justify some regulations as an exercise of police powers, which represent the inherent ability of governmental bodies to protect the public health, safety, morals, and general welfare. Governments have relied on these police powers to enact zoning ordinances, open-space requirements, mandatory dedications, and other similar land-use controls.

Normally, a regulation passed pursuant to the police powers will be enforced unless it is vague, arbitrary, or contrary to a constitutional provision. If a regulation limits the landowner's use too severely, a taking occurs and compensation must be paid. When a taking results and no compensation is forthcoming, the landowner either can have the regulation declared unconstitutional or can sue for monetary damages. This suit for damages, called an inverse condemnation action, is discussed in Section 16 below.

15. The Taking Issue

Courts have never defined the exact point at which a regulation goes too far and becomes a taking. With the ever-increasing volume of land-use regulations, the taking issue has become applicable to many land-owners. A land-use regulation generally is not ruled unconstitutional simply because it reduces the value of a parcel of land. It is only when a regulation deprives the landowner of the entire use and value of the property, or does not allow a reasonable return, that regulation is held unconstitutional as applied to that particular parcel. Several judicial tests have been used to determine whether a land-use regulation is a permissible use of the police power. These tests include (1) diminution of value and beneficial use, (2) harm versus benefit, and (3) public benefit versus private loss.

A regulation is considered a taking only when it deprives the land-owners of substantially all the beneficial use of their property. Thus, the question becomes—What constitutes a "beneficial use"? This issue arises most often when property is rezoned to a less intensive use. Land that was zoned for multi-family apartment complexes being rezoned to single-family detached homes is an example of *down zoning*. Courts are not in full agreement in resolving the question of whether down zoning is a taking. Most decisions have concluded that if the landowner is left with some appropriate, economically feasible use, no compensation is owed. In other words, a governmental body pursuant to the police powers can deny an owner the best use of land, as long as a beneficial use remains.

Regulations that are designed to prevent the private landowner from injuring the public are generally viewed favorably by courts. For example, laws that prohibit an owner of marshlands from filling in land without a permit have been upheld as a valid exercise of the police powers, even though the land's value would have been enhanced by filling in the wetlands.

Case 6.5

Ronald and Kathryn Just were owners of a 36.4-acre parcel of land with frontage along Lake Noquebay in Marinette County, Wisconsin. In 1967 Marinette County adopted a shoreline zoning ordinance which affected lands within 1,000 feet of high water elevation of navigable lakes and lands within 300 feet of a navigable stream or river. The ordinance clearly states that the purpose of the act is to prevent uncontrolled uses and subsequent pollution. It provides for certain permitted uses and for conditional uses upon proper issuance of permits. One portion of the Just parcel consists of "wetlands" as defined by the ordinance. Without proper permits, the Justs filled several hundred square feet to enhance market value. The Justs claim the ordinance is an unreasonable exercise of police powers and constitutes a constructive taking without compensation.

Issues: Do the restriction on use presented by the ordinance represent a taking without compensation?

Decision: No.

Reasons: The public has a right to have the shoreline preserved. This zoning ordinance preserves the nature and the natural resources of the shorelands as they were created. It does not create or improve the public's protection; it only prevents private landowners from harming or destroying the shoreline's nature. The public's rights may be protected by the exercise of police powers unless the landowner's damage is too great. Here the Justs have not lost all the beneficial use of their shoreline; indeed, the ordinance preserves the inherent value of the property's nature.

Just v. Marinette County, 201 N.W.2d 761 (Wis. Sup. Ct. 1972).

Finally, some courts have held that a regulation enacted pursuant to the police powers results in a taking when the detriment to the property owner outweighs the benefit intended for the public. A major issue in this analysis involves the determination of what values to balance. Because a balancing process is involved, it is difficult to make any generalizations about when a taking occurs. The following case, when compared to the preceding one, represents the judicial uncertainty when ruling on a valid exercise of the police powers.

Case 6.6

In February, 1961, the town of Fairfield, Connecticut, amended its existing zoning ordinances by creating a new classification called a "Flood Plain District." Whenever land was designated in a Flood Plain District, permitted uses were limited to parks, playgrounds, marinas, clubhouses, wildlife sanctuaries, farming, and motor-vehicle parking. Excavation and filling of such land was prohibited except under special permits. The town of Fairfield changed the classification of 170 acres of privately owned land from a "Residence B" classification to the new Flood Plain District. Many of these landowners challenge the new classification as a taking of their property without compensation and without due process.

Issue: Is the application of the new zoning classification to the plaintiffs' land an unreasonable exercise of the town's police powers?

Decision: Yes.

Reasons: The reclassification of the land here involved resulted in the owners losing practically all uses of their land. The permitted uses in a Flood Plain District are such that enforcement of the restrictions amounts to a confiscation of the land. Many times the private landowner must sacrifice so that the community's welfare is protected; however, that private sacrifice must not be as total as in this case. Furthermore, the town of Fairfield has failed to prove what public benefit is gained from the restrictions imposed. Therefore, the Flood Plain District classification as enacted cannot be applied to the plaintiffs' land.

Dooley v. Town Plan and Zoning Commission of the Town of Fairfield, 197 A.2d 770 (Conn. Sup. Ct. 1964).

16. *Inverse Condemnation*

As we have seen, governmental bodies, pursuant to the police powers, pass laws or take actions that interfere with landowners' property rights, but the government does not compensate these owners under the eminent domain power. Examples of these actions include zoning regulations or the construction of a public project near (but not on) an owner's land. In the past, landowners who suffered some governmental interference with their land have had two general causes of action. One remedy has been to sue to enjoin the government's action that caused the interference. This argument is based on the government's action being unconstitutional since just compensation was not paid.

A second cause of action has been to sue for damages caused by the loss of the property's use. This remedy is called a suit for inverse condemnation. *Inverse* or *reverse condemnation* is a legal action whereby a landowner seeks just compensation as a remedy for the government's "taking" of his or her land. It is not always easy to determine when governmental action results in a taking of land. Indeed, courts have struggled often with this issue. In a statement of judicial frankness, Mr. Justice Brennan of the United States Supreme Court wrote:

> The question of what constitutes a "taking" for purposes of the Fifth Amendment has proved to be a problem of considerable difficulty. While this Court has recognized that the "Fifth Amendment's guarantee . . . [is] designed to bar the Government from forcing some people alone to bear public burdens which, in all fairness and justice, should be borne by the public as a whole," this Court, quite simply, has been unable to develop any "set formula" for determining when "justice and fairness" require that economic injuries caused by public action be compensated by the government, rather than remain disproportionately concentrated on a few persons. Indeed, we have frequently observed that whether a particular restriction will be rendered invalid by the government's failure to pay for any losses proximately caused by it depends largely "upon the particular circumstances [in that] case."[3]

[3]Penn Central Transportation Co. v. New York City, 438 U.S. 104, 123–124 (1978).

Courts have found that an inverse condemnation action is an appropriate remedy when land is taken in one of three general situations. First, when an owner's use of land is prevented because of public improvements being made on adjacent land, an inverse condemnation is permissible. For example, construction of an interstate highway next to land used for a gasoline service station when there is no exit or entrance from the highway within a reasonable distance has essentially destroyed the land's value for use as a service station. Second, courts have compensated owners when a governmental body acquires an easement over or on land through a nonregulatory action. Review the case of United States v. Causby, found at the end of Chapter 1, wherein the extremely low overflights of military aircraft allowed the landowners to sue for monetary damages. Finally, inverse condemnation actions have been allowed when government regulation has unreasonably delayed condemnation proceedings or has lowered the land's fair market value prior to condemnation.

It is an unsettled question whether a landowner can sue for monetary damages pursuant to an inverse condemnation action when a zoning regulation substantially restricts the use of the land. Only the California Supreme Court has held that an owner is limited to challenging an excessive zoning regulation by seeking to have it declared unconstitutional. This suit for a declaratory judgment is based on the theory that the regulation resulted in a "taking" of private property without providing for just compensation.

Cases on Land-Use Controls

Lidke v. Martin
500 P.2d 1184 (Colo. App. 1972).

Enoch, J.:

This action was brought by certain residents of Hillcrest Heights Subdivision in Jefferson County to enjoin defendants from erecting two apartment buildings on the back portion of a platted lot owned by defendants and located in the same subdivision. The trial court entered judgment for plaintiffs on the grounds that the proposed apartment buildings would violate the subdivision's protective covenants. . . . We affirm this judgment.

The trial court based its conclusion that defendants' proposed apartment buildings would violate the subdivision's protective convenants upon the following clause of the covenants:

A. All lots in this subdivision shall be Residential One (R-1) only. No structure shall be erected, altered, placed, or permitted to remain on any lot other than one detached single-family dwelling not to exceed two and one-half stories in height, a private garage for not more than three cars, and other outbuildings incidental to residential use only.

Defendants concede that, if otherwise valid, this clause standing alone would prohibit the construction of the proposed apartment buildings. They contend, however, that another clause in the restrictive covenants incorporates existing zoning regulations into the covenants and since their property was rezoned to a zoning classification that allows apartment buildings, the apartment buildings would not violate the protective covenants. The clause relied on by defendants provides as follows:

L. None of the foregoing shall be construed as conflicting with any terms or regulations of the present or future Jefferson County zoning ordinance which shall form a part of this instrument and shall govern their use of all land herein described.

We do not agree with defendants that this clause allows a resident to make any use of his property permitted under applicable zoning regulations. Read as a whole, the protective covenants envision and provide for a single-family residential subdivision. To interpret *Clause L* in the manner argued for by defendants would render

these other covenants meaningless and allow their circumvention. Actually, *Clause L* provides a rule of construction for the covenants, the effect of which is to incorporate those portions of the applicable zoning ordinances which provide more restrictive standards than the covenants or which prescribe regulations not covered by the covenants. This result is consistent with section 31 of the applicable zoning ordinance which provides:

. . . It is not intended by this Resolution to interfere with or abrogate or annul any easements, covenants or agreements between parties, provided, however, that wherever this Resolution imposes a greater restriction upon the use of buildings or structures or required larger open spaces about buildings than are imposed or required by other laws, resolutions or by easements, covenants or agreements between parties, the provisions of this Resolution shall govern.

In this case, the new zone permitted the construction of apartment buildings. However, the covenants are controlling because they require a more restrictive use of the land than is permitted under the applicable zoning requirements. . . .

Affirmed.

Kelso Corporation v. Mayor and City Council of Baltimore
411 A.2d 691 (Md. App. 1980).

On March 14, 1978, the City of Baltimore filed a petition supported by affidavits for immediate possession and title of five lots owned by the Kelso Corporation. The petition was filed pursuant to the City's "quick-take" condemnation procedures. This land was being acquired in accordance with urban-renewal plans within the City. Also on March 14, 1978, the Court of Common Pleas issued an order that (1) the City be vested with possession of Kelso's property, and (2) title to the property "shall vest" in the City "ten (10) days after personal service" upon

Kelso of the quick-take petition and "this Order." The order further provided that the "vesting of such possession or title and possession in the . . . [City] shall in nowise act as a bar to trial of this matter to determine the fair value . . . [of the property] in accordance with the applicable provisions of law applicable thereto."

Within ten days after service of the petition, Kelso answered and alleged that the City lacked authority to acquire the land involved. The trial court held for the City, and Kelso appeals.

Melvin, J.:

Appellant contends that the appraisals filed with the quick take petition supporting the amount of money deposited into court as the City's estimate of the fair value of the property were "stale." The quick take statute requires that the amount deposited in court as the City's "estimate" of the fair value of the property to be acquired "be substantiated by the affidavits of two qualified appraisers, attached to said Petition." In this case, the affidavits of one appraiser, stating his opinion of value, were dated September 13, 1977, as to all five lots. The affidavits of a second appraiser, stating his opinion, were dated August 26, 1977, as to four of the lots, and February 2, 1978, as to one of the lots. As already noted, the quick take petition was filed March 14, 1978. Appellant argues that because the amount deposited did not represent the value of the property "at the time of the taking," the court had no right to vest *title* in the City by its order of March 14, 1978. The argument is without merit. . . .

The City's quick take statute does secure to the property owner just compensation. The payment into court of the City's estimate of fair value is specifically provided by the statute to be "without prejudice to either party and shall not be construed to prevent either party from requiring a subsequent trial to determine the value of the property." . . . [T]he March 14th order vesting title in the City specifically so provided. Moreover, although it

would have been better to have more current appraisals, we think the appraisals used here, on their face, were not so old as to require a holding invalidating the March 14th order. . . .

Appellant contends that "where the condemnor files a timely answer to the petition for immediate possession and title, the lower court may not award title or *possession* to the condemnor prior to a judicial hearing."

Subsections (c) and (d) of the quick take statute provide:

"(c) In cases where the City files a Petition for immediate taking . . . *possession and title* thereto shall irrevocably vest in the Mayor and City Council of Baltimore ten days after personal service of the petition upon each and every defendant *unless* the Defendants or any of them shall file an answer to the Petition within the said ten day period alleging that the City does not have the right or power to condemn *title* to the property. In the event the defendants or any of them should file an answer, the court shall schedule a hearing within fifteen days of the date of the filing of an answer, which hearing shall be only for the purpose of contesting the right or power of the City to condemn title to the property. The trial court shall render its decision within fifteen days from the final day of said hearing. . . .

(d) If it appears from a Petition for Immediate Possession . . . that the public interest requires the City to have *immediate possession* of said property, the court shall, within not more than seven days after the filing of said Petition, pass an order. . . directing that the City may take *possession* of said property after the expiration of thirty days from the filing of said petition or earlier, in the court's discretion. Upon passing such an order, the court may direct the City to give such notice of said order to the defendants as the court may deem proper, but the court's requirement of notice shall not extend the time within which the City may take possession of said property."

In the present case, as already noted, the quick take order of March 14, 1978, in addition to vesting the City "with possession" of the property also provided that "title . . . shall vest in the . . . [City] ten (10) days after personal service. . . ." This latter portion concerning vesting of title was technically erroneous, for the power to vest the city with *title* ten days after service would only exist if the defendant, "within the said ten day period," failed to file an answer to the petition "alleging that the City does not have the right or power to condemn *title* to the property." The order concerning title should have gone further and provided for this contingency. The fact that it did not so provide, however, resulted in no harm to the appellant. This is so because the effect of the appellant's timely answer challenging the City's "right or power to condemn title" was to suspend, by operation of law, the vesting of title until the issue was ultimately decided after a hearing.

The fact that appellant filed a timely answer to the quick take petition did not, however, affect the validity of that portion of the March 14th order vesting *possession* in the City. When subsections (c) and (d),

quoted above, are read together, it is clear that the filing of a challenge to "the right or power to condemn *title*" does not stay the effect of a prior order for immediate possession.

Following the hearing on the appellant's challenge to the March 14th quick take order, the court, on February 2, 1979, filed its "Ruling by the Court": . . .

> "Consequently, the Defendant's Motion to Vacate Order for Immediate Possession and Vesting of Title is hereby DENIED."

. . . we will modify the last paragraph and, as modified, affirm it. Without such modification, the effect of the February 2nd order is to leave standing that portion of the March 14th order that vested title in the City ten days after service upon the appellant of the quick-take petition and the March 14th order. As we have seen, such an order was technically erroneous. As modified, the last paragraph of the February 2nd order will read as follows:

> "Consequently, the Defendant's Motion to Vacate that portion of the order, entered in these proceedings on March 14, 1978, vesting the Mayor and City Council of Baltimore with *possession* is DENIED. It is Further Ordered that the portion of the aforesaid order entered on March 14, 1978, vesting *title* in the Mayor and City Council of Baltimore ten (10) days after service of the Petition for Immediate Possession, is hereby VACATED; and it is Further Ordered that title to the Defendant's property shall vest in the Mayor and City Council of Baltimore on this 2nd day of February 1979."

Judgment affirmed as modified.

REVIEW QUESTIONS

  1. Define and distinguish the following terms:
  a. Land-use controls
  b. Private controls and public controls

2. In this chapter, we discussed several ways restrictive covenants can be created. Discuss at least two of these methods.
3. In Chapter 2, we discussed conditional ownership interests. What is the primary difference between a restrictive covenant and a condition of ownership?
4. The Akins owned land they wished to develop into a residential subdivision. As they sold lots, they included in the deeds a restrictive covenant limiting the use of the land to single-family residential purposes. One lot was sold to the Knapps, who build a house as a residence for eight retarded, unrelated adults. When the Knapps' neighbors sought to enjoin this use, the Knapps argued that these neighbors cannot enforce a restrictive covenant in a deed between Akins and Knapps. When do parties, who are not parties to a deed containing restrictive covenants, have the right to enforce the covenant?
5. Based on the above facts, are the Knapps violating the single-family restriction by housing eight unrelated adults in one house?
6. Explain the difference between the terms "eminent domain" and "condemnation proceeding."
7. What are the two essential elements that must be present to justify the government's exercise of the eminent domain powers?
8. Joseph owned a parcel of land that was zoned residential. Because it was better suited for an office building than a house, Joseph sought to have it rezoned to a business category. Instead of granting the rezoning request, the town sought to acquire title in a condemnation proceeding. As to what was just compensation for the taking of his land, Joseph argued he should be paid the fair market value of the land as if it were zoned for a business use. The town claimed just compensation must be based on the value of the land as presently zoned. Which argument should prevail? Why?
9. State and local governments have the power to regulate use of private property by exercising the police powers. What is the limiting scope of these police powers?
10. Gorman owned and operated an upholstery shop just off Highway 25. In order to construct an improvement on this highway, the state acquired a temporary easement over Gorman's land. This easement effectively reduced Gorman's access or driveway to and from the highway from twenty-four feet wide to fourteen feet wide. Claiming that this narrowing of his driveway prevented vehicles larger than pick-up trucks from having access to the premises, Gorman sued for damages. What type of action did Gorman file? Do you think he will be successful? Explain.

7

Zoning and Other Land-Use Controls

1. Introduction

The uses of land are interdependent; that is, land use is greatly affected by other land uses and is heavily dependent upon public investments and the economic vitality of the surrounding neighborhood and community. It is this interdependence of land uses that leads to their control by governmental agencies. The use of land, more than the use of personal property, affects the owners of other property and creates costs for the public as a whole.

In this chapter we will examine some of the basic techniques and tools of local, state, and federal governments for controlling land use. These include control of nuisances, zoning, subdivision regulations, and environmental protection policies.

2. Control of Nuisances

One of the first methods for controlling the way in which land was used involved the law of nuisances. Beginning in English courts and continuing throughout our country's history, the law of nuisances has prevented owners of real estate from using their land in such a way as irreparably to injure another's property or body. Within the law of nuisances, there are two separate and distinct theories. The first theory is that of "public" nuisances. The second involves "private" nuisances.

A *public nuisance* occurs when a use of land or some other action affects the general public's right to use a common property interest. A public nuisance does not result when just one or only a few individuals are affected. Nevertheless, all members of the general public do *not* have to be adversely affected in order for a public nuisance to exist. For example, the permanent blockage of a public highway by a construction company deprives those who use the highway of that use. Although everyone in the community may not use this road, a public nuisance still would exist. The public has a right either to have the public nuisance enjoined or to bring criminal charges against its creator. These actions usually are filed by a governing body rather than by individuals.

A *private nuisance* is an unreasonable interference with the use and enjoyment of land. It differs from a public nuisance in that the former affects only a few individuals rather than the general public. Furthermore, a private nuisance can be remedied by the issuance of an injunction or by an award of monetary damages to the aggrieved party. There will be no criminal charges filed as a result of a private nuisance.

This private-nuisance theory relates to possession, rather than ownership or title of land. Therefore, a tenant, an adverse possessor, an easement holder, or any other party who has a real property interest can claim the protection provided against private nuisances. Because they do not have any real property interests, licensees and invitees cannot maintain an action to recover for a private nuisance.

Although many courts have dealt with the distinction between a private nuisance and a trespass, the differences are not always clear. Normally, a trespass involves the physical invasion of a person's exclusive possession of land, while a nuisance involves the mere interference with that person's use and enjoyment of the land. For instance, driving a car across someone's land is a trespass, and it may or may not cause great harm. On the other hand, the existence of a junk yard for wrecked cars across the street could be a nuisance due to the loud noises that are made. This type of private nuisance may be much more harmful to the injured party than a simple trespass. The practical distinction between a trespass and a private nuisance governs the decision as to when a cause of action against these acts must be filed.

The statute of limitations begins running on a trespass action when the actual invasion occurs. A private nuisance does not occur until substantial harm is done to the possessor of land; therefore, the statute of limitations does not begin to run until the harm of a private nuisance exists.

Today most lawsuits concerning private nuisances involve the uses of neighboring lands. As long as each use is reasonable in light of the other, no nuisance will be found. Because the standard is one of reasonableness, courts must balance the competing uses, as is demonstrated by the following case.

Case 7.1

The California Portland Cement Company manufactured cement on land that it owned for twenty years. When the company bought the land and began the manufacture of cement, the surrounding land was vacant and unimproved. Colbert, who raised citrus fruit and lived on land he owned near the plant, filed suit to have the plant enjoined as a nuisance because of the dust and smoke that it produced.

Issue: Is the farmer entitled to an injunction?

Decision: Yes.

Reasons: The plant produced about twenty tons of dust per day, part of which fell on the plaintiff's land, leaving a deposit of residue on his citrus trees and in his home. The right of people to use and enjoy their property is as supreme as their neighbor's, and no artificial use of it by either can be permitted to destroy that of the other.

Hulbert v. California Portland Cement Co., 161 Cal. 239, 118 P. 928 (1911).

Many present-day nuisance cases involve industrial or commercial uses of land that has been surrounded by residential or similar areas. Frequently, what is now a nuisance in an urban area was formerly a proper use of rural land. In other words, as areas urbanize, preexisting uses may become public or private nuisances. In order to reduce the possibility of these occurrences, governmental agencies need to exercise their police powers to limit the potential uses of real estate. A typical use of the police powers—zoning—to achieve these ends is discussed next.

Zoning

3. Introduction

The judicial techniques that were used to abate nuisances proved inadequate to regulate rapid urban growth. New York City passed the first comprehensive zoning ordinance in 1916, restricting the use and height of buildings in various districts of Manhattan, and other communities followed with similar laws.

Comprehensive zoning, by which land is divided into districts for the purpose of regulating the use of land and buildings and the intensity of various uses, gained increasing acceptance during the 1920s. The constitutionality of zoning ordinances was upheld by the U.S. Supreme Court in 1926.[1] Since that time, zoning ordinances and related land-use controls have been adopted in most areas of the United States. With the growing movement to control the quality of the environment, land-use regulations have increased in scope, causing considerable concern regarding both their cost and their impact on private property values.

The logical first step in the process of local land-use planning is the formulation and adoption of a *comprehensive general plan.* Such a plan is a statement of policies for the future development of the community. Since it serves as the basis for comprehensive zoning regulations, it should be a long-range plan that closely examines the community's physical needs for fifteen to twenty-five years in the future. Comprehensive plans usually contain the following elements: (1) an analysis of projected economic development and population change; (2) a transportation plan to provide for necessary circulation of people and vehicles; (3) a public-facilities plan that identifies such needed facilities as schools, parks, civic centers, and water and sewage-disposal plants; and (4) a land-use plan. The comprehensive plan may also include other elements, such as housing redevelopment and historic preservation. It should not be a static document; rather, it must be continually revised as conditions change.

The following sections discuss how zoning works, how it is changed, and some of the important legal issues that arise from zoning regulations.

[1]Village of Euclid v. Ambler Realty Co., page 182.

4. Zoning Classifications

Zoning laws divide land within a local jurisdiction into zones and include regulations relating to the type and intensity of land use. The three main classifications of land use are residential, commercial, and industrial. Each classification is usually divided into several subcategories based on the use of the land. For example, a residential area may be subdivided into single-family districts or multifamily housing. Similarly, commercial and industrial districts are usually subcategorized as "neighborhood shopping district," "highway commercial district," "light industrial district," and so on. In addition to the three main categories, most zoning ordinances contain such special-purpose districts as agricultural, flood plain, public lands, and research.

Intensity of use, also referred to as developmental density, is the extent to which the land within a given district may be used for its permitted purposes. The government can regulate intensity of use in several ways, including placing restrictions on building height and bulk, specifying minimum lot sizes, and establishing building setback requirements. Height limitations regulate the maximum height of buildings in feet or stories. Bulk regulations limit the percentage of the lot area that may be occupied by buildings. Both serve to control the volume of a structure on the land and therefore the intensity of use.

Another measure by which building volume may be controlled is the floor-area ratio—the relationship between the total floor area of a building and the total land area of the site. For example, an allowable ratio of four to one would permit a four-story building to occupy the entire area of its lot; an eight-story building would be permitted to occupy only half of the site's surface area; and a sixteen-story building could occupy only one-fourth of the land area.

The most common method of regulating development density is through provisions for a minimum lot size. Relatively large lots may be necessary for public health reasons if public sewer and water systems are not provided. However, requirements of very large minimum lot sizes may be challenged as depriving the owner of reasonable use of the property.

Zoning ordinances generally provide for setback of buildings from the street and minimum size of side yards in residential districts. Such restrictions may also, although less commonly, be applied to commercial and industrial districts.

Case 7.2

Ms. Road built a garage within four feet of her property line in violation of the setback requirements in the zoning ordinance of the city of Leadville, Colorado. The city brought an action to compel the removal of the structure. Ms. Road alleged that the zoning ordinance bore no relationship to the legitimate exercise of the municipal police power and as a result violated her constitutional rights to due process and equal protection of the law.

Issue: Is the setback requirement in Leadville's zoning ordinance constitutional?

Decision: Yes.

Reasons: The ordinance was directly related to a legitimate goal of government, and it was a proper use of the police power. The ordinance allowed the achievement of the maximum aesthetic benefit without arbitrarily burdening any particular property owners.

City of Leadville v. Road, 600 P.2d 62 (Colo. 1979).

5. Zoning Changes

A request to change a zoning ordinance frequently arises when circumstances have changed the practical uses of land. The property owner who desires relief from the zoning ordinance can seek to change it through legislative, administrative, or judicial means. If the property owner seeks a substantial change in the property's zoning, he can request it from the legislative authority that possesses the power to change the zoning ordinances, such as the city council or county commission. Zoning amendments generally require an advertised public hearing and some type of justification from the applicant demonstrating that changed conditions justify the zoning change. Usually there is a hearing before a planning board before consideration by the legislative body. These zoning hearings are frequently quite controversial, with spirited and often acrimonious public debate. The power of the legislative body to change a zoning ordinance can be constitutionally conditioned on a vote of approval by the public. In other words, some communities have required that any proposed zoning change approved by the city council or county commission then be voted on in a public referendum.

If the property owner seeks a relatively minor change, it can sometimes be accomplished administratively through a variance or special-use permit granted by a board of adjustments, zoning appeals board, or some similar body. Variances and special-use permits, which technically are not changes in a zoning ordinance, can make the ordinance much more reasonable and less burdensome to property owners. In order to avoid placing undue hardship on an owner, a *variance* permits land uses to deviate slightly from a strict interpretation of the zoning ordinance. A request for a variance should be filed prior to commencing construction that would violate existing zoning laws. Failure to secure a variance before beginning a project prohibited by zoning ordinances can result in an expensive mistake, in that the completed construction may have to be removed if the variance is not granted.

A zoning ordinance often permits special uses within districts if certain conditions are met. For example, a public-utility substation, church, school, or recreational facility may be permitted in a residential district if the board determines that the required conditions have been satisfied.

If the property owner is unhappy because the legislative or administrative relief sought is not granted, he may challenge the ordinance or administrative action in a court. A challenge may be based on the contention that the zoning ordinance is unconstitutional as a taking of the property without due process of law or that the law is arbitrary, unreasonable, or capricious. Zoning ordinances are usually upheld unless they involve clear abuses of power or are unduly restrictive.[2] As long as the enactment and enforcement of a zoning ordinance is reasonable, courts usually will not substitute their judgment for the reasoning of the legislative body.

However, zoning changes are sometimes invalidated by the courts if they can be shown to be *spot zoning.* This is zoning that singles out a particular parcel or limited area for special treatment or privileges that are not in harmony with other use classifications in the area when there are no apparent circumstances that call for different treatment. Tests to determine the existence of spot zoning are: (1) the use permitted by the rezoning is different from prevailing uses in the surrounding area; (2) the area involved in the rezoning is relatively small; (3) the change to a less restrictive classification provides a special advantage for a specific developer or a small geographic area; and (4) the rezoning is not in accordance with the adopted comprehensive plan.

[2]Westbrook v. Board of Adjustment, page 183.

Allegations of spot zoning may arise from legislative rezoning actions, variances, special-use permits, or other exceptions to the zoning ordinance. Generally, however, the courts will not invalidate such actions if they can be shown to be in accordance with the comprehensive plan or if they can be justified on the basis of major changes that have occurred in the area since the adoption of the original zoning.

Another type of rezoning that has sometimes been invalidated by the courts is *contract zoning,* defined as rezoning granted subject to additional restrictions placed on the land that is rezoned. For example, a municipality might grant a rezoning of a parcel from single-family residential to multifamily residential use, but only on the condition that no more than eight units per acre be construction when the general zone classification permits fifteen units per acre.

Contract zoning has been held invalid in some states on the basis that a city or county cannot bargain away its police power. Others have held that contract zoning is invalid because it is a form of spot zoning. A few states permit contract zoning, holding that the imposed restrictions are a valid exercise of the police power that permits real property improvements while avoiding harm to neighboring property.

6.   Noncomforming Uses

A noncomforming use is a continuing use of real estate that was legal before a zoning ordinance was passed or changed but which no longer complies with the current zoning law. Such a use is generally allowed to continue unless the nonconforming structure is substantially destroyed or abandoned. Regulations concerning noncomforming use usually do not permit the existing structure to be enlarged or substantially changed in use.

Case 7.3

Bylewski purchased a tract of land in an area where the zoning ordinance did not permit mobile homes. However, at the time of the purchase there was a mobile home located on the property, which was allowed to remain as a nonconforming use. Bylewski replaced the existing mobile home with a new one, and the county sued to force its removal, contending that the replacement violated the zoning code.

Issue: Did the replacement of the nonconforming mobile home with a new one terminate the protection given the nonconforming structure?

Decision: Yes.

Reasons: Any alteration of an existing nonconforming structure in excess of fifty percent of its value terminated the protection given the nonconforming structure under the zoning code. The Bylewskis were forced to remove the mobile home from their property.

County of Columbia v. Bylewski, 288 N.W.2d 129 (Wis. 1980).

7. Vested Rights in Development

A problem similar to nonconforming uses arises when zoning laws are changed during the course of a project's development. A land owner who obtains a building permit or receives subdivision approval based on existing zoning laws and expends a substantial sum after receiving this approval may obtain a vested right to complete construction or development. Under this vested right, the government cannot prohibit the construction or development of the project, even though it no longer complies with the zoning ordinance. In determining whether there is a vested right to develop, legal issues often arise relating to whether the building permit or subdivision approval was lawfully issued and whether there had been a substantial expenditure or commitment made by the developer.

8. Transfer of Development Rights

A relatively recent technique of land-use regulation, but one that has received considerable attention and seems to hold significant promise, involves transfer of development rights. Under a transfer system, a landowner can sell part of his bundle of rights to another landowner, who can then use his own land more intensively. Let us suppose that Mrs. Johnson owns a ten-acre wooded tract that she wishes to preserve as it is. Nearby Mr. Hite owns another ten-acre tract that he wishes to develop. Existing regulations require minimum one-acre lots in the area, so Mr. Hite could build only ten houses on his land. Mrs. Johnson, having no interest in developing her property, could sell her development rights to Mr. Hite, who could then build twenty houses on his ten acres while Mrs. Johnson's land remained in its wooded state. Proponents of this system contend that it is more equitable than one prohibiting such transfer of development rights, since it enables communities to preserve flood plains, open space, and historic structure without wiping out their property values.

Experience with transfer of development rights has been limited. Several communities in New Jersey and California are experimenting with the system in their efforts to preserve open space. Several cities, including New York, Chicago, and Washington, are using the transfer mechanism as a means of preserving historic landmarks. Floor-area ratios on such buildings can be transferred to other properties to allow denser development on those sites. It is interesting to note that the Supreme Court mentioned the value of transfer of development rights as part of the return that Penn Central could obtain from the existing use of Grand Central Terminal.

9.   Special Approaches to Zoning

Traditional zoning has been criticized for being inefficient, subject to poor administration and corruption, and for having little relationship to planning goals. Some attack it for its flexibility, charging that true separation of uses is seldom achieved because zoning boards submit to developer pressure to grant extensive rezonings. Others attack zoning for its rigidity, charging that its inflexible requirements stifle good design and foster inefficiency and rising costs. A few have come to the conclusion that zoning controls should be abolished, while others have attempted to improve the zoning process. The latter movement has led to some innovative techniques, including zoning for planned-unit development, performance or impact zoning, incentive zoning, and applications of down zoning.

A *planned-unit development (PUD)* is a method of residential development which can avoid some of the failings of traditional zoning practices. In a PUD, an area with specified minimum contiguous acreage is developed as a single entity according to an approved plan. This land is then zoned for a planned-unit development rather than any one specific zoning classification. Generally, dwellings are permitted close together in clusters, leaving substantial areas in a natural state. Many bulk and use regulations may also be waived to permit greater flexibility of design. Most planned-unit-development ordinances also permit some nonresidential uses such as convenience shopping. In return for this zoning flexibility, the community should receive the advantages of preservation of natural features, additional recreational and open space, greater housing choice, safer streets and pedestrian ways, reduced need for automobile travel, and lower housing costs.

Every person who owns land within a PUD becomes a member of the owners' association, which is considered the legal owner of all the recreational and open spaces within the development. In essence, a PUD is both a unique zoning development and method of ownership. It can be viewed as a cross between a condominium and a cooperative. A PUD is similar to condominiums in that all owners within the development actually have title to their land; the common areas are owned by a separate legal entity, very much like the corporation that owns a cooperative project.

Performance zoning, often known as "impact zoning," is a technique to relate permitted uses of land to certain performance standards, usually to protect the environment. Such standards, particularly industrial-use standards related to noise, smoke, smell, and the like, are sometimes quite detailed. Adoption of performance zoning generally results in simplified land-use controls. The performance standards relate land-use demands to land-use capacity, and they can be used to achieve better design and to reduce the cost of regulation as well as to protect the environment. The standards used are usually related to density, open-space ratio, impervious-surface ratio (surface-water runoff), and the number of vehicle trips generated by the site.

Closely related to performance zoning is incentive zoning, which encourages developers to provide certain publicly desired features in return for various incentives. For example, the San Francisco City Code permits increased floor area if the developer provides a pedestrian plaza or arcade. New York City provides similar incentives. Other communities permit higher densities for residential developments that provide such features as open space.

In most cases, rezoning is sought by the property owner to raise the potential value of his land by increasing the permitted intensity or type of use. For example, an owner might seek reclassification of the land from residential to commercial use or from low-density residential to high-density residential use. Sometimes, however, land will be rezoned from a higher classification to a lower classification, a practice that is known as *down zoning.* For example, the classification might be changed from commercial to residential or from multifamily to single-

family residential. As might be expected, such actions are often vigorously contested by property owners. Down zoning usually occurs as part
of a growth-management plan—that is, a plan designed to reduce the
population growth rate in a community. This larger issue of growth
management is discussed in Section 11, below.

Zoning Issues

10. Introduction

The use of zoning as a method of controlling land use has been accompanied by substantial legal issues. Examples of these zoning issues
include controlling growth and excluding people from certain areas
based on income or race. Other issues involving zoning have included
historic preservation, architectural controls, and aesthetic enhance-
ments such as the maintenance of open spaces. These various issues are
the subject matter of the next three sections.

11. Control of Growth

Historically, community growth has generally been regarded as highly
desirable. Communities whose populations were not expanding were
usually economically stagnant and unable to meet the needs of citizens.
The desire for growth changed drastically in many communities during
the 1970s. "No growth" often replaced "go-go growth" as an objective
in communities when citizens rebelled against the many problems that
often accompany rapid population expansion.

Communities attempting to restrict or manage their growth have
used a variety of methods, including: large-lot zoning; prohibitions on
multifamily units; restrictions on the number of bedrooms per dwelling
unit; minimum floor-space requirements; building moratoria; refusal to
expand municipal services, such as sewers and water lines; prohibitions
on mobile homes; and exclusions of low-income housing.

The stated purpose of such controls is to provide for the orderly
growth and development of the community consistent with physical,
environmental, social, and political resources and limitations. In other
words, their purpose is to help the community to develop or to curb
development as its citizens want. But they raise two basic policy issues:

Do growth controls violate the rights of private property owners?

Are growth controls exclusionary, serving to keep out racial minorities and low-income groups?

The techniques and issues involved in growth management are complex and controversial. Three techniques that have been utilized by communities are: (1) a growth cap; (2) a controlled-growth rate; and (3) a timed-growth policy.

First, a growth-cap technique is used when a community seeks to prevent growth over a certain size. A good example is Boca Raton, Florida. The population of Boca Raton stood at only 6,000 in 1960, but it had climbed to over 60,000 by 1980. This rapid growth, the loss of access to the public beach caused by private development of beach-front properties, and an influx of new residents concerned about maintaining the "quality of life" in Boca Raton combined to give impetus to the growth-control movement. This movement resulted in an initiative imposing a "growth cap" of 40,000 dwelling units. The city purchased $33 million worth of beach-front property to prevent its development, down zoning all multifamily zoning categories to reduce the density of such districts by 50 percent, and reducing the density in single-family zones.

A development company, which owned about 3,000 acres in Boca Raton and had seen the number of permitted dwelling units on its properties reduced from 18,000 to 8,000 filed suit against the city of Boca Raton to challenge the cap. While noting that growth caps could be constitutional, this one was struck down as bearing no rational relationship to municipal purposes.

Even though it was declared unconstitutional, Boca Raton's growth cap may have served its declared purpose. By the time the city finally lost its court fight in 1979, approximately 70 percent of the community had already developed, and the remainder was zoned for relatively low density under a new comprehensive plan that would yield approximately 41,500 units.

Another technique is to control the growth rate by establishing the maximum number of housing units that can be constructed during specific time periods. This is often coupled with a refusal to expand public services such as sewer and water lines to new areas. A good example is the growth policy of Petaluma, California. Petaluma was a small agricultural community north of San Francisco when the completion of a new freeway in the mid-1960s made it accessible to city commuters. An influx of new residents soon followed, straining the community's ability to provide the necessary housing and services.

Petaluma first placed a moratorium on rezoning, annexation, and development. It then developed a plan that allotted annual single-family and multifamily quotas to various sectors of the city and that included low- and moderate-income housing. It also set an "urban extension line" which defined the outer limits of the city's growth for the next twenty years or more, and beyond which it refused to extend city facilities.

Petulama's plan was upheld as constitutional when challenged by a construction industry association. The court stated that the concept of the public's welfare is sufficiently broad to uphold a city's desire to preserve its small-town character, its open spaces, its low density of population, and its orderly and deliberate growth rate.

The Petaluma plan appears to have achieved its objectives. The residential growth rate was reduced to the planned 6 percent per year (still much higher than the national or regional average), the mix of housing types shifted toward the desired multifamily development, and development pressure on the eastern agricultural valley was relieved as construction shifted to the more established western section of the city. The city's schools were returned to single sessions with manageable class sizes, and other public facilities were expanded to meet community needs.

The case which follows notes the limitations on the power of cities to refuse to extend necessary utilities as a means of controlling growth.

Case 7.4

Several developers sought to subdivide approximately seventy-nine acres of land northeast of Boulder, Colorado, and outside its city limits. The landowners proposed a residential development in conformity with the county's rural residential zoning. The city of Boulder, which operates the water and sewer and utility system which services this area, refused to serve the subdivision because the landowners' proposal was inconsistent with the Boulder Valley Comprehensive Plan and various aspects of the city's interim growth policy. The landowners filed suit seeking to require Boulder to serve their development.

Issue: Can the city of Boulder, in its role as a public utility, refuse to serve a development outside its corporate limits in order to further its growth-management objectives?

Decision: No.

Reasons: The court concluded that in its role as a utility, Boulder can only refuse to extend its service to landowners for utility-related reasons. Growth-control and land-use planning considerations did not suffice. Boulder had no land-use planning authority in the affected area.

Robinson v. The City of Boulder, 547 P.2d 228 (Colo. 1976).

A third method of controlling growth is to time it by tying it to the availability of public facilities. Ramapo, New York, is a good example of the use of this technique. Like Petaluma, California, Ramapo was a rural community until new highway facilities made it accessible to New York City commuters and transformed the town into a "bedroom community." Lacking adequate public facilities and development controls, the town was ill-prepared for growth. Local taxpayers finally revolted against the frequent and unpredictable tax increases necessary to meet the needs of the rapidly expanding population, and the town initiated a comprehensive planning program.

In response to research findings, Ramapo adopted a growth-management program that included a new zoning ordinance, a new official map, and revised subdivision and zoning ordinances as well as a special-permit system for residential subdivisions. Development could proceed only when certain public facilities and services were available. These community necessities included public sewers, downstream drainage facilities, public parks or recreational facilities, firehouses, and streets or roads. If the services were not available, developers would receive no permits unless they were willing to make the investment necessary to provide these facilities. At the same time, Ramapo adopted a capital-improvements plan designed to construct facilities to serve the entire township within an eighteen-year period.

When Ramapo's timed-growth policy was challenged by a developer who was unable to secure a subdivision permit, it was upheld. New York's highest court held that the plan was not exclusionary and did not exceed the limits of the police powers. The effect of this plan has been to stop the development of properties lacking the necessary public facilities and services. Ramapo's capital-improvements program fell behind almost from the start because of rapid inflation and unexpected costs. The net effect of this plan to time growth appears to have been a shifting of growth away from Ramapo to nearby communities.

12. Exclusionary Zoning

Several techniques are used to exclude certain types of housing from a community. Among those used to exclude low- and moderate-income housing are large lot requirements and minimum-floor-area standards. Large lot requirements often are justified by the desire to retain open space. This exclusionary zoning and large minimum-floor-area requirements as a practical matter prevent low- and moderate-income persons from acquiring land or building in a community, and they are not enforced if arbitrarily enacted.

Other zoning practices also tend to exclude low- and moderate-income families. For example, many communities seek to limit the number of mobile-home parks. Others seek to prevent multifamily dwellings. The constitutionality of these laws is challenged frequently. The case involving Mount Laurel, New Jersey, is a very good example. Mount Laurel Township contains approximately 14,000 acres in the path of suburban development for the Philadelphia metropolitan area. In 1950, before the completion of the New Jersey Turnpike, the town had only 2,800 residents, but by 1970 its population had increased to over 11,000.

Mount Laurel had passed zoning ordinances designed to make it a community of upper-middle- and upper-income families living in single-family detached homes. Attached residential dwellings, apartments, and mobile homes were not allowed within the township. The sole exception was one approximately 200-acre zone for a planned adult retirement community. The township also zoned nearly 2,800 acres for light industrial development, but fewer than 100 acres were in use for this purpose by the mid-1970s. Residential development was prohibited on this land.

Mount Laurel's zoning ordinance was attacked as being exclusionary and an example of "fiscal zoning," that is, zoning designed to keep out poor and large families who require extensive social and educational services, while attracting industrial firms and those wanting single-family detached dwellings—uses which require fewer services and yield higher taxes. In a potentially far-reaching decision, the New Jersey Supreme Court held that Mount Laurel had an obligation under the New Jersey constitution to provide for its "fair share" of low- and moderate-income housing for the region.

In a more recent decision, however, the New Jersey Supreme Court backed away from saying exactly what constituted a "fair share" of the requisite housing. The court held that land-use regulations were "exclusionary" if they tended to preclude the opportunity to supply substantial amounts of new housing for low- and moderate-income households in a municipality and in the appropriate region, whether or not such effect was intended.

Excluding low-income citizens often means excluding minority citizens, resulting in challenges based on discrimination. The United States Supreme Court has held that proof of discriminatory effect is not enough to nullify a zoning law. Discriminatory *intent* is required.[3]

13. Other Zoning Issues

There has been a growing awareness in recent years of our building heritage, and many communities have passed special zoning ordinances designed to protect historic structures or districts. As might be expected, these have often led to controversy when an owner was prevented from demolishing or altering property.

For example, New York City enacted a landmarks preservation law in 1965 for the purpose of establishing a citywide program of identification and preservation of historic structures and sites. Designation barred any construction or alteration of a building's exterior appearance without the approval of the Landmarks Preservation Commission. Grand Central Terminal, a structure in the Beaux-Arts style that was completed in 1913, was designated under the law in 1967. Subsequently, the Penn Central Railroad leased air rights over the terminal for a proposed fifty-five-story office tower. The Landmarks Commission rejected the plan, stating: "To balance a fifty-five-story office tower above a flamboyant Beaux-Arts facade seems nothing more than an aesthetic joke." Penn Central then turned to the courts for relief, contending that the landmarks preservation law took their property without just compensation.

The United States Supreme Court held that although the Landmarks Commission's refusal to grant a permit deprived the owner of approximately $3 million annually, Penn Central could still use the property as it had for sixty-five years, as a railroad terminal containing

[3]Village of Arlington Heights v. Metropolitan Housing Development Corporation, page 185.

office space and concessions. Writing for the majority, Justice Brennan said:

> It is, of course, true that the Landmarks law has a more severe impact on some land owners than others, but that in itself does not mean that the law effects a 'taking.' Legislation designed to promote the general welfare commonly burdens some more than others.[4]

Even so, the Court made it clear that preservation laws could not deprive the owner of a reasonable return on the property, but that it need not be the best possible return.

Zoning ordinances dealing with architectural controls and sign controls have a long history of legal controversy. Courts have almost always upheld regulations designed to control activities that are offensive to the senses of smell and hearing. The sense of sight has not fared nearly so well, primarily because of the difficulty in defining with any precision what is attractive and what is ugly. Beauty is in the eye of the beholder. However, today aesthetic regulations may be valid.

Regulations may be based solely on the desire of communities to improve their appearance. For example, the Massachusetts Supreme Judicial Court found constitutional the Town of Brookline's ordinance prohibiting all billboards. It held that aesthetics *alone* may justify the exercise of the police power—that within the broad concept of general welfare, cities and towns may enact reasonable billboard regulations designed to preserve and improve their physical environment.

In addition to historic preservation and architecture controls, there has been a move to maintain some areas as unimproved or open land. Approximately 1.2 million acres of open land in the United States are lost each year to urban development, most of it close to existing urban areas. These losses have led to problems in many states and communities in keeping land in agricultural use or in acquiring it as open space. Many communities have also attempted to retain open space through their zoning powers by enacting laws that severely limit the density of housing. These ordinances have often led to legal challenges charging that they constitute a taking of private property without compensation in violation of the Fifth Amendment or that they are exclusionary in nature. Like other challenges of land-use controls, the suits challenging open-space requirements must show that the zoning ordinance is either unreasonable or unconstitutional. Again, judicial reasoning normally will not be substituted for legislative enactments as long as the latter

---

[4]Penn Central Transportation Co. v. City of New York, 438 U.S. 104, 133 (1978).

are reasonable and within the bounds of applicable constitutional provisions.

Case 7.5

Donald Agins owned five acres in the city of Tiburon with an exceptionally good view of the San Francisco Bay. The city enacted a zoning ordinance that placed Agins' property in a residential classification allowing the development of only one to five residences on the five-acre tract. Without ever submitting a development plan for the city's approval, Agins filed suit seeking a judgment that the ordinance was unconstitutional.

Issue: Did the zoning ordinance, in denying Agins the most intensive use of his land, constitute a taking?

Decision: No.

Reasons: The zoning ordinance works to assure careful and orderly development of residential property with provisions for open-space areas. Agins will share with other owners the benefits and burdens of this legitimate exercise of the city's police power.

Agins v. City of Tiburon, 100 S. Ct. 2138 (1980).

Other Land-Use Controls

14. Introduction

The comprehensive plan and its land-use component are implemented through several tools of land-use control. As discussed above, the most prominent of these tools is comprehensive zoning. However, other items of importance in the application of land-use controls include the official map, subdivision regulations, laws on mandatory dedication of land, and building codes. Environmental laws at the federal and state levels also have a substantial impact on how land can be used.

The official map shows proposed streets and other public facilities identified in the comprehensive general plan. When an official map has been adopted, no building permits will be issued for construction on the land designated for such purposes. Granting variances or purchasing through the exercise of eminent-domain powers may be required if the ordinance can be demonstrated to result in undue hardship or deprivation of reasonable use. Generally, however, the official map can provide benefits for both private landowners and the public by prohibiting construction on land that will be needed for public facilities.

15. Subdivision Regulations

Subdivision regulations, another tool for implementing the community-planning process, establish the standards and procedures regulating the subdivision of land for development and sale. Their purpose is to protect both the community and future residents of the subdivision from poorly planned and executed developments.

The local planning board or other planning agency determines the standards that must be met for subdivision approval. Standards are provided for the design and construction of new streets, utilities, and drainage systems. The planning board also establishes an approval procedure, usually consisting of three distinct steps: a preapplication conference, approval of the preliminary plat, and approval of the final plat.

The purpose of the preapplication conference is to allow the developer to meet informally with the planning board before going to the expense of preparing a formal plat. Working with a sketch plan, the planning staff can review the proposal with the developer and make suggestions for changes that may be necessary in order to meet the subdivision regulations. The developer may also benefit from general planning efforts of the board that may affect his development.

The next step is for the developer to prepare and submit a preliminary plat for approval. The term "preliminary plat" is misleading, since all construction and mapping of the lots will be done on the basis of this plat. Detailed information is required, therefore, usually including topographic data on existing boundary lines, easements, streets, utilities, and ground elevations. Also included is the layout of the proposed subdivision, which consists of streets, other rights of way or easements, locations of utilities, lot lines and numbers, sites of special uses, and minimum building-setback lines.

After receiving approval of the preliminary plat, the developer can stake the lots and construct the streets and other required improvements. After these tasks are completed, or with the posting of a certified check or bond to guarantee completion, the developer can prepare a final plat and related documents.

The final plat is intended to be filed in the registry of deeds and must contain all information necessary for land titles, such as exact lot lines, street rights of way, utility easements, and surveying monuments. The required accompanying documents usually include a certification by a licensed engineer or surveyor regarding the accuracy of the details of the plat, plans concerning utility improvements within the subdivi-

EXHIBIT 7.1   FINAL PLAT

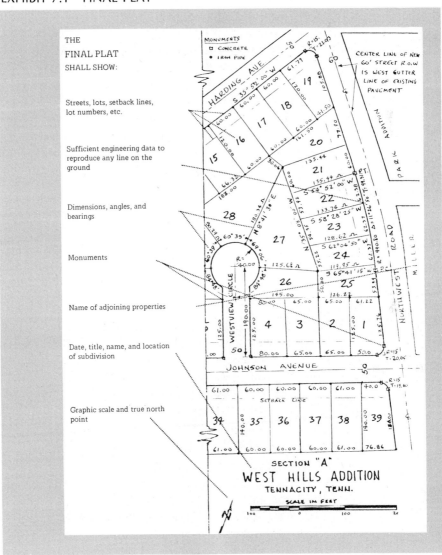

sions, and certification that the improvements have been constructed in accordance with the approved plans.

After approval by the planning board, the final plat will be recorded and the developer will then be permitted to sell lots in the subdivision. A typical plat is shown on page 175.

Closely related to subdivision regulations is site-plan review, the process of studying the proposed site plans of particular types of development before approval. Generally, site-plan reviews are undertaken for industrial parks, shopping centers, recreational areas, and multifamily residential projects, even when no subdivision of land occurs, in order to minimize the ecological, traffic, and other impacts of the proposed development. For example, alteration of surface drainage patterns or the paving of large areas may adversely affect nearby land. Similarly, an improperly located or designed driveway entrance may create a very dangerous traffic problem.

Generally, the site-review process requires the submission of a plot plan showing physical features, buildings, parking and loading areas, driveways, utilities, and similar features. Approval of the site plan is required before construction may proceed.

16. Mandatory Dedication

As part of the subdivision approval process, the developer is required to dedicate parts of the subdivision's land to such public purposes as rights of way for streets, utilities, and drainage. In some communities he may also be required to dedicate land for parks, open space, and schools. If the subdivision is small, payments in lieu of dedication are sometimes required.

Case 7.6

In 1975 the City of West Jordan, Utah, adopted an ordinance that required subdividers to dedicate 7 percent of the land area of any proposed subdivision to the city or pay the equivalent value in cash. These lands and monies were to be used for the purpose of providing flood control or recreation facilities. As developers, Hall and Jenkins were required to make a payment of $16,576 in lieu of land dedication before their subdivision would be approved. The two developers filed suit to challenge the validity of the ordinance, contending that (1) it is not within the city's granted powers, (2) the land or money required is not for the benefit of the subdivision but the benefit of the city as a whole,

(3) the city is attempting to exercise the power of eminent domain without following proper procedures, and (4) it unlawfully imposes a tax.

Issue: Did the city have the power to require mandatory dedication of land or payments in lieu of land from subdividers?

Decision: Yes.

Reasons: The ordinance falls within the scope of authority and responsibility of city government in its promotion of the health, safety, morals, and general welfare of the community. Requiring the dedication before approving the subdivision does not constitute a taking of private property.

Hall and Jenkins v. City of West Jordan, 606 P.2d 217 (Utah, 1979).

The mandatory dedication of land for parks and schools is understandably controversial. One view is that the need for such facilities is created by the new subdivision, while the opposing view holds that parks and schools are a general governmental responsibility that should be borne by the public at large. The courts are also divided on the issue, in some cases upholding mandatory dedication of land for such purposes and in other cases holding that the granting of the right to subdivide land on the condition that the developer donate land for parks and schools is a taking of property without due process of law. In some jurisdictions the developer is required to reserve the land only for a stated period of time, during which the municipality may purchase the property. If the land has not been purchased by the end of the period, the developer is no longer bound by the reservation.

17. Building Codes

The last tool for implementing a comprehensive land-use plan is the set of ordinances known as building codes, which establish detailed standards for the construction of new buildings and the alteration of existing ones. Their primary purpose is to protect health and provide safety, and they are primarily related to fire prevention, quality and safety of construction, and public health safeguards. They may also be used to promote energy conservation and other public purposes. Building codes are usually enforced through a system of building permits. Since

a building permit is required before construction can begin, local officials are enabled to ascertain that the proposed construction is in compliance with applicable building codes, zoning regulations, and
subdivision regulations, and that the site plan has been approved.

18. State Environmental Land-Use Controls

Until recently, land-use control in the United States had been almost
exclusively a prerogative of local governments. Today, we recognize
that land-use and environmental problems are often regional or statewide in scope and require some degree of state or regional participation
in their solution.

State land-use controls are largely a response to environmental
concerns, as are federal programs, such as the Coastal Zone Management Act of 1972, which provided planning funds for the thirty coastal
and Great Lakes states, and the National Flood Insurance Program.

In all, over half of the states now have some type of state-mandated
land-use controls. Most of these states have designated certain areas or
classes of land as areas of "critical state control." Areas of great scenic
value, such as New York's Adirondack Park, the Florida Keys, North
Carolina's Outer Banks, and California and Nevada's Lake Tahoe, fall
into this category. More generally, the states often single out particular
types of land for control: wetlands, shorelines, aquifer-recharge areas,
beaches, flood plains, and mountains. In some states the desire is to
protect agricultural land.

Case 7.7

As part of its statewide planning efforts, Oregon mandated the
preservation of certain types of land for agricultural use. A developer wished to subdivide a 119-acre tract that fell into this classification into thirty-four lots of various sizes. The parcel was
located near a rural area that had been zoned rural residential.
The county approved the subdivision, reasoning that the parcel
could not be farmed economically. A neighboring property
owner appealed the decision, alleging that the subdivision would
be an inappropriate use of the land under statewide planning
goals. He further argued that the board had failed to consider
alternative agricultural uses.

Issue: Should the subdivision be permitted even though it violated state
planning goals?

Decision: No.

Reasons: The commissioner did not consider possible agricultural uses of
the land other than grazing. There was no evidence presented
that the land could not be farmed profitably, and the board failed
to address the implications of the statewide planning goals with
regard to this parcel.

Hillcrest Vineyard v. Board of Commissions of Douglas County, 608 P.2d 201
(Or. 1980).

A. Hawaii

Hawaii passed the first statewide land-use control law in 1961, and it
remains the only example of state zoning in the United States. Since
much of Hawaii's land is mountainous and not suitable for cultivation,
the state has two land-use policy goals—protecting agricultural lands
and curbing urban sprawl. All land in the state was zoned in one of three
categories: agricultural, conservation, or urban. The amount of land
classified as urban is designed to provide just enough room to accommodate the orderly expansion of existing urban areas, and within these
districts local governments can impose their own more detailed zoning
criteria.

The law has made Hawaii's urban growth more compact and generally has confined expansion to less productive agricultural land. Oppo-
nents charge that the commission's policies have been politically
inspired and the restriction of urban areas has led to greatly increased
housing prices.

B. Vermont

In the 1960s, Vermont was eagerly promoting all types of economic
growth, styling itself the "beckoning country." The state's efforts were
successful, and its population grew more during that decade than during the previous fifty years. Pressures from this growth, and particularly
from burgeoning vacation-home developments, led to the passage in
1970 of the Vermont Environmental Control Act, providing for one of
the most comprehensive state land-use regulation systems in the nation. It includes a permit procedure for all projects over a certain size,
development performance standards, property tax relief for agricultural land, and a capital-gains tax on land sales. A state zoning
plan also was proposed, but this feature was not implemented by the
legislature.

Every commercial development of over one acre, every subdivision of more than ten lots, construction of more than ten housing units, and all construction at altitudes of more than 2,500 feet require a permit from one of nine district environmental commissions. In order to receive a permit, the development must meet specified environmental criteria, some of which are open to varying interpretations. As might be expected, the law has generated considerable controversy. Some observers feel it has probably restricted growth somewhat, but that it has also been very effective in improving the quality of development. Others contend the law has merely added to developers' costs and consequently to the cost of vacation housing.

C. CALIFORNIA

California's system of state control over construction along its entire 1,072-mile coastline generally is considered the boldest example to date in state land-use regulation. Passage of the original act in 1972 was sparked by public concern over dwindling access to beaches, high-density development along the coast, and environmental degradation. The law establishes a state coastal zone commission and six regional bodies. In addition to formulating a plan for conservation of the coastal zone, the commission was given the power to approve, modify, or veto all development in a 1,000-yard strip of land inland from the ocean's edge. During the first four years following passage of the act, nearly 25,000 permit applications were processed. Despite the controversy that was generated by some decisions, the legislature passed the California Coastal Act of 1976, which continues a modified and somewhat simplified permit and planning procedure.

19. Federal Environmental Legislation

A great deal of federal environmental legislation was enacted during the late 1960s and early 1970s. Some of the most important acts were the Air Quality Act, Clean Water Act, Coastal Zone Management Act, and the National Environmental Policy Act. Although this legislation and the regulations it has spawned have had considerable impact on real estate development, most has been of an indirect nature. For example, increased water-quality requirements have mandated local sewerage projects which in many cases have led to increased development costs. Environmental requirements have delayed or forced the cancellation of highways or other federally-funded projects, thereby adversely affecting private developments that would have received the benefits of these public projects. Other legislation, however, has had a direct impact on real estate development. For example, state and local regulations required under the Coastal Zone Management Act have restricted development in some areas. Similarly, the National Flood Disaster Protection Act, which provides flood insurance, mandates local flood plain zoning before a community is eligible to participate.

Among its provisions, the National Environmental Policy Act (NEPA) requires an environmental impact statement for any major federal action significantly affecting the "human environment." Generally these environmental impact statements have been required only for federally-financed construction projects, although the requirement has been expanded to encompass public-housing projects and military-base closings. However, at least a dozen states followed the federal example and enacted NEPA-like statutes at the state level. Several of these "little NEPAs," most notably those in California, Washington, and Florida, require an environmental-impact statement for certain private land developments. At times, these have led to the delay or cancellation of a number of proposed projects, as this next case indicates.

Case 7.8

A developer applied for a use permit to build a 128-unit motel on a 3.8-acre parcel of land near Carmel, California. The environmental-impact statement that was required under the California Environmental Quality Act disclosed several negative environmental effects of the development, including increased need for water and sanitation services, traffic congestion, and a displacement of sixteen families in an old apartment building that was to be removed for the project. Even so, the County Zoning Administrator issued a use permit for the project. The City of Carmel and an environmental group sought to compel the County Board of Supervisors and County Zoning Administrator to withdraw the use permit, contending that the adverse environmental effects of the project had not been adequately considered.

Issue: Did the Zoning Administrator have to consider possible adverse environmental effects before issuing the use permit?

Decision: Yes.

Reasons: Under the California Environmental Quality Act, zoning officials are required to give environmental-impact reports a significant role in considering use-permit applications. In this case the Zoning Administrator did not adequately consider evidence that might override the adverse effects disclosed by the environmental-impact statement.

City of Carmel-by-the-Sea v. Monterey County Board of Supervisors, 139 Cal. Rptr. 214 (Cal. 1977).

Cases on Zoning and Other Land-Use Controls

Village of Euclid v. Ambler Realty Co.
272 U.S. 365 (1926).

Ambler Realty owned a sixty-eight-acre tract of land in the Village of Euclid, Ohio, that it hoped to sell for industrial development. Euclid adopted a comprehensive zoning ordinance in 1922 which zoned part of the tract for residential use only. Ambler Realty attacked the ordinance on the ground that it was a "taking" of its property without just compensation. The district court agreed and declared the ordinance null and void. The village appealed to the U.S. Supreme Court.

Sutherland, J.:

. . . The ordinance now under review, and all similar laws and regulations, must find their justification in some aspect of the police power, asserted for the public welfare. The line which in this field separates the legitimate from the illegitimate assumption of power is not capable of precise delimitation. It varies with circumstances and conditions. A regulatory zoning ordinance, which would be clearly valid as applied to the great cities, must be clearly invalid as applied to rural communities. . . .

We find no difficulty in sustaining restrictions of the kind thus far reviewed. The serious question in the case arises over the provisions of the ordinance excluding from residential districts, apartment houses, business houses, retail stores and shops, and other like establishments. This ques-

tion involves the validity of what is really the crux of the more recent zoning legislation, namely, the creation and maintenance of residential districts, from which business and trade of every sort, including hotels and apartment houses, are excluded. . . .

The matter of zoning has received much attention at the hands of commissions and experts, and the results of their investigations have been set forth in comprehensive reports. These reports, which bear every evidence of painstaking consideration, concur in the view that the segregation of residential, business, and industrial buildings will make it easier to provide fire apparatus suitable for the character and intensity of the development in each section; that it will increase the safety and security of home life; greatly tend to prevent street accidents, especially to children, by reducing the traffic and resulting confusion in residential sections; decrease noise and other conditions which produce or intensify nervous disorders; preserve a more favorable environment in which to rear children, etc. With particular reference to apartment houses, it is pointed out that the development of detached house sections is greatly retarded by the coming of apartment houses, which has sometimes resulted in destroying the entire section for private house purposes; that in such sections very often the apartment house is a mere parasite, constructed in order to take advantage of the open spaces and attractive surroundings created by the residential character of the district. Moreover, the coming of one apartment house is followed by others, interfering by their height and bulk with the free circulation of air and monopolizing the rays of the sun which otherwise would fall upon the smaller homes, and bring, as their necessary accompaniments, the disturbing noises incident to increased traffic and business, and the occupation, by means of moving and parked automobiles, of larger portions of the streets, thus detracting from their safety and depriving children of the privilege of quiet and open spaces for play, enjoyed by those in more favored localities,—until, finally, the residential character of the neighborhood and its desirability as a place of detached residences are utterly destroyed. Under these circumstances, apartment houses, which in a different environment would be not only entirely unobjectionable but highly desirable, come very near to being nuisances.

If these reasons, thus summarized, do not demonstrate the wisdom or sound policy in all respects of those restrictions which we have indicated as pertinent to the inquiry, at least, the reasons are sufficiently cogent to preclude us from saying, as it must be said before the ordinance can be declared unconstitutional, that such provisions are clearly arbitrary and unreasonable, having no substantial relation to the public health, safety, morals, or general welfare. . . .

Under these circumstances, therefore, it is enough for us to determine, as we do, that the ordinance in its general scope and dominant features, so far as its provisions are here involved, is a valid exercise of authority, leaving other provisions to be dealt with as cases arise directly involving them. . . .

Reversed.

Westbrook v. Board of Adjustment
262 S.E.2d 785 (Ga. 1980).

Marshall, J.:

The appellant's application to rezone his lot in the Town of Trion from residential use to commercial use, for proposed use as a self-service or convenience store, was denied by the Board of Adjustment of the Town of Trion, as recommended by the town's planning commission. The denial was affirmed by the town's Board of Zoning Appeals. The appellant filed an equitable complaint to require the town to rezone the property, . . . After a hearing, the trial judge denied relief to the plaintiff, and he appeals. We affirm.

The appellant's lot is located in the northeast corner of the intersection of U.S. Highway 27 with Third Street, fronting 132.6 feet on the east side of the highway, with 68.3 feet on the north side of Third Street. There is *no* conflict in the evidence that all of that area on the east side of the highway where this lot is located is an old residential neighborhood; that there has been no change in the zoning thereof as residential, including property to the north, east and south of appellant's lot, since adoption of Trion's zoning ordinance in 1962; and that, although the lot is vacant, a dwelling had been located thereon for many years, having burned some years before the appellant bought the property in 1970 with knowledge that it was zoned residential. . . .

The appellant testified to a beauty parlor being operated three or four blocks north of his lot on the same side of the highway, but there was evidence that a lady had been operating this business out of a small part of her home when the zoning ordinance was adopted, and that she had been permitted to continue so doing as a nonconforming use. . . .

Except for the vacant lots of the appellant and the adjoining lot, all of the property in this area on the east side of the highway is occupied by houses.

All of the testimony emphasizes the existing heavy vehicular traffic on the highway and, in particular, the congestion that exists for three one-hour periods during each day when the work shift changes at the Riegel plant. This traffic volume is the basis of the contentions of both parties, the appellant urging that it renders the property unsuitable for residential use and the appellees urging that the problem would be worsened by commercial use. Witnesses for both the appellant and the appellees agree that the rezoning of the appellant's lot to commercial would increase the amount of traffic at the lot. The convenience store, which evidence showed would be the feasible use of the property if zoned commercial, would generate vehicular traffic going into and off of both adjoining

streets, creating a hazard for pedestrians crossing the streets. The mayor testified that this would create a traffic and safety hazard.

It is undisputed that commercial zoning would increase the market value of the lot. These amounts range from $1,000 residential value and $10,000 commercial value, according to the appellees' witness, to $500–$750 residential value and $30,000–$35,000 commercial value, according to the appellant's witness. It appears probable that the increase in value for commercial use would be attributable to the uniqueness of spot zoning for this lot in a residential area, the nearest commercially zoned property for retail business, shopping, etc., being located about a mile away. The appellant purchased the property knowing that it was zoned residential, undoubtedly paid a purchase price based upon its value as a residential lot, and his own witness acknowledged that the spot rezoning of this lot would adversely affect the surrounding residential properties' values.

"The police power generally supports an ordinance forbidding the erection in designated residential districts of business houses, retail stores, shops, and other like establishments; and such ordinances, apart from special applications, can not be declared arbitrary and unreasonable, and without substantial relation to the public health, safety, morals, or general welfare." Even if it be conceded that the property in question is in a "fringe" area, with bordering industrial use and heavy vehicular traffic lessening its value for residential use, nevertheless, the local governing body is the more appropriate one to shape and control the local environment according to the best interests of the locality and its citizens. Moreover, aside from the preservation of the surrounding residential area, the town's denial of rezoning was clearly within its police power with reference to at least the public safety and general welfare.

"A zoning ordinance is presumptively valid, and this presumption may be overcome only by clear and convincing evidence. The burden is on the person seeking to change the zoning to show the invalidity of the ordinance. The acts of the governing body of a municipal-

ity exercising zoning power will not be disturbed by the courts unless they are clearly arbitrary and unreasonable. It is not sufficient to show that a more profitable use could be made of the property."

Under the evidence, the trial judge did not err in holding that the denial of rezoning to the appellant was not unconstitutional.

Affirmed.

Village of Arlington Heights v. Metropolitan Housing Development Corporation
429 U.S. 252, 97 S. Ct. 555 (1977).

The Metropolitan Housing Development Corporation (MHDC) applied to the Village of Arlington Heights, Illinois, for the rezoning of a fifteen-acre tract of land from a single-family to a multiple-family classification. MHDC planned to develop a cluster of units for low- and moderate-income tenants. After the rezoning request was denied by the Village, MHDC filed a suit alleging that the Village's denial was racially discriminatory and therefore a violation of the equal-protection clause of the United States Constitution. The District Court held for the Village, finding there was no intent to discriminate. The Court of Appeals reversed because it found a discriminatory effect in the denial of the rezoning request. The Village's petition for a writ of certiorari was granted.

Powell, J.:

... Arlington Heights is a suburb of Chicago, located about twenty-six miles northwest of the downtown Loop area. Most of the land in Arlington Heights is zoned for detached single-family homes, and this is in fact the prevailing land use. The Village experienced substantial growth during the 1960's, but, like other communities in northwest Cook County, its population of racial minority groups remained quite low. According to the 1970 census, only twenty-seven of the Village's 64,000 residents were black.

The Clerics of St. Viator, a religious order (Order), own an 80-acre parcel just east of the center of Arlington Heights. ...

The Order decided in 1970 to devote some of its land to low- and moderate-income housing. Investigation revealed that the most expeditious way to build such housing was to work through a nonprofit developer ... MHDC is such a developer. ...

MHDC engaged an architect and proceeded with the project, to be known as Lincoln Green. The plans called for 20 two-story buildings with a total of 190 units, each unit having its own private entrance from outside. . . .

The planned development did not conform to the Village's zoning ordinance and could not be built unless Arlington Heights rezoned the parcel to R-5, its multiple-family housing classification. Accordingly, MHDC filed with the Village Plan Commission a petition for rezoning, accompanied by supporting materials describing the development and specifying that it would be subsidized under § 236. The materials made clear that one requirement under § 236 is an affirmative marketing plan designed to assure that a subsidized development is racially integrated. MHDC also submitted studies demonstrating the need for housing of this type and analyzing the probable impact of the development. . . . (The Court then reviewed the process by which the request for rezoning was denied and the decisions of the District Court and the Court of Appeals. The Court held that MHDC had standing to sue and then turned to the issue of discriminatory intent.)

Our decision last Term in *Washington v. Davis,* made it clear that official action will not be held unconstitutional solely because it results in a racially disproportionate impact. "Disproportionate impact is not irrelevant, but it is not the sole touchstone of an invidious racial discrimination." Proof of racially discriminatory intent or purpose is required to show a violation of the Equal Protection Clause. . . .

Davis does not require a plaintiff to prove that the challenged action rested solely on racially discriminatory purposes. Rarely can it be said that a legislature or administrative body operating under a broad mandate made a decision motivated solely by a single concern, or even that a particular purpose was the "dominant" or

"primary" one. In fact, it is because legislators and administrators are properly concerned with balancing numerous competing considerations that courts refrain from reviewing the merits of their decisions, absent a showing of arbitrariness or irrationality. But racial discrimination is not just another competing consideration. When there is a proof that a discriminatory purpose has been a motivating factor in the decision, this judicial deference is no longer justified.

Determining whether invidious discriminatory purpose was a motivating factor demands a sensitive inquiry into such circumstantial and direct evidence of intent as may be available. The impact of the official action—whether it "bears more heavily on one race than another,"—may provide an important starting point. Sometimes a clear pattern, unexplainable on grounds other than race, emerges from the effect of the state action even when the governing legislation appears neutral on its face. The evidentiary inquiry is then relatively easy. But such cases are rare, and the Court must look to other evidence.

The historical background of the decision is one evidentiary source, particularly if it reveals a series of official actions taken for invidious purposes. The specific sequence of events leading up the challenged decision also may shed some light on the decisionmaker's purposes. For example, if the property involved here always had been zoned R-5 but suddenly was changed to R-3 when the town learned of MHDC's plans to erect integrated housing, we would have a far different case. Departures from the normal procedural sequence also might afford evidence that improper purposes are playing a role. Substantive departures too may be relevant, particularly if the factors usually considered important by the decisionmaker strongly favor a decision contrary to the one reached.

The legislative or administrative history may be highly relevant, especially where there are contemporary statements by members of the decisionmaking body, minutes of its meetings, or reports. In some extraordinary instances the *members* might be called to the stand at the trial to testify concerning the purpose of the official action, although even then such testimony frequently will be barred by privilege.

The foregoing summary *identifies,* without purporting to be exhaustive, subjects of proper inquiry in determining whether racially discriminatory intent existed. With these in mind, we now address the case before us.

... The impact of the Village's decision does arguably bear more heavily on racial minorities. Minorities constitute 18 percent of the Chicago area population, and 40 percent of the income groups said to be eligible for Lincoln Green. But there is little about the sequence of events leading up to the decision that would spark suspicion. The area around the Viatorian property has been zoned R-3 since 1959, the year when Arlington Heights first adopted a zoning map. Single-family homes surround the eighty-acre site, and the Village is undeniably committed to single-family homes as its dominant residential land use. The rezoning request progressed according to the usual procedures. The Plan Commission even scheduled two additional hearings, at least in part to accommodate MHDC and permit it to supplement its presentation with answers to questions generated at the first hearing.

The statements by the Plan Commission and Village Board members, as reflected in the official minutes, focused almost exclusively on the zoning aspects of the MHDC petition, and the zoning factors on which they relied are not novel criteria in the Village's rezoning decisions. There is no reason to doubt that there has been reliance by some neighboring property owners on the maintenance of single-family zoning in the vicinity. The Village originally adopted its buffer policy long before MHDC entered the picture and has applied the policy too consistently for us to infer discriminatory purpose from its application in this case. Finally, MHDC called one member of the Village Board to the stand at trial. Nothing in her testimony supports an inference of invidious purpose.

In sum, the evidence does not warrant overturning the concurrent findings of both courts below. Respondents simply failed to carry their burden by proving that discriminatory purpose was a motivating factor in the Village's decision. This conclusion ends the constitutional inquiry. ...

Reversed and remanded.

Review Questions

1. Explain the difference in the application and effect of a public nuisance versus a private nuisance.
2. Zoning ordinances basically divide a community into various districts for the purpose of regulating the intensity of the use of the land and buildings. What are the three main classifications of land uses? What are some examples of the more specialized classifications?

3. Clarke applied for and received a building permit for a house but not for a carport. Even so, he built the carport, which extended to within 3'4" from his property line, even though the city's zoning ordinance required a 6'5" side yard setback. When notified that his structure did not comply with zoning requirements, Clarke requested a variance, which was denied. He then sued to require the city to grant him a variance, testifying that it would cost $500 to remove the carport and diminish the value of the total structure by $8,000. Was the city unreasonable in denying Clarke a variance? Why?

4. Webber owned 127 acres of land on which he drilled a well, installed a pump, constructed a large reservoir tank, and laid a water main along a public road which bisects his property. Webber spent $110,000 to develop the water system, which was designed to serve approximately 250 houses. This development plan was consistent with the current zoning ordinances, which allowed residential development at half-acre density. Subsequently, the county adopted a comprehensive plan that limited density of development to one dwelling per five acres. Is the construction of the water system prior to the adoption of the comprehensive plan sufficient to give Webber a vested right to continue development of his land at the half-acre density?

5. Define the following terms:
   a. PUD
   b. Performance zoning
   c. Down zoning

6. List the three techniques that have been used to manage a community's growth rate.

7. Whitemarsh Township's zoning ordinance prohibited mobile-home parks anywhere in the township. Harriet applied for a zoning amendment which would permit her to development a mobile-home park on a 44.5-acre tract of land. When her application was refused, she appealed to the courts. In general, is a prohibition of mobile-home parks in a community unconstitutional? Explain.

8. Several building firms sought to invalidate minimum-floor-area requirements in the zoning ordinances of four municipalities in their communities. They contended that these requirements were unrelated to the traditional purposes of the zoning power and had the effect of excluding lower- and moderate-income families from these communities. Are minimum-floor-area requirements for residencies traditionally a legitimate use of the police power?

9. Ordinances that regulate the development of subdivisions attempt to protect the community and future residents from poorly planned and executed development. Trace the typical steps a developer would have to complete in getting approval of plans for a potential subdivision.

10. Environmental concerns, which were emphasized greatly during the 1960s and 1970s, remain very important today. The National Environmental Policy Act regulates the use of land in some ways. Principally, this Act requires that an environmental-impact statement be prepared prior to any major federal action that might significantly affect the human environment. What is an environmental-impact statement? How do these apply to projects funded by the states?

8

Taxation and Real Estate

I. Introduction

Three types of taxes are of particular interest to owners and users of real estate. Ad valorem property taxes are levied on the value of the land and improvements. Income taxes are levied on the income earned from real estate or on the profits from its sale. Estate and inheritance taxes are levied on the value of real estate in a decedent's estate, and gift taxes are levied on the value of real estate given away during the donor's lifetime. Each of these will be discussed in this chapter.

The Property Tax

2. In General

The property tax is an ad valorem tax. It is levied as a percentage of the real estate's value, including improvements. This tax is *on the real estate* instead of *on the income earned* from it. The steps that governments follow in this taxing process are: (1) valuing and assessing taxable real estate, (2) developing a tax rate, and (3) billing and collecting the taxes.

The property tax has given rise to many controversies. Among other issues, they concern the uniformity of assessments, differential assessment of farmland and open space, special assessments, exempted property, and property-tax relief. These controversial issues are discussed after the following section on the real estate taxation process.

3. The Property Taxation Process

The first step in the property-taxation process is to value for tax purposes all properties within the jurisdiction—a process known as assessment. The government official responsible, usually called the assessor or tax assessor, must discover, list, and value all taxable properties.

An efficient assessor needs a complete set of maps showing each parcel of land and its measurements. The initial discovery of buildings and other improvements requires an on-site inspection; a system of continuing inspection of deeds and building permits is necessary to keep up with new construction and changes in property ownership.

After the property has been identified and described, the assessor is faced with the most difficult part of the job, that of valuing the property. Valuation is generally based on fair market value; this is considered to be the price that the property would probably bring in the market, given knowledgeable and willing buyers and sellers, acting under no abnormal pressure, and with a reasonable time to complete the transaction.

After making an estimate of the property's market value, the assessor then multiplies this value times some legally authorized fraction (such as 40 percent), to arrive at the assessed value, which is the value of the property used when computing property taxes. This assessed value is subject to review, and the results of the review process may be appealed by the taxpayer before an appeals board or court.[1]

Case 8.1

The owners of an apartment complex in Wilmington, Delaware, appealed from the County Board of Assessment Review's decision on the current assessment of their property, which was based on a general reassessment of all property in the county using 1970 as the base year. In 1975 the owners appealed to the County

[1]Valley Forge Apartments v. Board of Review, p. 214.

Assessment Review Board, contending that the fair market value of their property had fallen since 1970.

Issue: Did the constitutional mandate of uniform taxation force the County to use current market value as a basis for assessment?

Decision: No.

Reasons: The court held that assessments based on a complete reassessment of all property in the county five years earlier were more likely to produce the desired uniformity in taxation. Implementation of a system using present market value for only part of the properties without a general classwide reassessment would result in the application of different measures of assessment among taxpayers of the same class.

Board of Assessment Review v. Stuart, 378 A.2d 113 (Delaware 1977).

The second step in the property-taxation process is development of a budget and a tax rate by the city council, county commission, or other governmental body. The budget develops as the amount of public funds to be spent for operations and bonded indebtedness is determined. The amount of revenue coming from other taxes and from nontax sources is subtracted from the total budget; the remainder must be collected in property taxes. This amount is then divided by the total of assessed valuations to obtain the tax rate.

For example, suppose that property taxes to be collected amount to $10 million and the total of assessed values is $500 million. The tax rate needed to raise these revenues is:

$$\frac{\$10,000,000}{\$500,000,000} = 0.02$$

This rate may be expressed in three ways: (1) as dollars per $100 of assessed value ($2 in this example); (2) as a percentage of assessed value (2 percent in our example); or (3) as the rate per thousand of assessed valuation—the millage rate. One mill equals $0.001, or 1/1,000 of $1. In this example, $0.02 equals 20 mills.

As a matter of practice, of course, the local governing body does not just decide what it would like to spend and then set a corresponding tax rate. It may feel constrained not to raise the present tax rate, to raise it only slightly, or even to lower it. After the tax rate is set, the assessed values are multiplied by the tax rate to obtain individual tax bills. If a house in our hypothetical locality is assessed at $40,000, for example, the property tax would be $800 (20 mills x $40,000).

The final step in the property-taxation process involves the tax billing and collection procedures, which vary widely among the states. In some, property-tax bills are payable annually; in others they are payable semiannually or quarterly. Some states have special taxing districts that send their tax bills at different times of the year.

Property taxes become a lien on a fixed day each year. For example, in a typical state, property taxes for the year 1982 became a lien on January 1 of that year. This occurs even though the taxing authorities have not determined the tax rate or perhaps even the value of the property. After the taxes are computed, a tax bill is sent to the property owner indicating the amount of taxes and the due date of payment. The tax bill usually also includes an indication of the date after which the taxes would be delinquent. Indeed, payment dates and delinquency dates may even fall into a subsequent year. For example, the 1982 taxes may not become due and payable in some states until some time in 1983.

If property taxes are not paid by the delinquent date, interest and penalties are usually added to the bill. If not paid within a specified time, the taxing authorities may conduct a tax sale at which the property is sold for the unpaid taxes. The purchaser at the tax sale is given a tax deed, which in effect conveys title to the property to the purchaser. However, the law usually provides a period during which the former owner may redeem the property from the tax sale and clear the title of the tax lien or reobtain title to the property. The rights of the parties to a tax sale are similar to those in a mortgage-foreclosure process. This latter process is discussed in Chapter 14.

4.   Uniformity of Assessments

Properties throughout the jurisdiction must be uniformly assessed if the property tax is to be fair and equitable. It doesn't matter what percentage of market value is chosen, so long as all properties are assessed at the same percentage. For example, suppose that the $500 million in assessed values in our hypothetical community represented assessments at 50 percent of market value. If assessments were raised to 100 percent of market value, the total would rise to $1 billion, and the tax rate would be cut from 20 mills to 10 mills in order to raise the same

$10 million in revenue. The assessment on the house in the earlier example would rise to $80,000, but the tax would remain the same at $800 ($80,000 x 10 mills = $800).

The question of fairness arises when houses or types of property are assessed at varying percentages of market value. For example, it is a practice in many communities to assess property at the same figure year after year until it is sold. If market prices are rising, older properties that do not change hands will be assessed at a lower percentage of value than new properties, and their owners will pay a lower tax in relation to market value.

Certain types of property, particularly farmland and single-family residences, are typically assessed at lower percentages of value in many localities. This practice, which is permitted by the laws of some states, forces other taxpayers to carry the extra burden.

Case 8.2

The plaintiffs, owners of rental residential property in Memphis and Nashville, Tennessee, challenged the classification of property for property-tax purposes. Residential property containing two or more rental units was taxed on the basis of assessment at 40 percent of actual value, while assessments on other residential property was on the basis of 25 percent of actual value.

Issue: Did differing assessment ratios on different classifications of property violate the equal-protection clause in the United States Constitution?

Decision: No.

Reasons: These classifications are discriminatory but not arbitrary. Taxation on income-producing property at a higher rate than owner-occupied residences and farms does not violate the equal-protection clause. All property within each special classification is treated equally. All classifications do not have to be treated the same. "Perfection in the taxation of real property is neither required nor obtainable."

Snow v. City of Memphis, 527 S.W.2d 55 (Tennessee 1975), cert. denied, 423 U.S. 1083 (1976).

5. *Differential Assessment of Farmland and Open Space*

Beginning with Maryland in 1957, forty-four states have passed some sort of differential assessment program for farmland and other open space that is designed to give landowners an economic incentive to retain the land in its existing use. Generally the land is assessed on the basis of its value in agricultural use rather than the value it would have in residential or commercial use.[2] Often such programs contain provisions for deferred taxation, so that some of the forgiven taxes may be recovered for a specified number of years if the land is converted to an alternative use.

Both the objectives and the effectiveness of differential assessment programs are subjects of considerable debate. Many people contend that landholders on the urban fringe should be subject to economic pressures to convert their land to "high" uses, and that differential assessment will lead to economic inefficiencies. Others feel that the retention of farmland and open space is in itself desirable and will help to control urban sprawl.

Even if the objectives of the programs are accepted, the question of their effectiveness remains. The savings in taxes to the property owner may be enough to make a farming operation economically viable or to reduce to an acceptable level the cost of retaining a large tract. The owner may still put the property on the market, however, if the price rises high enough, or if urbanization makes it difficult to continue farm operations. Furthermore, the laws in many states are loosely drawn, extending tax reductions to lands owned by large corporations and land speculators.

Most studies have concluded that differential assessment can help to preserve farmland and open space, but that by itself it is not sufficient. A successful program must be combined with land-use controls, such as agricultural zoning or purchase of development rights.

6. *Special Assessments*

Special assessments are taxes collected only from specified property owners within a jurisdiction and then used to benefit the area from which they were collected. Some special assessments are collected to finance public-works projects that directly benefit the taxed property

---

[2]Dotson v. Henry County Board of Tax Assessors, page 216.

owners, such as sidewalks, sanitary sewers, drainage projects, or street paving. These are usually assessed on a basis that supposedly measures the benefit received, such as front footage of the lot or lineal feet of drainage pipe installed. Other special assessments take the form of additional property taxes within particular areas to finance special services such as downtown business district improvements, recreational programs, and additional fire protection. Property owners can challenge a special assessment in court, as the following case indicates.

Case 8.3

The City of Rosenville, Michigan, levied a $4-per-front-foot assessment to cover a portion of the costs of street widening, paving, and curbing along a section of Twelve Mile Road. The plaintiffs, who were property owners abutting the road, commenced a class-action suit to enjoin the city from levying the assessment, contending that the road did not benefit them but actually reduced their property values.

Issue: Did the road widening create special benefits for abutting property owners that justified the special assessment by the city?

Decision: No.

Reasons: The court found that no special benefit was conferred upon the property owners, but rather that the project benefited the public at large. The evidence also indicated that the widened street could be a detriment to abutting property owners.

Hack v. City of Rosenville, 239 N.W.2d 752 (Mich. 1976).

7. Exempted Properties

Some types of properties are exempt from taxation. Generally, such properties include government-owned property, colleges and universities, houses of worship, hospitals, and cemeteries. Often, however, exemptions are extended to properties that have little to do with the exempted organization's primary purpose. The twin towers of the World Trade Center in New York City generate no property taxes because they are owned by the Port of New York Authority, whose main purpose is to coordinate transit and shipping in Greater New York; the Port Authority uses only part of the building and rents space to other organizations. Similarly, no taxes are paid on the Chrysler Building because the land it occupies is owned by Cooper Union, an educational institution that was granted tax-exempt status by the New York Legislature in 1859.

Case 8.4

The Maine Turnpike Authority constructed two service areas consisting of restaurant and gas-station facilities adjoining the turnpike in the town of Kennebunk. The Authority, which had fee simple ownership of the land and buildings, entered into a lease with the Howard D. Johnson Company covering operation of the two restaurant facilities. The town assessed taxes on the land and buildings and billed them to Howard Johnson with the designation "real estate taxes." The company claimed that the tax was invalid because it was in fact assessed on the Turnpike Authority's fee simple interest in real estate and not on Howard Johnson's leasehold interest.

Issue: Could the town of Kennebunk charge the Howard Johnson Company real estate taxes on property that it leased from a public authority?

Decision: No.

Reasons: The legislative intent in creating the Maine Turnpike Authority was that the nonliability for the payment of property taxes should extend beyond the authority itself to the private lessee of the Authority's real estate, in this case the operator of restaurant facilities.

Howard D. Johnson Company v. King, 351 A.2d 524 (Me. 1976).

Partial exemptions for "homesteads," i.e., owner-occupied dwellings, are allowed in many states, and additional exemptions are sometimes granted to veterans, widows, the handicapped, and the elderly. Such exemptions are designed to promote homeownership and to provide tax relief to designated groups, but they necessarily add to the burdens of other property owners.

In all, one study estimated that approximately one-third of all real estate is exempt from property taxes.[3] Not only does this situation shift the burden to other taxpayers, but it often forces them to provide the services that are required by the users of the tax-exempt properties. For example, a local government must provide fire protection and the like to the residents of a university dormitory or a church-sponsored retirement home, even though those properties generate no property-tax income. Some such institutions, recognizing the inequity of accepting services that others must pay for, voluntarily pay the equivalent of a property tax to the community.

8. Property-Tax Relief

As property-tax assessment and rates rose in the 1960s and 1970s, resistance to further increases stiffened. Property-tax relief was sought both for lower-income taxpayers and for taxpayers in general.

One form of property-tax relief for retired persons and other low-income citizens is the so-called circuit breaker. Under this scheme, property taxes for homeowners are limited to some maximum percentage of income. In the states that have adopted the circuit breaker, the maximum tax has ranged from approximately 4 to 6 percent of income.

Various methods have been used to provide some measure of property-tax relief to taxpayers in general, and especially to homeowners. Some states have taken over the funding of some services formerly financed by local property taxes; some have given rebates, or cash refunds, to local taxpayers from state general-tax revenues.

The most celebrated property-tax-relief measure was the Jarvis-Gann tax limitation initiative in California, popularly known as Proposition 13. The proposal, which was passed in 1978, (1) limits property taxes to 1 percent of 1975 market value, (2) provides that assessments may be raised a maximum of 2 percent annually, (3) assesses new construction at its original value, (4) permits reassessment when property is improved or sold, and (5) requires a two-thirds vote of each house of the legislature to raise state taxes.

California property taxes were reduced by over 50 percent as a result of the amendment, and local governments were able to prevent large-scale cutbacks in services only through the imposition of new user

[3]Alfred Bolk, *The Free List: Property With Taxes* (New York: Russell Sage Foundation, 1971).

fees and extensive state aid from an existing state surplus. The impact in future years is uncertain, but unless the measure is modified, it is certain to produce growing tax inequities. The taxes on new construction or on properties that are sold or improved will be increasingly inequitable in comparison with those on properties that do not change ownership.

The amendment also led to raising protests by renters, who felt that their landlords were not passing on to them the reductions in property taxes that they were enjoying. In some cities the renters' protests led to imposition of rent controls. These controls are discussed further in Chapter 16.

Federal Income Taxation

9. Introduction

There are many factors that make real estate an attractive investment, including the potential for high return, appreciation of capital, protection against inflation, and the possibility of using financial leverage to an extent seldom available in alternative investment opportunities. In addition, even though tax benefits have been reduced in recent years, investments in real property still offer significant advantages as a tax shelter. One reason is that although a taxpayer may realize a gain on real estate sold, exchanged, or otherwise transferred, only a portion of the gain is recognized for tax purposes. Tax laws also favor the homeowner, encouraging and, in effect, subsidizing home ownership.

Any understanding of the tax advantages of real estate requires knowledge of the tax treatment of capital gains. Real estate owned for twelve months or longer is subject to the application of the capital gains formula. Profits that are entitled to capital-gains treatment create, in effect, a tax saving because a portion of the income is in effect not taxed at all. For example, at the present time, 60 percent of a profit or realized gain that qualified for long-term-capital-gains treatment does not have to be recognized as taxable. Thus, only 40 percent of a long-term capital gain is taxable, and this is subject to a maximum tax rate of 50 percent. Therefore, the effective maximum rate for the total long-term capital gain is 20 percent. The amount recognized is made a part of the taxpayer's ordinary income.

The federal income-tax laws have become increasingly complex. Legislation, regulations, rulings, and case law change constantly. Consequently, all that we can do here is to introduce a few basic concepts that are very important for owners and users of real property. An accountant or tax attorney should be consulted for answers to specific questions regarding the taxation of real estate.

10. Tax Aspects of Forms of Business Organization

There are many types of business organizations, each of which has advantages and disadvantages to particular investors with regard to liability, continuity of ownership, management, taxes, and financing. The basic types are proprietorships, partnerships, and corporations. These may be used by any type of business, including those primarily concerned with real estate. The real estate investment trust has also become an important form of organization in real estate investment.

The *sole proprietorship,* in which ownership is vested in one individual, is the simplest form. Income earned from sole proprietorships, including that from real estate, is considered income to the owner and is taxed at personal-income tax rates. The primary advantage of individual ownership is its simplicity and flexibility of management. The owner can make decisions unfettered by the responsibility of consulting with others. This freedom has a price however: the owner has responsibility for all management decisions and also faces unlimited financial liability. Further, the firm's management often lacks continuity, since title must pass to others at death. Also, the amounts of money that can be assembled by a sole proprietor are usually not large enough to finance most commercial or industrial real estate projects.

In a *partnership,* two or more owners combine their capital and expertise in a business venture. In a *general partnership,* each partner is responsible for all the actions of and debts incurred by the other partners in the conduct of the business. Although the partnership must file an informational return with the Internal Revenue Service, the organization does not pay any taxes. Profits or losses are passed through the organization to the partners and included in their personal returns.

A *limited partnership* is composed of one or more general partners who manage the business and are personally liable for its debts, plus one or more limited partners who contribute capital and share in profits and losses but take no part in running the business, and who incur no liability with respect to partnership obligations beyond their contribution to capital. Because of the limited liability of the limited partners, the organization is called a limited partnership.

The limited partnership as a tax shelter is of special value in many new businesses and especially in real estate ventures such as shopping centers and apartment complexes. It gives the investor limited liability and the operators control of the venture. It allows the maximum use of the tax advantages of depreciation and the investment credit. Depreciation often results in a tax loss in early years, which can be immediately deducted by the limited partner. However, there is usually a positive cash flow, notwithstanding the tax loss. Thus a limited partner may be able to receive income and at the same time show a loss for tax purposes. When such ventures start to show a taxable gain, the limited partnership is often dissolved and a corporation formed, or the venture may be sold.

A *corporation* is a form of equity ownership in which an entity is authorized to act as a private person and is legally permitted to receive, own, and transfer property, to make contracts, and to sue and be sued. The corporation is a taxable entity paying a tax on its earnings. The tax rates, which change from time to time, are graduated from relatively low rates on the first $25,000 of earnings to rates approaching 50% on corporate earnings over $100,000.

In addition to the direct tax, corporate income is taxed again when distributed to shareholders as a dividend or as a capital gain upon dissolution or sale of the property. The rate of this second tax depends on the tax rate of the persons receiving the dividend or distribution.

It is possible for a corporation to avoid in part the double taxation of corporate income. First of all, reasonable salaries paid to shareholder employees may be deducted in computing taxable income. This technique may avoid double taxation of substantial portions of income. The Internal Revenue Code disallows a deduction for excessive or unreasonable compensation and treats such payments as dividends. Therefore the determination of the reasonableness of corporate salaries is often an issue in closely held corporations.

Second, the capital structure of the corporation may include both common stock and interest-bearing loans from shareholders. For example, assume that a company needs $200,000 of cash to commence business. If $200,000 of stock is issued, there will be no expense to be deducted. However, assume that $100,000 worth of stock is purchased by the owners, and $100,000 is loaned to the company by them at 12 percent interest. In this case, $12,000 of interest each year is deductible as an expense of the company and thus subject to only one tax as interest income to the owners. Just as in the case of salaries, the Internal Revenue Code has a counteracting rule relating to corporations that are undercapitalized. In such a case, interest payments will be treated as dividends and disallowed as deductible expenses.

A third technique for avoiding double taxation, to some extent, is simply not to pay dividends and to accumulate the earnings. After the earnings have been accumulated, the shareholders can sell their stock or have the company dissolved. In either case, the difference between the original investment and the amount received is given capital-gains treatment. Here again, there are tax laws designed to counteract the technique. There is a special provision for an income tax imposed on "excessive accumulated earnings" in addition to the normal tax.

The purpose of the accumulated-earnings tax is to deter the use of the corporate entity to avoid personal income taxes. It compels companies to distribute any profits not needed for conduct of the business, so that individual shareholders will be liable for taxes on the dividends received. When earnings are retained in excess of the $250,000, the burden is on the taxpayer to rebut the presumption that earnings have been retained to avoid the second tax on dividends. The presumption may be rebutted by proof of needs of the business for the retained earnings. It is not sufficient to rebut the presumption by saying that tax avoidance was not the dominant reason for the accumulation, if it was in fact *one* of the reasons.

Finally, there is Subchapter S in the Internal Revenue Code which allows small, closely-held business corporations to be treated as partnerships for income-tax purposes and thereby to avoid having a tax assessed on the corporate income itself. These Subchapter S corporations cannot have over twenty-five shareholders, each of whom must elect to be taxed as a partnership, i.e., to have the corporate income allocated to the shareholders annually in computing their income for tax purposes, whether actually paid out or not. Subchapter S corporations cannot be used in most real estate ventures because the statute does not allow Subchapter S treatment for corporations receiving 20 percent or more of their income from rents, dividends, interest, or royalties. Therefore, such developments as apartment complexes and shopping centers cannot qualify for Subchapter S treatment.

Real estate investment trusts (REITs) were originally created for the purpose of extending the benefits of equity ownership to people who would not otherwise invest in real estate. The problem of double taxation inherent in the corporate form of ownership was solved when trusts were exempted from federal corporate taxes. Like shareholders, investors in REITs have only limited liability and can convert their investment to cash quickly because there is an organized market for REIT shares. These advantages attracted many small investors until the disastrous practices of many of the trusts during the early 1970s soured much of the investing public on this type of ownership.

11. *Depreciation*

The key to obtaining a profitable cash flow and a deductible tax loss is the expense of depreciation, which creates a deduction for tax purposes on the theory that the asset is being reduced in value and the owner will need funds with which to replace it. Each year a portion of the original cost is allowed as a charge against the income earned by the property. This allowable depreciation for tax purposes does not necessarily bear any relationship to the actual decrease in value of the property. Indeed, tax depreciation may be taken even though the property is actually increasing in value.

Land is not a depreciable asset; no deduction can be taken, nor can the original cost of the land be deducted over a stated period. However, if the land contains minerals such as oil, gas, sand, or gravel, a depletion allowance can be taken as the minerals are removed to compensate for the process of using up that portion of the land. The allowance available depends on the minerals being extracted.

Depreciation is allowable for improvements on the land, such as buildings, fences and tile on farmland, and for fixtures of all types. A depreciation expense may create a deduction and tax loss even though the value of the improvements may actually go up. Thus, the owner of a real estate investment may have a tax loss, cash return on investment, and an increase in the value of his asset.

This availability of the depreciation deduction provides real estate investment with a major tax advantage. For example, the dollar value of a building may be higher at the end of its "useful life" than it was at the beginning. Even though depreciation charges involve no actual cash outlay, they may be subtracted from income as "expenses," thus reducing the amount of income that is subject to tax. The goal is for the real estate investments to generate at least enough cash to cover mortgage payments, other actual cash outlays, and returns on investment, while depreciation charges create a loss for income-tax purposes that can be used to "shelter," i.e., diminish the reportable amount of, the investor's ordinary income.

The straight-line method of depreciation is the simplest way to measure tax depreciation. The salvage value of the property at the end of its useful life is subtracted from the original cost, and the result is divided by the number of years of the project's useful life. For example, in Table 8.1 a $150,000 improvement with zero salvage value is depreciated in fifteen years. The annual depreciation charge in this case is $10,000: (cost − salvage value) ÷ life = ($150,000 − 0) ÷ 15.

Depreciation charges serve to reduce taxable income, and generally the earlier the benefits can be received, the greater their value. Hence it is usually considered desirable to establish as short a useful life as possible in order to increase the amount of the annual depreciation deduction. The tax-cut legislation passed in 1981 established that the useful life of real estate improvements is fifteen years in most situations.

Further, an increase in the tax benefits of depreciation charges may be gained if deductions are increased in the early years through the use of accelerated depreciation, by which assets are depreciated at higher rates in the early years of a project's useful life and at lower rates in the later years. A commonly used accelerated-depreciation method is the declining-balance method.

In the declining-balance method, the depreciable value of the property is multiplied by 175 percent or 200 percent of the straight-line rate. The tax cut act of 1981 allows businesses to depreciate buildings by using a 175 percent declining-balance schedule. Low-income housing is subject to a 200 percent (double) declining-balance write-off

Table 8.1 Depreciation of $150,000 Improvement with a Fifteen-Year Life

Year	Straight-Line Method	175 Percent Declining Balance	200 Percent Declining Balance
1	$ 10,000.00	$ 17,500.00	$ 20,000.00
2	$ 10,000.00	$ 15,458.33	$ 17,333.33
3	$ 10,000.00	$ 13,654.86	$ 15,022.22
4	$ 10,000.00	$ 12,061.79	$ 13,019.26
5	$ 10,000.00	$ 10,654.58	$ 11,283.36
6	$ 10,000.00	$ 9,411.55	$ 9,778.92
7	$ 10,000.00	$ 8,313.53	$ 8,475.06
8	$ 10,000.00	$ 7,868.17	$ 7,345.05
9	$ 10,000.00	$ 7,868.17	$ 6,820.40
10	$ 10,000.00	$ 7,868.17	$ 6,820.40
11	$ 10,000.00	$ 7,868.17	$ 6,820.40
12	$ 10,000.00	$ 7,868.17	$ 6,820.40
13	$ 10,000.00	$ 7,868.17	$ 6,820.40
14	$ 10,000.00	$ 7,868.17	$ 6,820.40
15	$ 10,000.00	$ 7,868.17	$ 6,820.40
	$150,000.00	$150,000.00	$150,000.00

schedule. The advantage of these accelerated methods of depreciation can be seen in Table 8.1.

In the example used in Table 8.1, the straight-line rate of depreciation is 1/15 annually. Under the 200 percent declining-balance method, double this percentage of the undepreciated value would be applied each year. Thus, the first year's depreciation would be $20,000 (2/15 of $150,000), reducing the nondepreciated amount of $130,000. The second year's depreciation would decline to $17,333.33 (2/15 of $130,-000), while in the third year it would fall still further to $15,022.22. The taxpayer is allowed to shift to straight-line depreciation at any point.

12. Tax-Free Exchanges and Involuntary Conversions

Another important tax advantage of real estate is the possibility of tax-free exchanges. The owner may trade equity in one property held for investment or used in trade or business for equity in another "of a like kind" without having to recognize any of the realized gain. The requirement that the property be "of like kind" is broadly defined. For example, a taxpayer who is not a dealer in real estate can exchange city real estate for a ranch or farm. Likewise, an exchange of a leasehold of a fee for a term of thirty years or more for real estate with fee simple title is a "like-kind" exchange.

When a like-kind exchange occurs, each party involved must calculate its realized gains to determine what amount will be recognized for tax purposes. In calculating realized gain, one must know the extent of cash or other property received, that is, the *boot,* and (in the case of mortgaged property) the extent of mortgage reduction. Any mortgage assumed by one party is treated as cash paid by the party assuming the mortgage to the party relieved of the mortgage obligation. After the exchange occurs, each party involved must adjust its basis in the new property received.

The *realized gain* is calculated by taking the fair market value of the property received and subtracting the basis in the original property (that which was exchanged for the new property), the amount of boot paid, and the extent of mortgage assumed, while adding the amount of boot received and the extent of mortgage reduction. The *recognized gain* is the amount of the boot received plus the amount of the mortgage reduction. Finally, the *adjusted basis* is determined by taking the basis in the original property and adding the amounts of the recognized gain, boot paid, and mortgage assumed, while subtracting the amount of boot received and the amount of the mortgage reduction.

Although these rules may sound complex, they are not difficult to apply in most exchange transactions. Suppose Bob and Carol own rental property that has a fair market value of $100,000. Their basis in this property is $60,000. Further assume, Ted and Alice own a farm worth $150,000, in which they have a basis of $90,000. Now suppose these couples exchanged their ownership in these properties with each other, and that Bob and Carol paid Ted and Alice $50,000 in cash at the time of the exchange.

First, what are the consequences of this exchange to Bob and Carol? They will have a realized gain of $40,000 ($150,000 – $60,000 – $50,000). None of this realized gain has to be recognized by Bob and Carol. Their adjusted basis in the farm will be $110,000 ($60,000 + $50,000). These figures are determined by the formulas discussed above. Review these calculations and then determine the consequences of this exchange on Ted and Alice.

Ted and Alice will realize a gain of $60,000 ($100,000 – $90,000 + $50,000). Of this, $50,000 must be recognized by Ted and Alice. This amount is subject to capital gain application if the farm had been owned by Ted or Alice for at least twelve months. Their adjusted basis in the rental property acquired is $90,000 ($90,000 + $50,000 – $50,000).

If Ted and Alice had had a $50,000 mortgage on their farm and this mortgage had been assumed by Bob and Carol instead of them paying $50,000 in cash, the results of this exchange would have been exactly the same as discussed above. However, assume that Bob and Carol have a $30,000 mortgage on their rental property and Ted and Alice have a $60,000 mortgage on their farm. Also suppose Bob and Carol pay $20,000 in cash and the mortgages are assumed by the parties receiving the exchanged properties.

What are the tax consequences for each couple? Bob and Carol will have a realized gain of $40,000 ($150,000 – $60,000 + $30,000 – $20,000 – $60,000). They would not have to recognize any of their realized gain, since the boot paid and mortgage assumed is greater than the mortgage of which they are relieved. Their adjusted basis in the acquired farm would be $110,000 ($60,000 + $20,000 + $60,000 – $30,000).

Ted and Alice will have a realized gain of $60,000 ($100,000 – $90,000 + $20,000 + $60,000 – $30,000). Of this, $50,000 must be recognized for tax purposes, since the boot received and amount of mortgage reduction exceeds the mortgage assumed by $50,000. Ted and Alice will have an adjusted basis in their new property of $90,000 ($90,000 + $50,000 + $30,000 – $20,000 – $60,000).

A like-kind exchange of real property may not be the ideal transaction for all situations. There are some disadvantages inherent with exchanges. For example, any loss realized in the transaction cannot be recognized as a tax loss. Furthermore, a taxpayer may wish to have a high basis in real property to permit large amounts of depreciation. In that case, it may be better to sell the property, pay the taxes, and reinvest the proceeds rather than exchange the property with the resultant adjusted basis.

Despite these disadvantages, like-kind are exchanges likely to become more frequent in the future.

Case 8.5

On April 1, 1967, T. J. Starker entered into a land exchange agreement with the Crown Zellerbach Corporation. On May 31, 1967, Starker deeded timberland, worth $1,502,500 to Crown. Crown agreed to acquire suitable property in the future to be exchanged for Starker's timberland. Between May 31, 1967, and May 21, 1969, Crown acquired rights to twelve parcels which were deemed equal in value to the land transferred by Starker. Nine of these parcels, which were commercial property, were deeded by Crown to Starker. Two parcels were deeded by Crown to Starker's daughter at his direction. Starker used one of these as his residence. The final parcel involved Crown assigning Starker a third party's contract to purchase. The Internal Revenue Service sought to collect taxes claiming Starker had sold his timberland to Crown. Starker argued that his timberland was exchanged for the twelve parcels, all of which qualified as like-kind property; therefore, he claimed he did not have any recognizable gain.

Issue: Does this transaction qualify as a tax-free like-kind exchange?

Decision: Yes. All parcels transferred by Crown are subject to the exchange provisions except for the two parcels transferred to Starker's daughter.

Reasons: Section 1031 of the Internal Revenue Code requires that property in a tax-free like-kind exchange be used in a trade on business or held for investment and be transferred between the parties involved. There is no time period within which the exchange must occur, as long as it is clear the exchange is part of one transaction. The parcels transferred directly to Starker's daughter are nonqualified property, since the title was not transferred to Starker. Furthermore, using a parcel as a residence indicates that property is not used in a trade on business or held for investment. The last parcel does qualify as exchanged property because Crown gave Starker the opportunity to acquire title by assigning the contract to purchase the property. The other nine parcels qualify as like-kind property, since their use is of a commercial nature and title was deeded directly to Starker.

Starker v. United States, 602 F.2d 1341 (9th Cir. 1979).

An involuntary conversion occurs when property is taken through eminent-domain proceedings or is converted to cash through destruction by fire, theft, or other losses that yield insurance proceeds. Since the owner has no control over the transaction, requiring him to pay a capital-gains tax on the involuntary conversion of the property would weaken his ability to make himself whole out of the conversion proceeds by reinvesting them in a new property. Accordingly, the federal income-tax laws allow the owner to transfer his basis over to another similar property without paying capital-gains taxes if the property is replaced within two years. For business or investment property that is condemned, the allowable replacement period is three years. In essence, these involuntary conversions are treated like the exchanges of property, discussed above.

13. Tax Advantages for Homeowners

Definite encouragement for home ownership is provided through tax breaks that are not given to renters. First, the homeowner is allowed to deduct mortgage interest and property taxes from taxable income if deductions are itemized. This reduces the after-tax cost of ownership and gives it a favored tax status versus renting.

An additional important tax advantage for homeowners is the deferral of capital-gains taxes. Taxes on the gain realized from the sale of an owner-occupied dwelling do not have to be recognized if another house of equal or greater value is purchased within twenty-four months. This provision enables a homeowner to transfer equity without being taxed on the gains. The basis in the new residence is adjusted by reducing the amount paid by the gain not recognized.

Another provision of the tax law makes it possible to avoid paying income tax on these profits altogether. Taxpayers who are age fifty-five and over are allowed a once-in-a-lifetime election to exclude from taxable income up to $125,000 of any gain from the sale of a principal residence. Thus a family can defer taxation on profits from the sale of several principal residences over the years and then finally exclude up to $125,000 of these gains from taxation if in later life they wish to move to a smaller home or rental housing.

14. Residential Energy Credit

A tax credit for federal income-tax purposes may be taken for certain expenditures for home-energy conservation and for use of renewable energy sources such as solar energy conductors. The credit is based on the cost of items installed after April 19, 1977, in principal residences that were substantially completed before that time.

A credit for up to $300 is allowed for energy-conservation items such as insulation, storm windows or doors, caulking or weather stripping, thermostats with automatic set-backs, furnace replacement burners that reduce the amount of fuels used, devices for modifying flue openings for making a heating system more efficient. A renewable-energy-source credit for up to $4,000 can be taken on solar, wind, and geothermal energy items which heat or cool a principal residence or provide hot water or electricity for it. These items include solar-energy collectors, heat exchangers, solar panels, and windmills that produce energy in any form for the residence.

15. Business Use of a Residence

If a family rents out a portion of its home, expenses that apply to the rented part may be deducted. General expenses that cannot be directly attributed to either the rented or the owner-occupied portion are allocated on the basis of the percentage of the dwelling occupied by each use. For example, if one-fourth of the house is rented, then one-fourth of the general expenses can be deducted as a business expense. In addition, one-fourth of depreciation on the home can also be deducted as an expense. Depreciation on the portion used as a residence is not deductible.

Expenses associated with maintaining an office in the home may under very limited circumstances be claimed as a deductible business expense. The Tax Reform Act of 1976 severely restricted deductions for home offices. The taxpayer must prove that the office in the home is used "exclusively" and on a "regular" basis as (a) a "principal place of business"; (b) a regular place to meet patients, clients, or customers; or (c) an office in connection with a trade or business of an employer who provides no office for the employee. The taxpayer must also prove that the use of the office at home is for the convenience of the employer and not for his own convenience. Even if these tests are met, homeowners' expenses are limited to the gross income from the use of that office, less interest and taxes allocable to that office.

16. Vacation Home Deductions

Many families and individuals purchase a vacation home and rent or attempt to rent it when they are not personally using it. The net rental received may offset the expense of the upkeep and the cost of holding the property and may even generate a tax loss. The Tax Reform Act of 1976 limited this practice of deducting these expenses.

If the property is used by the taxpayer for personal purposes for more than two weeks per year or more than 10 percent of the annual rental days, whichever is greater, deductions otherwise allowable for depreciation, maintenance, utilities, etc., are limited. They cannot exceed the gross income for the rental of the property, reduced by interest and taxes which are allowable in any case.

The Federal Estate and Gift Tax

17. Introduction

Several decades ago, in order to break up large accumulations of wealth and property, Congress enacted a federal estate tax on testamentary transfers of property and a gift tax on lifetime transfers of property. These taxes were part of the philosophy that taxes should be used to redistribute wealth. When originally enacted, they were to apply only to the rich. However, as inflation escalated and created sizeable estates for numerous people, these taxes became a concern to the average citizen, and the field of estate planning, using techniques to reduce these taxes, flourished. This was due in part to the fact that life insurance generally was subject to the tax. In addition family businesses and farms often had to be sold to pay the tax, but proper planning could solve the problem to some extent. In 1976 a change of attitude began that resulted in Congress providing some relief for farmers and small businessmen. The 1976 law was also changed to gradually raise the amount of property exempt from the tax from $60,000 to $175,000. For estates subject to taxation, the beginning tax rate was 32 percent and it rose to 70 percent. Therefore, taxes still had a heavy impact on many people, especially those owning real estate.

In 1981 Congress enacted tax-cut legislation that dramatically changed the impact of the federal estate and gift taxes on most people. The law is directed once again at only the very wealthy. Only very large estates will be taxed, and these taxes will be of little concern to over 95 percent of all citizens. Complicated estate planning will not be necessary for most people. The use of trusts to avoid transfer taxes will no longer be very common.

Prior to the 1981 law, which became effective in 1982, a unified estate and gift tax applied to gifts made during the donor's lifetime of over $3,000 a year per donee and to estates over $175,000 in value. Beginning in 1982, lifetime gifts up to $10,000 a year per donee will be tax free. This means a husband and wife jointly can make any number of gifts of $20,000 a year per donee without tax liability. By 1987 the estates of decedents whose combined lifetime taxable gifts added to the estate at death are under $600,000 will not be subject to the transfer tax. This $600,000 figure will be achieved by stair-stepped increases from $175,000 over the years 1982 through 1987. The maximum tax rate will be reduced to 50 percent by 1985.

In addition to the increased exemptions from taxes on gifts and death transfers, the 1981 law states that any amount given to a spouse during one's lifetime or at death qualifies for a marital deduction and is not taxed at all. The new law allows a couple to avoid the tax until both the husband and wife pass their property to their heirs and beneficiaries.

The 1981 law does not eliminate the other methods that have been used to reduce estate and gift taxes in the past. For example, landowners may continue to value their real estate as it is currently used (special use valuation) instead of at its highest and best use value. (See Section 19.) The provision for extending payments of estate taxes also are still applicable. (See Section 20.) Life estates and remainders can be utilized in order to skip generations' ownership of fee simple interest in real estate and thus avoid the tax in their estates on the transfer of such real estate. Finally, the basis of real estate will continue to be stepped up to its current fair market value when it is transferred upon the owner's death. This stepped up basis may be a real advantage because it helps to reduce capital gains taxes whenever the property is sold.

Although some of these provisions just discussed may sound complicated, federal estate and gift tax should become less applicable and, therefore, less complex for all but the largest estates over the next few years. The real impact of the 1981 tax act legislation will be seen only as it becomes fully implemented in 1987.

18.   Calculation of the Estate Tax

The first step in determining the estate tax is to ascertain the total value of the decedent's gross estate. In the case of a living gift, it is the value of the gift itself that must be ascertained. The value of the gross estate includes the value of all property (except real property situated outside the United States) to the extent of the decedent's interest therein at the time of transfer. However, the gross estate also may include property in which the decedent did not have an interest at the time of his death. A decedent's gross estate for federal estate-tax purposes may therefore be very different from the same decedent's estate for local probate purposes. Examples of items which may be included in a decedent's gross estate and not in his probate estate are the following: property transferred by the decedent within three years of the date of death or in which the decedent retained a life estate; property held jointly by the decedent and others; property over which the decedent had a general power of appointment; proceeds of certain policies of insurance on the decedent's life; annuities; and dower or curtesy of a surviving spouse or a statutory estate in lieu of those interests.

The value of property includible in a decedent's gross estate generally is its fair market value at the time of the decedent's death, except that if the executor elects the alternate valuation method, it is the fair market value thereof six months later. The fair market value is the price at which the property would change hands between a willing buyer and a willing seller, neither being under any compulsion to buy or to sell, and both having reasonable knowledge of relevant facts. The fair market value of property includible in the decedent's gross estate is not determined by a forced-sale price. Livestock, farm machinery, harvested and growing crops must generally be itemized and the value of each item separately returned. Property values are not based on the value at which the property is assessed for local tax purposes unless that value represents the fair market value as of the applicable valuation date. Using the fair market value of the property justifies the application of the stepped-up basis principle. For example, although a decedent may have paid $20,000 for a piece of real estate in 1950, the value of the property is stepped-up to the current fair market value at the owner's death. The beneficiary's basis in this property will be stepped-up to the fair market value.

For farm land and real estate owned by a closely held business, there are special provisions which allow it to be reported at less than fair market value. This special use valuation is discussed in the next section.

The second step in determining the tax is to ascertain the value of the adjusted gross estate. This value is determined by subtracting from the value of the gross estate the authorized deductions. Under various conditions and limitations, deductions are allowable for expenses, indebtedness, taxes, and losses during administration.

The third step is to compute the taxable estate. This is achieved by deducting charitable gifts and the marital deduction from the adjusted gross estate. Based on the 1981 changes, the marital deduction is the value of all property passing to a surviving spouse.

The fourth step is to add taxable gifts during the decedents lifetime to the taxable estate. This sum is then used to compute a tentative tax by using the tables previously set forth. From this tentative tax, any gift taxes paid during the decedent's lifetime are subtracted, giving the gross estate tax due.

The final step is the determination of the net estate tax payable, by subtracting from the gross estate tax the unified credit to the extent it was not used during lifetime as well as the other authorized credits against tax. Under certain conditions and limitations, credits are allowable for the following:

1. State death taxes paid in connection with the decedent's estate;
2. Gift taxes not previously deducted;
3. Foreign death taxes paid in connection with the decedent's estate; and
4. Federal estate taxes paid on transfers of property to the decedent.

19. Special-Use Valuation

As previously noted, property is usually includible in a decedent's gross estate at its fair market value as of the date of decedent's death or as of the alternate valuation date six months later. In determining the fair market value of property, one important factor has been the "highest and best" use to which the property could be put, rather than the actual use of the property.

The law now provides that, if certain conditions are met, real property that comprises a family farm or is utilized by a closely-held small business may be valued on the basis of "current" use rather than "highest and best" use. By 1983, this special valuation process will be available to reduce the value of an estate up to $750,000. Therefore, to the extent that a decedent's estate includes qualifying property which exceeds this limitation, a dual valuation process is necessary. The current-use valuation takes into account the rate of return from the land. As a result, land that would sell for several thousand dollars per acre may be valued at less than a thousand per acre because the rate of return on its actual use greatly reduces its value for transfer-tax purposes.

Any tax benefits realized by the estate because of the special-use valuation are subject to recapture if the property passes out of the family or ceases to be used as a farm or small business within fifteen years of the decedent's death (with a phase-out of the amount recaptured during the eleventh through the fifteenth year).

In order to qualify for the special-use valuation: (1) the value of the business assets (real and personal property) must be at least 50 percent of the gross estate, (2) the value of the real property must be at least 25 percent of the gross estate, (3) the property must pass to a qualified heir, which usually means members of the deceased's family, and (4) the real property must have been used by the decedent or a member of his family as a farm or other closely held business, and he, or a member of his family, must have participated materially in its operation during five of the eight years preceding his death. The law contains an exhaustive list of farming activities. Finally, if farm property qualifies, it is valued on the basis of a formula of cash rentals, real estate taxes, and effective interest rates, or pursuant to certain specified factors. If closely held business property qualifies, its valuation is determined by various factors including capitalization of income or rent, assessed land values, comparable sales, etc.

It should be noted that the "special-use" valuation applies only to that portion of a closely held business comprised of real estate and does not affect the valuation of the other activities carried on in corporate or unincorporated form. Thus, for other than farms and similar real estate-intensive business activities, no valuation relief has been provided.

20. *Extended-Payment Provisions*

There are provisions which allow estates containing real estate to extend the time of payment of the federal estate tax. First, there is the ten-year rule, under which the tax may be paid in annual installments up to ten years if the business or farm assets exceed 35 percent of the adjusted gross estate or 50 percent of the taxable estate.

Second, there is the fifteen-year rule, under which an executor may defer all payments of tax for five years and pay only interest for that period if certain conditions are met. Thereafter, the tax is payable in equal installments over the next ten years (years six through fifteen after decedent's death). For the estate tax on the first $1 million in value of a farm or closely held business, a special 4 percent interest rate is provided. Qualification for these special payment rules is met only if the interest in the farm or closely held business exceeds 65 percent of the decedent's adjusted gross estate.

The time for the payment of tax under this provision will be accelerated if one-third or more of a decedent's interest in a qualifying trade or business is disposed of or a withdrawal of money or other property is made in an amount equal to one-third of the value of decedent's interest.

Finally, farms or closely held business interests comprising any portion of an estate, as well as other estate assets, may allow an executor to qualify for the ten-year installment payment of estate tax attributable thereto provided that "reasonable cause" is shown. This can be used when the percentages previously noted are not met.

These techniques greatly reduce the cash requirements in estates with significant real estate assets.

Cases on Taxation and Real Estate

Valley Forge Apartments v. Board of Review, 239 N.W.2d 148 (Ia. 1976)

LeGrand, J.:

Valley Forge Apartments owns and operates a multiple-apartment complex in Iowa City which was assessed for tax purposes in the amount of $1,133,820. Valley Forge's protest to the Board of Review was unavailing. Upon appeal to the district court, the assessment was reduced to $1,031,040.

Valley Forge raises only one issue. It asserts the court incorrectly used a capitalization rate of 10.5 percent in arriving at a valuation of the assessed property when the rate should have been 11 percent.

The Board's appeal challenges the reduction of the assessment, insisting the trial court erred for reasons set out in our later discussion.

We consider first the Board's appeal.

I. Plaintiff's property was valued by the assessor at $1,144,820, a figure adopted by the defendant Board on plaintiff's protest from the assessor's determination. On appeal to the district court, the valuation was changed to $1,031,040, a reduction of $113,780.

This figure was arrived at by combining separate valuations for the land ($79,740) and buildings ($951,300). The valuation on the land was left as established by the assessor. It is not an issue on this appeal. We are concerned only with the valuation of $951,300 placed on the buildings.

The basis for the assessment of real estate is found in . . . [t]he code which directs that real estate subject to taxation shall be valued at its actual value and then assessed at 27 percent thereof. Actual value is there defined as the fair and reasonable market value of the property. . . .

While the manner of ascertaining actual value under the statute may change, the ultimate goal is always the same—to fix market value. All parties agree the comparable sale method is here unavailable. Market value must therefore be ascertained by the alternative method, taking into consideration the applicable factors listed by the statute.

. . . Valley Forge produced two disinterested witnesses—both real estate salesmen and appraisers—who testified the market value of the property was less than that fixed by the assessor. Under the statute, it then became the Board's burden to uphold the valuation as reasonable and proper. As we understand the trail court's decree and the Board's appeal therefrom, the decisive question to be decided is

whether the Board sustained this burden. The trial court found the Board failed to do so, and our de novo review of the record leads us to the same conclusion.

We say this because we find the assessor and the Board relied almost exclusively on certain guidelines as to cost and other data prepared by its appraiser, Vanguard Appraisal Company, to the complete exclusion of evidence offered by Valley Forge and its witnesses.

These guidelines were in the form of arbitrary amounts computed on the basis of the past experience of Vanguard Appraisal Company and used by it in numerous appraisals made by that company. They were not related to the property here involved, and, in fact, the evidence shows Vanguard Appraisal Company in "all cases: used its own schedules despite what evidence there might be to the contrary." The Board's expert unequivocally stated he would always rely on these schedules, regardless of what the testimony might show in a particular case.

The trial court found, and we agree, this type of appraisal fell far short of overcoming Valley's direct and positive contrary evidence. The rule for which the Board argues would make it virtually impossible for a taxpayer to successfully challenge a valuation of his property since actual cost figures would perforce give way to the appraiser's all-purpose guidelines.

Our statute contemplates no such result. We have approved the use of guidelines to assist in reaching a true valuation, but we have said they may not be the sole method by which a result is reached nor may they serve as a substitute for the exercise of the assessor's judgment. Yet that is how they were used in the present case. Valley's data was totally disregarded because the appraiser "didn't believe them."

Like trial court, we find this explanation entirely unsatisfactory. We point out the trial court specifically stated the Board's attack on the credibility of Valley's witnesses was unwarranted. From our review of the transcript, we reach the same conclusion.

Patently the appraiser (and the assessor) refused to accept Valley's cost figures simply because they conflicted with his own prepared cost schedule.

Viewing the entire record before us, including the transcript of evidence, we conclude the trial court's determination of value should be affirmed. The Board failed to sustain its burden to show its valuation was correct.

In attacking the decree, the Board asserts the trial court failed to recognize or give effect to evidence concerning the equalization of assessments on apartment buildings in the Iowa City area.

We find no merit in this complaint. No matter how desirable equalization in tax assessments may be, the assessor may not use it as an excuse for failure to discharge his statutory duty with respect to burden of proof.

The judgment is affirmed on the Board's appeal.

II. There remains for determination Valley's appeal challenging the capitalization rate of 10.5 percent used by the trial court in fixing the value of the apartment buildings. Valley's witnesses had placed this figure at either 10.9% or 11%.

Capitalization of net income is one of the recognized methods of computing the value of income-producing real estate. After probable net income has been determined, that figure is capitalized to establish the actual value of the property. Capitalization is accomplished by dividing the net income by the reasonable rate of return the property should yield. The higher the divisor (rate of return), the lower will be quotient (value of the property). Hence Valley argues for a higher rate of return than the trial court used. If successful, Valley would be entitled to a substantial reduction in valuation.

As shown by the testimony in the present record, use of the capitalization method is far from an exact science. There are always differences among the experts concerning not only a reasonable rate of return but also regarding items of cost and operating expenses to be considered in arriving at net income in the first place.

Valley Forge would have the trial court accept its testimony in its entirety. Of course, the trial court was not obliged to do so. The result reached is supported by the record, is eminently fair, and should not be disturbed.

III. The judgment is accordingly affirmed on both appeals.

Affirmed on both appeals.

Dotson v. Henry County Board of Tax Assessors, 271 S.E.2d 691 (Ga. App. 1980).

Deen, J.:

This case involves an appeal from the assessment of real estate taxes for the year 1979 on the appellant's 266 acre farm, a part of which was open meadow land used to graze dairy cattle, a part woods, a part flood plain, and a part on which the farmhouse was located. The main contentions are that the appraisal methods did not comply with Code § 92-5702, that the taxes assessed are confiscatory in nature, and that the finding violates uniformity and equality in the assessment of rural property.

The appellant and her husband have lived on and run the acreage as a dairy farm for the past twenty years, during which time ad valorem taxes have increased from $200 to $4,300. The farm has expenses of approximately $5,000 per year for dairy feed, fertilizer and veterinary services, and constitutes the family's sole income except for Social Security and a small pension. It is uncontroverted that taxes assessed cannot be paid without selling off timber or otherwise going into capital. The owner therefore appealed the valuation of $1,425 per acre to the Board of Equalization, which lowered it to an average of $1,220.77. This ruling was appealed to the Henry County Superior Court and by that judge lowered to $1,088 per acre. From the latter assessment the case comes to this court.

In arriving at valuation, the assessors considered five "comparable" sales, one in the neighborhood of $2,200 per acre, and another witness, an appraiser, testified that he based his valuation on five such sales, four of which were speculative and the other one for a private airport.

The plaintiff's witnesses, who zeroed in on the value of the land for its existing uses of timber and grazing land, placed values of between $200 and $700 per acre. A careful reading of all the testimony, as well as the brief of the appellee, make clear that the underlying disagreement here is the extent to which, in an area believed to be shifting from traditional agricultural to speculative subdivision and commercial uses, "highest and best use" shall take precedence over "existing use" in the determination of value. Counsel states: "Appellee submits that Appellant's view of 'value' is based on something other than Ga. Code Ann. § 92–5702, which clearly defines 'value' in terms of an exchange, not in terms of present use." We disagree with this conclusion, based on an analysis of the statute itself and on the latest decision of the Supreme Court on this subject.

The prime duty of this court is to construe the intent of the Legislature in the wording of the statute. The last amendment, while substituting "fair market value" for "cash sale" specifically retained the classic definition of market value in terms of willing buyer/willing seller arms length transactions, as modified by three specific criteria to be used in determining this value (zoning, existing use, and deed restrictions) plus a catchall phrase allowing the use of "any other factors deemed pertinent." It is significant that while under this fourth criterion highest and best use may be considered, the Legislature did not base market value on highest and best use, nor did it list highest and best use as a specific criterion. An honest evaluation of the state of real property sales in the present economy of this country fosters the conclusion that in an area such as that described in rural Henry County in the 1970s a basing of fair market value primarily on sales for developmental purposes (as the testimony shows was done in the instant case) will in 100 percent of the cases yield a figure having no relation to that obtained by a willing seller/willing buyer contract for the purpose of continuing the existing agricultural or dairy use of the property. In such an economy basing market value for tax purposes on acreage intended for income from agriculture on the basis of prior speculative acreage sales has two disadvantages: first, the speculative use indubitably ballooned the value at the time of that sale, and secondly, if subdivision and commercial expansion did not follow rapidly on sales, the remaining land would not in fact bring an equivalent price in the open market. "Highest and best use" is thus itself a much more speculative assigned value than existing use. Large tracts of acreage in Henry County, under the evidence here, are not worth more than $200 to $700 for agricultural purposes—in fact one of the defendant's witnesses said he knew of no sales for purely agricultural purposes; yet, this part of the county is admittedly rural and in general the existing uses are agricultural uses. It is true that one of the assessors stated that they took these facts into consideration and in fact assigned values somewhat lower than what they would expect the land to bring on a speculative sale, but the point is that the existing use is agricultural and the assigned value is at least twice the estimated appraisal value for use as woods or dairy farming. In considering existing use, where the use is income producing, it would appear that the income capitalization method used by one of the plaintiff's expert witnesses should at least be considered [as] being a standard method of arriving at value.

It might further be pertinent to point out that the subdivision (a) (knowledgeable buyer/willing seller definition of market value) cannot be determined until after subdivision (c) (existing use, etc.) has been used as a yardstick. It follows that where the assessed value is based primarily on sales of other property, and all the so-called comparable sales are for speculative or development purposes (with the exception of one which was intended for use as a private airport) the formula has not been properly applied.

The trial court here correctly held that the assessors erred in considering foreclosure sales as comparable sales, and held that they erroneously over-valued a restricted use flood plain which comprised a significant portion of the land being appraised. The court erred, however, in approving a valuation which tilted market value in favor of an assumed "highest and best use" to appear from future speculation and development, rather than first determining the criteria for zoning, existing use, and deed restrictions, if any, at which time other pertinent factors may be considered.

Judgment affirmed in part and reversed in part.

REVIEW QUESTIONS

1. This chapter deals with three principal types of taxes affecting real estate. What are these types and what are their effects?
2. List the steps that make up the process of real property taxation.
3. Do most states allow the real estate to be valued only on the way in which it is being used or on the way in which it could best be used? What is the significance of these alternatives?
4. It has been universally accepted that owning one's personal residence creates substantial tax advantages. To which type of tax does this statement refer? What are these advantages?
5. List the various types of business organizations that can be used to own or develop real estate. How is the income of each organization taxed?
6. The Subchapter S corporation may have very limited usefulness as an organization created to own or develop real estate. Why?
7. Investors seeking to use real estate as a tax shelter often build low-income residential housing. What is the tax advantage of doing this?

8. Abbott owns real estate with a fair market value of $75,000 in which he has an adjusted basis of $60,000. Brock owns real estate with a fair market value of $50,000 in which his basis is $40,000. Assume these parties exchanged titles to these properties, with Brock paying $25,000 to Abbott. What are the tax consequences of these exchanges to each party?

9. Recently, the estate tax laws were changed. By 1985, what will be the maximum tax rate applicable to even the largest estate? By 1987, an estate will have to be valued at a certain minimum amount in order to be subject to estate taxes. What will that minimum amount be?

10. A couple purchased a 150-acre farm in 1930 for $2,000. Today that farm is worth over $200,000. An attorney would be wise to advise the couple not to sell or transfer the farm during their lifetimes. Why?

9
General Agency Principles

1. Introduction

Few people have the time and the knowledge to accomplish all their goals; therefore, they hire other people to assist them. These situations are recognized by the law as creating agency relationships which involve a *principal* and an *agent*. Principals are those persons who authorize agents to act on their behalf. Agents typically deal with third parties as they represent the principal's interests. Specific rights and duties of each party result from an agency relationship.

This chapter concentrates on the general aspects of an agency relationship, especially as they apply to real estate sales transactions. The next chapter examines some of the specific applications of these principles to real estate brokerage.

A common issue in agency relationships involves whether a principal and third party are bound by an agreement negotiated between an agent and third party. In addition, issues of liability between the principal and agent are very important. These are among the issues examined in this chapter and the next. However, prior to concentrating on these specific relationships, the scope of the general agency relationship is discussed hinging on the authority of an agent to act on behalf of a principal. Any agent's authority must be either actual or apparent in nature.

2. Actual Authority

The actual authority that a principal gives to an agent may be either expressed or implied. Expressed authority includes any written or spoken agreement between the principal and the agent. Because a written document provides specificity and clarity, it usually is best to define the scope of the agent's authority in writing. Nevertheless, a principal who orally states the agent's responsibility has given expressed authority to that agent. As we shall see, some states require that the authority given by a seller to a real estate agent must be in writing in the form of a listing agreement.

Implied authority can be derived from the expressed authority or from the customs or prior associations of the principal and agent. Implied authority is necessary in order to accomplish the purposes of the agency relationship. For example, if a broker told a salesperson to show a customer a residence, implied in those instructions is the salesperson's authority to drive to the house, to unlock and enter the house, and to present the house's features to the customer. Whether an agent has implied authority to justify certain conduct is narrowly construed.

An agent must act within the authority expressed or implied before the principal can be held liable for the agent's actions. The third party with whom the agent deals has the burden to show that the agent's performance was within the actual authority given or implied before the principal is liable to such third party. Suppose a salesperson orders personal calling cards from a local printing office. Is the brokerage firm liable to the printer for these calling cards? The printer would have to show that the salesperson had the broker's express authority to charge these cards or that this charge was reasonable on the basis of implied authority. If the printer cannot prove that this salesperson had the firm's expressed or implied authority to buy calling cards, the printer probably can collect only from the salesperson.

Sellers and buyers generally limit the actual authority given to a real estate agent. For example, these agents are to locate buyers for sellers or property for sale for buyers. Normally, these principals do not grant their agents actual authority to negotiate and sign a sales contract on their behalf.

3. Apparent Authority

A distinction must be made between the actual authority of an agent to act for a principal and apparent authority. Whereas the existence of actual authority is determined by the principal-agent relationship, apparent authority is based more on the principal-third party relationship. For example, assume that the above-mentioned brokerage firm always has paid for its salespeople's calling cards. In the past, the printer had no trouble collecting from the firm. Now suppose this firm has informed its sales staff that the firm will no longer pay for personal calling cards. Furthermore, assume that the firm failed to notify the printing company it has dealt with of this change in calling-card policy. If a salesperson placed an order for cards with the printer and refused to pay, could the brokerage firm be held liable by the printing company? The answer should be yes. Although this salesperson (agent) lacked actual authority to bind the brokerage firm (principal), the printing company (third party) can recover from the principal because apparent authority existed. In essence, the principal is estopped from denying liability since that principal allowed it to appear to the third party that the agent had proper authority to act.

As applied to a seller-agent or a buyer-agent relationship, the agent's apparent authority will be very limited if not nonexistent. This is because most states require a written document authorizing a real estate agent to enter into a written contract on the principal's behalf. Absent such a writing, the third party should realize there is no apparent (or actual) authority.

4. Ratification

Generally when an agent acts without authority, the principal is not bound by the agent's action. Ratification is an exception to this general rule. If a principal approves or ratifies the unauthorized acts of an agent, that principal is liable to the third party. The third party has the burden of proving that the agent's acts were either authorized or, on the other hand, ratified. The following case is one example when ratification was not proven.

Case 9.1

One of several owners of a parcel of real estate granted an option to Pettit to buy the land. The party granting the option claimed to be the sole owner and did not purport to be the agent of anyone. The other owners refused to go along with the sale. The consideration for the option benefited all the owners in that it had been used to pay expenses connected with the land.

Issue: Is the option binding on all owners? (Has there been a ratification?)

Decision: No.

Reasons: The owner granting the option could not have been an agent of the other owners because an agent's authority to bind his principal on a contract to sell real estate must be in writing according to the statute of frauds. The doctrine of ratification does not apply to an act claimed to have been ratified by a principal unless the original act was done by one who purported to act as an agent for a principal. Here he claimed to be the sole owner.

Pettit v. Vogt, 495 P.2d 395 (Okla. 1972).

Agency Relationships in Real Estate Transactions

5. Introduction

For the purposes of this discussion, examples of agency relationships are limited to transactions involving the sale of real estate, even though similar relationships do exist with respect to the rental and development of real estate. In a real estate sales transaction, several different agency relationships may be created.

First, real estate brokers may hire salespeople to assist in the business of listing and selling real estate. Chapter 10 includes a discussion distinguishing between a broker's and a salesperson's license. For our purposes in this chapter, it is sufficient to understand that a salesperson usually works for or on behalf of a broker. Second, a seller of real estate may list property with an agent. Third, a potential buyer may solicit the aid of an agent in searching for available property.

Throughout this chapter, the general principles of agency relationships are discussed with respect to sellers, buyers, brokers, and salespeople. The first relationship, mentioned above, involves a broker as the principal, a salesperson as the agent, and sellers and buyers as the third parties. In the second relationship, a seller is the principal, a broker or salesperson is the agent, and prospective buyers are the third parties. In the third relationship, a buyer is the principal, a broker or salesperson is the agent, and sellers are the third parties. These latter two relationships will be referred to generally as client-agent relationships. It is important to keep these changing positions in mind as we look at the rights and duties of all the parties involved.

6. Broker-Salesperson

Real estate salespeople generally work for brokers, and their relationship can be established by contract. A salesperson either is an employee or an independent contractor hired by the broker, depending on the extent of control that the broker exerts over the salesperson's duties. The greater the control exercised, the more likely it is that the salesperson is an employee. The status of a broker's sales staff is important for at least two reasons.

First, the laws of agency relationships are more directly applicable to an employer-employee than to a proprietor-independent contractor association. Contracts that employees enter into within the scope of their authority are binding on the principal-employer. Any third person who is injured by an employee while that employee is acting within in the scope of employment can recover from the principal-employer. Contracts signed by an independent contractor or injuries caused by such person are not binding on or attributable to the proprietor. In essence, an independent contractor is hired to produce a specified result without being told how to accomplish that goal.

The second reason to distinguish whether members of a real estate sales staff are employees or independent contractors concerns the broker's responsibility to file government reports. A broker must file reports related to social security, tax withholding, unemployment compensation, and workers' compensation for employees. These reports are not required if the sales staff consists of independent contractors.

7. Seller-Agent

In this section and the next, use of the terms "broker" and "salesperson" should be considered interchangeable unless otherwise indicated. The word "agent" is used in a broad sense and is synonymous with either "broker" or "salesperson." In other words, the real estate agent who deals with sellers and buyers may be a broker or a salesperson. Throughout the following sections, whenever the text states an agent is liable to a client, remember that the agent could be either a salesperson or a broker. In addition, as long as a salesperson is acting within the scope of authority granted by a broker, that broker is liable for the salesperson's actions.

If the real estate is not for-sale-by-owner, sellers generally give the real estate agent actual authority to sell their property. This authority is expressed in the various types of listing agreements discussed in the next chapter. Although many states allow the listing agreement to be oral, a written contract is preferable to help clarify the relationship and to establish the duties owed. Indeed, in about twenty states an agent is not entitled to a commission unless the listing agreement is in writing. For more on this writing requirement, see Section 6 of the next chapter.

Real estate agents who exceed their authority are personally liable for their actions. Typically, these agents are considered to be independent contractors. This status means that the agent cannot bind the principal (seller or buyer) to a contract signed by the agent. Furthermore, any injuries that the agent causes to third parties are not the principal's responsibility.

Generally, an agent may not delegate to another agent the duty to represent the seller. However, it is best to permit brokers to employ the services of their salespeople to assure a wider exposure of the property. Thus, the listing agreement should include a provision allowing the broker to delegate duties to that broker's sales staff.

8. Buyer-Agent

Potential buyers of real estate often create legal relationships with real estate brokers or salespeople. The buyer usually seeks the aid of an agent in locating property for sale. As a general rule, the buyer-agent relationship comes into existence much more informally than does the agent-seller relationship. Therefore, the agent and buyer seldom sign a written agreement governing their obligations. Indeed, an anxious buyer may enlist the aid of several different agents at the same time. A buyer can initiate an agency relationship by simply walking into a brokerage firm's office or calling an agent on the telephone inquiring about available property. How an agent who appears to be representing the buyer is compensated is discussed in Section 15, below.

9. Termination

If the principal and agent do not specify a date when their relationship will terminate, their agency is terminable at the will of either party without liability for damages caused. Even if the relationship is to last for a stated time period, courts generally will not specifically enforce an agency relationship. In other words, either the principal or the agent can terminate the agency with the understanding that that party will be liable for any damages caused by the premature termination.

Most legal issues concerning termination of real estate agency associations involve the seller-agent relationship. Since the buyer-agent relationship likely is entered into informally, the termination of such relationship is less complicated. The desired conclusion of either relationship is the successful negotiation of a purchase and a sale. However, if a purchase does not occur, the buyer may decide that the agent's assistance is no longer needed. As long as the buyer does not purchase property first shown by that agent, the buyer has no liability to the agent. Normally, an agent will be liable to a buyer for wrongful termination only when that agent has been paid and has failed to perform reasonably the duties promised.

If the property is not sold, the time period provided in the listing agreement governs the duration of the seller-agent relationship. At the expiration of that term, the relationship terminates. To avoid any potential problems associated with terminating the agency relationship when the property does not sell, a time period or term of the relationship should be specified in the listing contract. If such a date is not stated, the agency relationship lasts for a reasonable time. The most common reasonable term for listing agreements seems to be three to six months, depending on the type of property listed. These periods are commonly applicable to residential and commercial property, respectively. What period of time is reasonable often must be determined by the court; therefore, absence of a specific term in the listing agreement may result in expensive litigation.

The agency relationship between an agent and a seller can end by their mutual agreement. Some circumstances make it more beneficial to all parties to relieve the agent of the duties to locate a buyer and to relieve the seller of the duties owed to the agent. Such agreement to terminate the relationship may occur prior to the expiration of the listing agreement's term.

Even without the consent of the listing agent, the seller can at any time revoke the listing agreement which established the agency relationship. This revocation releases the agent from all duties to actively locate a buyer. Of course, the seller who breaches the listing agreement is liable to the agent for damages; however, the determination of an agent's damages may be rather difficult. It seems clear that an agent is not entitled to a commission when the seller revokes their agreement unless that agent already had found a ready, willing, and able buyer. To avoid liability upon termination of a listing agreement, the seller must act in good faith at all times.

Case 9.2

Snyder, a licensed broker, entered into a contract in May 1972 to sell real property belonging to Schram. In May 1973, Schram terminated the agreement. The Post Office bought the property in August 1973. Snyder had been negotiating with the Post Office prior to the time his listing agreement was terminated. Snyder commenced this action to recover a sales commission.

Issue: Was Snyder entitled to a commission?

Decision: No. The agreement was not terminated for the purpose of avoiding payment of a commission.

Reasons: Even though Schram could rightfully terminate the listing agreement in 1973, Snyder could nonetheless recover a commission on the subsequent sale of the land if Schram terminated the agreement in bad faith, i.e., to avoid payment of a commission to Snyder. The Post Office had notified Schram in April 1973 that it was not at that time interested in his property. Thus, when Schram terminated the agreement in May, he felt that nothing was being accomplished with regard to a sale to the Post Office. His termination was therefore in good faith.

Snyder v. Schram, 577 P.2d 935 (Ore. 1978).

Since the listing agreement creating the seller-agent relationship is a contract personal to the parties, loss of contractual capacity by either party terminates the relationship. This loss of capacity may result from death or insanity of either the principal or the agent. Also, destruction of improvements on the listed property should terminate the agency relationship. In summary, the seller-agent relationship can be terminated when

1. The listed property is sold,
2. The term of the listing agreement expires,
3. The parties agree,
4. One party breaches his duties,

5. One of the parties becomes contractually incapacitated,
6. The listed property's improvements are destroyed, or
7. The listed property is taken by the government under the power of eminent domain.

Termination of the broker-salesperson relationship follows the general rules stated at the beginning of this section. That is, either party can terminate the association without liability if it is terminable at will. If these parties have a contract that is to last for a stated time period, courts usually will let either party end the relationship but that party may be liable for any damages the early termination caused.

Fiduciary Duties

10.   Introduction

Generally, an agency also is referred to as a fiduciary relationship. This means that the principal places trust and confidence in the agent's ability and representation. Therefore the agent must always act with good faith, diligence, and loyalty toward the principal's interest. A breach of a fiduciary's duties may occur as a result of the agent's failure to follow the principal's instructions, to keep the principal informed, to account to the principal, and to refrain from negligence. A principal also can breach the duties owed to an agent, as when the principal fails to compensate an agent.

11.   Duty of Loyalty

At the very basis of all agency relationships is the duty of loyalty. This duty means that an agent cannot engage in self-dealing. In other words, an agent cannot take for himself an opportunity that was intended for the benefit of the principal. An agent breaches this duty of loyalty by appropriating any trade secrets or customer lists that are confidential. However, knowledge that an agent gains through experience may be used by the agent after the agency relationship has been terminated. For example, if a salesperson has become acquainted with a broker's customers, there is no law that would prohibit this salesperson from leaving the broker's employment and contacting these customers. Brokers may wish to include in employment contracts a covenant restricting a salesperson from competing with the employer after the termination of the contractual relationship. These covenants will be upheld as long as they are reasonable as to the time period and geographical area of restriction.

The most common breach of the duty of loyalty in client-agent relationships occurs when an agent begins to represent both the seller's and the buyer's interest.[1] This situation is referred to as a dual agency.

In simplest terms, the seller's agent's fundamental responsibility is to find a ready, willing, and able buyer of the property at the *highest* price possible. An agent representing the buyer should attempt to find suitable property at the *lowest* price possible. Obviously, these interests are in direct conflict. Nevertheless, any real estate agent often has the opportunity to represent both the seller and the buyer, an opportunity which would appear to be ideal, since that agent would not have to share the commission. However, this situation, known as a dual-agency relationship, requires the agent to inform both the seller and the buyer that neither of them can expect the agent's undivided loyalty. Consent of all parties must be obtained before the agent continues to represent both sides to a transaction. Even after all parties consent, the agent in a dual capacity must take precautions not to favor one party's position over the other.

The law requires that an agent act for only one principal at any given time. Therefore, a real estate agent's failure to inform all parties that a dual-agency relationship exists can result in (1) that agent losing the entire commission, (2) the damaged party rescinding or cancelling the sales contract without obligation, and (3) the agent possibly having his real estate license suspended temporarily or withdrawn permanently. These dangers of the dual-agency relationship apply not only when the same salesperson represents both seller and buyer. In the following case, a seller and buyer were assisted by different salespeople within the same brokerage firm. The court had to determine whether a dual-agency relationship existed.

Case 9.3

As a real estate broker, Mr. A. R. Hughes employed several salespeople. One of them obtained a listing agreement from Mr. and Mrs. Cecil Robbins. Another salesperson employed by Hughes listed the property of Mr. and Mrs. Hood. During the

[1]Meerdink v. Krieger, page 237.

course of their jobs, these two salespeople arranged for the Robbins and the Hoods to exchange their properties. A formal contract was drafted and signed by both couples. Although the actual sale-exchange between the Robbins and Hoods never occurred, the A. R. Hughes Realty Company sued both couples to recover the commission provided in the sales contract. The Robbins and the Hoods claimed that no commissions were owed because the Hughes Realty Company was acting as an agent of both couples and failed to give notice of this situation.

Issue: Was the Hughes Realty Company involved in a dual-agency relationship that deprived it of commissions?

Decision: Yes.

Reasons: The brokerage firm, not the individual salespeople, acts as the real estate agent. Therefore, this firm was representing both parties in a real estate transaction. A finding that there was no unfairness, misrepresentation, or fraud on the part of the salespeople does not change the existence of a dual-agency relationship. The broker or the salespeople must notify all parties involved in the transaction and obtain their consent to proceed. One principal's knowledge is not enough for the broker to avoid the loss of a commission. Even though the Hoods had been informed of the dual-agency relationship, the Robbins had not been notified. Under these facts, the broker cannot recover a commission from either couple. All principals must have knowledge of, consent to, and acquiese in these double employment situations.

Hughes v. Robbins, 164 N.E.2d 469 (Ohio Ct. Com. Pleas, 1959).

An important reason for discouraging dual agencies, when the parties are not fully informed, concerns the possible abuse of the agent's discretion. Discretionary actions of the agent who favors the seller (or buyer) when loyalty is owed to both seller and buyer necessarily harms the other party. When an agent does not have to exercise discretion or advise either customer, the interests in the seller's and buyer's transactions are not in conflict. Therefore, an agent may act solely as an intermediary in bringing a seller and buyer together. In other words, if the agent is not involved in the contractual negotiations, a dual-agency relationship is not created. Thus, an agent will not jeopardize the right to a commission when all parties are informed of and consent to the dual agency or when the agent simply introduces the seller and buyer and does not actively engage in their negotiations.

12. Duty to Follow Instructions

An agent must obey the instructions given by the principal. It is not the agent's right to question the wisdom of the instructions given. As long as the principal's instructions involve legal activities and no emergency situation dictates an alternative course of action, the agent must follow the instructions.

When a principal expressly authorizes an agent to do an act, that principal is in essence, giving instructions. Therefore it is logical that agents are responsible for staying within the boundaries of actual authority. One who exceeds the authority or instructions given becomes liable for any damages caused by these actions.

In a situation involving real estate sales contracts, an agent who signs on behalf of a seller or buyer without authority is personally liable to the third party and the principal for damages caused. Likewise, a salesperson who fails to obey the broker's instructions is liable for any harm caused to the broker.

13. Duty to Inform

In all agency relationships, the knowledge that an agent gathers from third parties or other sources is imputed to the principal. The reverse is also true: the principal's knowledge is imputed to the agents. From this legal principle concerning the imputation of knowledge between principals and agents arises the important duty to share information.

As with the other fiduciary duties owed, the duty to inform applies to both client-agent and broker-salesperson relationships. Implicitly it is understood in their relationship that the seller must cooperate with the agent to sell the property. Thus, the seller must provide pertinent information to the agent or potential buyer. At all times during contractual negotiations, the buyer and seller must be kept fully informed. In other words, it is the agent's responsibility to relay every offer, counteroffer, or other communication. Failure to keep the client fully informed can result in the agent's liability for the damages caused.

Case 9.4

George Glass, as executor of the estate of Walter Glass, entered into a thirty-day listing agreement with Burkett for the sale of a thirty-acre tract owned by the estate. The asking price for the entire tract was $50,000, and Glass instructed Burkett to sell the property in one tract. Burkett bought the property for himself within the thirty-day period for $40,420. Burkett did not communicate to Glass that he had an offer from a third party to buy 1½ acres of the land for $25,000, nor did Burkett disclose various other offers to buy the whole tract. After he had purchased this land, Burkett sold the 1½ acre tract to the third party for $25,000 and then sold the remaining acreage to another third party for $35,000. When Glass discovered these sales by Burkett, he brought this action to recover both actual and punitive damages for breach of a fiduciary duty.

Issue: Did Burkett breach a fiduciary duty owed to Glass?

Decision: Yes. Glass was entitled to actual and punitive damages.

Reasons: Since there is no question that a fiduciary relationship exists between a broker and his client, Burkett was clearly a fiduciary with respect to Glass. When a fiduciary relationship exists at the time of the transaction and the fiduciary appears to gain personally, the transaction is deemed presumptively fraudulent. This presumption is not conclusive and may be rebutted by the broker's proof that he exercised good faith and has not betrayed the confidence entrusted in him. To overcome the presumption of fraud, the broker must show (1) full disclosure of all relevant data to his client, (2) adequate consideration paid, and (3) competent and independent advice to the client. Since Burkett had not disclosed the offers to buy the property in parcels or in whole, he violated his fiduciary responsibilities to Glass. Because Burkett's actions were intentional, not in good faith, and with knowledge that his own advantage would be a loss to Glass, Glass was also entitled to punitive damages, as well as attorney fees.

Glass v. Burkett, 381 N.E.2d 821 (Ill. App. 1978).

Typically, a buyer must rely on the real estate agent to obtain information concerning the property for sale. If an agent makes a fraudulent statement or misrepresents the property's condition, the buyer can sue either for damages or for rescission of the contract. *Fraud* is present if an agent, (1) with the intention to mislead, (2) makes a false statement, material to the transaction, (3) that is justifiably relied on by his client, (4) resulting in injury to that person. The elements of *misrepresentation* are the same as these of fraud, except that the intention to mislead is not essential. For example, assume an agent listed as residential lots land that was partially on the flood plain. Although this land might appear suitable as a residential site, it would have to be filled in prior to any construction. A knowledgeable agent must inform any interested buyer that substantial work would have to be done before building could commence. An agent has this obligation when in possession of material facts. If the seller misinforms the agent who misinforms the buyer, the agent may not be liable.[2] This duty to give accurate information to a prospective buyer extends to the seller and seller's agent as well as to the buyer's agent.

Case 9.5

During 1972, First Church was planning to build a new church and a retirement home. Dunton Realty, the buyer's agent, was attempting to locate suitable property for this church project and found a tract listed for sale by Sherwood & Roberts, Inc., the seller's agent. Dunton secured a plat describing the property and naming three parcels of land within the tract. Sherwood purposively did not tell Dunton that the property it listed for sale was only one of the parcels. Dunton then pointed out to First Church the boundaries of the entire tract, including the two parcels which were not being offered for sale by Sherwood. Relying on Dunton's representations, First Church entered into a contract to purchase the listed property. The transaction was subsequently closed, and Dunton noticed "for sale" signs on the two parcels which he believed First Church had just acquired. When First Church learned of the misrepresentation of boundaries by Dunton and Sherwood, it brought this action against both of them to recover damages.

Issue: Could First Church recover damages from these two brokers?

Decision: Yes. First Church was entitled to damages.

[2]Nordstorm v. Miller, page 238.

Reasons: A selling agent is liable to a third party for misrepresentation of boundary lines of property offered for sale. The fact that Sherwood did not deal directly with First Church does not absolve it of liability. Dunton was authorized to offer the tract for sale to First Church and in this regard was authorized to transmit to this prospective purchaser the legal description supplied by Sherwood. Because the First Church relied on Dunton's expertise, Dunton also was liable for negligently failing to ascertain the actual property for sale.

First Church of the Open Bible v. Cline J. Dunton Realty, Inc., 574 P.2d 1211 (Wash. App. 1978).

14. Duty to Account

When an agent is entrusted with money, a duty to account to the principal arises. A typical application of this duty to a client-agent relationship occurs when a buyer deposits earnest money with an agent. At the closing or at some other appropriate time, the agent must make this money available as instructed by the principal. Failure to make an accurate accounting results in the agent being liable for damages suffered by the principal. In addition, real estate agents found to have commingled their personal funds with their clients' money likely will have their licenses suspended or permanently revoked.

The duty to account also applies to the broker-salesperson relationship. Whenever a salesperson decides to end an association with a broker, that salesperson must make an accounting to the broker. As the following case indicates, this reporting procedure ultimately is for the public's protection.

Case 9.6

Parkinson was employed as a licensed salesman by Reese Realty until September 1975, when he decided to go into the real estate business for himself. In August 1975 he obtained a listing of real property for sale. Parkinson planned on leaving Reese Realty at the time he obtained the listing, but he did not inform Reese of the listing prior to his departure. He received a $14,200 commission on the subsequent sale of the property. Parkinson received a commission of $10,000 on another sale which was listed with him prior to his departure from Reese Realty. The State Real Estate Commission learned of Parkinson's actions and suspended his broker's license for five months. Parkinson then commenced this action for a determination that his license should not be revoked.

Issue: Should Parkinson's license be suspended?

Decision: Yes. The decision of the Commission was not an abuse of discretion.

Reasons: A real estate broker has ultimate responsibility to the public, and the public has a right to rely on that accountability. The requirement that a salesman who is leaving the employ of a broker turn in to the broker all his listings serves a public-policy purpose of casting accountability on the broker, since not all salesmen leave a broker's employ to become brokers themselves. Thus, even though no harm came to the clients involved, the Commission may discipline a salesman for failure to turn over his listings and contracts.

Idaho Real Estate Commission v. Parkinson, 593 P.2d 1000 (Idaho 1978).

15.   Duty to Refrain from Negligence

Previously it was stated that a principal is liable for the actions of an agent acting within the scope of employment. This concept of placing liability on the principal applies to contract as well as tort (personal- or property-injury) matters. Holding a principal responsible for the negligent acts of an agent is based on the doctrine of *respondeat superior*—"let the superior respond." Normally this doctrine arises in employment situations when the employer has the power to control the employee.

Because a principal may be liable for an agent's negligence, the law places on the agent a duty to refrain from being negligent. In essence, an agent who is negligent breaches this duty and ultimately is liable to the principal for the damage caused. This duty seldom will apply to a client-agent relationship in a real estate transaction, since the agent generally is considered an independent contractor hired by the seller or buyer. Remember, one employing the services of an independent contractor is not liable for the latter's actions.

The duty to refrain from negligence is more applicable in the broker-salesperson relationship, since the salesperson may be considered to be an employee of the broker. To avoid potential liability for a salesperson's negligence, brokers attempt to establish their salespeople as independent contractors. A salesperson's negligence could create issues of ultimate liability in the case of an automobile accident that happens while the salesperson is transporting a buyer-client to view property for sale. The issues to be resolved include: (1) Was the salesperson an employee or an independent contractor? (2) If an employee, was he or she acting within the scope of employment? (3) If yes, was the employee actually negligent? If the answer to the last question is yes, the broker is liable to the third party (a buyer in our example), and the salesperson (agent) is liable to the broker (principal).

16. Duty to Compensate

In all agency relationships, the agent is entitled to be compensated for the services rendered. As between sellers and real estate agents, the listing agreement should dictate the rights and the duties relative to compensation. The various types of listing agreements are discussed in the next chapter.

When buyers deal with real estate agents, various issues on compensation arise. The buyer's responsibilities to a real estate agent employed to assist in a search for available property are less formalized but just as important as the seller's duties, which were mentioned above. Generally, a buyer must abide by any agreement that he may have entered into with an agent. For example, if a buyer agreed to pay a fee to the agent when a sales contract was signed, such agreement would be binding.

Many times buyers will be assisted by agents who will be able to share in the commission paid by the seller. (See Multiple Listings in Chapter 10.) In actuality these agents are treated as subagents for the seller. In this fairly typical situation, the buyer should realize that the agent is not representing the buyer's interest. Likewise, the agent must remember that it will not be possible to represent the buyer's interests without falling into the dual-agency trap.

Regardless of the foregoing situations between buyers, agents, and sellers, a buyer who is shown property by an agent may not feign disinterest in such property and then make arrangements to purchase the same property through another agent or directly from the seller. Such deception would be a breach of the principal's duty of loyalty to an agent.

Finally, a broker's duty to compensate a salesperson is a matter for negotiation between these parties. As with other contractual agreements, it is best to have a written document as evidence of what compensation is due when. Absent a written or oral agreement, courts have stated that a principal (broker) must pay an agent (salesperson) reasonable compensation based on the relevant facts.

Cases on General Agency Principles

Meerdink v. Krieger
550 P.2d 42 (Wash. App. 1976).

Green, J.:

Plaintiffs, purchasers, brought an action against defendant realtors, alleging nondisclosure of a dual agency relationship. Defendants appeal from a verdict in favor of plaintiffs. . . .

Plaintiffs, widowed sisters contemplating retirement, desired to exchange their homes for an apartment house in which they could live and receive rental income. They contacted defendant Glen Bunger, a real estate agent, seeking his advice and expertise to help them find an apartment house in the $80,000 to $90,000 range. Plaintiffs, unknowledgeable in real estate and business transactions, told Mr. Bunger they were depending solely upon him for advice. Unable to find a suitable apartment house, Mr. Bunger suggested that plaintiffs build one. He stated they could expect to receive a total net credit of $46,000 for their homes on a trade with a builder. Mr. Bunger and his employer, Mr. Krieger, d/b/a/ Krieger & Associates, introduced Mr. Johnson, a builder, to plaintiffs who stated their desired $80,000 to $90,000 price range. Mr. Johnson obtained plans which were viewed by plaintiffs who were then presented with an offer to purchase, prepared in Mr. Krieger's office and citing a purchase price of $120,000. Upon inquiry, plaintiffs were told that this figure had to be high to cover unforeseeable problems and, if possible, it would be adjusted downward to allow a small profit over costs. Plaintiffs were reluctant, but a few days later, signed the offer to purchase, relying on Mr. Bunger's statements that the transaction was a "good deal" and that they should pay more so that they could "get more money out of it." This offer was later accepted by Mr. Johnson with the following additional term:

> I agree with the above sale and the foregoing terms and conditions and agree to pay Krieger & Associates, as agent, a fee of $10,000 for services.

Upon receipt of a copy of the accepted offer, plaintiffs did not notice the additional recitation. Thereafter, they attached no legal significance to it but thought, throughout the transaction, that they were obligated to pay a commission.

During construction, plaintiffs continued to express to Mr. Bunger their dissatisfaction with the price and their reservations about going through with the transaction, but he advised them that they could not lose and urged them not to back out. At the suggestion of Mr. Bunger, plaintiffs put their residences on the market through a listing agreement with him, reciting selling prices of $35,000 for Mrs. Meerdink's home and $15,000 for Mrs. Cranfill's home. No results were obtained and plaintiffs ultimately conveyed their properties to Mr. Johnson, receiving a total net credit of $33,000 for both homes. Upon completion of construction, plaintiffs executed a real estate contract for a purchase price of $115,000. Thereafter, Mr. Bunger and Krieger & Associates held an open house to obtain tenants for the apartment units.

Plaintiffs testified that they thought Krieger & Associates and Mr. Bunger were working for them; that it was never discussed how they were to pay defendants for services; that they did not know the builder was paying a commission and that they would not have gone through with the deal had they known the defendants were not working for them. Mr. Johnson, the builder, testified that he knew plaintiffs were relying on Mr. Bunger and depending upon him for advice. It was further apparent to Mr. Johnson that the plaintiffs had very little knowledge of realty transactions and he questioned Mr. Bunger as to whether plaintiffs should be getting into the deal. Mr. Johnson stated that the price was reduced by $5,000 out of kindness and a desire to be fair to the plaintiff "neophytes." He testified the actual cost of the apartment house was around $80,000 and his usual profit was 15 percent. Both parties produced expert testimony regarding the value of the apartment house, ranging from $87,500 to $115,000. . . .

We begin with the fundamental rule that a real estate agent has the duty to exercise the utmost good faith and fidelity toward his principal in all matters falling within the scope of his employment. Such agent must exercise reasonable care, skill and judgment in securing the best bargain possible, and must scrupulously avoid representing interests antagonistic to that of the principal without the explicit and fully informed consent of the principal. Further, the agent must make a full, fair and timely disclosure to the principal of all facts within the agent's knowledge which are, or may be, material to the transaction and which might affect the principal's rights and interests or influence his actions. Consequently, a dual agency relationship is permissible "when both parties have full knowledge of the facts and consent thereto."

Before such consent can be held to exist, clear and express disclosure of the dual agency relation and the material circumstances that may influence the consent to the dual agency must be made.

Whether defendants violated these obligations raises questions of fact for the jury under proper instructions. . . .

Defendants also assign error . . . contending that the only proper measure of damages is refund or forfeiture of the commission paid. We disagree.

An agent is subject to liability for any loss to the principal arising from breach of duty. Breach of duty by an agent may result in forfeiture of the agent's commission as well as liability for damages. . . .

Affirmed.

Nordstorm v. Miller
605 P.2d 545 (Kan. 1980).

Herd, J.:

This is an action to rescind a contract for the purchase of real estate on the grounds of fraud and misrepresentation and to recover punitive damages. The defendants countersued to foreclose the purchase contract. The trial court rendered judgment for the plaintiffs. We affirm.

Carl and Cleo Nordstrom, plaintiffs, entered into a contract with John Lee and Marilee Miller, defendants, for the purchase of 480 acres of farm land located two miles west and ten miles north of Holcomb in Finney County. . . . The purchase price was $480,000.00. . . . Defendants listed the land for sale with Legere Real Estate & Auction Co., Inc. of Hays. . . .

Its newspaper ad read as follows:

480 acres of Prime Developed irrigated land located northwest of Garden City in Finney County, Kansas. Two irrigation wells and approximately 14,000 ft. of underground pipe. This land is flood irrigated and all runs are one-half mile long. New Brick 3 bedroom home, 2,000 sq. ft. with double car garage, also 50' x 70' Machine Shed, new. POSSESSION: To be worked out between buyer and seller. TERMS: Excellent on this Prime Irrigated Farm. "THIS IS ONE THAT YOU HAVE TO SEE TO BELIEVE."

Robert Legere, real estate broker with the company, contacted the plaintiffs and showed Carl Nordstrom the farm on November 23, 1975. Nordstrom, in the company of defendants, inspected the buildings, the land and the two irrigation wells. Plaintiffs again viewed the farm on December 15, 1975 with their family, and paid Legere a $15,000.00 downpayment on the land. Thereafter, plaintiffs sold their home and store in Colorado and moved their belongings and a few pieces of farm machinery to the Millers' farm. The transaction was closed on March 2, 1976, by the signing of a formal contract and the payment of an additional $75,000.00. . . .

During the second application of irrigation water to the milo in the summer of 1976, one of the two irrigation wells went dry. Upon further investigation, Nordstrom found there was insufficient available water to supply either well and the farm could no longer be operated as an irrigated farm due to geological limitations. . . .

Plaintiffs confronted defendants with this information and demanded rescission of the contract and the return of their money. Defendants offered to drill another well at no cost to plaintiffs, change the structure of payments under the purchase contract and defer the next payment due thereunder. The offer was refused and on August 12, 1976, plaintiffs instituted this action for rescission and damages for misrepresentation and fraud against the Millers and Robert Legere and Legere Auction & Real Estate. The trial court granted a motion for summary judgment as to Legere and the case was tried to the court November 9–11, 1977. The court rendered its decision for plaintiffs on April 12, 1978, and ordered rescission of the contract, awarding the plaintiffs $90,000 with interest at the statutory rate to accrue as of the date of the order. The request for punitive damages was denied. The Millers appeal. The Nordstroms cross-appeal against the trial court's actions in sustaining the motion for summary judgment on behalf of Legere and Legere Real Estate & Auction Co., Inc. and in overruling the plaintiffs' request for punitive damages.

We will first consider the cross appeal against Legere Real Estate & Auction Co., Inc. and Robert Legere. Plaintiffs claim Legere fraudulently conspired with Miller to sell the land as irrigated land when in truth it was dry land, incapable of natural irrigation. They claim Legere flatly stated the irrigation water would last a hundred years. They also point out the land was advertised for sale as irrigated land. They claim they were induced to make the purchase by the false and fraudulent representations of Legere and they should be awarded rescission and damages against him. The defendants Legere Real Estate & Auction Co., Inc. and Robert Legere contend all representations concerning the real estate were provided by Miller to Rodney Einsel, a Legere employee. Robert Legere states he used that information in his presentation to Nordstrom and believed it to be true, having no personal knowledge of his own.

The relationship between a principal and a real estate broker is essentially that of agency. We have held that in order for an agent to be liable for fraud there must be a fraudulent intent to deceive. . . .

Legere admits he represented to Nordstrom the irrigation wells were good and would last a long time, but claims he was merely reflecting information furnished by Miller. . . .

All representations made by Legere to Nordstrom were made innocently and in good faith and therefore do not amount to fraud. The trial court did not err in granting summary judgment as to Legere and Legere Real Estate & Auction Co., Inc. . . .

The judgment of the trial court is *affirmed.*

REVIEW QUESTIONS

1. Define and distinguish the following terms:
   a. Principal, agent, and agency relationship
   b. Actual authority and apparent authority
   c. Express authority and implied authority
2. Steven had been employed as a salesman for the Pioneer Realty Company. During his employment, Steven had worked with several people, including Tom Pierson on several deals. Due to his lack of attention to details, Steven's relationship with Pioneer Realty was terminated. Because no announcement was made about this dismissal, Tom continued to work with Steven as a representative of Pioneer Realty. If Steven is negligent and causes Tom damage by having him sign an inaccurate contract, can Tom recover from Pioneer Realty? Explain.
3. In this chapter, we discussed several possible agency relationships that can be involved in a typical real estate sales transaction. What are these relationships?
4. An owner who wished to sell some property entered into an agreement to have Clements Realty represent her. The Haas Agency, representing a prospective buyer, delivered an offer to purchase to Clements Realty, which delivered the offer to the seller. The seller counteroffered by insisting that she retain a security interest in the property sold. In closing the transaction, a security interest was not retained by the seller. She now sues the Haas Agency for breach of its agency obligations to her. Should the seller be successful?
5. List at least five ways in which a seller-agent relationship can be terminated.
6. On July 1, Nance, as a real estate agent, and McDougald, as a property owner, signed a listing agreement giving Nance an exclusive right to sell McDougald's movie theatre. This listing was to last for thirty days. On July 2, McDougald

called Nance and revoked their agreement. Nevertheless, Nance searched and found a ready, willing, and able buyer on July 17. Nance now sues McDougald for the real estate commission provided in the listing agreement. Should Nance succeed? Why?

7. This chapter included six fundamental duties that are implied in every agency relationship. List these six duties.

8. Dayton, a licensed real estate agent, showed Raach, a prospective buyer, resort property on a lake. Dayton told Raach that the property included 107 acres and one-half mile of lakeshore. Raach purchased the resort property and subsequently discovered he had purchased only sixty acres and one-fourth mile of lakeshore. Raach sought damages against Dayton. What is the basis of Raach's claim? Should he be successful? Explain.

9. Jensen owned a trailer park and listed it for sale with Peterson, a licensed real estate agent. Peterson located Beckman, who agreed to pay $45,000 for the trailer park. Rather than informing Jensen of this offer, Jensen offered to buy the trailer park for himself at a price of $35,000. Jensen agreed to this price. Later Peterson sold the trailer park to Beckman for $45,000. When Jensen discovered the true facts, he sued Peterson to recover the $10,000 profit which Peterson had made. Should Jensen succeed? Why?

10. Roger, a licensed real estate agent, received a $1500 check from Catherine as a good-faith deposit to accompany her offer to purchase. Roger had the bank deposit Catherine's check into his business' general operating account. Are there any problems with Roger's actions? Explain.

10

Real Estate Brokerage

1. Introduction

The agency principles discussed in the previous chapter become directly applicable to real estate transactions when a person seeks the assistance of a real estate agent. In this chapter, the term *agent* is used to include brokers and salespeople, unless otherwise indicated. These agents may be of importance to a sale or lease transaction because they possess knowledge and expertise that the typical seller and buyer or landlord and tenant lack.

Real estate agents must be licensed before they can offer their services. The distinction between a broker and a salesperson, and the general licensing requirements for each, are discussed in the next sections. Listing agreements and when an agent is entitled to a commission also are examined. Finally, recent applications of the antitrust laws to the real estate brokerage industry are explained.

Real Estate Licenses

2. In General

Every state and the District of Columbia have mandatory educational or experience requirements for real estate salespeople and brokers. Before these licensing laws were passed by the state legislatures, anyone could engage in the real estate sales business. Because these agents deal with the public, it was decided that some minimal level of competency should be established. Beginning in 1919, real estate licensing laws have become commonplace. New Hampshire and Rhode Island were the last states to adopt licensing requirements, and they did so in 1959.

As a threshold requirement, all applicants for a real estate license must demonstrate that their moral character and reputation within their community are good. Furthermore, the standards that must be met to obtain a real estate license are divided into categories for salespersons and brokers. Generally a salesperson works for a broker, who has greater experience and education than the salesperson.

3. Salesperson's License

The majority of states have established a minimum age of eighteen for a real estate salesperson. The sales license applicant must have completed high school or a course concentrating on real estate principles. The most common educational requirement for a sales license is a course involving thirty hours in the classroom or the college equivalent. This mandatory course should contain material on real estate transactions, legal documents involved, financing the transaction, appraising or evaluating the property, as well as material on ownership interests, land-use controls, agency relationships, and fair-housing laws.

Prior to 1970, each state prepared, administered, and graded the tests for their applicants. However, with the increasing number of applicants and with the need for higher standards throughout the United States, separate examinations for each state became unworkable. Therefore, both the Educational Testing Service of Princeton, New Jersey, and the California Department of Real Estate developed objective tests that are partially uniform for use in all states and partially directed toward specific regulations of the applicant's state. These tests cover some, if not all, of the topics described as the contents of the required educational course. Because each state's requirements for the sales license vary, interested students should contact their local or state realty board for full details on licensing prerequisites.

4. Broker's License

To obtain a broker's license in most states, a person must have gained some experience as a real estate salesperson or completed advanced educational requirements or both. Generally the potential broker needs two or three years of sales experience plus forty-five to sixty hours of in-class instruction. The broker's examination, while similar to the salesperson's test, necessarily goes into greater detail in all the subjects covered. The majority of the states use one of the uniform objective tests. However, since not all states have adopted one of the multistate exams, each applicant should find out from local or state realty boards the precise requirements and the kind of test given to obtain a broker's license.

5. Constitutionality of Licensing Laws

People who make their living in the real estate sales industry constantly seek to make their trade more "professional." State legislatures and courts are concerned with protecting the public from unqualified real estate brokers and salespeople. While raising the minimal prelicensing standards is perhaps the best way to upgrade the licensees, increasing the prerequistes can create a claim of illegality.

For example, applicants who fail to pass the real estate exam might argue they are being discriminated against. Most courts that have addressed these licensing issues hold that if the prelicensing requirements are reasonable in order to protect society's health, morals, safety, or general welfare, the licensing law is valid. Furthermore, the requirements must be reasonably related to the salesperson's or broker's job. An arbitrary requirement that all brokers be over fifty years old would unjustifiably exclude all qualified younger people. Any license requirement that amounts to an unreasonable restraint on a person's choice to enter the real estate sales business without providing protection to the public should be declared unconstitutional.

Whenever a court analyzes the constitutionality of a licensing regulation, it should address the following questions:

1. Does the regulation help protect the public from incompetent brokers and salespeople?
2. Does a rational relationship exist between the regulation and the job to be performed?
3. Can diligent people reasonably satisfy the regulation?
4. Does the regulation cause a disproportionately adverse affect on any minority group?

Affirmative answers to the first three questions demonstrate support for the licensing regulations' constitutionality. An affirmative answer to the fourth question must be balanced against the need for the regulation.

The most common challenge to licensing laws seems to involve nonlicensed persons suing for a commission. Generally, failure to have the proper license precludes the collection of any commission, even though a real estate license is obtained later. Having a real estate license in one state does not necessarily mean that the licensee can properly conduct business in another state.

Case 10.1

Stinson was a real estate broker licensed in Kentucky to deal in real estate transactions. In 1974, he entered into a contract with Potter to sell Potter's coal mining operation located in Tennessee, which included all assets of the operation. When this agreement was negotiated, Stinson did not have a Tennessee broker's license. Another broker consummated the sale of the operation in 1975, approximately one month before Stinson was licensed in Tennessee. When Stinson learned of the sale, he brought this action against Potter for a sales commission.

Issue: Could Stinson recover a commission from Potter?

Decision: No. The contract was unenforceable.

Reasons: The sale of the coal mining operation was a sale of a going business, which Stinson asserted did not require a real estate broker's license. While this is the view taken by courts of several states, this Tennessee court held that Stinson's contract for the sale of Potter's coal mining operation fit within the category of a sale of any interest in land and therefore required a licensed broker to negotiate the sale. Since Stinson was not a Tennessee-licensed broker while negotiating the sale of the operation, he could not recover any commission on its sale.

Stinson v. Parker, 568 S.W.2d 291 (Tenn. App. 1978).

Listing Agreements

6. Introduction

As indicated in the previous chapter, many sellers of real estate have neither the time nor the knowledge to search for prospective purchasers, and they therefore hire real estate agents to assist them. The seller and the real estate broker or salesperson create an agency relationship. The purpose here is to examine how the seller-agent relationship is created.

Sellers of real estate who seek the aid of an agent generally give that agent actual authority to locate buyers for their real estate. This authorization normally is expressed in a written document called a listing agreement. All the essential requirements of a binding contract must be present for the listing agreement, which is contractual in nature, to be enforceable. Approximately twenty states (including Alaska, Arizona, California, Florida, Idaho, Indiana, Kentucky, Michigan, Montana, Nebraska, Nevada, New Jersey, New Mexico, New York, Ohio, Oregon, Rhode Island, Texas, Utah, Vermont, Washington, and Wisconsin) require listing agreements to be in writing. Even in those states that permit oral listings, a written contract is preferable to help clarify the relationship established and the duties owed. The following case demonstrates why all listing agreements should be in writing.

Case 10.2

Howard, a real estate agent, noticed a newspaper announcement that a new federal courthouse was scheduled to be built in his city. Upon seeing this announcement, Howard contacted a number of people who owned property which might serve as a site for the courthouse. Among those contacted was Summersett, with whom Howard spoke by phone three or four times. There were never any express words between the parties whereby Summersett agreed to have Howard act as his agent or to pay Howard a commission. The parties never agreed to the terms of a sale of Summersett's property. When Summersett later sold the property to the federal government under threat of condemnation, Howard played no part in arranging that sale. Nonetheless, Howard brought this action to recover a commission when he discovered the sale.

Issue: Was Howard entitled to a commission?

Decision: No. There was no listing agreement.

Reasons: In order for there to be a binding listing agreement, there must be a mutual manifestation of assent to the terms. The purchase price is considered an indispensable term of a binding contract. No sales price was ever set by Summersett and communicated to

Howard. Therefore, there was no listing agreement, and Howard was not entitled to a commission.

Edens v. Laurel Hill, Inc., 247 S.E.2d 434 (S.C. 1978).

A listing agreement sets forth a description of the property, the asking price, the duties of the agent, the extent of authority given, and the rights of the agent to a commission. There are various forms of listing agreements, each with a different legal impact. The more common types of agreements are the open listing, the exclusive-agency listing, the exclusive-right-to-sell listing, and the multiple listing. These listing agreements create certain obligations between the agent and the seller, the extent of which depends on the type of agreement signed. The basic distinguishing factor among these different types of listings consists in the determination of when a commission is due and owing to an agent.

7. Open Listings

By signing an open listing, the seller authorizes an agent to find a willing, ready, and able buyer. Nevertheless, it is clear that the seller reserves the right to authorize any other agent to locate a potential buyer. In addition, the seller may sell the property without the aid of any agent. Under this open-listing agreement, the agent is entitled to the stated commission only if a buyer is successfully brought to the seller. An agent under an open listing would not receive any commission if either another agent or the seller sold the property.

The language commonly used to establish an open-listing agreement might appear as follows:

Seller and Agent understand and agree that this is an open-listing agreement and Seller reserves the right to sell the property himself or through any other agent without payment to Agent of the commission established herein. Agent shall be entitled to such commission only in the event that

(a) Agent procures a prospect ready, willing, and able to purchase the property on the terms established herein;

(b) Agent procures a buyer who does in fact purchase the property; or

(c) the property is sold, leased with an option to buy, or otherwise transferred, by Seller or any other person, at any time during this listing agreement or within two (2) months after its termination, to a prospect first submitted, directly or indirectly, to Seller by Agent.

This open listing has its advantages and disadvantages. The sellers have a great deal of flexibility under this agreement, since they are not limited to using only one agent. However, a disadvantage to the sellers arises from the agent's lack of incentive to concentrate on selling the property under an open listing. Since real estate agents have no assurances of receiving any compensation when they enter into an open listing, the use of this type of agreement may be discouraged by some agents.

8. Exclusive-Agency Listings

The exclusive-agency listing differs from an open listing in that the seller cannot authorize another agent to find a buyer as long as the agreement is effective. Despite the limits placed on the use of additional agents under an exclusive-agency listing, the seller reserves the right to sell the property without becoming liable to pay the agent a commission.

An exclusive-agency listing agreement will contain a paragraph similar to the following:

> Seller and Agent understand and agree that this is an exclusive-agency listing, and Seller reserves the right to sell the property himself without payment to Agent of the commission established herein. Agent shall be entitled to such commission in the event that
>
> (a) Agent procures a prospect ready, willing, and able to purchase the property on the terms established herein;
>
> (b) Agent procures a buyer who does in fact purchase the property;
>
> (c) the property is sold by any broker during the term of this agreement; or
>
> (d) the property is sold, leased with an option to buy, or otherwise transferred, by Seller or any other person, at any time during this listing agreement or within two (2) months after its termination, to a prospect first submitted, directly or indirectly, to Seller by Agent.

The exclusive-agency listing may seem most beneficial to sellers, since they have an agent acting as their exclusive agent and can sell their property themselves without becoming liable for the commission. However, the agent may not be totally dedicated to advertising this property, since all rights to the commission are lost on a sale-by-owner transaction. To avoid this possibility, agents have devised the next type of listing agreement.

9.   Exclusive-Right-To-Sell Listings

An exclusive-right-to-sell agreement may be the most common type of listing contract used today. A seller who signs this type of listing will be subject to terms similar to the following:

> Seller and Agent understand that this is an exclusive-right-to-sell listing. Agent shall be entitled to the commission established herein in the event that
> (a) Agent procures a prospect ready, willing, and able to purchase the property on the terms established herein;
> (b) Agent procures a buyer who does in fact purchase the property;
> (c) the property is sold by anyone, including Seller, during the term of this listing; or
> (d) the property is sold, leased with an option to buy, or otherwise transferred, by Seller or any other person, at any time during this listing agreement or within two (2) months after its termination, to a prospect first submitted, directly or indirectly, to Seller by Agent.

By this language the listing agent is guaranteed a commission regardless of whether that agent sells the property or whether another agent or the seller does.[1] Of course, this exclusive right to sell lasts only as long as the listing agreement states, typically three months. This time period usually is shorter than that provided in an open or exclusive-agency listing. Under an exclusive right to sell, the listing agent has the greatest incentive to promote the availability of the property, since receipt of a commission is assured if the property is sold. Often this exclusive-right-to-sell listing is also the most advantageous to the owner, since the agent is encouraged to locate a ready, willing, and able buyer as quickly as possible.

10.   Multiple Listings

Frequently an exlusive-right-to-sell listing will be obtained by an agent who is a member of a multiple listing service (MLS). A local MLS is an association of real estate brokers and salespeople who agree that all the

[1]Wade v. Austin, page 262.

listings they obtain will be shared with one another. The concept of multiple listing services has been subject to litigation. As long as all local brokers and salespeople are permitted to participate in this service, the MLS concept is legal. The litigation involving these services is discussed in detail in Section 19, below.

Pursuant to the typical multiple listing, the listing agent must make the pertinent information available to all other MLS members with a specified time period after the listing agreement is signed. Through a MLS, the sellers' properties get the greatest exposure, and potential buyers usually have access to the bulk of all properties for sale.

A multiple listing usually is a variation of an exclusive-right-to-sell agreement, under which the listing agent might typically receive forty percent of the total sales commission. Suppose that an agent other than the listing agent assists the buyer. Two agents are then involved in the potential sales transaction. If the buyer's agent completes the required acts, that agent receives the remainder of the commission. Today, the going real estate commission is generally 7 percent of the property's sale price. Thus, if the agreed-upon split is forty-sixty and the seller's and the buyer's agents are different, each will receive 2.8 percent and 4.2 percent, respectively, of the selling price.

For example, a seller grants a multiple listing to the Stevens Realty Company covering a house to be sold for $60,000. Pursuant to the multiple listing, the Baxter Realtors find a buyer who agrees to pay the asking price. Under a forty-sixty-split agreement with a 7 percent commission rate in effect, Stevens will receive $1680 and Baxter is entitled to $2520 of the total commission ($4200). It is possible, of course, that the seller's agent may find a buyer for property under a multiple listing. In such cases, the listing agent must be careful to represent only the seller's interest to be entitled to receive the entire commission. Representing the buyer's interests can place the agent in the hazardous position of being involved in a dual-agency relationship, as was discussed in the previous chapter.

11. Net Listing

In a net-listing agreement, the seller indicates that he must receive a stated amount for the real estate sold. Any amount in excess of the seller's price for which the agent can sell the property is the commission. For example, a seller may list a house for $60,000 under a net-listing agreement. If the agent procures a buyer at the price of $65,000, the agent's commission is $5,000. If the price is $80,000, the commission becomes $20,000. This net listing generally is disfavored today because it may encourage fraudulent activities. Indeed, the agent is induced to convince the seller that the real estate being listed is less valuable than a fair appraisal might indicate. Some states actually have made the use of a net listing illegal.

The Right to a Commission

12. Introduction

Most real estate agents make their living by earning commissions on sales or lease transactions. Therefore, a fundamental requirement in the real estate brokerage industry is to know when a commission is due and owing. Usually the listing agreement defines what performance is sufficient to earn a commission. Normally a commission is payable when the agent either procures a ready, willing, and able buyer or sells the property. The following sections discuss these aspects of the listing agreements, including procuring and on-sale clauses. The troublesome areas that might cause an agent to lose a commission are also considered.

Through an agreement among local real estate agents, the commission paid by the seller may be divided between the listing agent and the buyer's agent. The amount of the commission normally is established in the listing agreement, of which, as just discussed, there are several types. Indeed, the most important distinguishing factor of these agreements relates to when a commission has been earned.

Agents should be aware of the problem of introducing a buyer to the property and losing the commission when the buyer waits to purchase until the listing agreement expires. To avoid this loss of a commission, it is reasonable for an agent to include in the listing agreement a provision like the following:

> Agent shall be entitled to the commission provided herein in the event the property is sold, leased with an option to buy, or otherwise transferred, at any time during this listing agreement or within two (2) months after its termination, by Seller or any other person, to a prospect first submitted, directly or indirectly, to Seller by Agent.

The typical listing agreement expires three months (for residential property) to six months (for commercial property) after it is signed. The period of protection following the agreement's termination must be reasonable. A one-to three-month time period seems most appropriate.

13. Procuring Clause

A ready, willing, and able buyer is one who wants to purchase the property and has the financial capability to do so. If such a buyer is found and agrees to pay the asking price, the agent is entitled to a commission even if the seller refuses to sign or perform a sales contract. This provision is called a procuring clause. A listing agreement, regardless of type, may contain a procuring clause similar to the following: "Agent shall be entitled to the commission provided in the event that Agent procures a prospect ready, willing, and able to purchase the property on the terms established in this agreement."

Case 10.3

Lloyd and Edna Evans desired to sell their property. They employed the services of Fleming Realty and Insurance, Inc., a corporation engaged in providing real estate brokerage services. These parties entered into an exclusive-right-to-sell listing agreement, which contained a procurement clause that required the Evans to pay a commission if Fleming obtained a ready, willing, and able purchaser. The broker located Neal Hasselbach, who signed a standardized purchase agreement offering to buy the Evans' property on the terms specified in the listing agreement. In essence, this document signed by Mr. Hasselbach was an offer to pay the asking price to the Evans. Based on their fears that Mr. Hasselbach was not financially able to purchase their property, Mr. and Mrs. Evans refused to sign a sales contract with this buyer.

Issue: Did Fleming Realty procure a ready, willing, and able buyer such as to entitle it to the agreed upon commission?

Decision: Yes.

Reasons: The evidence at the trial court showed that Hasselbach had a net worth, in cash and property, in excess of $250,000. The proposed contract for the Evans' land totalled $155,840, to be paid by a down payment of $35,000 and ten annual installments of $12,184 each. The jury's conclusion that Hasselbach was financially able to perform this sales contract was reasonable. Since the buyer fulfilled the requirements of the listing agreement's procuring clause, the broker may collect the commission established even though the sale was not closed.

Fleming Realty and Insurance, Inc. v. Evans, 259 N.W.2d 604 (Neb. 1977).

14. On-Sale Clause

Less common is the listing agreement that contains only a commission-on-sale clause. If that provision was controlling, an agent could not receive a commission if the seller refused to sign a sales contract. However, if an agent finds a buyer who offers the asked price without additional conditions placed in the contract, a seller who refuses to accept that offer becomes liable for the commission even though a commission-on-sale clause appears to control. Thus, the distinction between the procuring and the commission-on-sale provisions becomes less clear when a ready, willing, and able buyer offers the asking price.

15. Losing a Commission

Real estate agents must be cautious that their actions do not cause them to lose commissions. An agent may not be entitled to payment if any duty owed to the principal is breached, which may occur if the agent (1) is negligent, (2) is disloyal, (3) fails to follow instructions, (4) fails to keep the principal fully informed, or (5) fails to account for monies received.

Since all agents occupy a fiduciary capacity, any misrepresentation or fraudulent transactions should cause the agent to lose the commission. Any intentional misstatement of a material fact that is justifiably relied upon and results in injury satisfies the requirements of a fraudulent statement. If the misstatement is not made with intent to mislead, misrepresentation results. If an agent refuses to reveal a material defect in the real estate for sale, such silence may be equivalent to a positive misrepresentation or fraudulent statement. Not only do fraud and misrepresentation result in the loss of a commission; the agent also may be liable for any damages that occur.

Perhaps the most common breach of duty occurs when the agent begins to represent both the seller and buyer. Failure to inform all parties that a dual-agency relationship exists creates a breach of the duty of loyalty and the duty to keep the principal informed. Any agent acting as a dual agent, without notifying both the seller and buyer of this dual capacity, may lose the right to a commission.

All of the preceding discussion concerning situations in which a commission is earned or lost is based on the presumption that the real estate agent is properly licensed by the state. Anyone who acts as a real estate broker or salesperson but is not actually licensed is not entitled to a commission. This is true even if the purported agent rendered a valuable service.

Case 10.4

In November 1970, Cardinal Enterprises approached McFarlane regarding the sale of its eight apartment complexes. McFarlane was a C.P.A. who was not licensed to sell real estate. In December, Cardinal and McFarlane executed an agreement whereby McFarlane agreed to undertake to sell the complexes for a commission. McFarlane obtained his real estate license in 1971. McFarlane met with Adams in August 1972 regarding a possible purchase by Adams. Adams at that time said that he had no interest in acquiring the properties. Adams and a group of investors did purchase the complexes, however, on December 31, 1973. McFarlane brought this action to recover a sales commission.

Issue: Was McFarlane entitled to a commission?

Decision: No. The agreement by which McFarlane undertook to sell the property was void.

Reasons: McFarlane was not a licensed real estate agent at the time the agreement was made. Since he was not licensed, the agreement was void and unenforceable. It was not enough that he became licensed later.

Jolma v. Steinbock, 596 P.2d 890 (Ore. App. 1979).

Real estate agents can lose their commission if they interfere with the completion of the transaction. For example, a broker arranged for two parties to trade their real property interests. In return for this service, the broker was to be paid a commission in cash at the closing. When the broker's client indicated that he lacked the cash to pay the commission, the broker told him not to show up at the closing. Because this party did not appear, the transaction was not completed and the broker was not entitled to a commission.

Also, agents must refrain from all illegal activities, or their commissions may be jeopardized. The following sections examine certain situations that have caused some real estate agents considerable trouble.

Antitrust and Other Issues

16. Introduction

The real estate brokerage industry is subject to many government laws and regulations, including antitrust and fair-housing laws, violations of which can result in criminal and civil penalties as well as in loss of a commission. Another area of immense concern to real estate agents should be which of their actions are proper and which amount to the unauthorized practice of law.

The federal and state governments have antitrust laws that regulate the real estate brokerage industry. The federal Sherman Antitrust Act delineates two areas of concern—unreasonable restraints of trade and monopolization—of which the former is the more important for purposes of our discussion. Whether real estate agents are engaged in illegal restraints of trade involves issues of rate fixing and access to multiple listing services.

17. Rate Fixing

Generally real estate agents have enjoyed nearly uniform commission rates. Throughout the country, the standard real estate commission is 7 or 8 percent of the property's sales price. Due to the existence of uniform rates, real estate agents have been accused of rate fixing, which would be a restraint of trade in violation of the federal and state antitrust laws. A criminal violation of the Sherman Act can be penalized by three years in prison or $100,000 or both for an individual and by $1,000,000 in fines for a business organization. Furthermore, the violator is subject to civil lawsuits wherein the plaintiff can recover three times the actual damages suffered.

Before rate fixing can be found illegal, at least two essential elements must be proven. First, it must be shown either directly or through factual circumstances that a group of real estate agents agreed they would charge the same commission rate. Unfortunately for the real estate brokerage industry's public image, these circumstances have been successfully proven in the past. In 1950, the United States Supreme Court held that real estate brokers in the District of Columbia were subject to the Sherman Act. In addition, the Court ruled that commission rates proposed by real estate boards amount to rate fixing when the local code of ethics required members to charge the standard rate.

The second element essential to a federal antitrust violation is that the agents either are engaged in or substantially affect interstate commerce. Because most brokerage firms do not do business that actually crosses state boundaries, they seldom are actively engaged in interstate commerce. Many real estate agents have argued (some successfully) that they could not have violated the federal law prohibiting rate fixing because they do not satisfy this interstate requirement. Governmental lawyers and scholars alike have stated that many agents are subject to federal antitrust laws since they have a substantial impact on interstate commerce. In a recent opinion, the United States Supreme Court agreed with this latter viewpoint.[2]

In addition to the federal Sherman Antitrust Act, most states have laws that regulate these same issues. Therefore, state laws must be consulted concerning these matters even when the agents' impact is entirely intrastate.

18. Interdependency of Agents

Despite the serious penalties for antitrust violations, real estate commission rates have remained fairly uniform. Many people have asked why these rates stay standardized in the face of legal pressures to increase price competition. One answer is the economic factor that real estate agents are interdependent and rely on one another. Through the multiple listing service (MLS), which is normally found in local communities, real estate firms and individual agents often share market information. Traditionally, the MLS calls for the commission to be shared between the seller's and buyer's agents. Since the MLS creates

[2]McLain v. Real Estate Board of New Orleans, Inc., page 263.

an environment for cooperative transactions, any agent would likely hesitate before listing a property at less than the standard commission rate. For example, a property listed at a 4 percent commission rate probably will not be shown by agents who have an opportunity to share a 7 percent commission on the sale of other listings. Although the economic environment of the real estate brokerage industry does create interdependency among agents, which may encourage uniform commission rates, it must be remembered that agreements between brokers and salespeople to fix these rates is a very serious antitrust violation.

19. Access to Multiple Listing Services

In most communities, brokers and salespeople involved in real estate have formed Realtor Boards. *Realtor* is a trade name which can be used properly only by Board members. Most Boards of Realtors have formed a multiple listing service (MLS), as previously discussed. Traditionally, access to MLS information has been limited to the local Board members who joined the MLS. In communities where membership in the local Board of Realtors is not open to all agents, nonmember agents are automatically excluded from sharing valuable MLS information.

Restrictions on joining the local Board of Realtors and on access to MLS information can result in a firm's or individual's inability to compete effectively. This is especially true when there are a few agents in a given community who are deprived of MLS access. The bulk of the courts that have considered the legality of restricting access to a MLS have decided that such restraints are illegal when they are unreasonable. These courts have declared these restrictions to be concerted refusals to deal, which are violations of the Sherman Act's section on restraints of trade as well as state antitrust laws.

20. Fair Housing Laws

In 1968, the United States Congress enacted into law the policy of providing fair housing throughout the United States. This law, which has become known as the Fair Housing Act of 1968, basically prohibits discrimination based on race, color, religion, sex, or national origin with regard to selling, renting, advertising, and financing real property. Discrimination in providing brokerage services is also prohibited.

The Fair Housing Act of 1968 does not apply to an individual, not in the business of selling or renting real estate, who sells or rents a single-family house without the aid of any brokerage service and without discriminatory advertisement. The rental of rooms or units of a dwelling is exempted from this law if the owner actually lives in the house and it is occupied by no more than four families.

Despite these exemptions in the 1968 law, any person still may be liable for discrimination based on race or color when such is related to property interests. The Civil Rights Act of 1866, which prohibits discriminatory action that interferes with a person's right to inherit, purchase, lease, sell, hold, and convey real and personal property, remains in effect today. Therefore, anyone who is not careful to avoid discriminatory practices related to housing faces potential civil liability for those practices.

Anyone who claims to have been injured by a discriminatory housing practice may file a complaint with the Secretary of Housing and Urban Development. These complaints must be filed within 180 days after the discrimination occurred. The Secretary shall investigate the basis of the complaint and shall indicate whether the grievance can be resolved administratively. If the Secretary is unable to obtain voluntary compliance with the Fair Housing Act within thirty days after the complaint is filed, the aggrieved party may file a civil lawsuit in the appropriate court. When a suit is filed, the Secretary shall cease all efforts to obtain voluntary compliance.

As an alternative to the administrative process just discussed, a private person may file suit in the appropriate federal or state court regardless of the dollar amount in controversy. The court has the power to grant any relief it deems appropriate, including temporary restraining orders, permanent injunctions, actual damages, punitive damanges up to $1,000, court costs, and attorney fees to a prevailing plaintiff who is not financially able to pay them.

To bring an administrative complaint or to be a plaintiff in a lawsuit alleging discriminatory housing practices, a person must have standing to sue. In essence, this concept requires that the complainant have a personal interest in the outcome of the litigation. Recently the United States Supreme Court broadened the concept of standing to sue. The result of the following case may have a substantial impact on the number of lawsuits brought against real estate agents asserting violations of the Fair Housing Act.

Case 10.5

This lawsuit, commenced by the Village of Bellwood, a Chicago suburb, a Negro and four white residents of Bellwood, and a Negro resident of neighboring Maywood, was filed against two real estate brokerage firms and nine of their employees. The parties to this litigation are collectively referred to as plaintiffs and defendants, respectively. The individual plaintiffs had consulted with the defendants about purchasing homes in the general suburban area, which included Bellwood. In fact, plaintiffs were not really buyers; they were "testers" attempting to determine whether defendants were engaged in directing prospective home buyers to different areas according to their race. These activities are known as "racial steering." The plaintiffs alleged that defendants "steered" black prospects to an integrated area of Bellwood and "steered" white customers away from this area. Four of the six individual plaintiffs lived within this integrated area of Bellwood. The complaint sought monetary, injunctive, and declaratory relief on the grounds that the Village of Bellwood had been injured by defendants illegally manipulating the housing market to the detriment of the Village's residents.

Issue: Did these plaintiffs have standing to sue for violations of the Fair Housing Act of 1968?

Decision: Yes, except for the two individuals who reside outside the target area in Bellwood, since they have alleged no injury to themselves.

Reasons: To have standing to sue, plaintiffs must show that they have suffered some actual or threatened injury as a result of a defendant's illegal conduct. By enacting the Fair Housing Act of 1968, Congress intended to provide two methods for resolving discriminatory housing practices. First was the administrative complaint to the Secretary of HUD, and second was the filing of a complaint in an appropriate court. Both these procedures were intended to provide protection to the widest possible class of complainants. The Village of Bellwood has standing to sue because racial steering can rob a community of racial balance and stability and thereby reduce property values and diminish the tax base. Those individual plaintiffs who reside within the Village of Bellwood have standing to sue as homeowners, in that the transformation of their neighborhood to a predominantly black community deprives them of "the social and professional benefits of living in an integrated society." In addition, these individuals may suffer a direct economic loss in the decreased value of their homes. The two individuals who reside outside the target area in Bellwood lack standing to sue since they failed to allege any personal injury or loss suffered.

Gladstone Realtors v. Village of Bellwood, 441 U.S. 91 (1979).

21.   Unauthorized Practice of Law

Over the years, many real estate brokers and salespeople have been sued for the unauthorized practice of law. Any agent who is not an attorney but who is acting as one is engaged in the unauthorized practice of law. A finding that an agent is engaged in law practice could result in (1) the sales transaction being unenforceable, (2) the loss of a commission, and, more seriously, (3) a possible contempt-of-court citation, (4) a fine or jail sentence, and (5) the loss of the brokerage or sales license.

What is the practice of law? This question is not easily answered. Agents seem to incur the most trouble when they prepare legal documents. Perhaps the best way to analyze this subject is to look at the agents' activities on a sliding scale. At one end are the agents' functions that are clearly not the practice of law. At the other end are those that clearly are improper. In the middle of this scale lie the functions that are neither clearly proper nor improper.

Typically, courts have allowed agents to prepare listing agreements, offers to purchase, and acceptances. Agents are allowed to draft these documents since they are required to assure that the agent is entitled to a commission. Other contractual devices enter the hazy middle ground. Options and sales contracts may be completed only if the agent fills in the blank spaces on forms which have been approved by a licensed attorney. Despite most agents being allowed to prepare these papers, a contract carefully drafted by an attorney is still best. A contract prepared especially for the particular circumstances in each transaction will help avoid potential misunderstandings between the buyer and seller.

The documents that must be prepared after a sales contract is signed but before the transaction is closed include the title abstract, the deed, and the financial papers such as the promissory note and mortgage instrument. Since these documents affect title to the property in some way, it is best to have them prepared by an attorney. Lawyers, not real estate agents, are trained to evaluate the validity of the title to real property. Nevertheless, several states have allowed agents to fill in the blanks on form deeds or mortgages. These states include Colorado, Idaho, Michigan, Missouri, New Jersey, Texas, and Wisconsin.

All states prohibit real estate agents from preparing documents in transactions in which they are not involved as agents. Accepting money above and beyond the sales commission as payment for drafting skills of any agent is strictly disallowed. Advising parties to a real estate transaction of their legal rights under a provision of any document must be reserved for lawyers.

The unauthorized practice of law is a serious offense. An agent found to be performing the function of an attorney can be held in contempt of court and subject to a fine or confinement or both. Such an offense may also lead to the agent's loss of the right to a commission. Courts have been concerned about the unauthorized practice of law in order to protect the public's interests. Real estate agents are parties intensely interested in the sales transaction. Therefore, a broker who is not legally trained will not likely be able to exercise unbiased judg-

Exhibit 10.1   Practice of Law by Real Estate Personnel

Functions that Are Not the Practice of Law	Middle Ground		Functions that Are the Practice of Law
1. Preparation of listing agreements, offers to purchase, and acceptances for transactions in which broker is involved in an agency capacity	1. Preparation of precontractual documents, such as options and rights of refusal	1. Preparation or filling in blanks on postcontractual documents, such as deeds, notes, and mortgages	1. Preparation of legal document when not otherwise involved in transaction
	2. Filling in the blanks on an approved-form sales contract		2. Accepting monetary reward above sales commission for preparing legal documents
			3. Giving advice about a buyer's or seller's legal rights

ment in preparing important legal documents. The buyer's and seller's interests are best protected by consulting a lawyer who is not financially interested in the outcome of the transaction.

In perhaps the majority of communities throughout the United States, the local bar and realty associations have entered into agreements governing the lawyer-agent interrelationship. If a question arises concerning how the issue of the unauthorized practice of law by real estate agents has been resolved in a particular community, both local associations should be contacted.

Cases on Real Estate Brokerage

Wade v. Austin
524 S.W.2d 79 (Tex. 1975).

The plaintiff, Austin, is a real estate broker licensed in Texas. Defendants, the Wades, listed their property with Austin under an exclusive-right-to-sell listing. After Austin had advertised and shown this property, the Wades sold their property directly to a buyer. The Wades refused to pay a real estate commission to Austin, and he sued. The trial court found that Austin was entitled to a commission under the signed listing agreement. The Wades appealed.

Ray, J.:

. . . Under the contract, appellee had the sole right to sell the property during the listing period, and the contract expressly provided that appellee would be compensated for services rendered in the event of sale, regardless of who sold the property. . . .

Appellants contend that appellee had not endeavored with all reasonable efforts to find a purchaser for appellants' real estate and, consequently, should not be compensated. However, the jury expressly found that appellee did endeavor with all reasonable efforts to find a purchaser for the property, and we have concluded that the record substantiates that finding.

Appellants . . . [next] contend that appellee Austin was not entitled to recover . . . because appellee, Jac A. Austin, was not

the procuring cause of the sale of the real property nor did he produce a purchaser ready and willing to purchase the property on the terms of the contract. . . . However, we are convinced that the "procuring cause" contention is without merit under an "exclusive right to sell" contract. The test is whether the broker rendered services as required by the contract and whether the property is sold during the listing period, regardless of by whom. The purpose of the "exclusive right to sell" contract is to avoid a broker rendering all reasonable efforts to sell a piece of listed property and then encounter the claim of the owner that the broker is not entitled to be compensated because the owners sold the property directly without the broker being the procuring cause. The "procuring cause" contention is tenable under an "exclusive agency to sell" contract but not "exclusive agency with sole right to sell" contract.

It is undisputed that the Wade property was sold to Florence during the listing period, and the jury found that appellee endeavored with all reasonable efforts to find a purchaser for the Wade real estate on the terms set forth in the exclusive listing agreement.

The evidence is undisputed that appellee performed the usual and customary services consistent with reasonable efforts to find a purchaser for the Wade real estate and only failed to perform those services which Wade asked Austin not to perform.

Appellee brought suit for specific performance under the contract asking to be paid for services rendered, as requested and contracted for by appellants. The exclusive listing contract provided, "If said property is sold prior to the termination of this agreement, whether by you, by me, or by any other person, or if the property is sold within 180 days after the termination of this agreement to anyone with whom you or any member of Multiple Listing Service negotiated during the period of this contract and of whose name you have notified me by written notice delivered to me personally or mailed to me at the address

stated below within ten days after the termination of this agreement, in either such event, I agree to pay to you in Dallas, Texas, a commission in cash equal to 6 percent of the selling price. . . ."

The contract for the sale of the real property was consummated between the Wades and Florence, during the ninety day period of the exclusive listing agreement, the property sold and title delivered with the advice of and consultation with appellee Austin and such other service as appellants would allow appellee to perform. The contract between the seller and purchaser of the real estate involved, was fully performed. Appellee had fully performed the obligations required of him under the terms of the exclusive listing agreement (a bilateral contract) and sought the specific performance of that portion of the contract allowing him 6 percent of the sales price for his realtors' commission. Appellants did not breach their contract by revoking the exclusive listing agreement, but only refused to pay the realtors commission. The amount of the attorney's fee having been stipulated between the parties, the liability therefore was established by appellee Austin. . . .

Affirmed.

McLain v. Real Estate Board of New Orleans, Inc.
100 S.Ct. 502 (1980).

McLain filed a class-action suit under the Sherman Antitrust Act on behalf of everyone who had employed real estate agents in New Orleans, Louisiana. The complaint alleged that the board members were guilty of fixing their commission rates. McLain sought treble damages and an injunction.

The defendants filed a motion to dismiss this complaint since their activities were not in the flow of interstate commerce. The district court dismissed the complaint, and the Court of Appeals affirmed. The Supreme Court then granted certiorari.

Burger, C. J.:

... The broad authority of Congress under the Commerce Clause has, of course, long been interpreted to extend beyond activities actually in interstate commerce to reach other activities that, while wholly local in nature, nevertheless substantially affect interstate commerce. This Court has often noted the correspondingly broad reach of the Sherman Act. . . .

The conceptual distinction between activities "in" interstate commerce and those which "affect" interstate commerce has been preserved in the cases, for Congress has seen fit to preserve that distinction in the antitrust and related laws by limiting the applicability of certain provisions to activities demonstrably "in commerce." It can no longer be doubted, however, that the jurisdictional requirement of the Sherman Act may be satisfied under either the "in commerce" or the "effect on commerce" theory.

Although the cases demonstrate the breadth of Sherman Act prohibitions, jurisdiction may not be invoked under that statute unless the relevant aspect of interstate commerce is identified; it is not sufficient merely to rely on identification of a relevant local activity and to presume an interrelationship with some unspecified aspect of interstate commerce. To establish jurisdiction a plaintiff must allege the critical relationship in the pleadings and if these allegations are controverted must proceed to demonstrate by submission of evidence beyond the pleadings, either that the defendants' activity is itself in interstate commerce or, if it is local in nature, that it has an effect on some other appreciable activity demonstrably in interstate commerce.

To establish the jurisdictional element of a Sherman Act violation it would be sufficient for petitioners to demonstrate a substantial effect on interstate commerce generated by respondents' brokerage activity. Petitioners need not make the more particularized showing of an effect on interstate commerce caused by the alleged conspiracy to fix commission rates, or by those other aspects of respondents' activity that are alleged to be unlawful. . . . If establishing jurisdiction required a showing that the unlawful conduct itself had an effect on interstate commerce, jurisdiction would be defeated by a demonstration that the alleged restraint failed to have its intended anticompetitive effect. This is not the rule of our cases. A violation may still be found in such circumstances because in a civil action under the Sherman Act, liability may be established by proof of either an unlawful purpose or an anticompetitive effect.

Nor is jurisdiction defeated in a case relying on anticompetitive effects by plaintiff's failure to quantify the adverse impact of defendant's conduct. Even where there is an inability to prove that concerted activity has resulted in legally cognizable damages, jurisdiction need not be impaired, though such a failure may confine the available remedies to injunctive relief.

. . . On the record thus far made, it cannot be said that there is an insufficient basis for petitioners to proceed at trial to establish Sherman Act jurisdiction. It is clear that an appreciable amount of commerce is involved in the financing of residential property in the Greater New Orleans area and in the insuring of titles to such property. . . . Funds were raised from out-of-state investors and from interbank loans obtained from interstate financial institutions. Multistate lending institutions took mortgages insured under federal programs which entitled interstate transfers of premiums and settlements. Mortgage obligations physically and constructively were traded as financial instruments in the interstate secondary mortgage market. Before making a mortgage loan in the Greater New Orleans area, lending institutions usually if not always required title insurance, which was furnished by interstate corporations. . . .

At trial, respondents will have the opportunity, if they so choose, to make their own case contradicting this factual showing. On the other hand it may be possible for petitioners to establish that, apart from the commerce in title insurance and real estate financing an appreciable amount of interstate commerce is involved with the local residential real estate market arising out of the interstate movement of people, or otherwise.

To establish federal jurisdiction in this case, there remains only the requirement that respondents' activities which allegedly have been infected by a price-fixing conspiracy be shown "as a matter of practical economics" to have a not insubstantial effect on the interstate commerce involved. It is clear, as the record shows, that the function of respondent real estate brokers is to bring the buyer and seller together on agreeable terms. For this service the broker charges a fee generally calculated as a percentage of the sale price. Brokerage activities necessarily affect both the frequency and the terms of residential sales transactions. Ultimately, whatever stimulates or retards the volume of residential sales, or has an impact on the purchase price, affects the demand for financing and title insurance, those two commercial activities that on this record are shown to have occurred in interstate commerce. Where, as here, the services of respondent real estate brokers are often employed in transactions in the relevant market, petitioners at trial may be able to show that respondents' activities have a not insubstantial effect on interstate commerce.

It is axiomatic that a complaint should not be dismissed unless "it appears beyond doubt that the plaintiff can prove no set of facts in support of his claim which would entitle him to relief." This rule applies with no less force to a Sherman Act claim, where one of the requisites of a cause of action is the existence of a demonstrable nexus between the defendants' activity and interstate commerce. Here what was submitted to the District Court shows a sufficient basis for satisfying the Act's jurisdictional requirements under the effect on commerce theory so as to entitle the petitioners to go forward. We therefore conclude that it was error to dismiss the complaint at this stage of the proceedings.

Reversed and remanded.

REVIEW QUESTIONS

1. Define and distinguish the following terms:
   a. Real estate salesperson
   b. Real estate broker
2. A seller sought the aid of a real estate broker to find a buyer for specified property. The broker did find a buyer and helped close the transaction. There-

after, the seller discovered that the broker was not licensed and refused to pay the commission. Can this person who acted as a broker use the courts to collect the stated commission? Why?

3. Define and distinguish the following terms:
   a. Open listing
   b. Exclusive-agency listing
   c. Exclusive-right-to-sell listing
   d. Net listing

4. Mrs. Pansey signed a standard form multiple-listing agreement which gave her real estate broker the exclusive right to sell her property. The MacKnights signed a written purchase-and-sale agreement offering to pay Mrs. Pansey's asking price. The broker signed the purchase-and-sale agreement in the space marked "realtor" and "salesperson." The space for the seller's signature was left blank. While she expressed satisfaction with the contract negotiated, Mrs. Pansey refused to sign the contract. The MacKnights sued, claiming that the real estate broker acted as an agent for Mrs. Pansey and bound her to the purchase-and-sale agreement. Was Mrs. Pansey contractually bound? Explain.

5. Define and distinguish the following terms:
   a. Procuring clause
   b. On-sale clause

6. Henry Dietz granted a listing to John W. Holland, a real estate agent. The listed property had an asking price of $6,000,000. Holland introduced Barr, who signed a contract to purchase the land subject to his ability to obtain an acceptable loan. When Barr failed to secure the needed financing and therefore refused to buy the property involved, Dietz refused to pay Holland the commission stated in the listing agreement. If Holland sued for the commission, should he succeed? Why?

7. As a real estate broker, Denver 1500, Inc., found a buyer who signed a sales contract with the seller. As compensation, the seller was to pay Denver 1500 a 7 percent commission in cash at the closing. The closing was delayed for two days when the seller could not raise the cash to pay the commission. An employee of Denver 1500 told the seller not to show up at the next closing date if he did not have cash to pay the commission. The seller failed to appear at the second scheduled closing, and the transaction was never closed. If Denver 1500 sues the seller for payment of a commission, should it win? Explain.

8 In recent years the United States Government has vigorously enforced the Sherman Act's restraint-of-trade provision as applied to the real estate brokerage industry's uniform commission rates. What are the criminal sanctions for violating this law? The civil sanctions?

9. Lawrence owned a home that had a garage-apartment which he rented. Since this was his only rental property, Lawrence understood that he did not have

to rent to any member of a minority who might inquire about the apartment's availability. Is Lawrence's understanding correct? Explain.

10. Robin, a licensed real estate agent, suggested that a prospective buyer enter into an option contract rather than a purchase-and-sale agreement. Robin advised that the sales price be left blank so that the buyer could lower the price at a later date. Discuss the propriety of Robin's actions.

11

Contracts in the Sales Transaction

1. Introduction

A contract is a legal device used to demonstrate that two or more parties have reached some agreement. Parties to a contract can include individuals, partnerships, corporations, or other business organizations. A contract can be expressed orally or in writing, or it can be implied from factual circumstances or legal situations. To be valid, all contracts must consist of certain minimal elements, including an offer, an acceptance, consideration, parties with capacity, and a lawful purpose. Furthermore, contracts involving real estate generally must be written. This chapter begins with a discussion of these necessary contractual requirements. Also included are types of contracts that relate specifically to the sale of real estate: (1) traditional sales contracts, (2) contracts for a deed, (3) escrow arrangements, (4) options, and (5) rights of first refusal.

Contract Requirements

2. Offer and Acceptance

Before any contract can be created, one person must make an *offer* to another. In essence, an offer is a statement specifying the position of the offer's maker. This party is called an *offeror*. The offeror implicitly states in the offer a willingness to be bound by the stated position. An offer may become an enforceable contract when it is accepted by the party receiving such offer. The receiving party is called an *offeree,* and an *acceptance* should result in a binding agreement. Together, the offer and acceptance form the mutual consent of the parties to be bound by their agreement.

Generally an acceptance must reflect the precise terms and conditions stated in the offer. If such terms are varied by the purported acceptance, no contract is formed. Rather, such an attempted acceptance becomes a *counteroffer.* With a counteroffer, the original offeror and offeree switch legal positions, and a contract may result when a counteroffer is accepted.

3. Consideration

The law requires that an exchange of *consideration* occur before a contract is enforceable. This concept of consideration is often described as incurring a legal detriment or foregoing a legal benefit. For example, assume Sam agrees to sell some real estate to Barbara for $50,000. What consideration is exchanged by these parties? The need for consideration is usually satisfied by the parties making mutual promises to one another. Sam is induced to transfer his real estate ownership to Barbara by her binding promise to pay $50,000. We say Sam receives the legal benefit of money in return for his promise to transfer title. Barbara suffers the legal detriment of having to pay that money. As an inducement for Barbara to pay the $50,000, Sam promises to transfer title to real estate to Barbara. Barbara will receive the legal benefit of ownership, and Sam suffers the legal detriment of foregoing his ownership of the real estate involved.

This analysis represents the consideration found in the typical real estate sales transaction. The seller relinquishes title to real estate in return for money. At the same time the buyer gives up the right to money and receives title to the real estate. Both parties' promises of performance are supported by consideration.

Once consideration is found in a contract, courts seldom will inquire as to the adequacy or sufficiency of the consideration exchanged. As long as the parties to the contract appear to have equal bargaining capabilities, the value of the mutual consideration is not important. Suppose a seller agrees to sell a piece of real estate for $25,000. After a binding contract is signed at that price, the seller would not necessarily be justified in refusing to perform because the property was appraised at $35,000. Only if the seller was taken advantage of could the contract be nullified or rescinded.

4. Competent Parties

In order to have an enforceable contract, the law insists that all the parties involved must have contractual capacity—the mental capability to know and understand what the contract represents. Most commonly, two classes of people are said to lack capacity to contract. First, insane persons (those either declared insane or acting under insane delusions) are protected from people who attempt to take advantage of their mental condition. Because the law cannot separate people with unjust intent from those with good intentions, insane persons can avoid all their contractual obligations. Therefore, these contracts are *voidable,* which means the agreement is binding against the competent party but can be rescinded at the election of the incompetent party. In some states, individuals who have been declared medically insane by a court lack a total capacity to contract. In these situations, an insane person's contracts are *void,* not voidable.

Minors are the second class of people who lack contractual capacity. Although some minors (typically defined as people under eighteen or twenty-one years old) have the intelligence to comprehend even the most complex transactions, the law provides them with protection. Any time before a minor reaches the age of majority and within a reasonable period thereafter, nearly all contracts that the minor has entered into may be avoided by the minor. Some states do not allow minors to rescind a contract until they reach the age of majority. This position seems to be counterproductive toward the goal of protecting minors who enter into contracts.

There are certain types of contracts involving a minor's purchase of necessaries that cannot be avoided. Since real estate is seldom considered a necessary, minors generally lack the capacity to purchase or sell it. Therefore, when one party to a contract involving the transfer of title to a real estate is a minor, that contract falls within the category of a voidable contract. Upon rescission of a voidable contract, the parties must return any consideration that was exchanged. All adults must beware of buying real estate from or selling real estate to a minor, since that transaction subsequently may be undone. Furthermore, adults must realize that a minor retains the right to regain title to real estate even though it has been transferred by the adult who dealt with the minor. The following case is an example of the problems created once a minor owns real estate.

Case 11.1

Oswell Ware, a minor, conveyed real property which he owned to his brother, Colley Ware. Colley then mortgaged the land to Mobley, who subsequently purchased the property at a foreclosure sale. Mobley was without notice that Colley had obtained the land from a minor. Oswell brought this action to establish that he was the owner of the land.

Issue: Was Oswell the owner of the land despite having conveyed it by deed?

Decision: Yes. Oswell may avoid the conveyance, since it was made during his minority.

Reasons: The right of an infant to avoid his contracts is an absolute and paramount right, superior to all equities of other persons, and may therefore be exercised against innocent purchasers from the minor's grantee, although they bought bona fide and without knowledge that their title came through an infant. In order to give vitality to the doctrine that an infant is incapable of irretrievably alienating his real property, it is necessary to hold that he can pursue his rights even as against an innocent purchaser. Therefore Oswell may avoid the conveyances to Mobley and Colley, even though Mobley was a bona fide purchaser.

Ware v. Mobley, 190 Ga. 249, 9 S.E.2d 67 (1940).

---

5.   Legal Purpose

A valid contract must have as its ultimate purpose some legal act or function. Any illegal means that must occur to achieve a lawful end also results in a void or unenforceable contract. Contracts involving real property seldom have illegal intentions; therefore, this essential element is usually less crucial than those requirements already mentioned.

One example of contracts that are illegal is agreement between a seller and a real estate agent whereby the stated commission amounts to rate fixing. This antitrust violation is discussed in more detail in

Chapter 10. Under any agreement that includes an illegally fixed commission, the real estate agent is not entitled to that commission. In addition, the agent may be guilty of a criminal violation as well as liable for monetary damages.

6. Statute of Frauds

Contracts may either be implied or expressed: expressed contracts may be oral or written. However, all contracts involving land or items attached to the real property must be in writing before a court will enforce them.[1] The original statute of frauds, which was enacted by the British Parliament in 1677, stated that certain contracts had to be written to be enforceable. The Statute's purpose was to remove the likelihood that one party could claim an oral contract existed when no such agreement did exist. Contracts involving real estate were required to be written by the original statute of frauds. Every state in this country has adopted some version of the statute of frauds that includes nearly all real estate contracts.

Contracts involving real estate must be written in order to minimize the possibility of a court being defrauded or tricked into ruling improperly when the subject matter is valuable real estate. The required writing does not have to be a formally drafted document. Indeed, any written words that indicate the parties' positions and is signed by the parties against whom enforcement is sought satisfies the statute of frauds. For example, writing on a piece of paper "I agree to sell my house to Timothy Vance for $70,000" is a contract enforceable by Mr. Vance if the paper is signed by the house owner. Of course, it is assumed that this owner had only one house; otherwise, it would not be clear what property the phrase "my house" meant. As stated in Chapter 1, an adequate written description of the real property being sold is essential. At times, courts have found that an enforceable real estate contract exists by reading two or more documents together.[2]

The writing requirement for real estate contracts does not prevent enforceability if the parties have partially performed their oral agreement. This partial-performance exception exists if a court can determine from the parties' actions what their intentions were. Generally,

---

[1]Contracts involving the sale of timber and crops may be oral and remain binding. The rules for these types of contracts are found in the Uniform Commercial Code. Each state's law should be consulted regarding the requisites of these contracts.

[2]Jones v. Olsen, page 291.

some payment plus possession by the buyer and physical, valuable improvements by that buyer point towards the existence of some kind of contractual understanding. However, the partial payment of the purchase price by the buyer or the payment of some expenses incurred by the seller are not sufficient to replace a written contract.

Case 11.2

A contract was drafted representing Baker's agreement to purchase farmland from Freeman. However, neither of these parties signed the contract. Baker failed to go through with the deal, and Freeman brought this action for damages incurred in attempting to close the deal, including survey and attorney fees.

Issue: Was there a valid contract between Baker and Freeman?

Decision: No. Accordingly, Freeman was not entitled to damages.

Reasons: An oral contract for the sale of realty is void under the statute of frauds. The statute of frauds, however, does not extend to the situation where there has been such part performance of the contract that the court can understand what the parties had agreed. The part performance must be sufficient to prevent any fraudulent result. In order to come within this part-performance exception, a party to the contract must perform some act essential to the performance of the contract which results in loss to him and benefit to the other party. The mere fact that one party relied upon the performance of the agreement but with no loss to him or benefit to the other party is not sufficient to take a contract out of the statute of frauds. The expenses incurred by Freeman were with a view toward consummating a sale, but expenses incidental or preparatory to performing a contract do not constitute part performance. The contract thus was void under the statute of frauds.

Freeman v. Baker, 248 S.E.2d 298 (Ga. App. 1978).

Because of the requirement that contracts involving land be in writing, parties to these agreements should be aware of the *parole evidence rule*. This substantive rule of law does not permit oral testimony about the oral negotiations that lead to a written contract. In other words, courts generally hold that all negotiations are merged into the written contract. Due to the parole evidence rule, all parties to a written contract must read their contract very carefully to make sure that it properly reflects their agreement. While the parole evidence rule prohibits oral testimony about the negotiations prior to the original written contract, it does not disallow oral statements about how a written contract was subsequently modified.

Traditional Sales Contract

7. Introduction

As indicated previously, a very common method of transferring ownership of real estate is through the sales process. Contracts representing agreements between two or more parties to sell and buy real estate are, in essence, gap fillers. Title or ownership of land is not transferred until the transaction is actually closed. (Title closings are the subject matter of Chapter 13.) The sales contract's purpose is to provide the rules governing the parties' rights and duties between the time the contract is signed and the transaction is closed. The following sections examine the methods of formalizing the typical sales contract and some of the basic provisions of that standard contract.

8. Negotiating the Contract

In a sale of personal property, a buyer and seller usually discuss orally what they are willing to pay and accept. Once a price and other terms are agreed upon, a valid, enforceable contract may exist. A sale of real estate is not so simple. Due to the required formalities of a written contract, parties to a real estate sale are more likely to have carefully thought out the sale or purchase and their obligations under such a transaction. These parties traditionally conduct their give-and-take sessions by exchanging written offers and counteroffers. Written offers are used in the negotiating stage so that a binding writing will exist if either party decides to accept the other's offer.

The parties to the sales transaction or a real estate agent, if one is employed, may use one of two methods during negotiations between a seller and a buyer. The first method is a two-step or binder approach to a formal sales contract. In step one, the buyer would sign a written offer to purchase, which would be delivered to the seller. This offer to purchase would name the parties involved, describe the property, indicate the amount of earnest money deposited by the buyer, state the price being offered, list any conditions the price was based on (such as the seller leaving the washer and dryer or painting the outdoor woodwork), and provide how long the offer will remain open for acceptance.

If this offer is unacceptable, the seller could ignore it or cross out the parts disagreed with and submit it to the buyer as a counteroffer. However, a seller who decided to accept the buyer's offer to purchase, could sign in the appropriate spot. Upon this acceptance, a binding agreement usually is formed. Indeed, an offer to purchase that has been accepted often is called a *binder*. This means that the buyer and seller are legally bound by what they have written, unless they state otherwise. In fact, these parties can specify that their agreement will be binding only when a formally drafted contract is signed. In no situation should a binder, which is merely the first step, be relied upon to resolve any potential disputes between the parties.

Step two involves having a lawyer draft a formal sales contract. This sales contract is necessary to provide for what happens in the transaction upon certain events, such as the buyer's inability to obtain adequate financing or the destruction of the property. Since it is merely a negotiating tool, the offer to purchase does not specify the parties' rights and duties concerning the earnest money deposit, the prorating of taxes, the type of deed, the inspection for pests, or the payment of an agent's commission, if any. These conditions and events must be foreseen and considered in preparing the sales contract; therefore, it is best to have an attorney, who is legally trained in the real property area, draft the contract.

Most states allow real estate agents to fill in the blanks on form sale contracts that have been approved by the state bar association or by a qualified attorney. Filling in the blanks on contractual forms provides the agent with the ability to formally bind the buyer and seller in one direct step. For example, a real estate agent could have the buyer make an offer by signing a completed standardized-form sales contract. If the seller is agreeable to the offer made, the seller's signature on the contract would represent acceptance and, at the same time, create an enforceable contract that hopefully provides for all possible contingencies.

9.   *Common Provisions*

Whether a real estate sales contract is drafted by an attorney or the parties use a standardized form, several key provisions, essential to assure that the transaction does not terminate prior to the transfer of title, should be included in the agreement. A well drafted contract will provide all the answers to the questions that arise during the time gap between reaching an agreement and the closing.

The first paragraph of the contract states that its purpose is for the purchase and sale of real estate. Then the names and addresses of the parties are stated.

A. PROPERTY DESCRIPTION AND FIXTURES

The next part of the sales contract states what property is being sold. This description must be sufficiently accurate to inform all those concerned what property is involved. While precise legal descriptions, as required in deeds, are not absolutely necessary to make the contract binding, the most accurate description is preferable to avoid dispute over the property. Reference to the city or county plat helps assure the property's location beyond simply giving a street address.

As defined in Chapter 1, fixtures are items of personal property which were once movable but have become attached to the land or to permanent improvements. A clause in the contract should provide that fixtures will remain on the property and title to them will pass to the buyer. The following is a typical provision relating to fixtures.

> Included as part of such property are all fixtures unless otherwise stated. Such fixtures include, but are not limited to, all lighting fixtures and TV antenna attached thereto; all heating, water heating, and plumbing equipment therein; and all plants, trees, and shrubbery now on the property.

Other fixtures that may be specified include carpets, draperies, drapery rods, or anything else the parties may stipulate.

B. PURCHASE PRICE

The traditional sales contract should state the purchase price and how it is to be paid. Such a provision could be like the following:

> The purchase price of this property shall be Sixty-two Thousand Dollars ($62,000), to be paid as follows:

(a) Buyer has paid in escrow One Thousand Dollars ($1,000), as earnest money, to be applied as part of the purchase of this property at the close of the transaction. If this sale, due to Buyer's default, is not consummated, then this earnest money shall be forfeited to Seller unless provided otherwise. In the event the sale is not consummated for reasons other than the default of the Buyer, this earnest money is to be refunded to Buyer. The forefeiture to Seller or return to Buyer of this earnest money shall not affect in any way either party's claims for damages or other remedies as a result of the failure to consummate this sale.

(b) The balance of the purchase price shall be paid from the proceeds of a conventional loan for a period not less than twenty-five (25) years at a rate of interest not greater than thirteen percent (13%). This loan shall be ninety percent (90%) of purchase price.

(c) Buyer agrees to pay all closing costs related to this loan.

(d) The balance shall be paid in cash at closing.

(e) If Buyer fails to secure adequate financing as provided herein, this contract may be cancelled at the Buyer's option.

The buyer usually is required to make a monetary deposit to demonstrate good faith. What is to be done with this deposit, called *earnest money,* must be stated in the sales contract. Normally, the earnest money is applied to the purchase price.

Due to the high cost of real estate, most buyers intend to finance all or part of their purchase. If the buyer, in our example, was not able to borrow $55,800 (90 percent of the $62,000 purchase price) and was still responsible under the contract, his or her financial position probably would be very poor. Therefore, it is of paramount importance that the contract be conditioned on the buyer's ability to obtain adequate financing. At all times the buyer must act in good faith to secure the financing required in the contract.

C. Title

The next paragraph of a sales contract concerns the type of deed to be delivered to the buyer by the seller. A general warranty deed, which is the most common, requires the seller to provide title to the property that is free from all restrictions except those specified. Such restrictions may include zoning ordinances affecting the property, general utility easements, subdivision covenants, and any other ownership encumbrances that are recorded.

This paragraph normally requires the buyer to search the public records for any title defects. The method and responsibilities of searching a legal title to real property and the ways of protecting that title are discussed in Chapter 12. Essentially, the buyer is required to discover any problems associated with the seller's title and give the seller written notice of these defects. Unless excused by the buyer, the seller must resolve these defects in the title or the contract is no longer binding. A typical contract clause that fulfills this requirement follows:

> Seller agrees to furnish good and marketable fee simple title to this property, as evidenced by a warranty deed. Buyer shall have a reasonable time to examine title to this property. If Buyer finds any legal defects to the title, Seller shall be furnished with a written statement thereof and given a reasonable time to correct any defects. If Seller fails to satisfy any valid objections to the title, then at the option of the Buyer, upon written notice to Seller, this contract may be cancelled and shall be null and void. Seller's warranty deed shall be subject to all easements and restrictions of record. It is agreed that "a reasonable time" means such a time period that would permit this transaction to close on or before the date provided in this contract.

D. ESCROW AND PRORATION

An escrow arrangement, whereby the buyer's earnest money and the seller's warranty deed are to be held by a third party until the sale is completed, may be established in some sales contracts. Often the sales contract will omit the requirement that the deed be delivered to an escrow agent. In that situation, the real estate agent may hold the buyer's earnest money in an escrow account. The advantages of using an escrow agent, other than the real estate agent, are discussed in Section 12 below. The following is a typical provision establishing an escrow arrangement.

> Escrow shall be open with The First National Bank, which shall hold the earnest money paid by Buyer and Seller's warranty deed, which shall be executed and delivered to the escrow agent within five (5) days of the execution of this contract by Seller. The earnest money and the warranty deed shall be held by the escrow agent until such time when the escrow agent is in a position to record all documents required hereunder and to make all disbursements provided under this contract. This transaction shall close as soon as practical after the parties have complied with all the conditions of this contract, but such closing shall occur not later than sixty (60) days after the execution of this contract.

A contract should also provide that any current taxes, other special assessments, and prepaid property-insurance premiums are to be pro-rated as of the date the transaction is closed. For example, if a sales transaction is closed on June 12, 1983, and if the property taxes payable for the calendar year are $368.65, the seller would pay $164.63 (163/365 of $368.65) and the buyer would pay $204.02 (202/365 of $368.65). Assessments and prepaid insurance premiums may be pro-rated in this same manner. Also, the contract should indicate when the transfer of possession or physical control over the property will occur. Generally possession is transferred when the title is transferred, which occurs upon closing the transaction unless otherwise stated.

E. Destruction of Property

A contractual clause designed to protect the parties' interest will specify their rights in case damage is done to the property. What if the improvements (house) on the property are destroyed or damaged by fire, wind, or other hazard during the time gap between execution of the contract and the closing? Does the seller or the buyer have the risk of loss during this period? The sales contract should specify the answers to these questions. When it does not, most courts have held that the buyer, as the equitable owner, remains liable to perform the contract at the stated purchase price. This result can be very harsh, because often buyers do not insure their interests until title actually has been transferred.

A few states (including Calfiornia, Hawaii, Illinois, Michigan, New York, North Carolina, Oklahoma, Oregon, South Dakota, and Wisconsin) have adopted the Uniform Vendor and Purchaser Risk Act. This act conditions the risk of loss on the right to possession or legal title. For example, if an improvement is destroyed through no fault of the buyer while the seller still has legal title and is in possession of the premises, the seller cannot enforce the contract. Under these circumstances, the buyer is entitled to have returned any portion of the consideration previously paid. On the other hand, if the buyer has obtained either legal title or mere possession, the risk of loss transfers to the buyer. In other words, under these latter circumstances, a seller can enforce the contract and the buyer is liable for the contractually stated purchase price. These principles of the Uniform Vendor and Purchaser Risk Act control unless the parties agree to the contrary.

A satisfactory provision that helps prevent harsh results is one that allows the buyer to choose between cancelling the contract or enforcing the agreement while collecting any insurance that is payable to the seller in the event improvements are substantially destroyed or damaged. Some time limit should be placed on the buyer's election under this section. An example of this type of clause follows:

Seller warrants that when the sale is consummated, the improvements on the property will be in the same condition as they are on the date of this contract, natural wear and tear excepted. However, should the premises be destroyed or substantially damaged before this sale is consummated, then at the election of the Buyer:

(a) this contract may be cancelled, or

(b) Buyer may consummate the purchase and receive the benefit of such insurance as accrues to the Seller on account of such loss or damage. This election is to be exercised within ten (10) days after the amount of Seller's insurance coverage is determined.

F. Miscellaneous Provisions

Frequently provisions are included in a sales contract to afford some protection to the buyer against pest infestation and to attest to the condition of appliances and utilities. For example, a seller should agree to furnish certification from a bonded pest-control company that the property is free from any wood-destroying organisms. With respect to appliances and utilities, the buyer should insist that the seller warrant these items to be in working order at the time of closing. It should be understood that the seller's compliance with these provisions does not afford the buyer absolute protection. Generally, the seller is not liable if pests invade a house or if the appliances break after title is transferred to the buyer. Therefore, the buyer may wish to have a building inspector go over the house, appliances, and utilities before the transaction is closed. This type of inspection, which is done at the buyer's expense, is discussed in more detail in Chapter 13.

G. Agent's Commission

When a real estate broker or salesperson is involved in the transaction, the sales contract generally contains a provision concerning that agent's right to a commission. Usually the agent's commission is deducted from the seller's proceeds. A seller who breaches the contract without justification must pay the commission anyway. A buyer who unreasonably refuses to perform his duties under the contract becomes liable for the entire commission. Sometimes this contractual provision states that the buyer's earnest money shall apply to the commission if the buyer breaches the contract. For example, if the buyer agreed to buy the seller's house for $62,000 and a $1,000 check was written as an earnest-money deposit, and if the buyer fails to purchase the house for reasons not provided in the contract, the $1,000 would go to the real estate agent. This buyer also would have to pay the agent an additional $3,340 in order to satisfy the full 7-percent commission on a $62,000 sale. A sample provision to this effect follows:

> In negotiating this contract, the Real Estate Brokerage Company has rendered a valuable service and is to be paid a commission which shall be 7 percent of the purchase price. This commission shall be payable to Broker from the Seller's proceeds. Seller agrees if he defaults and fails to consummate this sale, except for his exercise of some elective or optional right of cancellation hereunder or for his inability to cure any title defects, he shall pay broker the full commission, and the earnest money shall be returned to Buyer. Buyer agrees that if he defaults or fails to consummate this sale, except for the exercise of some elective or optional rights of cancellation hereunder or Seller's inability to cure title defects, Buyer shall pay Broker the full commission. In the event Buyer becomes liable for the commission, Buyer and Seller agree that Broker may apply the earnest money deposited by Buyer toward payment of that commission.

Because the entire earnest money goes to the agent when a buyer defaults, this provision may seem unfair to the seller. However, the harsh monetary penalty imposed on the buyer for breach will likely make any buyer think twice before refusing to complete the transaction. This same analysis can be used to show that this provision operates to the buyer's advantage. Most sellers would hesitate before becoming liable for a 7-percent real estate commission when the house is not sold due to their breach of the contract. Of course, all parties should be aware that this type of provision is drafted most favorably toward the agent. Ideally, the parties should have sufficient bargaining power to delete or modify this or any other provision. Circumstances in which an agent is entitled to a commission are discussed fully in Chapter 10.

H. COMPLETION OF THE CONTRACT

The traditional sales contract concludes with a provision that any changes in the agreement must be made in writing with all parties' consent. To be enforceable, the contract must be executed, which means the buyer, seller, escrow agent, and any other interested parties must sign the agreement. The date of the contract usually is that on which the last party signs it. This date will determine when the parties' performance is due.

The sample sales-contract clauses used in the preceding pages are for instructional purposes only. One of the great values of contracts is that they can be personalized to meet the needs of all parties in each situation. Because circumstances can change the provisions needed in a contractual agreement, no one form can be used universally.

Other Real Estate Contracts

10. Introduction

The most common contracts associated with a real estate sales transaction are the listing agreement and the traditional standardized-form sales contract. In addition to these, certain situations may require more specialized contractual agreements. Anyone who deals with real estate should have a basic understanding of a contract for a deed, an escrow arrangement, an option, and a right of first refusal. Each of these contracts is examined below.

11. Contract for a Deed

In certain situations, a special and very useful type of agreement is the contract for a deed. Because this instrument is often used when a buyer pays for vacant land over a specific time period, the contract for a deed is also known as an *installment contract* or a *land contract*. The contract for a deed is just what its name implies—an agreement to buy the deed (or title) to certain real property.

This type of contract differs from the more traditional sales contract in several important ways.

First, the parties to a contract for a deed understand that the purchase price will not be paid in a lump sum. In fact, in this transaction the buyer pays the seller on a regular basis (usually monthly) over a long period of time (perhaps ten, fifteen, even twenty or more years). In return for the buyer's payment over time, the seller does not have to give the buyer the deed to the property until all payments are completed.

A second characteristic of a contract for a deed is that the buyer does not have to obtain institutional financing. In essence, the seller furnishes the money needed to purchase the property. The seller is secured or protected against the buyer's nonpayment of principal and interest by retaining actual record ownership of the real estate.

A third distinction is seen in the lack of a formal closing in the contract for a deed transaction. Since title is not transferred until the entire purchase price and interest are paid, the typical closing (as described in Chaper 13) does not occur.

Finally, as indicated above, the written contract for a deed must fill a time gap between the execution of the agreement and the transfer of title. This time period usually is much longer (several years) than the time gap (sixty to ninety days) prior to the transfer of title pursuant to a traditional sales contract. Because a contract for a deed must govern the seller-buyer relationship for such a long time period, it must be very carefully drafted, and an escrow arrangement should be established. Absent a clear agreement to the contrary, most courts apply the doctrine of equitable conversion, which declares that the buyer should be treated as the owner and the seller should be treated as entitled to the purchase price. This doctrine is applicable particularly to situations under a contract for a deed when the buyer has paid a substantial portion of the purchase price. Furthermore, the buyer under a contract for a deed generally is treated as having an insurable interest to cover the risk of loss. The following case illustrates this point.

Case 11.3

In October 1954, Weiner agreed to purchase from the Briz-Ler Corporation a four-story hotel. A written contract for a deed was signed by these parties. Weiner paid $11,500 down, took possession of the hotel, and became liable for monthly installments. During 1957 a fire substantially damaged the hotel. Although it would have cost $107,000 to restore the hotel, Weiner settled with the insurance company for $31,500. This settlement was used to restore the first floor of the former building. A dispute over the contract arose, and Weiner abandoned the building. He now sues and asks that all the funds paid be refunded to him since Briz-Ler cannot deliver the four-story hotel.

Issue: Who has the risk of loss during the contract period in a contract for a deed?

Decision: Buyer.

Reasons: Generally a contract for the sale of lands requiring the seller to execute a deed conveying legal title upon payment of the full purchase price works an equitable conversion so as to make the purchaser the equitable owner of the land and the seller the equitable owner of the purchase money. In other words, the court of equity converts the buyer's contract interest from personal property (money) to real estate. It also converts the seller's interest (real estate) to personal property (money). Therefore the purchaser, or equitable owner of the land, takes the benefit of all subsequent increases in value, and necessarily all subsequent decreases in value.

Briz-Ler Corporation v. Weiner, 171 A.2d 65 (Del. 1961).

12.   Escrow Arrangements

Generally, before title to real property can be transferred, a deed must be delivered by the seller to the buyer. In the absence of this effective delivery, title is not transferred. The *escrow* is a legal device that assists in the delivery of a deed. An escrow arrangement can be created by a separate contractual agreement or within the contract covering the sale.

What would happen if the seller died or became incapacitated during the time gap prior to the closing under a sales contract, or before the buyer completed the payments under a contract for a deed? The seller could not sign the deed and deliver it to the buyer. Indeed, if the seller dies, title to his property would pass to those designated in his will or to his nearest relatives. Thereafter, the contract to sell property could become more difficult to perform. Indeed, the buyer may have to file suit against the deceased seller's estate or heirs. To prevent this potential obstacle, a simple escrow arrangement could be created. Once the seller has delivered the required deed to an escrow agent (some neutral third party named by the seller and buyer), courts have held that a buyer who completes his necessary performance can obtain the deed from the escrow agent. Of course, this agent must follow the instructions given by the parties to the contract so long as such instructions are reasonable and within the agent's powers.

The escrow arrangement protects the buyer's interest in that once the deed is delivered to the escrow agent and all other escrow conditions are satisfied, the seller's creditors can no longer levy on that property. In addition, if a seller is unmarried when the sales contract is signed but marries before the transaction is closed, the new spouse may have acquired certain marital rights (dower or curtesy) in the property to be transferred. In this situation, the seller who had placed the signed deed with an escrow agent prior to marrying would have avoided any questions about the new spouse's rights. Since the deed had been properly delivered, the transaction could have closed upon the buyer's performance being completed.

The basis of the protection provided by an escrow arrangement is the relation-back theory. In essence, courts have held that the delivery of the deed from the escrow agent to the buyer relates back to the date the deed was delivered to the escrow agent by the seller. In other words, the seller is divested of all ownership interests when the deed is delivered into escrow. This protection can be valuable to the seller as well as to the buyer. The following case indicates the advantageous position a seller is in upon delivery of the deed to the escrow agent.

Case 11.4

James Egan and Bessie Egan had a life estate in a tract of land, and Melford Egan owned the remainder. An agreement between the life tenants and the remainderman provided for a fifty-fifty division of the proceeds of any sale of the property, including a sale to the state in condemnation proceedings. On October 5, 1960, the parties under threat of condemnation executed a contract of sale and deed to the State of Missouri for a sale price of $30,500. The contract and deed were placed in escrow, to be held until a check in the amount of the purchase price was received from the state. The check was received November 9, 1960. James and Bessie Egan were killed October 25, 1960, and their estates claim one-half of the proceeds. Melford Egan contends that he is entitled to all the proceeds as the remainderman.

Issue: Was the delivery to the escrow agent effective to pass title to the state so that the life tenants were entitled to one-half the proceeds?

Decision: Yes.

Reasons: Upon final delivery of a deed deposited in escrow, the instrument will be treated as relating back to, and taking effect at the time of, the original deposit in escrow. This shall apply even though one of the parties to the deed dies before the second delivery. The relation of vendor and purchaser exists as soon as a contract for the sale and purchase of land is entered into. Equity regards the purchaser as the owner and the vendor as holding the legal title in trust for him. This equitable principle may be invoked in actions at law, even though the purchaser has not been put in possession. Delivery of a deed in escrow will also cut off attaching creditors of the seller and pass title clear of any claims perfected after the escrow.

Donnelly v. Robinson, 406 S.W.2d 595 (Mo. 1966).

13.   Options

There are times when a person may be interested in buying or selling property but may not be ready to enter into a sales contract. The option contract is one way to assure that the property will not be sold. Basically, the option contract is an offer that cannot be revoked for a stated time period. This type of irrevocable offer must be supported by consideration, typically some small amount of money. For example, in return for a buyer's payment of $100, a seller might promise to allow a prospective buyer to accept the outstanding offer during the next three months or a year or any other time period. This is known as an option to buy, since the choice to accept or reject the seller's offer rests with the buyer.

Of course, there is also an option to sell, which occurs when a buyer makes an irrevocable offer to buy. Now the seller must choose to sell or not. As a fundamental requirement of any option to buy or sell, the price must be specifically stated in the option. The specific price is essential to determine the rights of each party. A seller who agrees to sell vacant land to a buyer within the next six months at a price to be agreed upon is not agreeing to anything definite. On the other hand, if the price is stated as $10,000, both parties and neutral third parties can determine the rights of the seller and buyer. Implicit in any option contract is the understanding that the party holding the option cannot be forced to accept the offer and to enter into a formal sales contract. Such a result would be contrary to the nature of the option.

Option contracts are used frequently in connection with lease agreements wherein the tenant has an option to buy. Options also are tied to purchase agreements when the seller wishes to retain an opportunity to repurchase. The consideration for these options can be stated as a portion of the rental payment or the promise to sell the property. A major advantage of holding the rights under an option contract is that the decision to buy or sell can be made when the price is most advantageous. For example, a holder of an option to buy at a stated price may very well be able to obtain the appreciation that occurs during the option period. This advantage is the very nature of the option contract, which is enforceable so long as there is no fraud, misrepresentation, or undue influence present.[3]

14. Rights of First Refusal

Another important type of agreement related to real estate is the right of first refusal. This type of contract has less specific requirements than even an option. Pursuant to the right of first refusal, a seller promises to give the prospective buyer the first opportunity to purchase the property. Unlike the option contract, a right of first refusal does not have to include a specific price. However, the parties must conduct themselves at all times in good faith. A seller would be acting wrongfully to ask a price outrageously over the market value just to defeat a buyer's right of first refusal. As with the option contract, a party with a right of first refusal cannot be forced to enter into a sales contract. Often either an option or a right-of-first-refusal provision will be included in leases so that the tenant can purchase the property if desired.

Other Contractual Issues

15. Conditions of Performance

A typical contract provides that one of the parties will be excused or discharged from performance in the event certain things happen or fail to happen. Such events are called *conditions*. For example, most contracts provide that the seller's failure to correct any defects in the title to the real property will release the buyer from the duty to purchase. Likewise, contracts often stipulate that if the improvements on the property are destroyed or substantially damaged, the buyer is excused from performance if the buyer so chooses. Furthermore, the buyer's ability to obtain adequate financing usually is stated as a condition precedent to the buyer's duty to pay. This condition precedent prevents undue hardship on a buyer who, while acting in good faith, fails to obtain adequate financing. The acceptable financial consideration should be defined as a loan for a term of not less than a stated number of years at an interest rate not to exceed a stated percentage.

[3]Emerson v. King, page 292.

Case 11.5

Lach paid a deposit of $1,000 to Cahill for the purchase of a house. The sales contract recited that, "This agreement is contingent upon buyer [Lach] being able to obtain a mortgage . . . on the premises." Lach applied to a bank for a mortgage, but his application was denied. Thereafter, his application was denied by five other lending institutions. Cahill was unwilling to finance the house himself, and Lach notified Cahill that he was unable to secure a mortgage and that he wanted his deposit returned. When Cahill refused to return the $1,000 deposit, Lach brought this action to recover the deposit.

Issue: Was Lach entitled to the return of his deposit?

Decision: Yes. Lach was under no duty to buy Cahill's house.

Reasons: In order to recover his deposit, Lach was required to show: (1) that his ability to secure a mortgage was a condition precedent to his duty to perform under the terms of the sales contract; and (2) that he had made a reasonable effort to secure financing. A condition precedent is a factor or event which the parties intend must exist or take place before the duty of performance arises. If the condition is fulfilled, the right to enforce the contract does not come into existence. The language of the contract clearly showed that Lach's ability to secure a mortgage was a condition precedent to his performance. The condition, in addition, implies a promise by Lach that he would make reasonable efforts to secure a suitable mortgage. His attempts to find financing were reasonable under the circumstances, and Lach should accordingly recover his deposit.

Lach v. Cahill, 85 A.2d 481 (Conn. 1951).

Conditions of performance may be expressed or implied. An express condition is one that is stated in the contract. It must occur before a party is obligated to perform. It is best to state clearly all conditions intended by the parties. However, often parties to a contract fail to state express conditions of their performance. In these situations, courts must decide whether one party's performance is conditioned on that of another. Events which are vital or important to the parties' performance are held to be conditions. For example, a condition precedent often found in construction contracts is the requirement that the contractor obtain the architect's certificate of completion before the buyer or owner of the project has to make final payment.

16. *Substantial Performance*

In construction contracts, the issue often arises whether a contractor has substantially performed the work required so that the buyer becomes liable for payment. The concept of substantial performance allows the contractor to claim that the condition precedent to the buyer's performance has been satisfied even though the construction is not completely finished. Of course, a buyer can deduct any damages that result from incomplete performance, but that buyer is not excused altogether if the contractor's performance is substantially complete.

Case 11.6

Surety Development Corporation sold a prefabricated house to Grevas and agreed to have the house completed on a specified date. On that date everything was done except for a portion of the landscaping of the yard. Grevas refused to accept the house, contending that Surety had not completed the house on time. When Surety sued, Grevas argued he was excused from performance because Surety had failed to perform as promised.

Issue: Is complete performance by Surety required as a condition precedent to Grevas' performance?

Decision: No.

Reasons: The court stated that literal compliance with the provisions of the contract is not essential, but that it is sufficient if there has been an honest and faithful performance of the contract in its material and substantial parts. The court stated, "No substantial sum was required to complete the items left undone. Nor were they of so essential a character that defendants could not have been ensconced in their new home that night if they had so desired."

Surety Development Corp. v. Grevas, 192 N.E.2d 145 (Ill. 1963).

In construction contracts, delays in completion of performance usually are not material to contractual performance, especially if there is any justification for the delay. This general rule can be changed, and performance completed on time can be made a condition precedent by including in the contract a "time-is-of-the-essence" clause. This clause makes the time of performance a condition. When time is of the essence, even the slightest delay in performance is considered material to the parties' relationship. This clause should not automatically be included in every real estate contract. Many times a short delay in performance will not impair any party to the contract.

17. Remedies for Breach

Although a real estate sales contract is enforceable and binding, either the buyer or the seller could refuse to abide by the terms of their agreement. An unexcused failure to perform a required contractual obligation is called a *breach* of the contract. The refusal to perform because a condition precedent has not occurred is justified, and no breach occurs. However, when a party does breach a contractual promise, the nonbreaching party has a choice of remedies. Suppose that a written, enforceable sales contract is properly signed and then the seller unjustifiably refuses to transfer title to the buyer. This buyer may sue for monetary damages, for specific performance, or for the return of the earnest money deposit and rescission of the contract. These remedies are discussed in Chapter 1, Section 4.

18. Interpretation of Ambiguous Terms

It is always best to have a contract that is clearly written and is understood by all the parties. Unfortunately, the failure to reduce part of an agreement to written form or the imprecise use of language can result in ambiguities. The preceding discussion on substantial performance is one example of how courts attempt to resolve uncertain provisions in a contract. When the parties fail to specify a time for performance, a reasonable time will be inferred. Courts like to assume that most parties to a contract are reasonable and acting in good faith. Therefore, when a problem arises, courts try to interpret the ambiguity from the standpoint of a similarly situated reasonable person.

It is important to understand that the person who drafts the contract has the responsibility to avoid any unclear provisions. Courts generally will construe any ambiguities against the "drafting" party.

This result is particularly evident when the nondrafting party does not have bargaining power equal to that of the drafting party.[4] Relying on the courts to resolve any dispute that arises is very expensive and time-consuming. The material covered in this chapter should help heighten awareness to areas of concern related to real estate sales contracts. It is far better to take time in negotiating and drafting a contract than in trying to interpret one that was hastily signed.

Cases on Contracts in the Sales Transaction

Jones v. Olsen
400 N.E.2d 665 (Ill. App. 1980).

Woodward, J.:

This is an appeal from an order granting a motion by defendants, Paul and Catherine Cooper, to dismiss the complaint for specific performance of a purported real estate sales contract due to unenforceability under the Statute of Frauds. . . .

The complaint alleges that on February 16, 1978, plaintiff, William Jones, presented defendants with an unsigned form contract in writing for the purchase of certain real estate. . . . The complaint also alleges that plaintiff delivered a $12,000 check to defendants, payable to Paul and Catherine Cooper, the check stating on its face that it was earnest money for the purchase of 029 Lakeview, Mundelein. Defendants endorsed the check and negotiated it on or about February 25, 1978, but never signed the form sales contract. The transaction was not closed, the $12,000 was not returned, and plaintiff brought suit for specific performance of the contract. The contract was not signed by any of the parties, nor did the names of the seller or purchaser appear on the contract; nor did it contain a legal description, but it did include the address 029 Lakeview, Mundelein, with a lot size of "150 X 150"; it further provided that $12,000 earnest money in the form of a check, payable to sellers and to be deposited by sellers on acceptance of the contract, and that the contract was to be void if not accepted by February 28, 1978; the contract also contained the purchase price, method of payment, terms and conditions of sale.

On May 1, 1978, a commitment for title insurance was issued on Lots 28, 29 and 30 in Oak Terrace Subdivision, showing title to the land at the time of issuance to be in Kathryn M. Olsen, and while a legal description is shown, the common address is not. On May 19, 1978, a letter was sent to plaintiff from a law firm which stated that the purchase was being made from Mrs. Cooper and that she was being told that plaintiff would contact her "to obtain a deed into a trust from her daughter and son-in-law and trust agreement".

In granting the motion to dismiss, the trial court ruled that the contract violates

---

[4]Solomon v. Western Hills Development Co., page 294.

the Statute of Frauds for lack of signatures; that the check does not satisfy the signature requirement because it does not express the terms and conditions of sale; and that the letter from the law firm regarding the policy of title insurance does not satisfy the signature requirement because it was not signed by defendants or their authorized agent.

The Statute of Frauds requires that a contract for the sale of land must be in writing and be signed by the parties to be charged. . . . It is true, as both sides state, that a contract may consist of several documents. . . . However, where such a situation occurs it is necessary that the signed writing refer expressly to the unsigned writing or writings, or that the several writings be so connected, either physically or otherwise, that it may be determined by internal evidence that they relate to the same contract. . . . In the present cause, the signed writing (the check) does not state the price or the conditions of sale, nor does it refer specifically to the unsigned written contract; the check was in fact signed by plaintiff and both defendants. However, the form contract specifically calls for the purchaser of 029 Lakeview, Mundelein, to deliver to the "Owner of Record" a $12,000 check as an earnest money deposit, to be deposited by seller on acceptance of the contract; it further provides that the earnest money shall be returned and the contract rendered void if not accepted on or before February 28, 1978.

In light of the above, it is our opinion that the form contract and the check are, by their own terms, sufficiently connected as to allow them to be read together. Both documents refer to the same common address in the same municipality; the earnest money check is for the same amount as the earnest money specified in the contract; the check and the contract are dated with the same date; and defendants endorsed and cashed the check prior to February 28, 1978, as required by the contract. In reading the contract and the check together, it is apparent that the requirements of the Statute of Frauds were met, and that the trial court erred in ruling otherwise. In so holding, we do not comment on the enforceability of the contract by specific performance, nor on any of the requirements to obtain such relief. . . .

Reversed and remanded.

Emerson V. King
394 A.2d 51 (N.H. 1978).

Douglas, J.:

This case was brought as a bill in equity seeking specific performance of an option to acquire real estate. The property in question is a farmer's cottage plus ten vacant acres overlooking the Sandwich range in Sandwich, New Hampshire, . . . In the fall of 1952, the plaintiff, Denley W. Emerson, was approached by Miss Marjorie Thompson and her close friend, Miss Ida Pritchett, residents of Haverford, Pennsylvania. Both women were retired and unmarried, without family, dependents, or close relatives. They informed the plaintiff that they wished to buy the farmer's cottage as second home. The plaintiff eventually agreed to sell the house to Miss Thompson and Miss Pritchett subject to a repurchase agreement. The repurchase agreement reads:

The grantees by the acceptance of this deed hereby covenant and agree with the grantor that in the event that they or either of them should at any time wish to sell or otherwise dispose of or convey her or their interest in the premises herein described, or in any event upon the death of the eventual survivor of them, the grantor shall have an option to repurchase said premises together with any improvements thereon, for the total purchase price of $5,000.00, to be payable within sixty days of receipt of notice of such desire to sell or dispose of such interest from the grantee or grantees or the survivor of them or in any event within sixty days of the decease of the survivor of them, . . .

In 1955, Miss Thompson and Miss Pritchett approached the plaintiff regarding the purchase of the field adjacent to the cottage. Control of this field protects the view of the mountains from their cottage as well as the view from the homestead owned by the plaintiff.

After a long period of consideration, the plaintiff finally agreed to sell the field for $3,000. . . . All parties were represented by counsel in this transaction. The deed to the field was executed October 9, 1956, running to the two buyers as joint tenants with right of survivorship. It contains repurchase provisions similar to the provision in the 1952 deed for the farmer's cottage.

Miss Pritchett died in 1965. As surviving joint tenant, Miss Thompson became sole owner of their Sandwich real estate. . . . When Miss Thompson died on February 25, 1975, the defendants were named co-executors of her will. All of her real estate in Sandwich was devised to them. By letter dated April 8, 1975, the plaintiff notified the defendants of his intent to exercise the option for repurchase of both parcels of real estate at the agreed-upon price, and tendered an offer of the total purchase price of $8,000. The plaintiff brought this petition for specific perfor-

mance of the option agreements. The Trial Court denied the plaintiff's petition, ruling that . . . enforcement of the [repurchase] agreement in light of the increased value of the property would work an unconscionable result. A careful review of the facts of this case and the pertinent law persuades us that the trial court mistakenly denied the plaintiff's request for specific performance. . . . We therefore reverse.

. . .

The trial court erroneously found that enforcement of the option agreement would work an unconscionable result. The option agreement was included as a result of negotiations between two parties of equal bargaining strength. Each party was represented by able counsel. As we have noted above, it was only because the plaintiff's interest in the property was adequately protected that he agreed to sell. As Miss Thompson wrote her attorney, "we know we are being unbusinesslike and the terms are unusual but we are doing it with our eyes open." Even the defendant, Victor King, testified that no matter what advice they had received, these two women "would have gone right ahead and done it." The buyers were not coerced into accepting unfavorable terms of contract. Their overriding interest was in acquiring the land for their own use, as opposed for investment purposes. . . .

The defendants further argue that the improvements made to the cottage should not be allowed to benefit the plaintiff. Improvement to property alone is not a sufficient basis on which to deny specific performance. . . . There is evidence that these improvements were contemplated by both parties at the time of the sale and thus were part of the consideration which induced the plaintiff to sell the cottage. The fact that the deed expressly denies compensation for improvements lends support to our conclusion that the making of improvements was part of the consideration offered by the purchasers. Further, the improvements made on the house were used by the buyers for twenty-three years. There is no evidence in the record as to what extent the improvements actually increased the value of the cottage. This court has held that a person making improvements on property assumes the risk for the increase in value accruing to property when he or she is aware of the conditions attached to the estate. . . . All provisions of the deed were negotiated by two willing parties exercising their freedom to contract. . . . Neither party exerted undue influence on the other. On the contrary, through negotiations the parties were able to strike a bargain which benefitted them both. There can be no doubt that each party knew and fully understood what the agreement was; after long negotiations the second property transfer substantially adopted the terms of the first conveyance. The trial court made no findings of fraud, bad faith, undue influence or duress, which are the traditional bases for avoiding a contract. . . . Specific performance cannot be denied to permit persons to avoid improvident agreements. The provisions of the deed on these facts must be specifically enforced. . . .

Reversed.

Solomon V. Western Hills Development Co.
276 N.W.2d 577 (Mich. App. 1979).

Per Curiam:

On October 14, 1975, plaintiffs filed suit against defendants seeking specific performance of a real estate purchase agreement with Western Hills Development Company. Alternatively they sought damages for breach of contract. The suit arose as a result of an October 15, 1969, purchase agreement for sale of a lot in the Western Hills Subdivision #5. Defendants Claude O. Darby, Jr., Claude O. Darby, Sr., and Darby & Son, Inc., acted as agents for Western Hills Development Company in this transaction. The agreement stated that the purchase was to be consummated by a delivery of the deed in exchange for the purchase price "when plat is recorded." One hundred dollars in earnest money was paid by plaintiffs as part of this transaction.

Subsequently, Western Hills conveyed the property in question to defendants MacArthur and Banwell who recorded a plat for the subdivision. Efforts were then made to return the $100 to plaintiffs, with the explanation that Western Hills had abandoned the development. However, plaintiffs insisted upon performance of the agreement. . . . The trial judge . . . ruled that the October 15, 1969, purchase agreement was not an enforceable contract because it did not specify a time for performance. . . .

The crux of this case centers about the validity of the contract between the parties. On appeal plaintiffs contend that there was a binding contract between the parties and that a "reasonable time" requirement should be read into the contract to constitute the time of performance. Defendants . . . contend . . . that their recording of the plat constituted a condition precedent, the nonperformance of which excused their duty of performance.

We disagree with defendants' characterization of the clause "when plat is recorded." The clause does not read "*if* plat is recorded." If it had been so drafted we would agree that the recording of the plat constituted a condition precedent to their duty of performance under the contract. However, as drafted the clause is susceptible to the interpretation that the plat *will* be recorded at some unknown time in the future.

It is a general rule of construction that where a contract is ambiguous it will be construed against the party preparing it. . . . In the present case, the purchase agreement consisted of a standard form, filled in by Western Hills' agents. Accordingly, we construe the contract clause as a promise to record the plat at some future time, rather than a condition precedent to defendants' duty of performance under the contract that may be satisfied at their option.

However, the problem still remains as to the date of performance. No particular date is specified in the purchase agreement. For this reason, the trial judge ruled that the contract was unenforceable.

Michigan case law does not favor the destruction of contracts due to indefiniteness. . . . Where the time of performance is indefinite, performance may be required to be rendered within a reasonable time. What constitutes a "reasonable time" depends upon the facts and circumstances of the case, . . .

We conclude that such a "reasonable time" requirement should be read into the present contract. Therefore, we hold that the parties entered into a valid contract for the sale of property. As part of this contract defendant promised to deliver the deed to the property in exchange for the purchase price at the time the plat was recorded. Implicit in this promise was a promise that the plat would be recorded in a "reasonable time." Since the contract between the parties was valid the trial judge erred in granting defendants' motion for summary judgment.

Reversed and remanded.

REVIEW QUESTIONS

1. List and explain the elements essential to a valid contract.

2. Romain wrote a letter to Schwedes offering to sell a twenty-acre tract of land for $60,000. Schwedes communicated acceptance by telephone, and a closing date was set. Three days before the scheduled closing, Romain sold this property to a third party. Schwedes sued seeking specific performance of the contract. Should Schwedes succeed? Explain.

3. Assume in the above factual situation that Schwedes had paid to Romain $1500 as an earnest-money deposit and had secured a loan commitment for the desired amount from a financial institution. Should these facts change the court's decision on Schwede's suit for specific performance? Why?

4. Barber, as a buyer, and Stewart, as a seller, entered into a binding sales contract involving Stewart's house and lot. Property taxes for 1982, which were $1095.00, are payable on December 1, 1982. At the closing of this transaction, the property taxes are to be prorated as of that date. If the closing is April 15, 1982, how much does each person owe, and who would pay whom?

5. Why is it desirable to have a provision in the contract specifying which party has the risk of loss in the event the improvements are substantially damaged or destroyed after a sales contract is signed but before the transaction is closed?

6. How does a contract for a deed differ from a traditional sales contract? What other names are synonymous with a contract for a deed?

7. Joseph, a single man, agrees to sell his fifty-acre farm to Barry and Betty under the terms of a contract for a deed. These buyers are obligated to make monthly payments over the next ten years. Joseph signs a general warranty deed and delivers it to an escrow agent the day after the contract is signed. If Joseph marries Sarah two years later, and if the applicable state laws recognize dower interests, is Barry's and Betty's interest subject to Sarah's dower rights? Why?

8. Lessee sued lessors for specific performance of an option to purchase leased land and improvements. The lease provided that in order to exercise the option, the lessee must give notice at least sixty days prior to March 15, 1981. On January 15, 1981, the lessee gave the lessor written notice of his desire to purchase the property. Was this notice within the time allowed? Why?

9. Skogsberg agreed to purchase property from Petre in installments of $100/month. The contract included a forfeiture clause which recited that if Skogsberg defaulted in making payments, he forfeited his right to the property. The contract also contained a "time-is-of-the-essence" clause. Skogsberg began making payments irregularly, and these irregular payments were accepted by Petre for three years. At the end of the three years, Petre chose to exercise the forfeiture clause. Skogsberg brought this action for a declaratory judgment that he could retain the property upon further payment of amounts due. Does the "time-is-of-the-essence" clause require that all payments be paid promptly to avoid a default in this case? Explain.

10. Wolford and Kolls entered into a contract by which Wolford agreed to purchase certain real estate. Since Wolford delayed closing the sale for nearly a month, Kolls began negotiating with third persons interested in buying the property. One year later, Wolford filed this suit for specific performance of the sales contract. Should Wolford be entitled to specific performance?

12

Evidence of Title

1. Introduction

Title to real property signifies the legal right of ownership. In Chapter 11 we discussed contractual provisions for the transfer of title. This chapter is concerned with how the buyer acquires "good" title. The next chapter discusses preparation for transferring and the actual transfer of title.

Centuries ago in England, any person who possessed land was generally considered the landowner. In essence, possession and ownership were synonymous. In the presence of witnesses, this owner could transfer title to another person by simply going upon the land and handing the new owner a clod of dirt while verbally stating that title was transferred. This symbolic transfer of title by delivery of a piece of the land, which was called *livery of seisin*, caused great confusion, since there were no written records. The potential for fraud or a taking by force was limitless. Therefore, in 1677, the British Parliament enacted the Statute of Frauds, which required that all transfers of title of real property be in writing. As previously discussed, this provision has been adopted by every state in the United States. Thus, in order to transfer title to real estate today, a written deed must be signed by the grantor and delivered to the new owner.

Title to real property can be transferred during an owner's lifetime or upon the owner's death. An owner of real estate may voluntarily agree to sell or give his land to another. The most common voluntary transfer of title occurs under one of the types of sales contracts discussed in Chapter 11. An owner may also lose his title to real estate involuntarily. Adverse possession and easements can create limitations and restrictions on the owner's ability to transfer clear title to real estate. These and other limitations on ownership rights were discussed in Chapters 3 and 4.

Real property interests can survive the owner's life. Title transferred upon the owner's death is governed either by the owner's will or by the state's intestate succession law if no will exists. An executor is the manager of an estate distributed according to the deceased person's will. An administrator is responsible for the distribution of an estate when the deceased did not leave a will. The executor's and administrator's duties to transfer title are governed by the probate proceedings, as indicated in Chapter 4. And in Chapter 5, the use of special types of deeds, including the executor's and administrator's deeds, were discussed.

2. Good Title

In most transactions, a fundamental concern of the buyer of real estate is the acquisition of "good title" from the seller. "Good title" is a phrase that is usually used in combination with the words "marketable," "insurable," or "perfect of record." In essence, a buyer's desire to acquire "good title" generally means that the buyer wants ownership of the real property free from defects or encumbrances.

Specifically, "good and marketable title" indicates that the seller's title is free and clear from all past, present, or future claims to the title. "Insurable title" is title that a reputable title-insurance company is willing to insure. "Title perfect of record" means that the public record related to this particular title shows no defects or encumbrances whatsoever. For example, suppose the seller's title reveals that years ago a deed was improperly signed by a predecessor in title. This seller's title is not perfect of record.

Recording Statutes

3. Introduction

Every state has a statute that provides for a system for keeping records of every document affecting the title to real estate. Such documents include deeds, mortgages, leases, easements, contracts for a deed, and others. The location for recording real estate documents varies from state to state. Typically, the law establishes a recorder's office in the local courthouse. The official in charge of the recording system may be called the Recorder, the Registrar, or the Clerk of the Court. The next sections discuss the purpose of recording documents that affect title to real estate, as well as the various types of recording statutes, including notice, notice-race, and race recording statutes.

4. Purpose of Recording

A deed need not be recorded in order to transfer title from the grantor to the grantee. As between the parties to a properly delivered deed, the grantee receives title from the grantor even though that deed is not recorded. The purpose of recording the deed is to give notice of the transfer to third parties.

Case 12.1

Campbell purchased property from Storer in 1965. Campbell obtained a warranty deed which he did not record. In 1970, Storer conveyed the same land to another purchaser. Campbell brought this action for damages against Storer. Storer defended the suit on the rationale that the failure of Campbell to record his deed prohibited him from acquiring legal title to the property.

Issue: Did Campell acquire legal title?

Decision: Yes. Campbell was entitled to damages.

Reason: The mere failure of a grantee to record a deed is no defense to the grantee's action against the grantor for that grantor's act of conveying the property a second time. The failure to record affords protection to a subsequent purchaser of the property; it affords no protection to the original but forgetful or fraudulent grantor.

Campbell v. Storer, 368 N.E.2d 301 (Ohio App. 1975).

Because of the recording requirement and other public records (such as probate proceedings), anyone interested in the title to a piece of real estate may search the records to determine the identity of the owner and others with an interest in the land. In essence, the recording of all documents that affect title protects potential interest holders by enabling them to gain notice of others' interests through the public records. Notice may be either actual or constructive. Actual notice is given when a party sees the document as it is recorded. Constructive notice is given when a proper search of the record system would have revealed the existence of another's interest. The public has constructive notice of all properly recorded interests. For example, any buyer can determine whether the seller has deeded the property to anyone else.

Failure to record an interest (whether it is a fee simple interest, a lease, a mortgage, or other instrument) may result in the holder of that interest losing it to a subsequent party who acts in good faith. Parties act *in good faith* if they have no knowledge and no opportunity to learn that they are not entitled to the interest they receive. In most situations, a latter good-faith party has a superior claim, since there was no way of receiving notice of an unrecorded interest. Suppose Oliver had good marketable title to some land called "Blackacre." Assume Oliver sold this land and delivered a proper deed to Bailey. If Bailey failed to record this deed and if Oliver wrongfully sold "Blackacre" a second time to Gergory Francis Peck, who has superior title as between Bailey and Gregory Peck? The answer to this question might depend on the type of recording statute that the state has adopted.

5. Notice Statutes

When Gregory F. Peck searches Oliver's title, there will be no record that "Blackacre" had been sold to Bailey. Some states provide that since Peck had no notice of Bailey's interest, Peck would have superior title regardless of whether he filed his deed or not. These states have *notice* recording statutes, which determine who has superior title based solely on the opportunity to learn from the record that the grantor does or does not have title to transfer.[1] Therefore, Peck, as an innocent good-faith purchaser, wins over Bailey. Peck should record his deed to protect against losing title to another good-faith purchaser who takes a deed from Oliver.

6.   Notice-Race Statutes

Many other states would require that Peck, who took his interest without notice of Bailey's interest, record his deed before Bailey. In these states, which have a *notice-race* recording statute, the subsequent good-faith purchaser must be unaware of a previous purchaser and must file the deed in the record system first. Assume that Peck had no notice of Bailey's interest but that thereafter Bailey filed his deed before Peck filed: this second group of states would agree that Bailey now has superior title to "Blackacre."

In order for a deed to give notice of an existing claim to subsequent purchasers, there must be a clear and accurate legal description. The following case is an example of how someone with a recorded deed may not be protected.

Case 12.2

Mary Neeley and Clarence Kelsch became involved in a dispute over who owned a particular 8½ acre piece of land. They both based their claim on deeds they received from Arta Corbet. In 1957, Corbet conveyed title to some land to Clarence Kelsch. Although Kelsch thought this deed of conveyance included the land now in dispute, the metes-and-bounds description did not encompass this land. There was merely a reference to all land north of the County Road. Kelsch filed this deed on November 23, 1966. Subsequently, on May 30, 1968, Corbet signed and delivered a deed to Mary Neeley. This deed's description specifically did include the disputed land. Neeley had this deed recorded on June 28, 1968.

Issue: Under a notice-race statute, does Kelsch or Neeley have superior title?

Decision: Mary Neeley does.

[1]Fees-Krey, Inc. v. Page, page 314.

Reasons: The specific metes-and-bounds description in Kelsch's deed takes precedence over the general reference to land north of the County Road. Therefore, Kelsch's recorded deed was not effective to put subsequent purchasers on notice of his claim. Thus, when Mary Neeley acquired her deed for value, she was a good-faith purchaser without notice of any previous claim. When her deed was recorded, Neeley satisfied both requirements of Utah's notice-race recording statute.

Neeley v. Kelsch, 600 P.2d 979 (Utah 1979).

7. Race Statutes

A few states have adopted a pure *race* recording statute. In these states, the party who records the deed first has superior title, regardless of whether that party was acting in good faith at the time of purchase. For example, assume Peck knew that Bailey had received a deed from Oliver prior to Peck obtaining a second deed from Oliver. Peck could successfully claim superior title only in the few states that have a pure race-recording statute.

There are two distinguishing characteristics of these three types of recording statutes. These characteristics, summarized in Exhibit 12.1, concern when the subsequent party must be in good faith (without notice of a prior transfer) and when the document must be recorded first.

Despite the legal differences among the various recording statutes, anyone who receives an interest in real estate should record the document promptly. The recording system is the key element that creates an efficient method of transferring title or other interests in real estate. Without these public records, the confusion that existed in England centuries ago would still prevail. Prospective interest holders can gain near certainty as to their predecessor's title because of public records.

Exhibit 12.1   Characteristics of Recording Statutes

	Notice	Notice-Race	Race
1. Requirement that subsequent party be in good faith.	Yes	Yes	No
2. Requirement that document be recorded first.	No	Yes	Yes

In order to reach any level of certainty as to the validity of the real estate title or interest being transferred, the method of conducting a title search must be understood.

Examining the Record System

8. Introduction

The typical real estate sales contract provides that a buyer has a reasonable time to search the title and discover any defects or encumbrances to the seller's title. Some of the more common defects in title that might appear include a prior deed that was not properly executed, a prior deed that inadequately described the property, or the existence of another party claiming ownership of the same real estate. Common encumbrances that might appear on the record include mortgages, liens, easements, profits, restrictive covenants, or similar rights and uses. The presence of either a defect or an encumbrance on the seller's title means that the seller cannot deliver "good title."

Normally the buyer satisfies the duty to check the seller's title by obtaining a title opinion from an attorney or by having the seller purchase a title policy from a title insurance company. A thorough search of the public records allows a person trained in this area to give an opinion on the status of the title to a particular piece of real estate. As discussed in Section 12, title insurance companies usually maintain their own set of private records related to certain tracts of land.

9. Title Search

It is vitally important that real estate students recognize that real estate titles are searched by lawyers or abstractors, who are specifically trained in this field. Therefore, real estate brokers and salespeople should not become involved in a transaction as the title examiner. Any attempt by unqualified personnel to examine a title could lead to a claim of professional malpractice. Although real estate salespeople do not actually search real estate titles, it is important that they understand how such an examination is performed.

A title examiner must search the records to be sure that no defects or encumbrances exist from previous transactions or that existing defects or encumbrances are listed as exceptions on the title policy or in the lawyer's title opinion. The examiner is looking to make sure that the grantor has "good title" and has not previously conveyed that title. In the alternative, the examiner wants to make sure that defects which are found are cleared from the title. The search is accomplished by tracing the grantor's chain of title, which is the history of all the previous owners of the piece of real estate involved. The title search includes discovering who these owners were, when and how they became owners, and what they did with their interest. The chain of title can be followed by means of grantor and grantee indexes. Each county in every state maintains alphabetical indexes of the names of people who have given any interest in real estate to another (grantors) and of the names of people who have received such interests (grantees). The examiner begins by tracing the property involved back through the grantee indexes. Then the examiner searches the applicable grantor indexes to determine whether any improper grants have been made.

Case 12.3

Ms. Elliott, an illiterate eighty-seven-year-old widow, agreed to convey two acres of her land to Russell. Russell prepared the deed, but the property described in the deed consisted of about fifteen acres. Ms. Elliott signed the deed, unaware of the amount of property she was conveying. On February 11, 1972, Russell conveyed four of the fifteen acres to McClellan, and the deed was recorded on that date. Russell informed Ms. Elliott that there had been a mistake in the original deed and conveyed thirteen acres back to Ms. Elliott. This deed was recorded on February 16. McClellan then conveyed his four acres to Love on February 23. When oil was discovered on the McClellan-Love tract in May 1974, Ms. Elliott commenced this action for rescission of the deed she had given to Russell on the ground of fraud. These transfers can be summarized by the following chains:

Step 1. (1/31/72)

Step 2. (2/11/72)

Step 4. (2/23/72)

Elliott
↓
Russell ———————┐
↓   Step 3. (2/16/72)
        Elliott
McClellan
↓
Love

Issue: Did Love have notice of Russell's reconveyance to Ms. Elliott even though that transfer was not within McClellan's chain of title?

Decision: No. Love's title is superior to Ms. Elliott's as long as Love was not aware that Russell had defrauded Ms. Elliott with regard to thirteen acres.

Reasons: Ms. Elliott cannot claim title on the ground that Love had record notice of the reconveyance of thirteen acres to her on February 16. Although that transaction occurred one week before McClellan conveyed four acres to Love (on February 23), the transfer to Ms. Elliott was not in the same chain of title. In other words, a title examiner would not have to look at Russell, as a grantor, after February 11, 1972. This was the date McClellan recorded the deed received from Russell. Thereafter, any conveyance by Russell was not effective. Thus if McClellan and Love were bona fide purchasers without knowledge of any fraud by Russell, their claims are superior to Ms. Elliott's.

Love v. Elliott, 350 So.2d 93 (Fla. App. 1977), as modified by **McCoy v. Love,** 382 So. 2d 647 (Fla. 1979).

Examination of the grantor and grantee indexes should reveal whether anyone other than the grantor has an ownership interest in the property involved. This limited examination is not enough to assure a complete title search. The examiner must also check the tax records to discover whether the payment of any taxes is delinquent. Furthermore, the local court's records must be searched in case any judgment has been awarded against the grantor or any lien has been filed against the property. Delinquent taxes, judgments, and other liens are present or potential encumbrances that the grantee should require to be cleared before the transaction is closed. In addition, records of probate proceedings should also be examined. Only after all these records have been searched can a precise title opinion be given.

A search of the records relies on the grantor's name. In other words, any document filed under the grantor's name must be examined. However, only those documents that appear to relate to the parties presently involved must be checked for a legal description. Only if an encumbrance or an attempted transfer by a grantor concerns the property under contract does that record have to be considered thoroughly. Suppose Paul Purchaser is planning to buy "Tara" from Mr. Hugh

Landowner, who owns several different pieces of real estate. During an examination of Mr. Landowner's title to "Tara," his name likely will appear many times in the records. The examiner searching the title to "Tara" must decide which, if any, documents involve "Tara." This is determined by the legal description found in each document involving Mr. Landowner. Those documents concerning property other than "Tara" can be disregarded in this title search. This and other reasons for precise and complete legal descriptions were discussed in Chapter 1.

10. Abstracts of Title

Title examinations are made much easier through the title *abstract,* which is a compilation of all the recorded documents that affect a given piece of real estate. Generally, abstracts are prepared by employees of an abstract or title insurance company who, while not necessarily licensed lawyers, are specifically trained in searching titles. In some states, the public records are maintained in the form of title abstracts. Many title insurance companies maintain their own private title records. These records are often called tract indexes as well as title abstracts. When an abstract is readily available, the buyer's attorney does not have to go through the detailed search of the grantor and grantee indexes and other records. The attorney obtains the proper abstract, studies it, and issues his opinion to the buyer whether the seller has good or defective title.

When a title insurance or abstract company contracts to supply a title abstract, it is responsible for the accuracy of the abstract. If the abstractor has omitted a recorded document in the abstract or misrepresented the true nature of the records, the abstractor may be liable for any damages caused. In essence, whether it is a buyer, a seller, or an attorney who orders the abstract, that party is relying on the abstract's accuracy to make decisions. In the following case, the grantor (rather than the grantee) sought an abstract of his title so that he would know whether a previous transaction related to the same real estate had been recorded.

Case 12.4

Pepper gave a contract for a deed for property he owned to a grantee who recorded the contract. Subsequently the grantee defaulted in payment required under the terms of the contract, and Pepper found another buyer. Pepper gave the buyer a warranty deed and employed Lawyers Title Insurance Corp. to abstract the record title to the property. Lawyers Title performed the abstract but failed to discover that the prior contract for a deed had been recorded. The deal was closed, but the buyer later discovered that the contract had been recorded. Pepper was forced into a monetary settlement with the buyer and then commenced this action against Lawyers Title for damages.

Issue: Was Pepper entitled to damages from Lawyers Title due to its failure to discover a prior recorded contract?

Decision: Yes. Pepper could rely on the abstract.

Reasons: While Lawyers Title asserted that it could not be liable for damages for an omission of a document in an abstract where the person claiming damages had actual knowledge of the omitted document, there is a fundamental distinction between knowing about a previous transaction regarding property and knowing whether this transaction had been recorded, thereby creating a cloud on the title of the property. Since Pepper had employed Lawyers Title for the very purpose of telling him whether the contract had been recorded, Lawyers Title could not defend this action by contending that Pepper was aware of the contract.

Pepper v. Lawyers Title Insurance Corp., 357 So.2d 242 (Fla. App. 1978).

11. Title Opinion

Unlike the preceding case, it is typically the buyers who are most concerned with the title to the property involved. They usually are not concerned about what a title search is or how it is performed; they simply desire a professional opinion on the status of the grantor's title. Traditionally, buyers of real estate have relied on lawyers to determine whether the seller can transfer "good" title. A lawyer's title opinion frequently is expressed in the form of a letter to the buyer stating that the title appears to be marketable or that the title is defective for reasons set forth. Once again, these reasons might include the existence of an outstanding mortgage, a lien, an easement, an improper deed, or a claim of ownership by another person.

Most title-opinion letters will be conditioned on a number of things. For example, a lawyer might write that the grantor's title appears to be marketable subject to any claim of a person currently in possession. Most lawyers base their opinion solely on a search of the records rather than on a physical inspection of the property. This exception means that a lawyer is not liable if there is an adverse possessor on the land who is entitled to an ownership interest. Other common exceptions to a lawyer's statement that the grantor has "good" title could include the following:

1. Any outstanding mortgages,
2. Any restrictive covenants as recorded,
3. Any matter not properly recorded or indexed,
4. Any statutes, ordinances, or regulations that limit the use and enjoyment of the land, and
5. Any real property taxes for the current year not yet due and payable.

As with title abstracts, the title opinion must be accurate. Any negligence on the lawyer's part in misstating the condition of a grantor's title may cause the buyer damages. If an inaccuracy is proven to be the lawyer's fault, that lawyer should be held liable for damages that have resulted. Exhibit 12.2 is an example of a typical lawyer's title opinion.

12. Title Insurance

The lawyer's title-opinion letter is not the only way in which a buyer can be assured that the seller can deliver marketable title. Indeed, in many parts of the country today, title insurance is purchased to provide protection in case the acquired title is defective. As the lawyer does before writing a title opinion, the title insurance company will search the public records or their own private records to determine the condition of the title. In several cases, title insurance grew out of the expanded function of abstract companies or a group of lawyers. In addition to preparing abstracts or writing opinion letters, these companies or associations began to issue insurance that the title to a piece of real estate was "good and marketable."

Upon receiving a request for title insurance, the company will conduct its own search of the grantor's title. The company then evaluates the validity of this title and determines the risk it must take to insure the title's marketability. The title insurance policy includes a schedule of exceptions, which might list liens, easements, or other encumbrances

EXHIBIT 12.2 LAWYER'S TITLE OPINION

May 8, 1981

Mr. and Mrs. Nou Lund Owener
308 Hillman Circle
Development, Georgia

Re: Property designated as
Lots 5 and 6
of Hilman Subdivision,
Mayberry
County, Georgia

Dear Mr. and Mrs. Owener:

At your request, I examined the record title to the above-referenced property. This examination was limited to the time period from October 16, 1972, until 2:30 P.M. on May 8, 1981. The examination was conducted pursuant to the applicable title standards of the State Bar of Georgia. Based on this examination, I do certify that you have good and marketable title. Nothing appears in the records for the period searched that would constitute a lien upon or otherwise adversely affect your title, except as follows:

1. An outstanding security deed from Joseph P. Warlock to Citizens and Southern National Bank, dated October 16, 1972, and recorded in Deed Book 9, page 825, in the Mayberry County Superior Court Clerk's Office.

2. Any defects which would be revealed by an accurate survey or physical examination.

3. Protective covenants recorded in Deed Book 7, page 617, of the Mayberry County Records.

4. Any matter not properly recorded or indexed, including, but not limited to, the rights of any laborer, materialman, architect, engineer, or surveyor covering work performed or materials provided for the improvement of the above-referenced property.

5. The rights of any person currently in possession of the above-referenced property.

6. Any statutes, ordinances, assessments, or covenants restricting or regulating the use and enjoyment of the above-referenced property or the character or improvements which may be erected thereon.

7. Any real property taxes for the current year not yet due and payable.

I hope you enjoy your new home.

Sincerely yours,
I. M. A. Lawyer

that appear in an examination of the public record. Often the policy will state that all restrictions of record are excluded from coverage. In addition, the policy can exclude those defects created by any party who possesses the property at the time the policy is delivered. Other risks excluded might include defects revealed by an accurate survey or any defects that are not recorded as required. The insured under a title insurance policy must be certain what defects are excepted from the policy and either have the seller-grantor clear the title of these defects or encumbrances or else protect themselves by receiving credit from the seller for existing financial liens and thereafter paying them off.

In a real estate transaction, title insurance may be purchased for the buyer-grantee or by the party (mortgagee) who is financing the purchase price and is taking a security interest in the real estate. In the typical transaction, the policy is paid for by the seller or the mortgagor. Whoever the insured is, that person must realize that title insurance differs from liability, life, or property-hazard insurance in several important ways. First, the insured is charged a premium only once, and it is payable when the policy is delivered. Second, a title insurance policy protects only the named insured; therefore, when the insured transfers the title that is covered, the insurance does not protect the new transferee. However, title insurance companies have been ordered to pay the insured when that party is sued by a subsequent transferee. When title is transferred by the insured, the policy usually can be reissued for a low rate, particularly when it has been in force only a short period of time. Third, the policy protects against past rather than future events.[2] The schedule of exceptions normally exempts from coverage any liens, encumberances, or other defects that arise after the title is insured.

A title insurance policy may act as a substitute for the lawyer's title-opinion letter. Indeed, the practice in many states is to purchase a title policy rather than obtain a title opinion, because some people feel the title policy provides more protection at a better price. In the alternative, a title policy may be purchased as suppplemental protection to the lawyer's opinion. In essence, a title insurance company provides protection to the insured to the extent that the title was free from unknown defects when the insured acquired title. Primarily, this protection covers the possibility that the recording system has failed to disclose a proper claim to the property. For example, if a previous owner received title through a forged deed and later the true owner appears, the title

[2]National Mortgage Corp. v. American Title Insurance Co., page 316.

insurance company would be obligated to defend the insured's title in court or reach a monetary settlement. In these situations, title insurance can provide very valuable protection.

In some states the decision to purchase a title insurance policy is not automatic in all transactions. The nonexistence of title insurance does not prevent the grantee from filing suit against the grantor for breach of a warranty in the deed given. (See Chapter 5 for a review of the warranties and covenants that may be contained in a deed.) However, there is always the possibility that the seller may be insolvent and unable to pay any judgment the buyer might obtain. Furthermore, a title-opinion letter written by a lawyer after a title search or a review of the prepared abstract may provide adequate protection. If a defect in the title later comes to light and the defect was overlooked due to the abstractor's or the attorney's negligence, the title holder has a cause of action against the negligent party. Of course, recovering from a title insurance company normally will be much cheaper than having to pursue a lawsuit for negligence. In essence, buyers of real property should evaluate their needs and only then determine whether an attorney's search, or title insurance, or a combination of both provides the best and most economical protection.

The Torrens System

13. Introduction

In some states a search of title records by a lawyer or a title insurance company is not the only way to assure a buyer that the grantor has good title. Furthermore, recording a deed received from the grantor is not the only way to protect title to land against a subsequent good-faith purchaser. Both of these needs can be satisfied by registering the title to real estate. Some states provide a method of title registration as an alternative to the more traditional recording system.

The best-known scheme of title registration probably is the "Torrens System," which derives its name from Sir Robert Torrens, a resident of Australia during the nineteenth century. Becoming convinced that the methods for recording land ownership were cumbersome and inadequate, Torrens developed his own scheme similar to the registration of ship titles. The first Torrens Act was adopted in South Australia in 1858. Between 1895 and 1917, twenty states and territories in the

United States enacted the Torrens system of land registration, but since then no other states have adopted it. Indeed, eight states have repealed their Torrens Act. Today, only Colorado, Georgia, Hawaii, Illinois, Massachusetts, Minnesota, New York, North Carolina, Ohio, Oregon, Virginia, and Washington have valid Torrens systems.

14. How the Torrens System Works

The ultimate goal of the Torrens system is to provide the landowner with a certificate of title, similar to the certificates now used to show title to a motor vehicle. In order to obtain an original Torrens certificate of title, the purported owner must be willing to go through a legal registration proceeding. This process commences with the owner filing a petition for registration which contains the legal description of the land and all the claims that any person might have to the land. All the people who have potential interests in the land must be notified and made parties to the registration action, during which all parties with interests in the land attempt to prove them.

After determining who the rightful owner is, the judge will issue a decree naming the true owner of the land and any valid claims, such as mortgages, easements, or other restrictions, against the land. This decree is conclusive proof that all the other parties in the registration proceeding have no existing interests. The judge's decree is entered on the court's records, an original certificate of title is recorded, and a duplicate certificate is given to the landowner. To transfer title under the Torrens system, the old certificate of title must be returned to the official registrar, who then issues a new certificate to the new owner. The recordation of the new certificate is essential to the transfer of title. This requirement is the fundamental difference between the Torrens system and the more traditional delivery of deeds as an exchange of title. Furthermore, the necessity for possession of the certificate representing title is a major disadvantage of the Torrens sytem. When the certificate is lost or stolen, it is almost as difficult to reestablish title in the real estate as it was to register the title originally.

15. Use of the Torrens System

The Torrens system is used principally in Australia, New Zealand, and parts of Canada and England. Its most extensive application in the United States is found in Chicago, Boston, Minneapolis–St. Paul, and

New York City. Even in these areas the system's use is limited, since the registration of land is optional. A major advantage of the Torrens system is the protection it affords against claims that the land has been adversely possessed. Therefore, land which is not inhabited, like timberlands in Georgia, will often be registered under the Torrens system. Another advantage of the Torrens system is its use to clear defects from the recorded title. For example, if search of the record system revealed that a deed had not been properly executed, every heir of the grantor or beneficiary named to receive real property in that grantor's will would have to be located and would have to sign a quitclaim deed to clear the title. The difficulty of obtaining these quitclaim deeds may make it advantageous to register the title under a Torrens Act, if applicable. The following case is an example of both these advantages of registration under a Torrens Act.

Case 12.5

In 1905, Issac Moore owned land that was just north of Joseph Cotton's land. Cotton had a driveway built entirely on his land, but Moore was allowed to use it as a way of access to his garage. There was no doubt that Moore had acquired a prescriptive easement to use Cotton's driveway. During 1937, Cotton brought an action for title registration of his land which included the driveway. Cotton's application under the Torrens Act named Issac Moore as one of the defendants. Although he was properly served, Moore did not file an answer asserting his easement claim. After a Torrens certificate was issued, Cotton's land was transferred many times until Kent Henricksen purchased it in 1961. Prior to purchasing this land, Henricksen personally inspected the premises and learned of Carolyn Moore's use of the driveway. (Carolyn Moore was a descendant of Issac Moore.) A dispute arose between Ms. Moore and Mr. Henricksen, and he eventually barricaded the driveway, thereby blocking Ms. Moore's use of it.

Issue: Can a landowner who owns land pursuant to a Torrens Act title certificate deny the existence of a preexisting prescriptive easement that is not mentioned on the title certificate?

Decision: Yes. Henricksen had the right to block Ms. Moore's use of the driveway.

Reasons: The purpose of title registration under the Torrens Act is to give the certificate holder conclusive ownership and use, subject to the exclusions noted on the certificate. Since Moore's prescriptive easement was not recorded on the certificate, the easement is lost unless the certificate holder purchased the land in bad faith. Hendricksen's knowledge of Ms. Moore's use of the driveway did not amount to a bad-faith purchase. Indeed, to conclude that Henricksen was a purchaser in bad faith would put the buyer of property registered under the Torrens Act in a less favorable position than the original certificate holder. Finally, once land is registered, title or use by prescription cannot be obtained against the registered owner. Therefore, Issac Moore lost his prescriptive easement to use the driveway in 1937, and Ms. Moore's continual use until 1962 did not mature into a new prescriptive easement.

Moore v. Hendricksen, 165 N.W.2d 209 (Minn. 1968).

There are several reasons why the Torrens system has not gained wider acceptance in the United States. First, it is optional rather than mandatory. Second, the high cost of the initial proceeding discourages owners from having their land registered. Third, tremendous problems arise if the actual certificate is lost or stolen. Finally and perhaps most important, lawyers, abstractors, and title insurance companies have discouraged the use of the Torrens system, since land transfers would no longer require their services.

Cases on Evidence of Title

Fees-Krey, Inc. v. Page
591 P.2d 1339 (Colo. App. 1979).

Enoch, J.:

This is a quiet title action. Plaintiffs, Fees-Krey, Inc., appeal from a judgment quieting title in defendant, Page, Jr., on his counterclaim to a 2 percent overriding royalty on an oil and gas lease. Defendant never recorded his interest pursuant to the Colorado Recording Act, § 38–35–109, and plaintiffs subsequently acquired the lease without notice of defendant's overriding royalty. Neither plaintiffs nor any grantees prior to plaintiffs recorded their interests in the lease. Plaintiffs contend that § 38–35–109 is a pure notice statute, and that therefore plaintiffs have priority over defendant, because plaintiffs acquired their interest without notice. Defendant argues that the statute is a race-notice statute, . . .

We hold that the statute is a pure notice statute. . . .

The issue whether § 38–35–109 is a pure notice or a race-notice type of statute is critical in this case because the characterization will determine the priority between the competing interests. An overriding royalty carved out of the working interest in an oil and gas lease is an interest in real property . . ., and is therefore subject to the rules of priority of the Recording Act. If the statute is a race-notice type, a subsequent purchaser will prevail over a prior unrecorded interest only if he purchases without notice and records his interest before the prior interest is recorded. Even if the prior interest is never recorded, the subsequent purchaser must record his own interest before he can assert priority. Thus defendant would have priority here because plaintiffs, though subsequent purchasers without notice, failed to record. If, on the other hand, the statute is a pure notice statute, a subsequent purchaser who purchases without notice of a prior interest prevails over a prior unrecorded interest even though the subsequent purchaser does not record. Thus, plaintiffs, having purchased without notice of defendant's overriding royalty, would prevail under a notice type statute.

. . .

After careful consideration of the language and purpose of the statute, we are convinced that the better construction is as a pure notice statute.

Section 38–35–109 reads as follows:

All deeds, powers of attorney, agreements, or other instruments in writing conveying, encumbering, or affecting the title to real property . . . may be recorded in the office of the county clerk and recorder of the county where such real property is situated and no such instrument or document shall be valid as against any class of persons with any kind of rights, except between the parties thereto and such as have notice thereof, until the same is deposited with such county clerk and recorder. In all cases where by law an instrument may be filed, the filing thereof with such county clerk and recorder shall be equivalent to the recording thereof.

. . .

The statute reads like a pure notice statute, and the language is similar to pure notice statutes in other jurisdictions. . . . For example, the Illinois recording act, which is generally considered as a notice statute, . . . provides that:

All deeds, mortgages and other instruments of writing which are authorized to be recorded, shall take effect and be in force from and after the time of filing the same for record, and not before, as to all creditors and subsequent purchasers, without notice; and all such deeds and title papers shall be adjudged void as to all such creditors and subsequent purchasers, without notice, until the same shall be filed for record.

. . . By contrast, language in race-notice statutes, such as Michigan's, specifies that the subsequent purchaser must first record before he can have priority:

Every conveyance of real estate within this state hereafter made, which shall not be recorded as provided in this chapter, shall be void as against any subsequent purchaser in good faith, and for a valuable consideration, of the same real estate, or any portion thereof, whose *conveyance shall be first duly recorded.*

. . . Because § 38–35–109 does not specifically state that to assert priority a subsequent purchaser must record his interest, as well as acquire it without notice, we construe the statute liberally to protect those who take without notice of a prior unrecorded interest.

Our decision is buttressed by the fact that a pure notice statute serves to protect subsequent purchasers, allowing them to rely on the record title as it exists at the time of their purchase. The danger of a race-notice statute is that a prior interest holder who has failed to record may cut off the claim of a subsequent purchaser who relied on the record at the time of his closing but has not yet had time to record his own instrument. . . . Characterizing the statute as a pure notice rather than race-

notice statute will encourage purchasers to record their interests as soon as acquired. Although a subsequent purchaser need not record to protect his interest against prior unrecorded interests, unless he does record, his interest may be cut off by a purchaser subsequent to him.

. . .

The judgment is reversed and the cause is remanded with directions to enter judgment quieting title in plaintiffs to the 2 percent overriding royalty, and to order that all funds held in escrow pending this appeal be paid to plaintiffs.

Reversed and remanded.

National Mortgage Corporation v. American Title Insurance Company 261 S.E.2d 844 (N.C. 1980).

In 1967 Mr. and Mrs. Abernethy leased two undeveloped lots in Chapel Hill, North Carolina, to Jonas W. Kessing. This lease was for a sixty-year term. In order to assist Mr. Kessing's company in developing this land, the Abernethys agreed to subordinate their fee simple interest to any lien created by Kessing for the purposes of financing the erection, furnishing, and equipping of improvements on this land. This subordination agreement was conditioned on all borrowed money being used for improving the Abernethys' land. Kessing borrowed $125,000 from National Mortgage Company and granted a lien to it against the Abernethys' property. This lien was in the form of a deed of trust. The subordination agreement and deed of trust were recorded respectively at 12:23 p.m. and 12:26 p.m. on July 18, 1969. The National Mortgage Company purchased a title insurance policy to protect the lien interest it had received. The $125,000 borrowed was not used for improving the Abernethys' land. Therefore, their subordination agreement was not effective, and the Abernethys' claim to their land became superior to that of the National Mortgage Corporation. When this corporation lost its claim to the land for nonpayment by Kessing, it sued the American Title Insurance Company pursuant to the title policy it had purchased.

Huskins, J.:

... In the instant case both National Mortgage and American Title agree that the subordination agreement executed by the Abernethys is null and void as a result of which National Mortgage's lien on the Abernethy property is no longer valid. However, the parties disagree as to whether the events which caused the nullification of the subordination agreement and thus the loss of the lien are within the coverage of the title insurance policy. Consequently, the dispositive question on this appeal is whether the events which caused nullification of the subordination agreement were covered by the policy.

... [T]itle insurance operates to protect a purchaser or mortgagee against defects in or encumbrances on title which are in existence at the time the insured takes his title. ... "It is not prospective in its operation and has no relation to liens or requirements arising thereafter." ... "The risks of title insurance end where the risks of other kinds begin. Title insurance, instead of protecting the insured against matters that may arise during a stated period after the issuance of the policy, is designed to save him harmless from any loss through defects, liens, or encumbrances that may affect or burden his title when he takes it."

Here, the policy of title insurance issued by defendant insured the lien of plaintiff's deed of trust on the Abernethy property "all as of the 18th day of July, 1969, at 12:26 p.m. the effective date of this policy." ... The objective of this coverage is to protect against defects or other matters in existence at the time the policy is issued, unless otherwise excluded, which may, upon discovery at a later time, invalidate plaintiff's lien on the Abernethy property. Thus, the policy only insures: (1) that on 18 July 1969 fee simple title is vested in the Abernathys, and (2) that the subordination agreement and deed of trust are sufficient *on that date* to give plaintiff a first lien on the property. The policy does not insure against a breach of the subordination agreement by the Jonas W. Kessing Company or Village Associates of Chapel Hill after 18 July 1969 which invalidates the lien of plaintiff's deed of trust.

In the instant case the events which breached the condition of the subordination agreement and rendered it ineffective occurred outside the stated coverage of the policy. On 24 July 1969 plaintiff authorized the direct disbursement to Village Associates of Chapel Hill, a limited partnership controlled by Jonas Kessing, of $125,000 in loan proceeds which plaintiff knew were required to be used to construct improvements on the Abernethy property. This disbursement was knowingly made by plaintiff prior to the commencement of any construction on the property. No construction was ever begun nor were any funds ever expended for improvements on the Abernethy lots. Apparently, the moneys disbursed to Village Associates of Chapel Hill were misappropriated.

One of the conditions imposed by the Abernethys in return for their agreement to permit plaintiff's deed of trust to become a first lien on their property was that the proceeds of loans secured by said deed of trust would be utilized *for the construction of improvements on their property.* The 24 July 1969 disbursement of loan proceeds in the sum of $125,000 and the subsequent misappropriation of these funds made compliance with this condition impossible and resulted in the nullification of the Abernethy subordination agreement and the loss of plaintiff's first lien on the Abernethy property.

Due consideration of the record impels the conclusion that the 24 July 1969 disbursement and the subsequent misappropriation of the loan proceeds caused the nullification of the subordination agreement and the loss of plaintiff's lien on the Abernethy property. There were no breaches of the subordination agreement as of 18 July 1969. Nor were there any fatal defects in the drafting or execution of the agreement on or prior to that date. Thus, the failure of the subordination agreement and the consequent loss of the lien cannot be attributed to matters in existence on the date the policy was issued. We hold, therefore, that the loss incurred by insured is not covered by the policy of title insurance sued upon in this case.

. . .

Reversed and remanded.

REVIEW QUESTIONS

1. Define and distinguish among the following terms:
   a. Marketable title
   b. Insurable title
   c. Title perfect of record
2. If the mere acceptance of a valid deed by the grantee gives that party superior title to the grantor, what is the purpose of recording that deed?
3. What are the three types of recording statutes discussed in this chapter?
4. Rob sold and granted his interest in Blackacre to Diane on April 3, 1979. Diane did not record her deed from Rob until November 13, 1981. On February 6, 1980, Rob wrongfully sold and granted Blackacre to Justin, who recorded his deed on February 7, 1980. Assuming no other facts, who has superior title to Blackacre under each type of recording statute mentioned in your previous answer?
5. Now, assume that Justin actually was aware of Diane's claim to Blackacre prior to February 6, 1980. How would your previous answers change? Explain.
6. List and explain three ways in which a party can be fairly assured that a newly-acquired interest is taken free from the claims of others.
7. How does a title insurance policy differ from other insurance policies? Explain.
8. The District of Columbia Redevelopment Land Agency filed a condemnation complaint involving a tract of land. The Agency employed Lawyers Title Insurance Company to ascertain the owners of this property. The title report indicated that two charities each owned a 25 percent interest in the land to be condemned, with the remaining 50 percent owned by the heirs of Foller. None of the heirs contested the condemnation, and the two charities each received over $10,000, while the heirs received nothing. The heirs then brought this action against Lawyers Title, alleging that the two charities had no interest in the property condemned and that Lawyers Title had been negligent in its examination of the title. Could these heirs recover for the negligence of Lawyers Title?
9. What are the advantages and disadvantages of the Torrens system of land registration?
10. For what reasons has the Torrens system not been more widely adopted and used in the United States?

13

Closing the Sales Transaction

1. Introduction

The event at which title to or ownership of real estate is transferred from a seller to a buyer often is referred to as *closing* or *settling* the transaction. The term used usually depends on the geographic location of the parties and the property, but in this chapter they are used interchangeably. The following sections examine the duties of buyers and sellers prior to actually closing the transaction. Provisions of the federal Real Estate Settlement Procedures Act also are discussed. Finally, the events that occur at a real estate closing are developed.

Preparation for Closing the Transaction

2. In General

In a real estate transaction, there actually may be several closings. The borrower and the lending institution must close the loan; the escrow agent, if one is employed, must close the escrow arrangement; and the grantor and grantee must close or transfer the title to the property involved. Generally, but not always, these various closings occur at the same meeting. Therefore, the phrase "closing the transaction" can include the closings of several different relationships. It must be remembered that the ultimate purpose of the real estate sales process is to transfer title from the seller to the buyer. Before looking at the actual closing event, each party's responsibilities prior to closing must be examined.

3. Buyer's Duties—In General

When the buyer and the seller sign a sales contract, the real estate transaction has only started. In fact, during the time gap between signing a contract and closing the transaction, the buyer becomes responsible for obtaining financing, securing a title opinion or a title insurance policy from the seller, having the property insured and surveyed, and inspecting the property. If the purchase is for commercial purposes, the buyer should investigate the zoning restrictions on the parcel involved. It is recommended that a sales contract for commercial land be conditioned on the zoning allowing the contemplated use. A buyer of rental property should study the current leases' terms and conditions as well as the schedule of rental payments. Of course, since the parties are the masters of their contracts, a sales agreement may include other duties owed by the buyer prior to closing the transaction.

4. Buyer—Financing the Purchase

Purchasing a house may be the largest financial investment the average American family will ever make. Since very few families are able to pay cash for a home, most buyers must finance this purchase. Indeed, even those with large amounts of cash are encouraged to borrow money, since the interest paid is tax deductible and their money can be used for other investments. Typically, buyers of residential real estate finance seventy, eighty, ninety and even ninety-five percent of the total purchase price. The buyers' reliance on borrowing money requires that they insist on a contractual clause conditioning their performance on their ability to secure adequate financing.

Under such a conditional clause based on obtaining adequate financing, the buyer must act in good faith and with honesty in all attempts to borrow the required amount. This obligation includes applying for the loan within a short time period after the contract is signed. The buyer cannot delay this attempt to secure financing so that there is not enough time for the lending institution to approve the loan prior to the closing date. If failure to secure adequate financing is the buyer's fault due to lack of good faith, the seller has a cause of action for damages resulting from the buyer's inability to close the transaction. However, if the mortgage market is exceedingly tight, if the bank is unwilling to risk a loan based on the buyer's ability to pay, or if for whatever other reason, outside the borrower's direct control, the loan is not approved, the buyer is relieved of his contractual obligation.

Case 13.1

On July 25, 1975, Mr. and Mrs. Lanusse agreed to buy two vacant lots from Mr. and Mrs. Gerrets for $20,000. The contract signed by these parties was conditioned on the ability of Lanusses to borrow $17,000 using this property to secure the loan. The contract also provided that if a loan could not be obtained within thirty days after acceptance, the contract would be void. When the offer was made, the Lanusses deposited $2000 with an attorney who was directed to hold this money for the Gerrets' benefit. After several attempts to secure a suitable loan, the Lanusses were told that the lots were not worth $17,000. At that time, these purchasers sought to have their deposit refunded. Mr. Gerrets directed the attorney who held the $2,000 not to return it. The Lansusses then filed this suit.

Issue: When a contract is conditioned on a buyer obtaining financing, and good-faith attempts to obtain a loan are unsuccessful, are the purchasers excused from further performance and entitled to a return of their deposit?

Decision Yes.

Reasons: A sales contract is the governing document between buyers and sellers of real estate, who should make every effort to have the contract reflect their agreement. In this case the parties' contract was conditioned on the buyers obtaining a loan of $17,000 with the property as security. There is nothing inherently wrong with such a condition. Indeed, such provisions are often advisable. Based on the evidence presented, the Lanusses made many applications for a loan. All these applications were refused because the land was appraised for only $15,000 to $16,000. Having made these good-faith attempts to obtain an appropriate loan and having the protection of the stated condition which was not satisfied, the Lanusses are excused from further performance and shall receive a full refund of their $2000 deposit.

Lanusse v. Gerrets, 357 So.2d 45 (La. App. 1978).

Omission from the sales contract of the conditional clause based on obtaining financing can result in great hardship to the buyer. In this situation, failure to secure adequate financing does not relieve the buyer's contractual duties; therefore, a buyer who cannot pay the purchase price at closing has breached the contract and is liable for the seller's damages.

The details of how real estate is financed and how the buyer obtains that financing are discussed in Chapter 14.

5. Buyer—Securing the Title Opinion

After signing a sales contract, the buyer should always either employ a lawyer to give an opinion on the condition of the seller's title or insist that the seller furnish a title-policy commitment letter. Even though a seller may agree to pass title with a general warranty deed, the buyer should obtain a title opinion based on search of the public records for several important reasons. First, many sales contracts require the buyer to inform the seller of any defects or encumbrances found in the seller's chain of title. As previously discussed, the best way to discover whether the seller's title is defective is through a complete search of the public record.

Second, the general warranty deed signed by the seller may contain promises that there are no defects or encumbrances except those "restrictions or encumbrances of record." It then becomes the buyer's responsibility to learn of these restrictions or encumbrances of record, if any. Again, an examination of the recording system is the only way to gain this knowledge.

Third, an additional reason for the buyer to secure an accurate title opinion or a title-policy commitment letter is to avoid having to sue the seller for a breach of a warranty or covenant.

In essence, the title opinion written by a lawyer or the policy issued by a title insurance company often provides protection to the buyer when the seller's general warranty deed does not. Of course, as indicated in the previous chapter, all buyers must be aware of the limitations in protection that even title opinions and policies provide.

6. Buyer—Having the Property Insured and Surveyed

Because of the magnitude of real estate costs, most people cannot bear the risk of losing the property value due to potential hazards. Certainly when a buyer is borrowing money to purchase real estate, the lender will require that property-hazard insurance be purchased or that the seller assign the existing policy pursuant to a clause in the sales contract. Indeed, the lending institution usually will refuse to close the loan unless the borrower has given proof that insurance in at least the amount of the loan exists. This proof typically is provided by a letter from the insurance company to the lending bank or savings and loan association. Property insurance is indirectly vital to the title closing, since it must be obtained before the loan can be finalized, and the loan is crucial to the overall performance of the sales contract.

An actual survey of the property's boundaries is not always required before title is transferred. Indeed, in residential subdivisions which have been platted, the plat in the public records normally will suffice in lieu of a survey. However, if the lender requires that a survey be made, the buyer must pay for it unless the sales contract provides otherwise. Whenever there is a dispute or uncertainty over the actual boundaries, the parties should include in the sales contract a provision specifying whether the buyer or seller or both must pay for the survey.

7. Buyer—Inspecting the Property

For the purposes of this section, assume that the real estate involved has been improved with a building, such as a house. Except in unusual circumstances, a buyer will have visited the real estate once, twice, or many times before the sales contract is signed. Despite these numerous visits to view the property, prospective buyers seldom thoroughly investigate the plumbing, wiring, or heating system. At times they are subjected to pressure to sign a sales contract by sellers or their agents so as not to lose the opportunity to buy the particular house. Due to lack of time or for whatever other reason, the major utilities and appliances, if they also are sold, remain uninspected.

The high costs associated with the plumbing, wiring, heating/air-conditioning unit, stove, oven, dishwasher, and other appliances make it extremely important that these items be in good working order. If they are not, the buyer should know about it so that the offer to purchase can be adjusted accordingly.

Suppose that Christopher and Margaret Cook agree to buy a house from Donald and Elizabeth Wilson for $62,000. How can the Cooks be assured that the major appliances and utilities are in working order? One source of protection is a paragraph in the sales contract wherein the seller guarantees that all utilities and appliances will be working on the closing date. Although this clause provides some assurances to the Cooks, it is inadequate by itself. If the heating system works when the Cooks moved in but quits two weeks later, must the Wilsons fix it? No. The Wilsons only promised that the system would be working at the time of closing, and we assumed it was. In the absence of fraud, the Wilsons are relieved of any further obligation related to the heating unit or any other utilities and appliances.

The Cooks, in our hypothetical situation, like all other buyers, should inspect the premises during the time period before the closing. The seller must cooperate in allowing access to the buyer for this purpose. The expense of having someone knowledgeable inspect the major items of concern is far smaller than that of replacing the heating unit two weeks after closing the transaction. If something is found to be wrong with any of the utilities or appliances, the seller is responsible for repairing the defect before the closing. Depending on the materiality of the defect, failure of the seller to make the required repairs will either relieve the buyer of his contractual obligations or constitute a breach of the seller's promise concerning the utilities and appliances.

In recent years, the need to protect innocent buyers from poor residential construction has become obvious. In response to this need, real estate companies and builders have offered plans of buyer protection. Since the major problem seems to have been with newly constructed houses, builders have started to provide buyers with insurance coverage against major defects. One of the largest plans is called HOW —Home Owners Warranty. Under this program, qualified builders buy the purchaser a ten-year insurance policy against defects. During the first two years, the builder is to make the repairs needed. Then the insurance company will pay for the repairs of defects for the next eight years. If the builder fails to meet the obligations during the first two years, the insurance company will. Since the HOW coverage plan is transferrable during its ten-year life, it can be an advantage when selling a house. Absent this type of insurance, commercial builders generally are liable for defective construction. Courts have said builders implicitly give the buyer of a new home a warranty of habitability,[1] which is an implied promise that the house has been constructed in a workmanlike manner and is suitable for living.

Another very important reason for all buyers to inspect the premises carefully is to learn of any existing encumbrances that are not reflected in the recording system. As was previously pointed out, most title opinions and policies exempt from their coverage those defects or encumbrances that would be revealed by a physical inspection of the real estate. A buyer who fails to inspect physically when required to do so will be deemed to have constructive notice of everything that such an inspection would have reasonably revealed. Under circumstances when an encumbrance, such as a prescriptive easement, exists and is not covered by a title opinion or policy, the seller's warranty deed may provide valuable protection.

Case 13.2

A seller conveyed certain realty to a buyer by deed, with a covenant against encumbrances. Running across the property was an irrigation ditch that had been in existence so long that it could not legally be removed. The buyer had inspected the property and had seen the ditch but had concluded that it was abandoned.

Issue: Does a warranty deed with a covenant against encumbrances include a covenant against visible easements such as the ditch?

Decision: Yes.

Reasons: An easement that is a burden upon the estate granted and that diminishes its value constitutes a breach of the covenant against encumbrances in the deed. This is true whether the grantee had knowledge of its existence or whether the easement was visible and notorious. The intention to exclude an encumbrance should be stated in the deed itself. A resort to oral or other extraneous

[1]Glisan v. Smolenske, page 342.

evidence to negate an easement would violate settled principles of law in regard to deeds.

Jones v. Grow Investment and Mortgage Company, 358 P.2d 909 (Utah 1961).

8.   *Seller's Duties—In General*

The seller takes on the duties of obtaining the required deed, removing all unexcepted encumbrances including any outstanding loans, and furnishing a title-insurance-policy commitment letter if one is required by the sales contract. In the areas of the United States where termite or other pest infestation can cause substantial damage to a house, the buyer will want assurance that the property being purchased is without such infestation. Generally the sales contract should require the seller to furnish a certificate from a bonded pest-control company stating that the property is free from any wood-destroying organisms, in which case it is the seller's duty to obtain such a certificate before the closing. In addition, the seller sometimes will assign to the buyer the rights and duties under a service-maintenance contract with a pest-control company.

If the property being sold is commercial, the seller may have contractual duties to assist the buyer in changing the zoning restrictions. On closing rental property, the seller will have to turn over all valid leases to the buyer. In addition, rent schedules and letters to all tenants about the change of ownership must be provided. Once again, a sales contract can place special duties on the seller, which generally must be performed prior to closing the transaction.

9.   *Seller—Obtaining the Deed*

The seller's ultimate responsibility is to transfer title in order to close the transaction. In the vast majority of transactions, title is passed by delivery of a properly drafted and executed deed. Therefore, the seller has the duty to have a deed prepared and to sign it before the required number of witnesses and notaries. The type of deed that must be prepared depends on what is specified in the sales contract. As previously stated, most transactions involve title passing under a general warranty deed. However, if the contract is silent on the type of deed the seller

must deliver, most courts would rule that a bargain-and-sale deed satisfies this requirement. Remember, as was discussed in Chapter 5, nearly
all states require that the seller obtain the services of a lawyer to have
the deed drafted.

10. Seller—Removing Encumbrances

Frequently sales contracts place a duty on the buyer to inform the seller
of any defects that exist in the title to the property being sold. As
previously stated, the title opinion or policy usually is relied on by the
buyer as a means of learning about any defects or encumbrances
that might exist. After the buyer supplies this notice, it becomes the
seller's responsibility to clear these defects or encumbrances, if any,
from the title. If the seller cannot clear the title of existing claims,
the contract may provide that the buyer's duty to perform can be rescinded.

Even though a buyer may not notify the seller of existing defects,
there are circumstances that require the seller to remove encumbrances
or other defects in the title. For example, assuming that a deed other
than a quitclaim or a bargain-and-sale deed must be delivered to the
buyer, the seller covenants that the real estate title is free from all
encumbrances or defects except those specified in the deed. Certainly
no seller would purposely breach one of these covenants, since that
seller would ultimately be liable for such breach. Types of encumbrances that may have to be removed could include unrecorded claims
of ownership, encroachments by another, easements, and liens. To be
sure that the transaction can be closed properly and that the buyer has
no valid claim for a breach after title is transferred, the seller must take
steps to remove all defects and encumbrances from the title unless they
can be reasonably excepted in the deed.

Some states (including Connecticut, Florida, Illinois, Indiana,
Iowa, Michigan, Minnesota, Nebraska, North Dakota, Ohio, Oklahoma,
South Dakota, Utah, Vermont, and Wisconsin) have enacted statutes
that assist a landowner in clearing claims from the record title. Such
statutes frequently are known as Marketable Record Title Acts. Under
this type of law, if a person holds record title to a piece of real estate
for the statutory period (thirty to forty years is common) and no one
makes a claim against the property during that time, the title holder has
marketable title. These acts can result in awarding title to a person who

cannot claim through a valid chain of title, as is illustrated by the following case.

Case 13.3

In 1845, the State of Florida acquired from the United States lands under certain navigable water adjacent to Biscayne Bay in Miami. In 1898, Henry Flagler, without the right to do so, conveyed this land to the Florida East Coast Hotel Corporation. In 1919, the State of Florida properly conveyed the same land to the City of Miami. In 1944, the St. Joe Paper Company recorded a warranty deed to the same land from the Hotel Corporation. Over thirty years later, the City of Miami commenced this action asserting that it held legal title to the land. The Marketable Record Title Act, in effect in Florida, provided that any claim or interest in real estate is cut off unless the claimant preserves his claim by filing a notice within a thirty-year period.

Issue:

Does the Marketable Record Title Act operate to give St. Joe Paper Company legal title to the land?

Decision:

Yes.

Reasons:

The City argued that its claim was not barred by the Act, since the root of title relied on by St. Joe (i.e., the deed to it from Hotel Corporation) was a wild deed. The Act, however, can confer marketability on a chain of title arising out of a forged or wild deed. The purpose of the Act is to render marketable any estate in land recorded for thirty years or more and to make the estate free and clear of any interest arising from a transaction which occurred prior to the effective date of the root of title. "Root of title" is defined as the last title transaction recorded for at least thirty years. This allows persons to rely upon a deed recorded for a period of thirty years or more. The transfer from Henry Flagler to the Hotel Corporation was the root of St. Joe's title. Since the City did not record its interest during the thirty-year period commencing in 1944 when St. Joe acquired title through the wild deed, the City's interest was extinguished by operation of the Act. While the City asserted that the Marketable Record Title Act serves as a means whereby people may steal land, the City could easily have preserved its claim to the land by filing a notice within the thirty-year period.

City of Miami v. St. Joe Paper Company, 364 So.2d 439 (Fla. 1978).

The result in this case explains why more states have not adopted a Marketable Record Title Act. However, before condemning the concept, it must be stated that these acts would not deprive a long-time owner of real estate (like the city of Miami) of the property if that party had done one of the following:

1. Filed notice of ownership within the past thirty years or other statutory time period;
2. Remained in possession of the property; or,
3. Been assessed taxes on the property during the time provided (usually a short period such as three to seven years).

If a landowner fails to do any one of these required acts, the Marketable Record Title Act simply cuts off all claims of ownership. Those legislatures that have adopted this kind of act have facilitated land-title transactions by abolishing claims that become stale and unobvious. In essence, these acts limit the need to search a seller's title to only the past thirty or forty years (or whatever the statutory period is), rather than all the way back to the original grant from the sovereign. Despite Marketable Record Title acts, real estate still can be adversely possessed. Indeed, an adverse possessor is a type of encumbrance that must be removed by the seller.

11. Seller—Satisfying the Loan

Loans for the purchase of residential property usually are to be paid back over a period of twenty to thirty years. Due to the longevity of these loans, many owners do not complete their house payments before they sell the property. Therefore, a major encumbrance on the real estate being purchased is the seller's mortgage. Although it is an outstanding encumbrance prior to the closing, the buyer cannot claim to rescind the contract based on this encumbrance.

One of two things usually happens at closing with respect to the seller's loan: either it will be satisfied out of the sale's proceeds, or it will be assumed by the buyer. Whichever event is to occur, the seller must have the proper papers ready at the closing. With the aid of the seller's lender and lawyer, either a certificate of satisfaction, a release of the mortgage, or the loan-assumption papers must be prepared. For the purposes of our example below, the buyers are not assuming the sellers' loan; thus, a certificate or release stating that the sellers' loan and mortgage are satisfied is needed at the closing, and it should be recorded.

12.   Closing Costs

There are certain costs that must be paid by the buyer or the seller at the close of the transaction. Most of the buyer's costs relate to the financing of the purchase. Therefore, many buyers attempt to assume the seller's loan and mortgage in order to avoid the larger part of the closing costs. Specifically, the buyer normally must pay for the following in cash at closing: (1) loan origination fee, (2) loan discount points, (3) appraisal fee, (4) credit report fee, (5) lender's inspection fee, (6) mortgage-guarantee-insurance premium, (7) attorney's fees, (8) hazard-insurance premium, and (9) recording fees for the deed received and the mortgage given.

Often the loan origination fee, the discount points, and the mortgage-guarantee-insurance premium are calculated as a percentage of the loan amount. Typically, the other items of closing costs are flat fees regardless of the loan amount. In general, the total of all these costs may be from two to ten percent of the money borrowed. For example, assume that a buyer signs a contract to purchase real estate at $62,000 and plans to borrow ninety percent of this purchase price. On a loan of $55,800, closing costs could easily total $4000. Therefore, the buyer must have over $10,000 in cash to cover the down payment and closing costs. Of course, closing costs vary greatly according to location, the percentage loan, and other economic factors. For instance, the mortgage-guarantee-insurance premium usually is not charged on loans of eighty percent or less of the purchase price. Mortgage-guarantee insurance is discussed in detail in Chapter 14 on real estate finance.

The seller also is responsible for the payment of some costs at the closing. These frequently include (1) the real estate brokerage commission, if one is payable; (2) the attorney's fees for preparation of the deed or other documents; (3) the recording fee for the mortgage's certificate of satisfaction; and (4) the title policy premium. Coming up with the cash to pay these costs usually is not a major problem for the seller because they are simply subtracted from the proceeds of the sale.

The buyer's and seller's closing cost are examined further with the disclosure statement in Exhibit 13.1 in Section 14 below.

Real Estate Settlement Procedures Act

13. Introduction

Rising closing costs became a major concern of the United States Congress in the early 1970s. In hopes of keeping these costs down, Congress enacted the Real Estate Settlement Procedures Act (RESPA) in 1974, and amended it in 1975. (Some localities use the terms "settlement" and "settlement charges" instead of "closing" and "closing costs." For our purposes, these terms are synonymous.) The requirements of RESPA apply to virtually all original loans used to finance the purchase of one- to four-family properties.

Although Congress concentrated on high closing costs, RESPA does not establish a maximum level for these costs. Instead, the legislation attempts to prevent the occurrence of certain events that tend to drive the closing costs higher. The items covered include (1) disclosure of the closing costs to the buyer, (2) limitation on amounts of monthly reserve or escrow payments, (3) prohibition of referral fees or kickbacks, and (4) prohibition of the mandatory use of a particular title insurance company.

14. Full Disclosure

When a buyer files a loan application, the lender is required to provide a good-faith estimate of the closing costs. In addition, the lender must also give the buyer a copy of the Department of Housing and Urban Development's pamphlet entitled "Settlement Costs and You: A HUD Guide for Home Buyers." This booklet and the good-faith estimate of costs must be provided within three days of the loan application. The purpose of these requirements is to help educate borrowers and to encourage them to shop around for the best available credit terms.

Assuming that the buyer's loan is approved, the lender must comply with all the disclosure requirements of the truth-in-lending law. Basically, the truth-in-lending law requires that the finance charge and the annual percentage rate be disclosed to the borrower. Besides the items of disclosure already mentioned, the borrower can request the exact amount of the closing costs one business day prior to the actual closing. The costs are presented in the form of a closing statement such

EXHIBIT 13.1   RESPA CLOSING STATEMENT

A.	U.S. DEPARTMENT OF HOUSING AND URBAN DEVELOPMENT SETTLEMENT STATEMENT	B. TYPE OF LOAN

Conventional insured

ST. JOSEPH BANK
382 WEST BUTLER BOULEVARD
ST. JOSEPH, MISSOURI 64501

6. FILE NUMBER:	7. LOAN NUMBER: 28706-82
8. MORT. INS. CASE NO.:	

C. NOTE: This form is furnished to give you a statement of actual settlement costs. Amounts paid to and by the settlement agent are shown. Items marked "(p.o.c.)" were paid outside the closing; they are shown here for informational purposes and are not included in the totals.

D. NAME OF BORROWER:	E. NAME OF SELLER:	F. NAME OF LENDER:
CHRISTOPHER AND MARGARET COOK	DONALD AND ELIZABETH WILSON	ST. JOSEPH BANK

G. PROPERTY LOCATION:	H. SETTLEMENT AGENT: Ted Phillips of Phillips and Easton Law Firm PLACE OF SETTLEMENT: St. Joseph Bank	I. SETTLEMENT DATE: October 31, 1982
1097 Timbers Crossing St. Joseph, Missouri		

J. SUMMARY OF BORROWER'S TRANSACTION:		K. SUMMARY OF SELLER'S TRANSACTION:	
100. GROSS AMOUNT DUE FROM BORROWER		400. GROSS AMOUNT DUE TO SELLER	
101. Contract sales price	62,000.00	401. Contract sales price	62,000.00
102. Personal property		402. Personal property	
103. Settlement charges to borrower (line 1400)	4,230.40	403.	
104.		404.	
105.		405.	
Adjustments for items paid by seller in advance		Adjustments for items paid by seller in advance	
106. City/town taxes to		406. City/town taxes to	
107. County taxes to		407. County taxes to	
108. Assessments to		408. Assessments to	
109.		409.	
110.		410.	
111.		411.	
112.		412.	
120. GROSS AMOUNT DUE FROM BORROWER	66,230.40	420. GROSS AMOUNT DUE TO SELLER	62,000.00
200. AMOUNTS PAID BY OR IN BEHALF OF BORROWER		500. REDUCTIONS IN AMOUNT DUE TO SELLER	
201. Deposit or earnest money	1,000.00	501. Excess deposit (see Instructions)	
202. Principal amount of new loan(s)	55,800.00	502. Settlement charges to seller (line 1400)	4,403.20
203. Existing loan(s) taken subject to		503. Existing loan(s) taken subject to	
204. Loan Application fee	50.00	504. Payoff of first mortgage loan	32,800.00
205. Commitment fee	558.00	505. Payoff of second mortgage loan	
206.		506.	
207.		507.	
208.		508.	
209.		509.	
Adjustments for items unpaid by seller		Adjustments for items unpaid by seller	
210. City/town taxes to		510. City/town taxes to	
211. County taxes 1/1/82 to 10/31/82	638.40	511. County taxes 1/1/82 to 10/31/82	638.40
212. Assessments to		512. Assessments to	
213.		513.	
214.		514.	
215.		515.	
216.		516.	
217.		517.	
218.		518.	
219.		519.	
220. TOTAL PAID BY/FOR BORROWER	58,046.40	520. TOTAL REDUCTION AMOUNT DUE SELLER	37,841.60
300. CASH AT SETTLEMENT FROM ⊠⊠ BORROWER		600. CASH AT SETTLEMENT TO⊠⊠⊠⊠ SELLER	
301. Gross amount due from borrower (line 120)	66,230.40	601. Gross amount due to seller (line 420)	62,000.00
302. Less amounts paid by/for borrower (line 220)	58,046.40	602. Less reduction amount due seller (line 520)	37,841.60
303. CASH FROM BORROWER	8,184.00	603. CASH TO SELLER	24,158.40

L. SETTLEMENT CHARGES	PAID FROM BORROWER'S FUNDS AT SETTLEMENT	PAID FROM SELLER'S FUNDS AT SETTLEMENT
700. TOTAL SALES/BROKER'S COMMISSION based on price $ 62,000 @ 7% $4,340.00		
Division of commission (line 700) as follows:		
701. $ 4,340.00 to Real Estate Brokerage Company		
702. $ to		
703. Commission paid at Settlement		4,340.00
704.		
800. ITEMS PAYABLE IN CONNECTION WITH LOAN		
801. Loan Origination Fee 1 %	558.00	
802. Loan Discount 2 %	1,116.00	
803. Appraisal Fee to Gregory Atkinson	75.00	
804. Credit Report to St. Joseph Bank	30.00	
805. Lender's Inspection Fee		
806. Mortgage Insurance Application Fee to		
807. Assumption Fee		
808. Photographs		
809. Loan application fee	50.00	
810.		
811.		
900. ITEMS REQUIRED BY LENDER TO BE PAID IN ADVANCE		
901. Interest from to @ $ /day		
902. Mortgage Insurance Premium for 12 mo. to Mortgage Guaranty, Inc.	279.00	
903. Hazard Insurance Premium for 1 yrs. to (P.O.C.)	(521.00)	
904. yrs. to		
905.		
1000. RESERVES DEPOSITED WITH LENDER FOR		
1001. Hazard insurance 2 mo. @ $ 39.25 /mo.	78.50	
1002. Mortgage insurance mo. @ $ /mo.		
1003. City property taxes mo. @ $ /mo.		
1004. County property taxes 12 mo. @ $ 63.88 /mo.	766.50	
1005. Annual assessments mo. @ $ /mo.		
1006. mo. @ $ /mo.		
1007. mo. @ $ /mo. Total Reserves Deposited	845.00	
1008. mo. @ $ /mo.		
1100. TITLE CHARGES		
1101. Settlement or closing fee to		
1102. Abstract or title search to		
1103. Title examination to		
1104. Title insurance binder to		
1105. Document preparation to Little, Brown & Jacobs		30.00
1106. Notary fees to		
1107. Attorney's fees to Phillips & Easton	250.00	
(includes above items No.:)		
1108. Title insurance to		
(includes above items No.:)		
1109. Lender's coverage $		
1110. Owner's coverage $		
1111.		
1112.		
1113.		
1200. GOVERNMENT RECORDING AND TRANSFER CHARGES		
1201. Recording fees: Deed $ 9.00* ; Mortgage $ 6.00* ; Releases $ 4.00*	15.00	4.00
1202. City/county tax/stamps: Deed $; Mortgage $		
1203. State tax/stamps: Deed $ 29.20* ; Mortgage $167.40**	167.40	29.20
1204. * T.B. Strickland, Clerk ** Tax Commissioner,		
1205. Buchanan County		
1300. ADDITIONAL SETTLEMENT CHARGES		
1301. Survey to		
1302. Pest inspection to		
1303.		
1304.		
1305.		
1400. TOTAL SETTLEMENT CHARGES (enter on lines 103 and 502, Sections J and K)	4,230.40	4,403.20

as HUD's Uniform Settlement Statement in Exhibit 13.1. At the closing, the buyer and seller sign this statement and each receive a copy. Exhibit 13.1 is filled out in accordance with the Cook-Wilson transaction, pursuant to their sales agreement assumed earlier.

In addition to the fact that the sales price is $62,000, assume that the buyer is borrowing ninety percent of the purchase price, that the closing date is October 31, 1982, and that the 1982 city and county property taxes will be $766.50 and will become due on December 15, 1982. The buyer's closing costs include a loan origination fee of one percent of the loan, two discount points, a $75.00 appraisal fee, a $30.00 charge for the credit report, and a $50.00 loan application fee. Other information needed to complete this closing statement is the buyer's attorney's fee, which is $250 and includes a title search and opinion letter. The seller paid $30 for preparation of deed, and the sellers have an outstanding balance on their loan of $32,800 on date of closing. These figures are hypothetical, but they represent the figures involved in a typical residential sales transaction.

The preparation of a closing statement and the mortgage documents is the responsibility of the lender and the parties to the transaction. Usually this responsibility is delegated to a real-property lawyer. The real estate agent generally does not have an active role in the preparation of these documents.

Although this Uniform Settlement Statement appears rather complex at first glance, it really does simplify and summarize the financial transactions. Page 2 is a worksheet to help determine the seller's and buyer's closing costs. Upon studying this worksheet, most items should be self-explanatory. Lines 1000 through 1008 concern the reserves deposited by the buyer with the lender. These reserves also may be called escrow or impound payments. The limitation that RESPA places on the amount of these reserves is discussed in Section 15 below. The figures on lines 1201 through 1205 vary from state to state, as they are dependent on the amount charged for recording fees and other governmental taxes.

Returning to the first page of the closing statement, the buyer's transaction is summarized on the left side and the seller's on the right. In essence, the purchase price is the beginning point in both columns (lines 101 and 401). The Cooks, the buyers in our example, must pay for the items listed in lines 101 through 119 and totaled on line 120. Next, the Cooks are given credit for the amounts on lines 201 through 219, totaled on line 220. Line 303 shows the total amount of cash needed ($8184.00) by the Cooks at closing. The Wilsons, our sellers, are given credit for those items totaled on line 420. Then, the amounts that reduce the seller's proceeds are listed on lines 501 through 519 and totaled on line 520. The cash ($24,158.40) the Wilsons will receive at the closing is the amount on line 603.

Certain costs must be prorated or shared by the buyer and seller. These costs normally include state and local taxes, the hazard-insurance premium if that policy is to be assigned to the buyer, and the monthly mortgage payment if the buyer assumes the seller's loan. The costs of any other contracts that exist during the seller's and buyer's ownership should be prorated. For example, the cost of a pest-extermination contract purchased by the seller and not cancelled by the buyer must be shared. Whether this proration will appear as a credit to the seller or the buyer depends on which party pays the amount owed. In commercial sales, the collection or payment of rents also must be prorated equitably.

In our example, we assumed that the 1982 city and county taxes would not be due until December 15, 1982. Because the Cooks will be in possession of this real estate on that date, these taxes must be prorated so that the Wilsons contribute their share for January through October, 1982. This proration, shown on lines 211 and 511 of Exhibit 13.1, is calculated by multiplying the taxes due times the days each party possessed the house in 1982. For example, the Wilsons will have occupied the property for the 304 days of January through October. Thus, the taxes for which they are liable equals 304/365 X $766.50, or $638.-40. If the 1982 taxes are not known at the time of the closing, the amount of the 1981 taxes can be used as a reasonable estimate. When the amount of the 1982 taxes became known, adjustments may be made by the parties.[2]

15. *Limitation on Monthly Reserve Payments*

Another important protection provided by RESPA concentrates on the amount a lender can require a borrower to deposit on reserve to cover recurring expenses such as property taxes, hazard-insurance premiums, and other periodic assessments. A borrower's monthly housing payment always includes principal repaid on the money borrowed and interest charged for use of the money. In addition, it may include reserve payments, most commonly for taxes and insurance. These re-

[2]Wolfe v. Lake Shore Savings and Loan Association, page 344.

serve payments, also called escrow or impound payments, are deposited in a separate bank account, and the funds are used when needed to pay the recurring tax, insurance, and possibly other bills. Unfortunately for the borrower, RESPA does not sepcifically require that interest be paid on these deposited funds.

Case 13.4

Massachusetts had a law that required financial institutions to pay interest on real estate escrow-deposit funds. The Massachusetts Commissioner of Banks sought a declaratory judgment that this law was applicable to federally chartered savings and loan associations. Several of these federal associations argued that a federal regulation preempted this area of the law and made the Massachusetts law unconstitutional. The State Commissioner asserted that the Real Estate Settlement Procedures Act (RESPA) allowed the enforcement of such state laws.

Issue: Does RESPA validate a state law that requires interest to be paid on escrow-deposit funds?

Decision: No.

Reasons: [Having determined that the Massachusetts law requiring interest to be paid on escrow deposits was unconstitutional as a violation of the Supremacy Clause, the court addressed the application of RESPA.] RESPA does not carve out an exception that would permit the application of this state law. A state law must be complied with when the Secretary of Housing and Urban Development determines that the state law gives greater protection to the consumer than federal law does and settlement costs are involved. First, this Massachusetts law does not necessarily provide greater protection than does the federal law. Second, payment of interest on escrow deposits does not fall within the definition of settlement services given in RESPA. These services do involve title searches, title insurances, services rendered by an attorney, preparation of documents, property surveys, credit reports or appraisals, pest and fungus inspections, services rendered by a real estate agent, and the handling of the closing or settlement process.

Greenwald v. First Federal Savings & Loan Association of Boston, 446 F. Supp. 620 (D. C. Mass. 1978), aff'd 591 F.2d 417 (1st Cir. 1979).

Because there is no universal requirement that interest be paid on these escrow funds, RESPA provides a formula limiting the amount of reserves that the lender can collect at closing. A lender can require the borrower to pay for the months between the closing date and the last time the bill was paid. For example, we said that St. Joseph city and county taxes last were paid on December 15, 1981. From that date to October 31, 1982, the assumed closing date, is ten months. In addition, the lender can collect at closing a cushion of 1/6 (two months) of the amount payable. Thus, on line 1004 of the closing statement, the Cooks were assessed with a twelve-month reserve deposit for city and county taxes.

Now when the 1982 county taxes are due, the lender will have sufficient funds to pay them and still have a cushion left over. Any excess amount in the reserve or escrow account is refunded to the borrower when the loan is completely satisfied by payment. Line 1001 of the closing statement indicates only two months of advance payments for the hazard-insurance premiums. This is because the buyer had to purchase the entire first year of the policy outside the scope of the closing costs (see line 903).

16. Other RESPA Protections

Congress was concerned with lending institutions paying real estate agents or lawyers, or both, fees in return for these parties recommending that their customers and clients go to that lender to secure the necessary financing. The payment of referral fees or kickbacks probably was increasing the total amount of closing costs. Therefore, RESPA prohibits anyone from giving or receiving a fee or kickback under an agreement that business will be sent to the payor. This RESPA provision, of course, does not prevent the cooperative transactions between real estate agents and brokers within the multiple listing services.

Congress also was upset about the buyer's lack of choice in selecting a title insurance company if such insurance was purchased. Therefore, RESPA prohibits the seller and lender from requiring that the buyer purchase a title insurance policy from a particular company.

17. Remedies for RESPA Violations

Any buyer who feels that the RESPA requirements have not been followed should consult the party who conducted the closing. If an unfavorable response is encountered, the aggrieved buyer should contact a lawyer. RESPA provides remedies only when the prohibitions on referral fees and on mandatory title insurance companies are violated. These remedies allow the injured buyer to recover three times the amount of the referral fee of the title insurance premium as well as court costs and attorney's fees. In addition, there are criminal penalties for the payment of referral fees or kickbacks, up to a $10,000 fine or up to one year in prison or both. Any lawsuit seeking RESPA remedies must be filed within one year of the alleged violation.

Most closing agents are subject to the regulations of governmental agencies or the disciplinary procedures of professional associations. Any grievances also might be brought before these organizations. Copies of all complaints can be sent to the HUD Office of Consumer Affairs and Regulatory Functions, which has the primary responsibility for administering the RESPA program.

Despite the existence of RESPA, closing costs remain a major expense in many transactions today. Indeed, people who have never owned real estate can have tremendous difficulty in saving enough money for the down payment and the closing costs. Closing costs remain high because of certain inadequacies of RESPA as it now appears. For example, Congress refused to establish a percentage of the loan as a maximum for closing costs. Furthermore, the regulations are not strong enough to keep the costs down. Finally, the penalties imposed for violations of RESPA are weak. In fact, there is no apparent penalty suffered by a lender who fails to provide the required closing statement or who charges excessive reserve payments. In order to reemphasize its desire to hold closing costs to a minimum, Congress could tighten up the RESPA requirements.

Closing the Transaction

18. Introduction

After all the foregoing preparation has been completed, the actual closing can take place. During the closing, several transactions, including the financing, the escrow, and the passage of title, may be completed. Many times the parties involved leave a closing confused or uncertain about what has transpired. Although it may appear to be a large paper shuffle, an understanding of the closing is not difficult to grasp. First, everyone involved should know what to expect. Second, the actual events should be comprehended. Using the Cook-Wilson transaction represented in Exhibits 5.1 (the warranty deed) and 13.1 (the RESPA statement), we now examine a hypothetical closing.

19. Parties Present at the Closing

Although closings can be handled through the mail without ever having a group meeting of interested parties, a closing of a real estate transaction normally is held at the lending institution, the seller's lawyer's office, or the buyer's lawyer's office. Present at the closing will be the buyer, the seller, a representative of the lender, and the lawyer who represented the buyer. Other parties who may attend include the lender's lawyer, the seller's lawyer, a title insurance company representative, and the real estate broker. A real estate broker, if one was involved, attends the closing in order to collect his commission as well as to turn over any of the buyer's earnest money that the broker held pursuant to the sales contract.

In addition to those already mentioned, the escrow agent must be present if an escrow arrangement was used. Assume the Cook-Wilson sales contract provided that the Cooks would pay $1,000 as earnest money in escrow. Further, suppose the Wilsons were obligated to deliver the signed warranty deed to the escrow agent within five days of signing the contract. To close the entire transaction, the escrow must also be terminated, and that agent is needed to produce the earnest money and the deed. Since the escrow agent will often be the same bank that is lending the buyer money, the lender's representative may also represent the escrow agent.

20. Events at the Closing

The person in charge of the closing normally is the lawyer for one of the parties. After introductions, the lawyer will present the loan-related papers to the Cooks for their consideration and signatures. These papers will include the promissory note, which is the legal document stating that the Cooks, as borrower, will pay back the money loaned. In this case the Cooks are borrowing 90 percent of $62,000, or $55,800.

In addition to the promissory note, the Cooks will be presented with a loan-settlement statement, the required truth-in-lending papers (if they have not already received them), and the mortgage instrument. (See Chapter 14 for a complete discussion of these latter documents.) The mortgage, in essence, gives the lender a security interest or lien on the real estate subject to the loan's repayment. Some states use either a deed of trust or a security deed in lieu of the mortgage. These specialized deeds actually transfer the buyer's newly acquired title to a third party or the lender for as long as the loan is being repaid. A final, yet vital, document is the closing statement, a copy of which is given to the seller and buyer. The RESPA statement, discussed in detail under Section 14 above, often is used as this closing statement.

In some transactions, the buyer-seller relationship may be summarized by a simpler document. For example, if we suppose that the Cooks were assuming the Wilsons' unpaid mortgage, the closing statement might look like Exhibit 13.2. In this situation, closing costs are avoided to a substantial degree. While the Cooks are reading these loan papers, the lawyer in charge obtains the signed deed from the escrow agent or presents the unsigned deed to the seller for signatures. In our case, the Wilsons signed the warranty deed and delivered it to the escrow agent in accordance with the sales contract. The legal documents to be signed may be lengthy; nevertheless, the parties should read and study them before signing. No one should be afraid to take extra time or to ask questions to clarify ambiguous points. A real estate closing is an important event, and problem areas can be handled much more easily before

EXHIBIT 13.2   CLOSING STATEMENT

Property: Lot 3, Block G of Harris Billups Estate, Buchanan County, Missouri
Buyer: Christopher and Margaret Cook
Seller: Donald and Elizabeth Wilson

I.   Summary of Buyers' Transaction
     A.   Gross Amount Due from Buyers
          1.   Contract Sales Price $62,000.00
          2.   Transfer Fee to First
               Bank of St. Joseph   200.00
          3.   Recording Fees (Warranty Deed)   9.00
          4.   Attorney Fees   150.00

GROSS AMOUNT DUE FROM BUYERS $62,359.00

B.   Amounts Paid by or on Buyers' Behalf
  1.   Earnest Money Deposit $ 1,000.00
  2.   Amount of Loan Assumed   32,800.00
  3.   Items Paid by Buyer after
      Closing (Local Taxes
      1/1/82-10/21/82)   638.40

TOTAL AMOUNT PAID BY/FOR BUYERS   34,438.40

NET AMOUNT DUE FROM BUYERS   27,920.60

II.   Summary of Sellers' Transaction
    A.   Gross Amount Due Sellers
       1.   Contract Sales Price $62,000.00
       GROSS AMOUNT DUE SELLERS $62,000.00
    B.   Reductions in Amount Due Sellers
       1.   Amount of Loan Assumed $32,800.00
       2.   Earnest Money Received   1,000.00
       3.   Items Paid by Buyers after
          Closing (Local taxes
          1/1/82-10/31/82)   638.40
       4.   State Transfer Tax   28.00
       5.   Attorney Fees (drafting deed)   25.00
       TOTAL REDUCTIONS   34,491.40

       NET AMOUNT DUE TO SELLERS $27,508.60

III.   Distribution of Net Due From Buyers
     A.   Net Due Seller $27,508.60
     B.   Transfer Fee to Bank   200.00
     C.   Attorney Fees   175.00
     D.   Clerk Buchanan County
          Transfer Tax   28.00
          Recording Fee   9.00
       TOTAL DISTRIBUTED $27,920.60

The undersigned parties agree to the accuracy of this closing statement and acknowledge receipt of a copy of it.

_____   _____

Christopher Cook   Donald Wilson

_____   _____

Margaret Cook   Elizabeth Wilson

the documents are signed. Indeed, if all the papers are not properly prepared, the closing should be postponed until a later date.

Let us assume the Cooks' lawyer is satisfied with the various loan papers and they sign them. These papers are delivered to the lender's representative, and the loan is thereby closed. The Cooks must then write a check for the amount not covered by the loan. This amount covers the down payment plus closing costs. Exhibit 13.1 shows $8,-231.69 as the amount owed in cash. The $1,000 earnest money is received from the escrow agent and applied to the purchase price. After the purchase price and closing costs have been paid, the signed deed is delivered to the Cooks. Actually, the deed is taken by the Cooks' attorney to the courthouse to be filed with the public records. Thereafter, the Cooks will receive the deed in the mail. The buyer's attorney will examine the seller's title one last time to make sure no encumbrances have arisen between the date of the first title search and the closing.

Although the deed delivery represents passage of title, the closing is not yet completed. The money must be distributed. The Wilsons' lender is paid the amount remaining due on the Wilsons' loan and mortgage. Thereupon, that lender executes and delivers a certificate of satisfaction, which is also filed with the public records. Next the real estate broker receives the commission earned. Then whatever is left after these items are paid goes to the Wilsons. This amount is commonly called the seller's equity and profit. Exhibit 13.1 indicates the Wilsons will receive $24,158.40. The seller's equity may be held in escrow until the title search is conducted and the title is declared to be free from defects.

These events may take only ten to fifteen minutes in a simple residential closing or an hour or more in a more complex transaction. Regardless of how long it takes, a successful closing accomplishes its goal of completing the real estate transaction by transferring title from the seller to the buyer.

Cases on Closing the Sales Transaction

Glisan v. Smolenske
387 P.2d 260 (Colo. 1963).

Frantz, C. J.:

In the early months of 1957, Henry C. Glisan, who is a builder, was erecting houses in Holy Hills Subdivision in Arapahoe County, and the street on which some of these houses were being built is South Jasmine Place. Mrs. Smolenske, during the first days of March, 1957, had inspected a house then under construction at 2501 South Jasmine Place, had called the real estate agency handling its sale, and had an initial discussion with the agency and Glisan concerning the sale and purchase of the property.

A day or two later Mr. Smolenske, accompanied by his wife, looked at the premises. Negotiations ensued in which the Smolenskes, Glisan, and the agency participated. On the occasion of one of these meetings at the premises Mr. Smolenske observed that caissons were being constructed for the house next to 2501 South Jasmine Place, and upon inquiry was told by Glisan that due to soil difficulties he had to put in caissons in this property. To allay Mr. Smolenske's expressed concern about 2501 South Jasmine Place, Glisan assured Mr. Smolenske that he had undertaken structural measures to overcome the soil difficulties.

These structural measures were the use of spread footings, and of slightly heavier steel beams in the foundation of the house at 2501 South Jasmine Place than required by the building code. Their nature was unknown to the Smolenskes. It appears that spread footings were quite extensively used in the subdivision.

As a result of the negotiations the Smolenskes entered into an agreement on March 21 to purchase what in that document is described as a "home,"...

By the terms of the agreement the Smolenskes were required to pay $26,-700.00 for the property. A receipt for $500.00 earnest money was part of the agreement.

At the time of executing the agreement the house was still in the course of construction. Nor was the house completed on April 1, 1957, the "closing" date of the transaction. It was admitted that to the date of trial Glisan had failed to place tile in the

entry way and to enclose the furnace with plywood. As reason for not using a plywood enclosure Glisan asserted the risk of fire arising from such framework.

It was, therefore, contemplated that the house being built was a "home"; that the builder was "to include" certain items in the home; that the home was "to be completed in workmanlike manner"; and that possession of the home was to be given at the time of transfer of title. These were the material matter of the contract, and these formed the nature of the thing which Glisan, as vendor, was proposing to sell to the Smolenskes, as purchasers....

The Smolenskes occupied the premises on April 1, 1957, and they have lived there ever since. Shortly after they moved in, cracks started appearing in the surfaces of the house, and as time passed, these cracks enlarged. Doors and windows tilted. Other defects developed. All these imperfections resulted from contraction and expansion of the soil upon which the house rested, depending upon the dryness or dampness of the soil beneath the foundation.

The Smolenskes ... relied for a recovery of damages against Glisan upon a breach of implied warranty of fitness for habitation....

One of the early decisions in this country on the point is that written in the case of Vanderschierer v. Aaron, 103 Ohio App. 340, 140 N.E.2d 819. In that case the rule prevailing in England was adopted, and the Court held that an implied warranty of fitness for human habitation existed. We follow the Vanderschrier case.

A statement of the law often cited appears in the leading case of Miller v. Cannon Hill Estates, Ltd.:

... The position is quite different when you contract with a builder or with the owners of a building estate in the course of development that they shall build a house for you or that you shall buy a house which is then in the course of erection by them. There the whole object, as both parties know, is that there shall be erected a house in which the intended purchaser shall come to live. It is the very nature and essence of the transaction between the parties that he will have a house put up there which is fit for him to come into as a dwelling house. It is plain that in those circumstances there is an implication of law that the house shall be reasonably fit for the purpose for which it is required, that is for human dwelling.

Ordinarily, the measure of damages recoverable for a breach of warranty is the difference between the actual value of the property at the time of sale and what its value would have been if it had been as warranted. . . . But where the buyer has retained the property and uses it, as here, he may make reasonable expenditures to bring the property into conformity with the warranty, and such expenditures may represent the measure of the buyer's damages —another way of arriving at this difference in value. . . . The latter application was appropriately used in this case.

The judgment is *affirmed*.

Wolf v. Lake Shore Saving and Loan Association
253 N.E.2d 112 (Ill. App. 1969).

Dempsey, J.:

This is an appeal from an order dismissing the plaintiff's complaint.

The complaint contained the following allegations: The plaintiff entered into a contract with the defendant to purchase certain real estate. The contract provided that the buyer would take subject to general taxes due and payable after the year 1967, but that all unpaid taxes were to be pro-rated to the date of the closing of the transaction. The transaction was closed on February 28, 1967 and, because the amount due for the unpaid taxes for the year 1966 was not yet known or available, the taxes were pro-rated temporarily on the basis of the 1965 tax bill; this was in accordance with a common practice followed in most real estate transactions. When the 1966 tax bill became ascertainable, it was for an amount that was in excess of the sum credited to the plaintiff at the time the transaction was closed. The 1966 tax, and

the tax from January 1, 1967 to the closing date computed on the basis of the 1966 tax bill, was $2,004.77 more than the sum credited to the plaintiff.

The defendant advanced several grounds in support of its motion to strike and dismiss, but only two were of substance and neither of these justified dismissing the complaint. One of these was that at the time the deal was closed a statement pro-rating all taxes was accepted by the plaintiff. . . . The statement, however, did not support the defendant any more than it did the plaintiff. The cryptic notation in the statement did nothing more than confirm the undisputed fact that the taxes for fourteen months (twelve months of 1966 and the first two months of 1967) were pro-rated on the basis of the 1965 tax bill. The notation did not indicate whether the pro-ration was a temporary one as charged by the plaintiff or a final one as averred by the defendant. The unsigned closing statement of itself confers no contractual rights and it does not supersede the provisions of the previous contract or the subsequent deed. It may have evidentiary value to show the intention of the parties as to the terms of the contract but it was not dispositive of the issue between them. Likewise, a provision in the contract that "All pro-rating shall be as of the date of closing of deal and time is of the essence of this contract," has probative value and adds credence to the defendant's contention that the pro-ration in the closing statement was a final one. Standing alone, however, or read in conjunction with the statement, it does not establish this as a matter of law.

The other ground for dismissal which appeared to have substance was the averment that a deed was delivered to the plaintiff which provided that the premises were conveyed subject to taxes for the years 1966 and 1967. The averment was accompanied with the argument that all agreements between a seller and a purchaser in a real estate transaction are merged in a deed unless the contract provides for subsequent acts by either party. The legal argument was correct . . . but its application to the complaint was premature. The complaint alleged that a subsequent act was to be performed by the parties, that of pro-rating. The plaintiff asserted, without denial by the defendant, that it was agreed that this was to be done on the basis of the 1966 tax bill, and she alleged this was a common practice followed in most real estate transactions. These allegations were relevant to the issue of whether the contract merged into the deed and the plaintiff should be given the opportunity to prove them. . . .

The plaintiff's complaint stated a cause of action. It should not have been either stricken or dismissed upon the grounds urged by the defendant.

Reversed and remanded.

REVIEW QUESTIONS

1. The terms "closing the transaction" and "settling the transaction" often are used. What is the distinction between these phrases and what do they mean?
2. Both the buyer and the seller have certain acts they either must or should do after the sales contract is signed but before title is transferred. Briefly, what are the buyer's and seller's duties in general?
3. Barbara Barrett signed a sales contract that conditioned her performance on her ability to secure adequate financing. Because Barbara failed to apply for a loan, she did not make arrangements to borrow the money needed to meet the sales price. At the closing, will Barbara be excused from performing her duties under the contract? Why?
4. Assuming Barbara Barrett is not excused from her contractual promises in the previous problem, what is her potential liability? Explain.
5. In 1972, the Sage Construction Company built a house and sold it to the Hammonds. In 1975, the Hammonds resold the house to Barnes. Shortly after moving into the house, Barnes discovered that the basement leaked and that there were substantial cracks in basement walls. Should the Sage Construction Company be liable to Barnes for the cost ($4000) of these repairs? Why?

6. During 1974, the Nielsens hired an architect, contractors, and subcontractors to build a mountain home. After being unable to sell the house, the Nielsens moved into it. In 1976, the Mazureks purchased this house from the Neilsens. Shortly thereafter, the water supply diminished. The Mazureks ran tests and discovered that the well was not capable of producing enough water for household use. Based on these facts, are the Neilsens the type of seller-builder who implicitly warrant this house to be habitable? Would the water supply be included in an implied warranty of habitability? Explain.

7. What are the common elements of closing costs to be paid by the seller and the buyer at a closing of a residential sales transaction?

8. RESPA, the Real Estate Settlement Procedures Act, was enacted to control the amount of closing costs. What four things does RESPA attempt to do in order to achieve its purpose?

9. Assume in your community that real property taxes are due on December 1 of each year. If a buyer is closing a loan transaction on March 1, how many months of these taxes may the lending institution collect at closing? If closing was on November 1, how many months of taxes can be collected at the closing?

10. List, in order, the events that occur at a typical closing of a real estate sales transaction.

14

Real Estate Finance

1. Introduction

For the average American family, the largest financial transaction of their lives usually involves real estate. It is very seldom that buyers of real estate pay cash to close the transaction. Indeed, even if a buyer had sufficient funds to pay cash, Chapter 8 explained that tax laws actually encourage the financing of the real estate purchase. Typically, a buyer of real estate will borrow money from a financial institution, which will take a security interest in the real estate. Most frequently this security interest is based on a mortgage. The borrower who grants a security interest in real estate via a mortgage is called a *mortgagor.* The lender who receives the security interest is a *mortgagee.* This chapter will examine various types of mortgages, the mortgage transaction, the enforceability of mortgages, and the priority of mortgages.

2. Historical Development of the Mortgage Concept

Originally a mortgage was a pledge of real property to secure a debt. The concept is not new, but goes back to Egyptian, Greek, and Roman times. Under early Roman law, nonpayment of a mortgage loan entitled the lender to make the borrower his slave. These severe terms were later modified to permit the debtor to remain free while working off his debt. Still later, Roman law was changed to permit the unpaid debt to be satisfied by the sale of the mortgaged property.

Basic mortgage law in the United States goes back to English common law. Although the concept of using real estate to secure a debt was widespread in England by the eleventh century, Christian strictures against usury prohibited the charging of interest on loans. Christian lenders therefore took over a debtor's property and collected rents until the debt was paid. Not being bound by Christian rules, Jewish lenders charged interest and left the borrower in possession of his property. By the fourteenth century, however, the charging of interest while leaving the borrower in possession, known as *hypothecation*, became universal.

The relative rights of the borrower and lender with respect to the mortgaged property were still not resolved fully. Early mortgages provided that if the borrower met all of the terms of the loan and completely repaid the debt, the mortgage was then defeated and the title was returned. If any of the conditions were not met, however, the borrower lost all rights to the property, including all money previously paid, and the property was sold to repay the debt. Gradually a system evolved to give the borrower more rights and to enable him to redeem his property within a certain period of time after default by repaying the debt.

Today in the United States, the mortgage document and the rights given to the lender and borrower vary from state to state. The laws of some of the eastern states that were influenced greatly by the English common law provide that the mortgagee (lender) receives full legal title to mortgaged property. This is known as the "title theory" of mortgages. A few states follow the logic that a mortgage gives the mortgagee legal title but only for the purpose of protecting a security interest in the real estate. These states follow the "intermediate theory" of mortgages. The majority of states have laws which give the mortgagee only a lien against, not title to, mortgaged property. Mortgages in these states involve the "lien theory."

These various theories of mortgages were very important in determining the mortgagees' rights to possess and sell the real estate subject to the mortgage at the time the mortgage document was executed. Mortgagees in "title" states had greater rights to the property than did those in "lien" states, with mortgagees in "intermediate" states coming in between. Today, states following "title" and "intermediate" theories have eliminated most of the mortgagees' rights to the property unless they are necessary to protect the security interest in the real estate. Typically, mortgagors (borrowers) in all states remain in possession of the mortgaged property until a default occurs. At the time of default, mortgagees can either take possession immediately ("title" and "intermediate" theories) or can exercise legal rights that will result in gaining possession of the property ("lien" theory). In the discussion "Enforcing the Mortgage" (p. 367) the mortgagees' rights upon a default will be examined in more detail.

Types of Financing

3. Introduction

During periods of stable interest rates, the principal method of financing real estate transactions is through the conventional mortgage, pursuant to which the mortgagor grants a security interest in real estate in return for the money loaned. The mortgagor agrees to repay both the principal amount of loan and the interest in fixed monthly payments. The interest rate charged is the same throughout the life of the loan, usually twenty-five to thirty years. The mortgagee's security interest is dissolved when the final monthly payment is made or a lump-sum payment satisfies the obligation prior to the due date.

The use of this conventional mortgage fell out of favor during the 1930s because the borrowers' promises to repay were insured only by the value of real estate mortgaged. During the Great Depression, land values decreased to the point that lenders were no longer secure. As a part of the New Deal legislation, Congress created the Federal Housing Administration (FHA) to insure mortgage loans. In return for a fee that is usually one-half of one percent of the unpaid balance, the FHA acts as an insurer of repayment from borrowers to approved private lenders who actually make the loan. The FHA mortgage loan program has been extremely successful, although its importance to mortgage markets diminished during the seventies because of the availability of private mortgage insurance.

The Veterans Administration (VA) loan guarantee program was established during World War II. The VA mortgage guarantee is very similar to FHA mortgage insurance, except that no fee is charged the veteran for the guarantee. The government pays any losses out of general tax funds. The popularity of the FHA and VA programs reached a peak in 1955, when over 45 percent of outstanding mortgages were either FHA-insured or VA-guaranteed. By the late seventies, however, the number of new loans of this type had fallen to approximately 10 percent of all new mortgage loans.

The conventional mortgage loan is neither FHA-insured nor VA-guaranteed. However, the coventional loan may have private mortgage insurance. This availability of private mortgage insurance is the primary reason that conventional mortgages, rather than government-insured loans, have dominated the mortgage markets. Private mortgage insurance usually costs the equivalent of 2 percent of the loan amount. This amount can either be paid in cash at the closing or it can be financed. In the latter case, the borrower must pay ½ of 1 percent of the loan amount at closing, and the other 1.5 percent over a ten-year period. All financial institutions that make conventional loans require private mortgage insurance unless the loan is for 80 percent or less of the property value. Therefore, the higher the down payment a borrower can make, the less likely will be the necessity of paying for mortgage insurance when taking out a conventional loan.

In addition to the conventional mortgages, FHA-insured mortgages, and VA-insured mortgages, there are numerous other types of mortages, which differ in the legal positions of the parties and in the flexibility of interest rates charged. Sections 4 through 7 discuss some of these alternatives to the traditional, conventional, fixed-rate mortgage. Section 8 examines leasehold financing, which is an alternative to all types of mortgage financing.

4. Deed of Trust

In many states the *deed of trust* or *trust deed* has been the most commonly used mortgage instrument. It conveys title to the real estate to a third party, called the trustee, who holds it in security for the debt. Thus, whereas the conventional mortgage involves two parties—the mortgagor (borrower) and the mortgagee (lender)—the deed of trust involves three parties—the trustor (borrower), the trustee, and the trust beneficiary (lender).

The trustee's title lies dormant as long as the borrower is meeting the terms of the loan. However, in the event of default, the trustee sells the property to pay off the debt to the lender. Under this power of sale, the trustee transfers to the new purchaser all the right, title, and interest that the borrower had at the time the deed of trust was executed.

The deed of trust can simplify the foreclosure process, a topic to be examined in Section 16 below.

5. Purchase-Money Mortgage

When the seller of real estate lends the buyer the money that enables that buyer to make the purchase and takes a security interest in the property sold, a *purchase-money mortgage* is involved. Sometimes it is advantageous for the seller of a property, particularly the seller of raw land, to finance a sale himself, without involving a financial institution. Some of these advantages were discussed in Chapter 11, Section 11, under the heading "Contracts for a Deed." One reason for the seller to agree to a purchase-money mortgage is that it can reduce federal income taxes. If part of the purchase price is received in future years, the seller can treat the transaction as an installment sale and count as income only that portion of the profit represented by the year's payments. This device defers the tax due and may place the seller in a lower tax bracket by reducing income received in any one year.

In times of tight mortgage markets, sellers often will have to agree to finance the transaction in order to sell the property. If mortgage funds are not available or are at a very high interest rate, buyers will seek alternative sources of funds. Sellers who are financially able to carry a purchase-money mortgage make their properties more attractive from the financing standpoint. When the transaction involves vacant, unimproved land, a purchase-money mortgage frequently contains a subordination clause to allow the purchaser to obtain a first mortgage loan to finance the building of improvements on the property. In that case, the purchase-money mortgage becomes a junior mortgage. The priority of junior mortgages is discussed more completely in Section 20 below.

6. Variable-Rate Mortgages

Before the 1930s, relatively short-term mortgages with large balloon notes at the end of the term were the most commonly used type of mortgage instruments. If the mortgagor still met credit requirements, the mortgage was refinanced at the end of the term, usually around five years, at the then-current interest rate.

During the Great Depression, new programs such as FHA mortgage insurance led to the widespread use of the long-term, fixed-interest-rate mortgage, and this type of mortgage has been standard in the United States for the last half century. However, during periods involving high rates of inflation and the attendant rapidly rising interest rates, the fixed-rate mortgage is less popular among lenders.

Despite its common use in England, Canada, and many other countries, the *variable-rate mortgage* (VRM) was not adopted widely in the United States during the 1970s. In 1979 the Federal Home Loan Bank Board (FHLBB) authorized federally chartered savings and loan associations to issue variable-rate mortgages whose interest rate could be adjusted annually by as much as half a percentage point a year and up to two-and-a-half percentage points over the life of the loan in accordance with some predetermined relationships to an index of market interest rates, the lender's cost of funds, or the Consumer Price Index. Since the board also required the Savings and Loan Associations (S&Ls) to continue to offer fixed-rate mortgages, which consumers preferred, the idea did not catch on except in California, where S&Ls have used the variable-rate mortgage for several years.

In 1980, however, the FHLBB authorized the S&Ls to issue *renegotiated-rate mortgages* (RRM), or rollover mortgages, and allowed them to stop making fixed-interest-rate loans. Under this plan, home loans would be made for a term of thirty years but would "roll over" every three to five years at a renegotiated interest rate. The rate could rise as much as half a percentage point a year up to a maximum of five percentage points over the life of the loan. It could fall an unlimited amount.

Although the renegotiated-rate mortgage has been used for some time in several states (Wisconsin, Ohio, Florida, Washington, and the New England area), the plan was furiously attacked by consumer groups, while the savings and loan industry vigorously defended it. Periods characterized by volatile shifts in interest rates are likely to see the use of a range of these variable-rate mortgages, such as the renegotiated-rate concept.

One of the problems that may face many younger families is the difficulty of making the monthly payments required under a conventional fixed-rate mortgage during the first few years of the loan's life. Although it is not actually a mortgage with variable interest, the *graduated-payment mortgage* (GPM) is designed to help such families. Under the graduated-payment plan, payments are lower in the first five years than under a fully amortized mortgage, usually being insufficient even to cover fully the interest on the loan. For example, a standard FHA-insured mortgage for $50,000 at 9.5 percent interest requires a monthly payment for principal and interest of $420. Under the most popular type of graduated-payment mortgage, payments are $318 the first year and rise by 7.5 percent annually until they reach $457 monthly during the fifth year. They then remain at this level for the remaining life of the loan. It is hoped that use of the graduated-payment mortgage will help ease the strain on the budget of a new entrant into the employment market. Meanwhile, the increase in the monthly payment should be offset by increases in salaries during those first five years.

A variation of the graduated-payment mortgage that includes the concept of variable interest rates is the *graduated-payment adjustable mortgage* (GPAM). As with the graduated-payment mortgage, the initial payment would be lower but could increase substantially. The interest rate could be adjusted up or down a maximum of one-half of one percentage point a year. Without a maximum on the overall increase of interest rate, a GPAM instrument would allow monthly payments to increase very fast. For example, a thirty-year $50,000 loan at an initial rate of 13 percent would have an original GPAM payment of $428.09 a month. During the sixth year, if there were constant maximum interest rate increases, the monthly payment would be $657.46. These figures are compared with a $553.10 monthly payment for a fixed-rate mortgage at 13 percent. With these rapid increases, the borrower's income may not keep pace, resulting in an untenable situation for the borrower.

7. Other Types of Mortgages

In addition to influencing the creation of mortgage instruments that vary the interest rate over time, inflationary conditions and unstable interest rates have led to the development of mortgages that allow the lender to share in the possible appreciation in the value of the mortgaged property. These types of mortgages include the participation mortgage, the shared-appreciation mortgage, and the reverse-annuity mortgage. These same pressures also can lead to increased use of the wraparound mortgage.

A. PARTICIPATION MORTGAGE

Traditionally, real estate developers have taken the entire entrepreneurial role in developing commercial and industrial properties, reaping the benefits if the project is successful, while financial institutions have furnished most of the needed mortgage funds at fixed rates of interest. Quite often, lenders actually furnish 100 percent of the necessary funds, leaving the developer with little invested in the project but time. The lender participated fully in the risks of the project if it went sour, but reaped no additional benefits if the project was successful or if inflation increased its income.

The need of financial institutions to protect themselves against the ravages of inflation, in additon to the "seller's market" for mortgage funds that exists during tight-money periods, often leads many lenders to demand some form of equity-participation in their commercial loans. Such *participation mortgages,* as they are called, take a variety of forms, including: (1) a percentage of gross or net income; (2) "free equity," under which the lender, as a condition of the loan, acquires partial equity ownership; or (3) joint-venture arrangements, by which a partnership is created between the lending institution, which provides money, and the developer, who provides entrepreneurial skills.

Lender participation can be desirable for both borrower and lender. The participation feature usually allows the developer to borrow a larger amount than would otherwise be available and at better terms. If the lender agrees to participate in a percentage of gross or net income received above a certain level, the added burden of the participation agreement will not be felt until the project is successful. Joint ventures between developers and lenders may also enable developers to particpate in more projects and diversify their risk.

Equity participations can reduce the risk of inflation to the lender, but they can also increase financial risk. In the real estate boom of the early 1970s, some financial institutions became so enamored of the prospect of obtaining part of a project's equity that they failed to analyze its risk potential properly. During the recession that followed, some learned the painful fact that a fixed-return mortgage in a successful project is far more valuable than an equity participation in a failed project.

B. Shared-Appreciation Mortgage

The *shared-appreciation mortgage* (SAM) carries the principle of the participation mortgage into residential financing, primarily to assist first-time buyers. It bears a fixed interest rate set below the prevailing market rate, along with contingent interest based on the appreciation of the property at maturity or payment in full of the loan on sale or transfer of the property. For example, the share of the appreciation payable as contingent interest may not exceed 40 percent of net appreciation, and the maximum term of the loan may be ten years with guaranteed long-term refinancing.

The shared-appreciation mortgage likely will see increased use during periods of inflation or rising interest rates. Because the lower interest rates mean lower monthly payments, it may permit some buyers to purchase homes that otherwise would be beyond reach. Being able to buy a house that should appreciate in value may outweigh the potential appreciation given up in the form of contingent interest. The alternative during tight money markets may be to forego the purchase because affordable funds are not available.

C. REVERSE-ANNUITY MORTGAGE

Another type of mortgage is the reverse-annuity mortgage (RAM), designed for older homeowners who want to get some of the equity out of their house without having to sell and move elsewhere. Under this concept, the owner of a home that is fully paid for may secure a mortgage for approximately 80 percent of appraised value. The proceeds of this loan are used to purchase an annuity whose monthly proceeds pay the interest on the loan and provide income for the owners. The principal amount of the loan is paid from the owner's estate or from sale of the home at time of death.

D. WRAPAROUND MORTGAGE

Although it does not involve the concept of the mortgagor and mortgagee participating in or sharing the appreciation, inflationary circumstances and rising interest rates have encouraged many people to use the wraparound mortgage. A *wraparound mortgage* is a second mortgage that includes an existing first mortgage. It is used when the interest rate on the existing mortgage is below the rate currently charged on new loans. The existing mortgage remains on the property and the new loan "wraps around" it.

For example, suppose a commercial property that is sold for $500,-000 is subject to a $250,000 mortgage at 8 percent interest which has fifteen more years to run. If current mortgage interest rates are fourteen percent, a new lender might be willing to make, say, a $400,000 loan on the property at 11 percent. This would consist of the existing loan plus an additional loan of $150,000. The new lender would be responsible for making payments on the first mortgage, at 8 percent, while the mortgagor was making payments on the new loan of $400,000 at 11 percent. This transaction produces a net yield of 16 percent for the second mortgagee. The advantages of the wraparound mortgage are that the mortgagor can borrow money below the current interest rate while the second mortgagee nets a yield above the current rate.

8. Leasehold Financing

Leases may be used as substitutes for fee ownership and mortgage financing by business firms. Leasing may offer several advantages to business firms, including the freeing of long-term capital for current uses and substantial tax benefits. Long-term leases may vary only slightly (except in legal terms) from fee simple ownership and mortgage financing. For example, a business firm (lessee) may arrange to have a developer purchase land and construct improvements for its needs, which the developer will then lease to the firm. Under the long-term lease, the rental payments will often completely amortize the investment and provide a return to the owner (lessor). It is not uncommon for title to the property to pass to the lessee at the end of the lease period, making the lease very similar to the purchase of the property with a 100 percent fully amortized loan.

One variation on leasehold financing is the sale-leaseback arrangement, under which the owner sells his property and simultaneously leases it back from the buyer. The buyer gets a profitable investment, and the seller-lessee frees his money for other purposes. This type of sale-leaseback arrangement can be used with older properties as well as new projects. In the latter case, the sale-leaseback arrangement may be known as a buy-build-sell lease.

Why would a firm enter into a long-term lease agreement rather than own and finance the property? There are several reasons:

1. Under a lease, the user of the property can in effect get 100 percent financing. As owner, the firm would commonly have to supply a portion of the purchase price from equity funds.
2. In the case of an older property, the firm will be able to convert illiquid equity funds to working capital without surrendering the use of the property.
3. The firm will be out of the real estate business. Many companies consider this to be a great advantage of leasing, since they feel that their funds can be used most effectively and profitably in

their special area. Many others take the opposite view, of course, feeling that real estate is a very profitable investment.

4. Leasing offers major tax advantages. The development of urban properties requires large outlays for the purchase of land, but such expenditures cannot be depreciated. If the owner sells the property and leases it back, however, all of the lease payments are tax-deductible business expense. In other cases, it may be advantageous to sell the property because the present owner has already fully depreciated it, while a new purchaser could receive tax benefits by depreciating it all over again.

The Financing Transaction

9.   Introduction

Chapter 12 included a discussion of closing a real estate sales transaction. Contained within that chapter was a reference to the typical financing transaction, which usually consists of a borrower applying for a loan, the lender making a commitment to grant the loan, and the preparation and execution of legal documents. Federal and state laws substantially affect the entire financial transaction, because they insure that disclosure requirements are met and that fair-lending practices are satisfied. Throughout the following sections, a conventional mortgage transaction is examined. Any of the other types of mortgages just discussed could be substituted, and the transaction would remain about the same.

10.   Loan Application and Commitment

The loan application is a most important source of information used by the lender in determining whether the prospective borrower has the ability and probable desire to fulfill faithfully the mortgage loan agreement. This application is usually supported by other confirming documents, such as verification of bank deposits, credit report, verification of employment, and appraisal of the property. For commercial properties, the application and supporting documents would, of course, be much more elaborate and detailed.

If the lender is satisfied that the applicant has the ability and willingness to repay the loan, and that the property offered as security has a market value that will exceed the unpaid balance of the loan throughout the life of the mortgage, he will issue a commitment letter. This sets forth the terms of the loan and the conditions that must be met before closing. The latter might include the completion of a property under construction, or the successful sale of a currently-owned home and satisfaction of the mortgage on that property.

In some states the commitment both obligates the lender to make the loan at the specified terms and the borrower to pay a commitment fee even though the loan is never actually closed. In most states the commitment is considered an offer by the lender which must be accepted by the prospective borrower within a certain time period. If the applicant accepts, the lending institution is obligated to make these funds available for a specified period, usually several months, in return for the commitment fee, which often is one percent of the loan amount.

Case 14.1

Selective Homebuilders was constructing a garden apartment complex, known as Park Terrace, in Bensalem Township, Pennsylvania. In March 1974, the Hudson City Savings Bank made a commitment to make a permanent loan of $1,200,000 on the project. This commitment would automatically expire unless the loan was closed by January 1, 1975. Selective proposed in November that the loan be closed with a small "holdback" until minor work on some of the units was completed. The savings bank led the construction company to believe that such a closing might be possible but notified it on December 24 that the project would have to be fully completed, ready for occupancy, and the loan closed by January 1 or the commitment would be null and void. Selective was unable to comply with the conditions of the notice, and as a result the closing did not take place. Selective argued that the Hudson City Savings Bank was committed to make the loan.

Issue: Was the lender required to honor the commitment to make a permanent loan even though the property was not 100 percent completed?

Decision: Yes.

Reasons: There was no requirement expressly stated in the commitment that the construction be 100 percent completed, nor was there any implied provision. "Substantial" completion is compliance with this type of contract in the absence of any expressed agreement to the contrary. The lender was required to make the loan and to pay damages of $9,100 to cover additonal costs incurred by the builder because of the lender's failure to close the loan.

Selective Builders, Inc. v. Hudson City Savings Bank, 349 A.2d 564 (N.J. 1975).

11. Legal Documents

At closing of the financial transaction, the borrower is required to sign a legal document that represents the borrower's promise to repay the loan amount at a specified interest rate over a stated time period. This document is called a *promissory note.*

In addition to making the promise to repay the debt, the borrower grants to the lender a security interest in the real estate involved. As previously stated, this security interest usually is transferred through the legal document called a mortgage. Since a mortgage is a type of contract, it must satisfy all the essential elements of a contract. In addition, a mortgage must be in writing and must contain: (1) the names of the mortgagor and the mortgagee, (2) a description of the mortgaged property, (3) the terms of the debt and the duties of the mortgagor with regard to taxes, insurance, and repairs, and (4) the mortgagor's signature. Finally, this document must be delivered to the mortgagee.

The mortgage can be a rather lengthy document, because it can include many provisions describing the rights and duties of the mortgagor and mortgagee. Some of these more common provisions might be (1) covenants requiring the mortgagor to keep the property in good repair, to insure it against loss, to pay taxes, and not to remove or demolish any of the buildings or other improvements; (2) a defeasance clause, which voids the mortgage upon payment of the debt; and (3) an acceleration clause, which gives the mortgagee the right to call for immediate payment of all sums due and payable in case of default or other breach of contract by the borrower.

The mortgagor can discharge the mortgage through periodic payments over the life of the loan or in a lump sum payment before the due date in accordance with the prepayment clause. Either type of repayment extinguishes the mortgagee's security interest in the property. The mortgagee's interest is defeased or terminated. Even though the obligation ceases to exist and the mortgage is extinguished when payment is made in full, the discharge of the obligation should be recorded in the real property records to remove the mortgagee's existing security interest on record.

An acceleration clause enables the lender to declare the entire outstanding balance immediately due and payable if the borrower defaults on any one payment. Otherwise, the mortgagee could not foreclose on the property until the last payment was due. The loan may also be accelerated if the borrower defaults on any other provisions of the loan, such as failing to pay taxes and insurance premiums promptly, failing to keep the property in sound repair, or selling it without notifying the lender.

The *due-on-sale clause* is a specialized type of acceleration clause which gives the mortgagee the option of declaring the entire debt due and payable upon the sale of the property. This clause protects the lender if the purchaser is not credit worthy. During periods of rapidly rising interest rates, however, it has been used by lenders for a new purpose—to raise the interest rate upon the sale of the property.

During these periods it has been advantageous for the mortgagor to allow a purchaser to assume the existing mortgage, since it will usually carry a lower-than-current market interest rate. In such situations, the mortgagor can usually obtain a higher selling price on his property because the purchaser can benefit from the lower interest rate on the existing loan. The buyer will assume the loan and pay the balance of the purchase price in cash or perhaps with a combination of cash and a second mortgage given to the seller.

Quite naturally, the mortgage lender desires to receive a higher interest rate in such circumstances. These lenders have been using the due-on-sale clauses in existing loans to generate a higher return even though the new owner is credit worthy and poses no threat to the security of the loan. This use of the due-on-sale clause has also quite naturally produced considerable controversy, both in the courts and in the legislatures. As of early 1981, the prevailing legal view seems to be that lenders can use the clause to exact higher interest rates when properties are sold. One such case follows, while an opposing opinion is included at the end of this chapter.[1]

[1]Wellenkamp v. Bank of America, page 377.

Case 14.2

Ms. Crockett sold three apartment buildings to the Proctors on the condition that they were able to secure written approval from the lender to assume the outstanding balance of the existing mortgage at the 7 percent interest rate specified in the note. The savings and loan association agreed to transfer the note to the Proctors, but only if the rate of interest were raised to 9.75 percent. The Proctors already had a loan with the association which was current, and the refusal to transfer the loan was not based on any fear that the secured property might become impaired. Ms. Crockett then filed this suit.

Issue: Does a lender have a lawful right to require the proposed purchasers of a property secured by a deed of trust to agree to pay an increased rate of interest as a condition to its assent to a transfer of a secured property and the assumption of the loan?

Decision: Yes.

Reasons: The due-on-sale clause was validly exercised even though the secured property was not impaired and the transfer of the security property did not affect repayment of the original loan. In the absence of the due-on-sale clause, the borrower would receive a premium for a favorable loan assumption when he sold his realty. It seems fair for the lender to be able to contract to receive an increased interest rate in the event the original purchaser decides he is not going to continue ownership or pay off the loan so as to have full equity in the realty. The due-on-sale clause is employed by sensible lenders to minimize their risk and avoid losing the benefit of future increases in the interest rate.

Crockett v. First Federal Savings and Loan Association, 224 S.E.2d 580 (No. Car. 1976).

In an attempt to circumvent court rulings that have refused to enforce due-on-sale clauses, the Federal National Mortgage Association has approved a plan that allows mortgagees to call due thirty-year mortgage loans at the end of seven years. At that time the mortgagee can renegotiate a higher interest rate if current rates are higher than that specified in the mortgage. As of the end of 1980, this plan had been approved for mortgages in Arizona, California, Colorado, Georgia, Illinois, Iowa, Michigan, Minnesota, New Mexico, South Carolina, and Washington.

12.   Disclosure Requirements

Title I of the Federal Consumer Credit Protection Act of 1969, commonly known as the Truth in Lending Law, requires disclosure of credit terms in consumer credit transactions. The law was implemented by Regulation Z, issued by the Federal Reserve System. Regulation Z applies to any person or organization that in the ordinary course of business arranges or extends credit. It does not apply to the individual seller of a home who might take a note for part of the purchase price.

Under the Act, the lender must disclose to the prospective borrower the actual cost of credit, including the "finance charge" and the "annual percentage rate." Finance charges, which must be expressed in terms of a dollar amount, include interest loan service fee, discount points, commissions, and other fees. The total dollar amount of finance charges does not have to be disclosed on first mortgage loan transactions when the loan proceeds are used to purchase a residence. The annual percentage rate (APR) is the relationship between the annual finance charge and the amount borrowed. It is expressed in terms of a percentage rate. Since it includes fees and discount points, it often will be higher than the contract rate appearing in the loan agreement.

The purpose of these disclosure requirements was to encourage a borrower to shop around for credit. It is debatable whether the Truth in Lending law has achieved this purpose. However, other provisions of the law do provide the borrower very valuable protection. For example, borrowers have the right to cancel a credit transaction involving their principal residence within three business days. This right of rescission extends for a longer time period if full disclosure is not made by the lender.

Case 14.3

Willie and Betty Jean James were in a difficult financial situation. They would lose their house unless they could borrow $6,165.40 to repay a second mortgage loan on which they had defaulted. After trying many lenders to no avail, they went to Mr. Ragin, a real estate agent who had originally sold them the property. He offered them the following deal:

1. The Jameses would sell the house to him for $22,457.21, an amount equal to the outstanding first and second mortgages and approximately $3,000 less than the fair market value of the property at the time of the transaction.

2. The Jameses would pay rent of $254.10 per month for six months. This amount was $100 more than the monthly payment on the first mortgage.

3. At the end of six months, the Jameses could repurchase the property for $23,456.21, or $1,000 more than the purchase price six months previously. The net effect of the agreement was that the Jameses would pay Mr. Ragin $1,600 over a period of six months on a loan of $6,165.40, a return of more than 50 percent on an annual basis. Even though the terms were harsh, the alternative was to lose their house, so the Jameses accepted the agreement. However, after paying the specified rent for several months they sought to rescind the agreement. They contended that Mr. Ragin did not inform them of their rights under the Truth in Lending Act to rescind the agreement anytime within three days. Because of this omission, as provided under the Act, they could rescind the agreement anytime within three years. Mr. Ragin contended that he was not subject to the Truth in Lending Act.

Issue: Was Mr. Ragin a "creditor" subject to the Truth in Lending Act?

Decision: Yes.

Reason: On at least ten occasions in five years, Mr. Ragin had taken promissory notes and second deeds of trust to finance portions of the purchase price of homes that he had sold. He was acquainted with the requirements of the Truth in Lending Act and was subject to the act as a "creditor." He was required to give the Jameses a warranty deed to the property in return for a payment of $6,165.40, an amount equal to the "loan." He was also required to return all the interest paid by the Jameses plus pay them a penalty of $1,000.

James v. Ragin, 432 F.Supp. 887 (W.D. No.Car. 1977).

In an attempt to protect borrowers from very high interest rates, many states have enacted *usury laws* that set a maximum rate on interest that can be charged on a loan. The provisions and penalties under these laws vary greatly from state to state. In some states certain transactions may be exempt, such as loans to businesses or loans over a certain amount. In others, fees for services such as appraisals and credit reports are exempt, while some states also exclude discount points.

If a loan is found to be usurious, the penalty also varies widely. In a few states the lender forfeits both principal and interest, while in others only the interest or a portion of the interest is forfeited. In a few states the penalty is some multiple of the interest charged.

As prevailing interest rates in the economy rose rapidly during the past decade, the usury laws in many states began to have unforeseen consequences. Mortgage lenders refused to make loans in states where the interest-rate ceiling was much lower than the market rate. Many of these ceilings were raised, but the legislative process was often too slow to prevent harm to housing markets.

The Federal Depository Institutions Deregulation and Monetary Control Act of 1980 preempted this field by eliminating all state usury ceilings on first mortgage residential loans unless a state adopts a new ceiling before April 1, 1983. The Act permits an interest rate of not more than 5 percent above the Federal Reserve discount rate on ninety-day commercial paper. If a lender knowingly charges a higher rate than this ceiling, all interest is forfeited, making the loan interest free. If a debtor has already paid an illegal rate, he can recover in a civil action an amount equal to twice the amount of interest paid.

13. Fair-Lending Practices

In evaluating the credit worthiness of mortgage loan applicants, lenders have traditionally engaged in practices that could be considered discriminatory against female borrowers. For example, a working wife's income was usually not given as much weight as the husband's income because of the fear that the wife would drop out of the labor force. Single women were sometimes required to have additional cosigners to their notes where single males would not have this requirement. Such practices were made illegal by the *Equal Credit Opportunity Act* of 1974 which prohibited discrimination in credit transactions because of sex or marital status. The act was amended in 1976 to extend these prohibitions against discrimination to include other factors such as age, race, color, religion, national origin, or the receipt of welfare benefits.

In addition to prohibiting discrimination, the act requires that lenders notify credit applicants of the action taken on their application within thirty days. If the application is denied, the creditor must inform the applicant of the reasons for the rejection. Violation of the act makes the lender liable for actual and punitive damages sustained by the aggrieved applicant.

Perhaps no issue in mortgage lending is more controversial than *redlining,* the alleged practice by lending institutions of refusing to grant home mortgages or home-improvement loans for properties in older urban neighborhoods. Redlining may consist of more subtle practices than the blunt refusal to lend in designated areas. Such subtle practices might include (1) requiring higher down payments and earlier loan-maturity dates; (2) charging higher interest rates or special discount points for mortgages in redlined areas; (3) establishing "minimum loan amounts" that exclude lower-priced, older urban housing; or (4) underappraising properties in redlined areas.

Whether redlining actually exists is hotly debated. Some studies have used deed records to indicate that commercial banks, mutual savings banks, and savings and loan associations have put more of their money into the suburbs than into the central cities. Other studies conclude that redlining is largely a myth. They contend that the relative paucity of loans in the central city is more a product of lower demand there, in response to general urban decay. Some even assert that central-city borrowers receive preferential treatment because of the greater risk and cost of administration of loans in those areas.

The question of how to evaluate risk is at the heart of the redlining controversy. Community groups opposing redlining practices (sometimes known as "greenliners") feel that mortgage lenders are discriminating against older properties and the people who live in those neighborhoods. They contend that redlining is a self-fulfilling prophecy. If lenders deny mortgage funds to an area because they feel it is declining, then the neighborhood will decline because homeowners cannot improve their properties and prospective homeowners cannot finance their purchases.

Many financial institutions take an opposite view. They point out that they have the responsiblity to invest the savers' funds in a sound and prudent manner, and that this requirement dictates that they follow sound business practices in evaluating risks. In fact, many contend that they are now subsidizing inner-city neighborhoods by making loans on properties with greater potential for loss at terms similar to those found in the suburbs.

The "greenlining" activists charge that redlining is a direct cause of and principal contributor to neighborhood decline, and they seek additional legislation to force financial institutions to make more loans in older neighborhoods. They argue that the increased flow of funds would revitalize the inner-city and halt urban decay.

The financial institutions and their supporters assert that where redlining exists it is a consequence of decline already long underway. Neighborhoods first deteriorate; lenders are then more cautious about making loans there. Their policy prescription is for the community to examine the real causes of urban decay and to establish programs and strategies to deal with those problems. If this is done, they contend, the mortgage funds will definitely follow.

In any case, the Community Reinvestment Act of 1977 specifically prohibits discrimination in lending on the basis of the age of the dwelling or its neighborhood. The act also requires lending institutions to keep records on applicant characteristics such as race, sex, age, and neighborhood, and to make them available for inspection. Racially discriminatory lending practices also are prohibited by the Fair Housing Act of 1968.

Case 14.4

John and Susan Harrison were living in an apartment in a racially-mixed area of Toledo, Ohio, called the Old West End. They decided to buy a house in the area and sought financing from the Heinzeroth Mortgage Company. When an employee of the company, Mr. Haugh, found out where the house was, he told the Harrisons that this was a bad area because it was racially transitional. He told them that the only conventional financing available there was with a 50 percent down payment, but if they would look for property elsewhere he would probably be able to get the financing they wanted. The Harrisons sued, contending that the mortgage company had engaged in racial discrimination in housing, in violation of the 1968 Fair Housing Act.

Issue: Did the mortgage company violate the 1968 Fair Housing Act?

Decision: Yes.

Reasons: The evidence established that Mr. Haugh, the employee of the mortgage company, violated the Act by refusing to offer racially-neutral financing terms for the purchase of a house located in a racially-mixed neighborhood. The mortgage company was deemed responsible for the employee's wrongful actions, even though these actions were in violation of his duties and his employer's instructions. Harrison was awarded damages of $2,500 from Haugh plus $5,000 compensatory damages and attorney's fees from the mortgage company.

Harrison v. Otto G. Heinzeroth Mortgage Company, 430 F.Supp. 893 (N.D. Ohio 1977).

14. The Mortgage Closing

The closing of a mortgage transaction usually takes place at the same time that the real estate transaction is closed. This process was described in Chapter 13. Other mortgage loans not made in conjunction with a sale are closed separately, of course. At this closing, the mortgagor will be asked to sign both the promissory note and the mortgage. As previously mentioned, these documents are of vital legal importance and should be read very carefully. The mortgagor should not feel embarrassed by taking time to review all these documents before signing. If something appears to be inaccurate, it is much easier to correct before the document is signed.

After the note and mortgage are properly executed and delivered to the mortgagee, the loan amount minus any closing costs not paid in cash will be disbursed. These closing costs may include a loan origination fee, loan discount points, a credit report fee, an appraisal fee, attorneys' fees, cost of survey, a premium for the mortgagee's title insurance, and a mortgage-insurance premium if the loan is protected by private mortgage insurance. The mortgagee may also deduct certain prepaid items or those placed in escrow accounts, such as hazard-insurance premiums and property-tax payments.

After this closing is completed, the mortgagee will want to have the mortgage recorded in the appropriate office so that its security interest in the real estate will be apparent to anyone who searches the record title of that property.

Enforcing the Mortgage

15. Introduction

A lender's purpose in having a security interest in property is to have a second source from which satisfaction of a debt can be obtained. In the real estate financing transaction, a lender hopes that the borrower makes full repayment. However, such a lender is much more comfortable knowing that the value of the real estate is another source from which the debt can be collected. If the borrower fails to make full repayment, the secured lender can require that the mortgaged real estate be sold to pay off the entire debt. The process of selling such property is known as *foreclosure.* These next sections examine that procedure and the rights of the mortgagor and mortgagee.

16. Foreclosure

If the mortgagor fails to make payments as due or defaults on other terms of the mortgage agreement, the mortgagee can begin foreclosure proceedings. Usually, however, the mortgage holder will attempt to work out some type of alternative payment program. Not only is this practice much better for the mortgagee's community relations, it also avoids the time-consuming and expensive foreclosure process. Foreclosure is, for the most part, only a last resort for the mortgagee.

There are two methods used to sell mortgaged real property in satisfaction of a defaulted mortgage: (1) foreclosure by judicial sale, and (2) foreclosure by power of sale. Foreclosure by judicial sale is a predominant method of foreclosure in the United States, even though it is complicated, costly, and time-consuming. It involves a preliminary legal process including a hearing, the issuance of a decree or judgment, notice of sale, actual sale, and additional legal proceedings following the sale. The sale itself is usually at public auction held by the sheriff or other officer of the court. If the proceeds exceed the amount necessary to satisfy the debt, they will be distributed among other lien holders. If there are no other liens, the excess proceeds go to the mortgagor.

Foreclosure by power of sale under a deed of trust or a power-of-sale clause in a mortgage is a simpler procedure which is permitted in most states. Under this procedure, the foreclosure sale may be held without a judicial hearing or decree. After varying types and degrees of notice, usually through newspaper advertisements, a public sale is conducted either by a public official such as a sheriff, by some third party such as a trustee, or by the mortgagee. Unless otherwise specified, the mortgagee can always bid at the public sale and may be the ultimate foreclosure purchaser.

17. Rights of Redemption

A mortgagor who is in default on a note secured by a mortgage can terminate the foreclosure process prior to its completion by exercising a right called the *equity of redemption.* Upon the mortgagor's payment of an amount equal to the debt then owing plus interest and any expenses incurred by the mortgagee, the mortgagor's interest in the property is restored. In other words, the debt and the mortgage will be reinstated if the mortgagor redeems his or her interest by making payment prior to the foreclosure sale.

Any person who acquires the mortgagor's interest while a default situation exists also acquires the right to redeem the property interest equitably prior to foreclosure. Because the mortgagee may have the right to accelerate the amount owed upon default, the entire debt may have to be paid in order to redeem the interest. Normally the mere payment of the amount in default is not sufficient if the debt has been accelerated properly.

Case 14.5

When Bay Side, Inc., failed to make a loan payment to the MFS Service Corporation, the latter commenced foreclosure proceedings on Bay Side's real estate which secured the loan. Although MFS had called the entire amount due upon Bay Side's default, Bay Side sought to terminate the foreclosure proceedings prior to completion by paying the amount of the original default plus expenses. When MFS refused to withdraw the foreclosure proceedings, Bay Side appealed.

Issue: After a debt has been properly accelerated due to the debtor's default, can the equity of redemption be exercised through a partial payment?

Decision: No. The full amount owing at the time of payment must be satisfied.

Reasons: The parties are governed by any legal agreement into which they enter. The right to accelerate a debt in default is lawful. Partial payment made after acceleration of the entire debt is not sufficient to cure the default and thereby redeem interests and terminate the foreclosure process.

Bay Side, Inc., v. MFS Service Corp., 407 A.2d 206 (Del. 1979).

In many states (including Alabama, Arizona, California, Colorado, Connecticut, Hawaii, Idaho, Illinois, Indiana, Iowa, Kansas, Kentucky, Maine, Michigan, Minnesota, Missouri, Montana, Nevada, New Jersey, North Dakota, Oregon, South Dakota, Utah, and Washington), the mortgagor is allowed to redeem his property even after foreclosure. This right to redeem property after a foreclosure sale is called the *statutory right of redemption.* The statutory redemption period varies from state to state, being as short as six months and as long as two years. The most common statutory period is one year. In states that have this statutory right of redemption, the purchaser at a foreclosure sale does not obtain full and clear title until the statutory period of redemption has passed.

18.   *Deficiency Judgment*

It was previously noted that if the proceeds of a foreclosure sale exceed the amount of the outstanding mortgage, other lien holders or the mortgagor receive the balance. Conversely, if the proceeds are not large enough to satisfy the debt, in some states the mortgagee can obtain a deficiency judgment against the mortgagor for the balance due. This may cause other assets of the debtor to be seized and sold by an officer of the court to satisfy the deficiency.

Property that is sold at a foreclosure sale seldom brings a price that reflects the market value of the property under normal circumstances. During the Great Depression of the 1930s, prices at foreclosure sales fell to extremely low levels, often leaving debtors with large deficiency judgments against them even after they had lost their mortgaged property. As might be expected, a great deal of antideficiency legislation was passed during this period. Some states prohibit a deficiency judgment when foreclosure has been by the power of sale. Others base the deficiency not on the foreclosure sale price but on some "fair value" determined by the court or by appraisers. Indeed, a mortgagee should have the foreclosure price approved by a court with jurisdiction prior to or concurrently with filing a motion for a deficiency judgment.[2] A few states (including Nebraska, New Jersey, and Oregon) have completely abolished deficiency judgments.

For the mortgagee, foreclosure is a long and expensive process that ties up the property for a considerable period of time. For the mortgagor, foreclosure can also be expensive in money, in harrassment, and in harm to reputation. In addition, in states which permit deficiency judgments, the mortgagor may not only lose the property but end up with a lien on other property as well. To avoid these problems, the parties may agree to the mortgagor giving the mortgagee a deed for the property in satisfaction of the mortgage debt. This is known as a deed in lieu of foreclosure.

Although the deed in lieu of foreclosure offers many advantages for both parties, the mortgagee must be aware of certain pitfalls in the procedure. Unlike foreclosure, a deed in lieu of foreclosure does not

[2]Reliable Life Insurance Co. of St. Louis, Mo. v. Cook. see page 378.

extinguish any other liens that may be on the property. Moreover, the mortgagee could become involved in legal actions with other creditors regarding the adequacy of compensation if the mortgagor is insolvent.

Priority of Mortgages

19. Introduction

The security interest held by a lender is valuable only if the secured property's value exceeds the amount of the debt. How valuable a security interest is often depends on what priority the lender has to claim the secured property. The higher the priority, the more valuable the security interest. Suppose a landowner had a house built on his or her real estate. Further assume this owner had borrowed $10,000 from the First Bank to finance the purchase of the lot. Next, the owner borrowed $40,000 from the Second Savings and Loan Association to finance the construction project. Also assume that during this project the owner bought on credit a central air-conditioning unit to be installed in the new house and failed to pay the electrician for wiring the house. If this house and lot were sold to satisfy all these debts, which creditors would be paid and in what percentage if the sales price were insufficient to pay everyone entirely?

The answer to this question is determined by which creditors had priority to claim the sales proceeds. This hypothetical situation requires at least three types of analysis. First, the electrician who provides labor or materials may have a mechanic's lien. This special type of lien is the subject matter of the next chapter, and priorities between mechanic's liens and mortgages are discussed in Section 14 there. The second issue between the bank and the savings and loan association concerns priorities between two mortgages. Finally this example involves a creditor who financed a fixture—the air-conditioning unit. How priorities are determined in these second and third situations are discussed in the following sections.

20. Junior Mortgages

A mortgage that holds senior priority on a property and that will be paid first in the event of default and foreclosure is known as a first mortgage. The amount of money that can be raised through a first mortgage is often less than the buyer needs to complete a purchase. In such cases *junior mortgages*—that is, second, third, and fourth mortgages, which are subordinate to the first mortgage—are sometimes used. Such mortgages carry more risk than first mortgages and are usually issued for shorter periods of time and at higher interest rates.

The priority given to various mortgages on the same real estate normally is determined by which mortgagee is the first to record the mortgage document with the public records. However, order of recording is not always determinative of priority. One mortgagee whose mortgage is already on record may agree to subordinate its priority to another mortgagee. This subordination often occurs between a financer of vacant land and a financer of an improvement project. In our example above, the First Bank that holds a security interest in the vacant land probably would agree to let the Second Savings and Loan Association have priority if the construction of the house will increase the land's value by more than the amount of the additional mortgage.

Junior mortgages also are commonly used to help in the financing of the sale of an existing home or income properties. For example, a homeowner may be able to get a higher price for his house if the purchaser can assume an existing mortgage at an interest rate lower than those currently charged by banks. The required down payment may be larger than the buyer can pay, however, and the seller may be willing to take a second mortgage for part of the purchase price. As was seen in Section 5 above, such mortgages are known as purchase-money mortgages. Furthermore, second mortgages commonly are used for home-improvement loans. A family that wants to add a room or make extensive repairs to its home can usually get the money to do so at a lower rate through a junior mortgage than by taking out a personal installment loan.

21. Fixture Financing

As was seen in Chapter 1, fixtures are defined as personal property that becomes firmly affixed to real estate. Unless specified otherwise, a fixture generally is treated as part of the real estate. Very often when an item of personal property is financed, a conflict can arise if that personal property becomes a fixture. This conflict exists between the owner or mortgagee of the real estate and the financer of the fixture.

For example, who has a superior claim to a central air-conditioning unit that is firmly installed in a mortgaged house—the mortgagee or the air-conditioner financer? In order to answer this question, an understanding of secured transactions is necessary. Article 9 of the Uniform Commercial Code (which is law in every state except Louisiana) provides for the methods by which lenders can take security interests in items of personal property.

In order to have a valid security interest, the lender must either (1) take possession of the personal property or (2) enter into a written security agreement that describes the collateral and is signed by the debtor. In addition to either of the above requirements, the lender must give value in return for the security interest, and the debtor must have rights in the collateral. Together, all these steps are known as *attachment* of the security interest to the collateral.

After their security interests have been created, lenders will want to perfect these interests so that they will have priority to the collateral if the debt is not paid. Although there are several ways to perfect a security interest, we will concentrate on the filing of a *financing statement.* A financing statement is a document that must contain the names and addresses of the debtor and the secured party, a description of the collateral, and at least the debtor's signature. (The 1962 version of Article 9 required the secured party's signature as well as the debtor's.) When this financing statement is filed in the appropriate office that maintains Article 9 records, the lender's security interest becomes perfected. The filing of a financing statement gives constructive notice to all interested parties that a security interest exists.

Now, as between a lender that finances real estate and one that finances personal property that becomes a fixture, Article 9 contains a section that establishes which lender has a superior claim or priority to the fixture. Unfortunately, there are two different versions of this section. The original Article 9 commonly is called the 1962 version. Due to a number of problems with the original draft, several changes were recommended. This latter version is referred to as the 1972 revision. Because both versions are the law in various states, we will look at each of them in the following sections.

22. § 9–313—1962 Version

The section of Article 9 dealing with the priority to fixtures is numbered 9–313. Under the original version, a lender whose security interest *attached* to the personal property and was *perfected* before the collateral became a fixture would have an absolute priority over a holder of a mortgage on the real estate. For example, assume that ACE Air Conditioning Company sold a central air-conditioning unit to Del Debtor on credit. If ACE had a valid security interest and perfected that interest by filing a financing statement before the unit was affixed to Del's building, ACE would have priority over a preexisting or subsequent mortgagee of the land and building.

Even if ACE had failed to perfect the security interest before the unit became affixed to the real estate, it would still have priority over all preexisting mortgagees if the security interest attached to the collateral prior to the unit becoming a fixture. This priority is given to the fixture lender, despite lack of perfection, because the addition of a new fixture presumably will increase the overall value of the mortgagee's interest in the real estate. ACE's failure to perfect by filing a financing statement prior to the unit becoming affixed means that a subsequent real estate mortgagee or purchaser would have priority over the creditor claiming an interest in the fixture. If a subsequent mortgagee or purchaser of the real estate acts without actual or constructive knowledge of ACE's interest in the air-conditioning unit, ACE will not have priority because of the failure to perfect the security interest.

When a debtor defaults on a loan repayment, the lender with priority has first claim to the value of the collateral. In our example, assuming it has priority, ACE would be allowed to remove the air-conditioning unit from the real estate in order to sell it. ACE would have to reimburse the mortgagee or the owner, if the real estate owner is not the debtor, for any damage caused to the physical structure upon removal of the fixture.

23. § 9–313—1972 Revision

One of the major criticisms of the 1962 version of Article 9 concerned this fixture-priority section. It was felt that the rules described in the previous section did not take into account some basic principles of real estate law. In light of these criticisms, § 9–313 was modified greatly in the 1972 revision. Like the 1962 version, the revised § 9–313 does not attempt to define when personal property becomes a fixture. However, the revision does state that a security interest cannot be created in ordinary building materials that are incorporated into an improvement or real estate. Such materials include lumber, bricks, shingles, sheetrock, concrete, and other similar items.

A major distinction in the revised section on fixture priority is the creation of a *fixture filing*. Under the 1962 version, a financing statement properly filed would never appear in the real estate records. Therefore, a party interested in buying or financing the real estate could search the real estate records and never learn of a security interest in a fixture. The "fixture filing" concept requires that a financing statement be filed in the office where a real estate mortgage would be recorded. In addition to this requirement, a typical financing statement for fixture filing must contain a description of the real estate involved and the name of the record owner if different from the debtor. For example, if a tenant is financing the purchase of a fixture, the fixture filing must contain the landlord-owner's name as well as the tenant-debtor's.

Case 14.6

A dispute arose between two banks as to which one had the better rights to grain bins located on the debtor's real estate. The Bank of Rector had financed the debtor's purchase of the real estate involved and had recorded its mortgage on May 17, 1976. The Corning Bank had previously financed the grain bins and had filed a financing statement on March 19, 1976. This financing statement did not describe the real estate where the bins were located nor was it referenced into the real estate records. When the debtor became insolvent, these banks sought a judicial determination establishing which one had priority to the grain bins.

Issue: Does the filing of a financing statement prior to the recording of a mortgage give the Corning Bank priority to the grain bins?

Decision: No.

Reasons: The court held that these grain bins were firmly attached to the real estate and thus were fixtures. Under the applicable 1972 revision of § 9–313, a financing statement filed as a fixture filing must contain a sufficient description of the real estate involved so that constructive notice of the financer's interest will be given to anyone searching the applicable real estate records. Furthermore, the Corning Bank failed to have its financing statement cross referenced in the real estate records. Failure to abide by these essential requirements results in a subsequent mortgagee having priority to the grain bins located on the secured real estate.

Corning Bank v. Bank of Rector, 576 S.W.2d 949 (Ark. 1979).

A party that lends money which enables the debtor to buy an item that becomes a fixture will have priority over a preexisting mortgagee or owner if that lender's security interest is perfected by a fixture filing prior to or within ten days after the item becomes a fixture. This ten-day grace period is allowed only to the lenders that make the fixture purchase possible. This lender is said to take a *purchase-money security interest.*

In situations that do not involve purchase-money security interests, a lender that takes a security interest in a fixture must perfect that interest by a fixture filing before a mortgagee's or owner's interest is recorded. In other words, the party who is first on record has the best priority when purchase-money security interests are not involved.

The revised § 9–313 establishes a category that must be considered pseudo-fixtures or soft-fixtures. A party who finances readily removable factory or office machines or readily removable replacements for domestic appliances, consumed by the purchaser, has priority if a security interest is perfected by any of the methods allowed under Article 9. Basically this provision should be a warning to a mortgagee or purchaser of real estate to check whether these items are encumbered. A mere search of the real estate records is not sufficient when dealing with items like typewriters, adding machines, and replacements for dishwashers, stoves, ovens, refrigerators, and other similar machines or appliances.

Finally, the 1972 revision recognizes the need to give the construction mortgagee priority over all security interests in fixtures if the personal property items become fixtures prior to the completion of the construction. All that is necessary for the construction mortgagee to have priority is to record the mortgage before the personal property becomes a fixture. This subordination of fixture filings occurs regardless of whether the security interest was perfected before or after the collateral became affixed during the construction period.

A similarity to the 1962 version exists in giving the lender with priority the right to remove the fixture upon reimbursement to the mortgagee or owner, if different from the debtor, for damage done to the physical structure. As of the end of 1980, approximately one-half of the states had adopted the 1972 revision of Article 9. These states include Arizona, Arkansas, California, Colorado, Connecticut, Florida, Georgia, Hawaii, Idaho, Illinois, Iowa, Kansas, Maine, Massachusetts, Michigan, Minnesota, Mississippi, Nevada, New York, North Carolina, North Dakota, Ohio, Oklahoma, Oregon, Texas, Utah, Virginia, West Virginia, and Wisconsin. If past history of the acceptance of the Uniform

Commercial Code is any indication, the other states likely will adopt the 1972 revision in the near future.

Cases on Real Estate Finance

Wellenkamp v. Bank of America,
582 P.2d 970 (Cal. 1978).

Cynthia Wellenkamp purchased real property from the Mans, agreeing to assume the balance of their loan from the Bank of America. The bank notified Ms. Wellenkamp that if she did not agree to an increase in the interest rate from 8 to 9¼ percent they would accelerate the loan. When she refused, the bank filed a notice of default and elected to sell under the deed of trust.

The plaintiff then filed the present action in which she sought an injunction against enforcement of the due-on-sale clause. She also sought a declaration that exercise of such a clause, without any showing that defendant's security had been impaired as a result of the sale of the property to plaintiff, constituted an unreasonable restraint on alienation in violation of California law. The superior court dismissed the complaint and this appeal followed.

Manuel, J.

We addressed today the question whether enforcement of a due-on clause, contained in a deed of trust securing real property, constitutes an unreasonable restraint on alienation in violation of California law. . . .

The complaint herein alleges a controversy over the legal rights and duties of plaintiff and defendant under the deed of trust containing a due-on clause. Plaintiff contends that this clause is unenforceable absent a showing by the lender of impairment to its security; whereas defendant contends that it can automatically enforce the clause without any further showing. . . .

Outright sales of real property commonly involve different types of financing arrangements depending upon the circumstances existing at the time of sale. Thus, when new financing is available and eco-

nomically feasible, a buyer will be able to arrange to pay the seller the purchase price in full, in an "all cash to seller" arrangement. When, however, new financing is unavailable or is economically unfeasible, the buyer may arrange, as did plaintiff herein, to pay the seller only the amount of the seller's equity in the property, agreeing to assume or take "subject to" the existing deed of trust, in a "cash to loan" arrangement.

The availability of new financing often depends upon general economic conditions. In times of inflation, when money is "tight" and funds available for real estate loans are in short supply, new financing may be difficult, if not impossible to obtain. The same result may occur when interest rates and the transactional costs of obtaining new financing are high, making it economically unfeasible for the buyer to acquire a new loan. When economic conditions are such that new financing is either unavailable or economically unfeasible, the seller and buyer will normally agree to a form of financing arrangement wherein the buyer will assume the seller's loan. In such circumstances, if the lender is unwilling to permit assumption of the existing loan, and instead elects to enforce the due-on clause, transfer of the property may be prohibited entirely, because the buyer will be unable to substitute a new loan for the loan being called due, and the seller will not receive an amount from the buyer sufficient to discharge that loan, particularly when the balance due is substantial. Even when the lender is willing to waive its option to accelerate in return for the assumption of the existing loan at an increased interest rate, an inhibitory effect on transfer may still result. The buyer, faced with the lender's demand for increased interest, may insist that the seller lower the purchase price. The seller would then be forced to choose between lowering the purchase price and absorbing the loss with the resulting reduction in his equity interest, or refusing to go through with the sale at all. In either event, the result in terms of a restraint on alienation is clear. . . . We furthermore reject defendant's contention that the lender's interest in maintaining its loan portfolio at current interest rates justifies the restraint imposed by exercise of a due-on clause upon transfer of title in an outright sale. Although we recognize that lenders face increasing costs of doing business and must pay increasing amounts to depositors for the use of their funds in making long-term real estate loans as a result of inflation and a competitive money market, we believe that exercise of the due-on clause to protect against this kind of business risk would not further the purpose for which the due-on clause was legitimately designed, namely to protect against impairment to the lender's security that is shown to result from a transfer of title. Economic risks such as those caused by an inflationary economy are among the general risks inherent in every lending transaction. They are neither unforeseeable nor unforeseen. Lenders who provide funds for long-term real estate loans should and do, as a matter of business necessity, take into account their projections of future economic conditions when they initially determine the rate of payment and the interest on these long-term loans. Unfortunately, these projections occasionally prove to be inaccurate. We believe however, that it would be unjust to place the burden of the lender's mistaken economic projections on property owners exercising their right to freely alienate their property through the automatic enforcement of a due-on clause by the lender. . . .

For the foregoing reasons, we hold that a due-on clause contained in a promissory note or deed or trust cannot be enforced upon the occurrence of an outright sale unless the lender can demonstrate that enforcement is reasonably necessary to protect against impairment to its security or the risk of default. . . .

The judgment is *reversed*.

Reliable Life Insurance Co. of St. Louis, Mo. v. Cook
601 P.2d 455 (Okla. 1979).

Hodges, J.
This is an appeal by appellant, J. J. Cook, from the entry of a deficiency judgment of $247,611.84 against him following

the foreclosure sale of an apartment complex owned by appellant.

On June 17, 1974, a foreclosure judgment was entered against appellant for $933,375.62, plus 10% interest from September 1, 1974, until paid, and for $93,337.56 in attorney's fees. A public sale of the property was held August 5, 1975, whereby appellee purchased the property for $620,100 which met the two-thirds of market value requirement. Appellee also filed a motion to confirm the sale on that same day and that motion was affirmed on August 11, 1975. The appellee next filed this action for a deficiency judgment on October 16, 1975, and the appealed judgment was entered on October 15, 1976.

The appellant alleges that 12 O.S.1971 § 686 requires that a motion for deficiency judgment must be filed simultaneously with a motion to confirm. The sentence in § 686 that appellant relies upon reads:

> Simultaneously with the making of a motion for an order confirming the sale or in any event within ninety days after the date of sale, the party to whom such residue shall be owing may make a motion in the action for leave to enter a deficiency judgment upon notice to the party against whom such judgment is sought or the attorney who shall have appeared for such party in such action.

Appellant claims the meaning intended by the provision is that the two motions must be filed together and they must be filed within ninety days.

We find the claim without merit. The plain language of the statute in its ordinary meaning indicates an option to the filing party. The filing party may or may not file the motion for deficiency judgment with the motion for confirmation and, regardless of whether he files them together, the motion for deficiency judgment must be filed within ninety days of the sale.

The appellant also asserts that § 686 as construed by this Court is unconstitutional as a deprivation of due process. Appellant bases his claim on the fact that, if the motion for deficiency judgment and the motion to confirm are not required to be filed simultaneously, the mortgagor has no notice to the motion to confirm. Appellant, therefore, states the mortgagor has been subjected to the exposure of a deficiency judgment without notice.

The statutory provision, however, provides the appellant, mortgagor, sufficient protection within the proceedings of the deficiency judgment. The deficiency judgment is the amount appellant is liable for, less either the market value or the sale price of the property, whichever is higher. Although the sale price may be confirmed by the mortgagee in a hearing, without formal notice to the mortgagor, the mortgagor can still protect himself by introducing evidence as to the market value of the property in the deficiency proceedings. Accordingly, we find that the appellant has not been deprived of due process of law.
Affirmed.

REVIEW QUESTIONS

1. Define the following terms:
   a. Mortgage
   b. Mortgagor
   c. Mortgagee
2. Distinguish between the following:
   a. Mortgage and deed of trust
   b. Purchase-money mortgage and contract for a deed

c. Participation mortgage and shared-appreciation mortgage

3. A sale-leaseback transaction may be an attractive alternative to traditional financing as a way to free funds that are tied up in real estate investments. List the advantages of this transaction to both the seller-tenant and buyer-landlord.

4. Mortgages containing due-on-sale clauses, due-on-emcumbrances clauses, due-on-default clauses, and similar clauses have created considerable controversy. What type of general mortgage provisions do these clauses represent? What effect have courts given to these clauses?

5. Sims, a partner in a construction company, had borrowed money from First Bank in order to build a house for resale. Due to financial difficulties, Sims was unable to complete the house on schedule. Concerned about the unfinished nature of their security, the Bank required Sims to grant a mortgage on her personal residence as additional security. There was no disclosure of a finance charge or an annual percentage rate with respect to this mortgage. When Sims was unable to pay the debt owed, she sought to rescind the mortgage on her residence since the Truth in Lending Law had not been followed. Is this financial transaction exempt from the disclosure requirements of the Truth in Lending Law? Why?

6. When the Pleasant Valley Campground, Inc., purchased land and a mobile home from Krauz, it signed a purchase-money mortgage describing the land but excluding the mobile home. Later, Campground, Inc., defaulted on its payments, and Krauz foreclosed the mortgage. At a public sale, it was announced the sale would not include the mobile home located on the property. Nevertheless, the buyer at the foreclosure sale took possession of the mobile home and refused to recognize anyone else's claim to it. Could the Pleasant Valley Campground, Inc., successfully claim that the buyer had taken the mobile home by wrongful conversion? Explain.

7. This chapter discussed two types of redemption rights. What are these two rights, and what is the feature that distinguishes between them?

8. Bennett borrowed money from Leonard and mortgaged some real estate as security for the loan. Bennett defaulted, and Leonard foreclosed. At a public sale the highest bidder was Alfred, an agent of Leonard's for the purposes of bidding. If the amount of the sale proceeds does not equal the debt owed, can Leonard sue Bennett for the deficiency? Explain.

9. On April 27, Citibanc obtained a judgment against the Potters for $20,000. This judgment was recorded that same day. Subsequently, the Potters purchased a lot and granted a mortgage to the Exchange Bank to cover the costs of constructing a home on the lot. Thereafter, when the Potters were unable to pay their debts, Citibanc sought to have the real estate sold to satisfy the judgment. Which party has priority to the proceeds of any forced sale? Why?

10. Under the 1972 revision of Article 9, a purchase-money security interest involving personal property that might become affixed to real estate gives its holder an advantage over secured parties that are not involved in a purchase-money transaction. What is meant by a purchase-money security interest? What is the advantage given to this type of fixture financer?

15

Mechanic's Liens

1. Introduction

A *lien* exists when a creditor has a claim to property for payment of some debt or obligation. Most landowners are well aware of taxes and mortgages as major liens against real estate. Probably far fewer owners have a working knowledge of the encumbrance known as the mechanic's lien. A *mechanic's lien* is a statutory claim on real estate to secure the compensation of persons who are directly or indirectly under contract with an interest holder (usually the owner) to furnish labor or materials for the improvement of the real estate. The concept of mechanic's liens must not be confused with the lien that an automobile mechanic may have against a car that is repaired. These real estate mechanic's liens were in existence long before automobiles had any impact on our society.

In a general sense, mechanic's liens benefit laborers and materialmen who contribute to the improvement of real estate. An improvement is any addition to the land. Construction of a building or an addition to an existing structure are common examples of improvements. Other examples might include landscaping or work done on the land to aid in its cultivation, such as drainage tile or irrigation systems.

While the term *improvement* does not necessarily mean that the land's value is increased, most improvements usually do increase the value of the real estate.

Based on the idea that an improvement has added some value to the landowner's property, the law created mechanic's liens. If a person who is partially responsible for the improvement is not paid for the work or material provided, that person may obtain an interest in the improvement and the land as security for payment. Often mechanic's liens are given preference over other claims because the improvement made has increased the value of all parties' interests. In order to understand how mechanic's liens are used to secure payment for an improver, we will look at the following elements: (1) the nature of mechanic's liens, (2) the creation and perfection of mechanic's liens, (3) the enforcement of mechanic's liens, and (4) the termination of mechanic's liens.

Nature of Mechanic's Liens

2. In General

A mechanic's lien is a statutory lien. All fifty states have statutes that control the existence and operation of mechanic's liens. Although the statutes vary in their detail, the general framework of mechanic's liens is similar throughout the country. The laws of the various states may differ on who is entitled to a lien, against whom the lien may be asserted, when and how notice of a lien must be given, the priorities of the lien compared with other claims, and the causes for which the lien may be terminated. This chapter concentrates on the general aspects of mechanic's liens statutes. During this discussion it must be remembered that the statute of the state where the real estate is located must be examined in order to determine the rights of the parties in any particular case.

By its nature, a mechanic's lien may be a secret lien. Some states do not require the parties entitled to the lien to notify the landowners or other interested parties that a mechanic's lien is being filed. Therefore, mechanic's liens may exist without the affected parties having knowledge of them.

3. Parties Entitled to a Lien

Let's assume that Fred Thompson owns a vacant lot and builds a house on it. During this construction, how will the mechanic's lien law apply? Mechanic's liens can give protection to all who directly or indirectly contract with the owner to furnish labor or materials to improve real estate. Typically, those protected can include general contractors, sub-contractors, laborers, and suppliers of materials. Frequently, a land-owner will hire a *general contractor* to oversee the entire construction of an improvement. If Fred Thompson hires the Evans Construction Company to build his house, there is a direct contractual relationship between the owner and the general contractor. Due to its overall contribution to the construction project, Evans would be entitled to a mechanic's lien.

In this example, the Evans Construction Company likely will contract with others in several areas of the project. For example, the electrical wiring, the plumbing, the roofing, the cabinetry, and the masonry are often subcontracted. Suppose the general contractor agrees to have A & E Electric Company do all the wiring in Mr. Thompson's house. The A & E Electric Company, as a *subcontractor,* contributes to the improvement of Fred Thompson's real estate. Although subcontractors are associated only indirectly with the landowner, they are entitled to claim mechanic's liens for the work provided.

Both the general contractor and the subcontractors usually hire individuals to do the physical labor involved in the improvement. These workers, who are called *laborers* in most statutes, are indirectly hired by the landowner. When Fred Thompson pays Evans Construction Company, he expects Evans to pay the subcontractors who in turn pay their laborers. If the laborers are not paid, they may have a valid claim to a mechanic's lien against the improvement.

The issue has arisen whether those who furnish professional services are entitled to mechanic's liens. When the performance of an architect, an engineer, or a surveyor contributes to the improvement of real estate, should mechanic's liens be applicable? States generally have resolved this question through court decisions or statutory enactment. Although their services may not add to the physical construction of an improvement, professionals usually are entitled to a mechanic's lien as long as they can show how their services increased the value of the land. When an architect's or an engineer's services do not result in actual enhancement of real estate values, mechanic's liens are not available to secure payment. For example, an architect who draws a plan that is never used cannot validly obtain a mechanic's lien.[1]

In a position somewhat similar to laborers are those people who furnish supplies or materials that make the construction project possible. These *suppliers* or *materialmen* may deal contractually with the general contractor or the subcontractors. Suppose that A & E Electric Company ordered a circuit-breaker panel especially for the Thompson construction project from a General Electric distributor. Because of its contribution to the construction of Mr. Thompson's house, this supplier has the right to file a mechanic's lien if it is not paid. The supplier of this distributor generally cannot claim a mechanic's lien, because the material furnished to the distributor was not explicitly intended to be used only for a specific project.

Of the people entitled to mechanic's liens, only the general contractor must have a direct contract with the owner. Of course, this does not preclude a laborer or a supplier from having a direct relationship with the owner, too. Although a subcontractor, a laborer, and a supplier may not sign a contract with the owner, these parties must establish some agreement that shows they have furnished services or supplies to the improvement. This requirement places a burden on the suppliers of construction materials, such as lumber, to know into which projects their supplies went. Failure to establish the essential requirement of a direct or indirect contract means that these parties are not entitled to mechanic's liens.

4.   Property Subject to a Lien

The law of most states provides that a mechanic's lien cannot be attached to nonpossessory interests such as an easement or a license. Fee simple ownership interests and possessory leasehold interests may be subject to mechanic's liens. Generally they must be asserted against the true owner of the improved real estate. The true owner is the person who has legal title to the land. Only when the true owner has consented to the contract under which the improvement is made can the mechanic's liens be enforced.

The landlord is the true owner of leased property. Due to the rule just expressed, improvements ordered by a tenant do not necessarily give rise to an enforceable lien. A landlord has liability for the improve-

---

[1]Gollehon, Schemmer & Associates, Inc. v. Fairway-Bettendorf Associates, page 400.

ments made only when the landlord gave expressed or implied consent to the contract. When a landlord lacks knowledge that an improvement is being made, a valid mechanic's lien cannot be filed against his property. However, when a landlord is aware of improvements ordered by the tenant, the issue becomes—Did the landlord consent to the contract under which the improvement is made? In order to avoid the problem of silence being interpreted as implied consent, some states require that the landlord give *notice of nonresponsibility* to the parties making the improvements. State statutes vary as to whether this written notice must be clearly posted on the real estate, filed in the place of public records, or personally delivered to those making the improvements. A landlord who learns that a tenant is having improvements made on the real estate should immediately find out what is required by the mechanic's-lien law in the state where the real estate is located.

In certain situations it is possible that a long-term tenant can subject his or her interest to a mechanic's lien while not subjecting the landlord's fee ownership interest to the same lien. The following case is an example of such circumstances.

Case 15.1

Jack Endo Electric, Inc., supplied to J. A. Thompson & Son, Inc., a contractor, materials which were used in the construction of a real estate development. The real estate was being developed by a lessee, Lear. The Bishop Estate was the lessor and fee owner of the land. When Endo was not paid by Thompson, Endo filed a claim of lien which was served on Thompson and Lear. The Bishop Estate was neither named in the lien nor served. Thompson contended that the lien claim was invalid because it failed to name the fee owner, as required by the mechanic's lien statute.

Issue: Was the lien valid against Thompson and Lear?

Decision: Yes. Endo intended only to encumber the interests of Thompson and Lear, and intended no interference with the fee interest.

Reason: The statutory requirement that the owner of the fee title be served with notice of the lien claim is directory and not mandatory. Its objective is to give notice to all persons who might be affected by the proposed lien so that they might take steps to preserve their interests. The lien was therefore valid as against Lear and Thompson, since the failure to notify the fee owner would be a defense available only to the Bishop Estate. Lear and Thompson were not prejudiced by the absence of notice to the fee owner.

Jack Endo Electric, Inc. v. Lear Siegler, Inc., 585 P.2d 1265 (Hawaii 1978).

An interest in real estate may be held by a married individual in his or her name only or as a joint owner with the spouse. If the property is held by an individual, an improvement ordered by the spouse does not automatically mean that a valid mechanic's lien can be created. Only when the spouse has permission to act as the true owner's agent is there a possibility that a contract exists between the owner and the person furnishing labor or supplies to the improvement. Once again, this contract must be established explicitly or implicitly by the improver in order to justify a mechanic's lien. It must be remembered that a husband-wife relationship does not in and of itself create the requisite authority to order an improvement.

When land is owned jointly (whether by spouses or others), an improvement ordered by one owner is not considered as an order by the other unless it can be shown that the other owner consented to the improvements being made. What happens if one joint owner hires a carpenter to build a new barn over the expressed objection of another owner, and the carpenter is not paid? Let's assume Larry and Ervin own a farm as tenants in common. If Larry employed a carpenter over Ervin's protest, the unpaid carpenter and any of the other laborers or suppliers could file a mechanic's lien against Larry's one-half interest. Based on this example, no lien can attach to Ervin's interest because there is no contractual agreement between him and the persons supplying labor or material.

As was discussed in Chapter 11, minors do not have the legal capacity to contract in most situations. An exception to this rule concerns contracts for necessaries. The courts in nearly all states universally agree that improvements on real estate are not necessaries. Therefore, mechanic's liens generally cannot be acquired against the real estate of a minor.

Property owned by the federal, state, or local government is not subject to mechanic's liens even if the government falls behind on paying for a contracted improvement. Public policy has been interpreted to prohibit a forced sale of governmental property; thus a mechanic's lien would be of very little value even if it were permitted to be filed against government land.

Creation and Perfection of Mechanic's Liens

5. Introduction

The statutes of the various states provide for the steps to be taken to create and perfect a mechanic's lien. The term creation describes the way in which a person entitled to a mechanic's lien establishes the right to it. Perfection is a more difficult concept. To perfect an interest (lien) in another's property means to take those steps to assure that the lien will not be lost, thereby lessening the lienholder's chances of receiving what is owed by the debtor.

The steps to create and perfect mechanic's liens differ from state to state. Creation usually requires substantial performance of the contract and notice to the landowner. Perfection involves filing a claim of lien with the public record keeper of documents relating to real estate. The failure to follow these statutory procedures does not mean that the landowner's obligation to pay ceases to exist; it merely means that the obligation is not secured by a lien against the owner's real estate.

6. Substantial Performance of the Contract

As stated previously, a laborer or supplier must establish a direct or indirect contractual relationship with the landowner to be entitled to a mechanic's lien. In addition there must be proof that the contract has been substantially performed. While the degree of performance required to justify a mechanic's lien can vary from case to case, most courts ask whether the landowner has received essentially what was expected. If the general contractor has completed only one-half of the building under contract, the landowner can refuse to pay the agreed-upon price and sue the contractor for breach of contract. When the amount of work completed is insufficient to support the laborer's or supplier's claim for payment, a mechanic's lien cannot be properly created.

7. Preliminary Notice

Many states require that any laborer or supplier who has not directly contracted with the owner must deliver to the owner *preliminary notice* of a potential mechanic's lien. This notice informs the owner that services or materials are being provided to make the improvements possible. Furthermore, it lets the owner know that if this laborer or materialman is not paid, a lien may be claimed against the described property. Generally the states that require a preliminary notice do not make it necessary for parties that deal directly with the landowner to deliver this notice. The contract itself serves as notice of the general contractor's potential claim. In a previous example, we assumed that Evans Construction Company, as the general contractor, subcontracted with the A & E Electric Company to do the electrical wiring. Those states that require a preliminary notice would usually require it to be delivered by A & E but not by Evans.

The purpose of this preliminary notice is to make the landowner aware of who has the potential right to claim a mechanic's lien. It is assumed that any owner of real estate who deals directly with a laborer or supplier will know that these parties can claim a mechanic's lien. Therefore, only those who do not contract directly with the owner must deliver a preliminary notice when the statute so requires.

Most of the states that provide for this preliminary notice of a lien require that it be delivered to the owner within a short time period, such as sixty days, after the work has begun or the supplies are delivered to the job site. These statutes usually allow the preliminary notice to be delivered to the landowner by hand, by mail, or by leaving the notice in an obvious place at the location where the improvements are being made.

Failure to follow the statutory requirement of delivering a preliminary notice when required will result in the claimed mechanic's lien being declared invalid. The following case is an example of this result.

Case 15.2

Booth was a subcontractor who performed work on a roadbed owned by Lombardi. When Booth was not paid by the contractor for his work, he filed a claim of lien against Lombardi's property. At no time during the performance of his work did Booth deliver a preliminary notice of a potential lien. Despite this statutory requirement, Booth argued that his mechanic's lien should be enforced.

Issue: Was Booth's claim of a mechanic's lien properly perfected and valid against Lombardi?

Decision: No. Notice to the landowner was a condition precedent (or a prerequisite) to a perfected mechanic's lien.

Reason: The mechanic's lien statute provided that "[a]ll lienors . . . as a prerequisite to perfecting a lien . . . and recording a claim of lien, shall be required to serve a notice on the owner. . . ." Booth's failure to give Lombardi the required notice precluded any right to a mechanic's lien against Lombardi's property.

Booth v. Joe Lombardi, Inc., 309 So.2d 51 (Fla. App. 1975).

8.   Filing the Claim of Lien

Whereas some states require that a preliminary notice be delivered as an initial step in perfecting a mechanic's lien, all states' statutes provide that a document indicating the existence of the lien be filed with the public record keeper. The states vary in the terminology used. Some states call the required document a claim of lien, a certificate of lien, a statement of lien, or a notice of lien. In those states that call it a notice of lien, the document filed should not be confused with a preliminary notice of a potential lien. Depending on the applicable state statute, this filing requirement is either the first or second step in perfecting a mechanic's lien. In either case, it is mandatory in order to have a valid lien.

In addition to filing a claim of lien in the public records, a copy must be served on the party against whose interest the lien is being claimed. Once a proper claim of lien is filed on public record and served, it gives notice of the existence of the mechanic's lien to anyone who has or may receive an interest in the land. To be effective in giving this notice, the claim of lien usually must include (1) the name of the party against whose interest the lien is claimed, (2) a description of the property against which the lien is filed, (3) a statement of the services or materials provided for the improvement, (4) the amount claimed to be owing to the lien holder, (5) the name and address of the lien holder, and (6) a sworn statement verifying the accuracy of the document's contents. Failure to meet these essential requirements will make the lien ineffective.

Most courts have held that the first two essential elements are necessary to give the owner notice that a lien has been filed and to identify the real estate subject to the mechanic's lien. The third requirement means that a supplier must be able to trace the materials furnished to particular construction projects.[2] This requirement is of essential

[2]Bowen v. Collins, page 402.

importance and often is difficult for suppliers of lumber, bricks, sheet-rock, and similar materials to satisfy.

Failure to include all essential elements in the required document will defeat the lien. However, a claim of lien that fails to satisfy precisely all the statutory prerequisites may still be effective if the noncompliance is minor. As in many areas of the law, substantial compliance, not perfect compliance, is all that the law requires. Strict application of all requirements sometimes would frustrate the purpose of the mechanic's lien law. Therefore, insubstantial omissions are overlooked at times. Of course, what a court may decide is substantial compliance with the statute is always in doubt. Thus, anyone who is attempting to file a claim of lien should have it prepared by an attorney. Problems similar to those in the next case could be avoided by having complete knowledge of the legal requirements. Fortunately for the lienor, the court concluded that the legal requirements had been substantially met.

Case 15.3

Tesauro demolished a building, filled and graded the area, and prepared for construction of a new building, all under contract with the property owner, Baird. After completing the work, Tesauro filed a mechanic's lien claim and served copies of the claim on Baird. The copies showed the court and the term in which the original was filed, but did not show the term number or the date of filing of the claim, as required by statute. As a result of the omission of the number and date, Baird contended that he had not been served with proper notice of the lien claim and that the lien was therefore ineffective.

Issue: Did the failure of the lien claim copy served on Baird to state the term number of the court and the date of filing result in the claim being ineffective?

Decision: No. Tesauro substantially complied with the service requirements.

Reasons: The right to file a mechanic's lien is of statutory origin; no right to such a lien existed at common law. Therefore, if a party desires to avail himself of the lien, he must strictly comply with the statutory provisions. If there had been no notice to Baird, the lien claim would have been clearly invalid. Adherence to the terms of the statute is indispensable, but the rule should not be pushed into such niceties as to perplex and prevent a remedy intended to be simple and summary. A substantial compliance with notice requirements is sufficient to satisfy the statute. Thus, the notice to Baird, even though lacking the court term number and date, substantially complied with the law and was therefore valid.

Tesauro v. Baird, 335 A.2d 792 (Pa. Super. 1975).

---

9. Time Period for Filing

Mechanic's lien statutes usually provide a time period during which a claim of lien must be filed and served on the proper parties. Typically the time for filing begins to run when a laborer has finished providing services or a supplier has completed delivery of materials to the construction site. Although the laws vary, the time for filing the claim of lien is quite short in most states. Thirty-, sixty-, or ninety-day time periods after the lienor's performance is completed are common in most states.

The failure to file a claim of lien within the statutory time period means that the lien is ineffective. An issue that frequently arises concerns when a laborer's or supplier's work is finished so that the time period for filing begins to run. If the time for filing is about to expire, will another small amount of work start the period over? In other words, when is work really completed for filing purposes? The best and most widely accepted rule is that a minor detail that is completed after the contract has been basically completed will not extend the filing-time period.[3] Some states allow the landowner to post a notice on the construction site that the work is deemed completed. This notice of completion commences the time period for filing. A few states allow the landowner to shorten this time period when the notice of completion is filed.

10. Foreclosing the Lien

The final step in perfecting a mechanic's lien usually is filing a lawsuit to foreclose or to enforce the lien. The next few sections of this chapter involve the enforcement of the lien; therefore, the lawsuit is discussed there. However, it may be emphasized here that there is a statutory time period within which the lawsuit must be filed. As with filing the claim of lien, failure to bring this lawsuit for enforcement within the time allowed results in an ineffective lien.

[3]Mitchell v. Flandro, page 403.

A one-year time period for filing a lawsuit is typical of many mechanic's lien laws. This time period usually begins to run upon completion of the laborer's work or the supplier's delivery. As in the case of the time period for filing a claim of lien, a minor incident that actually completes the contractual performance cannot be used to extend the time period after the work has been substantially completed.

Case 15.4

Carlisle furnished labor and materials for a maintenance building owned by Cox. The work was completed on December 6, 1968, except for the installation of one heating register. This heating register, which cost $2.26 and represented .0011 percent of the total value of the work, was not installed until February 19, 1969. The register had been in the front seat of Carlisle's truck for over a month before it was installed. Carlisle commenced this action on February 17, 1970, to recover the value of his material and labor furnished to Cox. A statute required that such an action for enforcement of a mechanics' lien be commenced within one year from the last date materials were furnished or labor performed.

Issue: Did Carlisle commence the action within a year after materials were furnished or labor performed?

Decision: No. The action was thus barred.

Reasons: When a building has been substantially completed and has been accepted by the owner, the contractor may not thereafter at his own instance perform some minor omitted part of the contract and thereby extend the one-year period. The building had been accepted by Cox, and Cox had made no request for the heating register. The one-year period could, therefore, not be extended by the later installation of the register.

Carlisle v. Cox, 506 P.2d 60 (Utah 1973).

Enforcement of Mechanic's Liens

11.   Introduction

The enforcement of a properly created and perfected mechanic's lien involves the process by which the lien holder (lienor) collects the money due for services or materials furnished for an improvement of real estate. The process shows the advantages that a secured creditor has over an unsecured general creditor. The typical enforcement mechanism is the lawsuit that must be filed after a claim of lien has been filed and served on the interested parties. During this litigation, the lienors have the burden of proving that they are protected by a valid mechanic's lien and are entitled to the amount claimed. Issues that may arise in the lawsuit might include whether the mechanic's lien statute is constitutional, how this lien is properly foreclosed, and what priority the lien has when compared with other claims against the property.

12. Constitutionality

For a number of years constitutional attacks on mechanic's lien statutes have been frequent. Historically, most of these objections have been held to be without merit, and the statutes have been upheld on a regular basis. Perhaps the most frequent claim is that a mechanic's lien deprives the property owner of the use of the property without due process of law. When a mechanic's lien law permits the creation of a lien without the owner receiving preliminary notice, that owner does not have a valid claim of unconstitutionality. However, when a lien can be enforced without judicial supervision through a lawsuit, these laws have been declared invalid as a taking of property without due process. To avoid this constitutionality issue, all states now require that a lawsuit be filed to enforce a mechanic's lien. When this judicial supervision is present, the statute should survive constitutional attacks.

Case 15.5

Associates, a partnership owning a tract of real estate, entered into a contract with Metro to have a shopping center built on their land. Samas furnished building materials to Metro, and when Samas was not paid for the supplies, Samas filed a mechanic's lien against the property. Associates brought this action against Samas to have the lien removed, alleging that the statute under which Samas claimed the lien was unconstitutional since it permitted a person claiming to be a creditor to deprive and interfere with the use of the property by its owner without judicial supervision and without immediate opportunity for a hearing.

Issue: Was the mechanic's lien statute unconstitutional?

Decision: No. Samas' lien was valid.

Reasons: Although some use of the owner's property is curtailed by a lien claimed under authority of the statute, the owner is not legally precluded from selling, encumbering, renting, or otherwise dealing with the property as he chooses. There is an important interest served by the imposition of a lien in favor of the supplier. The statute accordingly did not deprive owners of a significant property interest without due process.

Fayetteville-85 Associates, Ltd. v. Samas, Inc., 243 S.E.2d 887 (Ga. 1978).

13.   Foreclosure

The ultimate purpose of the lawsuit is to have the court declare the amount owed to the lienor and order that the improved real estate be sold to pay the debt. The lienor must prove in court that there was a direct or indirect relationship with the landowner, that the contract was substantially performed, that the lien was created and perfected within the statutory requirements, and that the lawsuit was properly and timely filed.

If the party claiming the rights to a mechanic's lien is successful in proving these elements, the court can order that the lien be foreclosed. Foreclosure of a mechanic's lien means that the real estate involved will be sold as provided by the statute, and the sale proceeds will be paid into the court. From these proceeds the creditors, who had a security interest in the real estate, including the mechanic's lien claimant, will be paid. If these proceeds are insufficient to pay all creditors, the extent to which each will be paid depends on the laws relating to priorities.

14.   Priorities

The higher the priority of a lien, the more likely that upon foreclosure the lien will be entirely paid. In other words, it is better to be first in priority than second or some lower priority. In order to be able to determine the priority of any particular mechanic's lien, we must know when the lien attached. Although a few states differ as to the time of a lien's attachment, the majority of states' statutes specify that the attachment of a properly created and perfected mechanic's lien relates back to the time work was begun by the laborer or supplier. For example, suppose Evans Construction Company begins a project on June 3,

1982. If this project continues until July 8, 1984, and Evans files a mechanic's lien within the statutory time period, most states' laws would say this lien attached as of June 3, 1982. This date of attachment is crucial for priority purposes.

There are two basic problems that may arise in connection with the issue of a mechanic's lien's priority. The first concerns priority among similar mechanic's liens. The second hinges on the priority of mechanic's liens compared with other claims against the same real estate. If against the same real estate there are several mechanic's liens filed that arose out of different improvement projects, the priority of each of these liens is based on the date it attached. In the majority of states, if several liens arise out of the same improvement, they are considered equal. If the proceeds of a foreclosure are insufficient to satisfy all these debts, the lienors must share the proceeds on a pro-rata basis equal to the percentage of the entire project that their work represented. A few states (including Florida, Georgia, Michigan, New Jersey, New York, Ohio, and Oklahoma) provide that certain lienors who contributed to the same improvement take priority over other lienors, even though the date on which their liens attached may be the same. For example, the liens for laborers' wages have priority over subcontractors' liens, but subcontractors' liens take precedence over a general contractor's lien.

The priority given to a mechanic's lien compared with other liens against the real estate depends on the state's statute. A typical situation involving the issue of priority concerns a mechanic's lien and a mortgage. A mortgage is a document which grants a lender a security interest in real estate in return for making a loan. The mortgage often is used to finance a construction project or the purchase of real estate. The mortgage document is the subject matter of Chapter 14 on financing real estate.

When determining the priority of a mechanic's lien and a mortgage on the same property, the date of attachment remains crucial. Nearly all states provide that a mortgage attaches when it is properly recorded. If the state where the land is located is one of the few providing that a mechanic's lien attaches when a claim of lien is filed, then priority is given to the creditor who is first to file.

As mentioned above, the majority of states' laws on mechanic's liens say that these liens attach when work first begins or when supplies are first delivered. In these states a mortgage may be filed before a claim of lien is filed, and yet the lien has priority. A lender who takes a mortgage must therefore make sure there are no potential mechanic's liens or obtain an agreement from laborers and suppliers that their liens are subordinated to the mortgage. Absent these actions, a mortgage holder may lose all or at least part of the foreclosure proceeds to a mechanic's lienor. Such was the outcome in the following case.

Case 15.6

New Georgia Plumbing furnished labor and materials to an apartment complex owned by Accent. Work commenced in November 1972 and was completed in November 1973. Shortly thereafter, Accent obtained a loan from Old Stone Mortgage, and a mortgage was given as security. The mortgage was recorded on November 19, 1973. Old Stone had actual notice that New Georgia was claiming money was due it from Accent. On December 17, 1973, New Georgia filed its claim of lien. New Georgia commenced this action for a declaratory judgment that its mechanics' lien was entitled to priority over Old Stone's mortgage.

Issue: Was New Georgia's mechanics' lien entitled to priority over the mortgage?

Decision: Yes. The lien attached at the time work commenced.

Reasons: A mechanic's lien attaches from the time work is commenced or material is furnished. If the lien is thereafter filed in the manner prescribed by statute, the lien is effective from the date of attachment. New Georgia had complied with the recording requirements and its lien was thus entitled to priority over the mortgage, which was recorded after the lien attached.

Old Stone Mortgage and Realty Trust v. New Georgia Plumbing, Inc., 231 S.E.2d 785 (Ga. App. 1976), aff'd 236 S.E.2d 592 (Ga. 1977).

Still other states give priority to mechanic's liens over a previously recorded mortgage because the lienor increased the value of the property. This added value should be evident in the greater proceeds obtained at the foreclosure sale. After the lienor is paid, the mortgagee still has the remaining proceeds, which should be about the same as if no improvements had been made at all.

Termination of Mechanic's Liens

15. Introduction

There are several ways in which laborers' or suppliers' rights to a mechanic's lien may be terminated. Under some circumstances a lien may be prohibited by agreement. The rights of a lienor may be abolished as a result of such actions of the lienor as the waiver or release of the lien or the failure to perfect the lien within the statutory time period. Still other means that terminate a mechanic's lien include actions by the real estate owner, including payment of the contract price or filing a bond as a substitute for the lien.

16. By Agreement of the Parties

Mechanic's liens must grow out of a contractual relationship between the landowner and the laborers and suppliers. As was seen in Chapter 11, a contract governs the rights and duties of the contracting parties. As long as the contract is legal, it will be the law between the parties who agree to it. Therefore, there is nothing wrong with the owner and those involved in making the improvement agreeing that there are to be no rights to mechanic's liens. This kind of agreement is frequently referred to as a no-lien construction contract.

In addition to an expressed no-lien contract, courts have found that certain implied agreements preclude the existence of a mechanic's lien. If a laborer or supplier agrees to do the work or furnish the material on credit, normally no mechanic's liens can be filed. The extension of credit requires the improver to make some other arrangements to secure that full payment will be forthcoming. This rule does not generally apply when the parties have agreed to payments on account thirty days after the work is performed or the material is furnished.

17. By Acts of the Lienor

A laborer or supplier who may have the right to claim a mechanic's lien under the applicable state law may lose this right under certain circumstances. In essence, the agreement of the parties to enter into a no-lien contract may consist of the improver waiving all rights to claim a lien. A *waiver* is the voluntary relinquishment of a right. Any laborer or supplier can waive the right prior to filing a claim of lien on record. A waiver may be expressed in written form or implied from the factual situation surrounding a construction project.

For example, assume that a materialman and a contractor were engaged in several different projects. The materialman must maintain separate accounts of the supplies furnished for these various projects. If the contractor makes a partial payment to the materialman, it is the materialman's responsibility to find out on what accounts the payment was made. By failing to maintain these accurate records, the material-man implicitly waives the right to a lien on the owner's property. Once a waiver is established, the materialman can look only to the contractor for payment.

Even after a claim of lien is filed on record, a person who contributes to an improvement can extinguish his or her right to enforce the lien. This post-filing process is known as a *release* of the lien. Frequently, the concepts of release and waiver are confused. Most accurately, a waiver occurs before a claim of lien is filed, whereas a release is used after there has been a public filing. A lien is perhaps most commonly released when the landowner pays the lienor after a claim of lien has been filed. The owner must obtain and file a signed release so that the public records will indicate that the mechanic's lien no longer exists.

Finally, as previously mentioned, a party who has the statutory right to claim a mechanic's lien may lose that right if the statute's requirements are not substantially fulfilled. It is important to remember that there are various time limits within which a preliminary notice must be delivered (if one is required), a claim of lien must be filed and served, and a lawsuit must be commenced. If any one of these time periods is not complied with, a mechanic's lien will be ineffective.

18. *By Acts of the Owner*

Normally the landowner who has hired laborers and suppliers or a general contractor, as supervisor, can prevent the existence of or terminate existing mechanic's liens by paying the lienors in full or by substituting a bond for the liens that may arise.

Logic seems to dictate that a landowner should have to pay only once for improvements made. Some states place the burden of receiving payment on subcontractors, laborers, suppliers, or other parties who deal indirectly with the landowner. In these states, once the owner has proven that the general contractor was fully paid, the owner is not liable if the contractor failed to pay other lienors.

Not all states, however, follow this procedure favoring the land-owner who has fully paid the general contractor. Precise knowledge of the law of the state where the land is located is essential to avoid double payment. For example, some states place a duty on the landowner to learn whether the subcontractors, laborers, and suppliers involved in the improvement project are paid by the general contractor. They re-quire that the owner obtain an affidavit (a sworn statement) from the general contractor concerning the existence of any mechanic's liens, or stating that all potential lienors have been paid. This affidavit must be obtained before the owner makes final payment to the contractor. When the applicable mechanic's lien statute requires this action and the landowner fails to obtain the affidavit, the owner's land still may be subject to valid mechanic's liens.

Case 15.7

McDonald, a homeowner, entered into a contract with "Mr. Ex-teriors" to remove rotted wood from the exterior of his house and to replace it with aluminum siding. Mr. Exteriors picked up the building materials from Crown, a supplier. When the work was complete, McDonald paid Mr. Exteriors in full. McDonald had no knowledge of Crown and did not know that Crown was unpaid. He did not ask for or receive from Mr. Exteriors a con-tractor's affidavit that all labor and materials had been paid. A week after payment was made to Mr. Exteriors, McDonald re-ceived a "Notice to Owner" from Crown, notifying him that Crown had not been paid. Several months thereafter, McDonald received a copy of Crown's claim of lien. McDonald then com-menced this action seeking a judgment that the lien be vacated.

Issue: Should Crown's lien against McDonald's property be cancelled?

Decision: No. The lien was enforceable.

Reasons: McDonald's payment to Mr. Exteriors was improper under the mechanic's-lien statute because of the failure to obtain the con-tractor's affidavit asserting that all had been paid or listing those who were unpaid. An owner pays the contractor at his peril when he does not demand and receive the affidavit as required by this state's statute.

Adams v. McDonald, 356 So.2d 864 (Fla. App. 1978).

In some states, merely obtaining a contractor's affidavit is not sufficient to relieve the owner of liability even after the contractor has been fully paid. There is a further requirement that the landowner must have made the final payment in *good faith* that all improvers had been paid. The owner's failure to prove a good-faith payment means that liens are still possible. Therefore, because a contractor's affidavit contains false information, the owner may still be liable for lienor's claims. Just because the owner acquires a contractor's affidavit does not mean that good faith exists. In other words, good faith must be proven, and obtaining an affidavit from the general contractor is just one thing to be considered in determining the owner's good-faith payment.

As a substitute for full payment of a lienor's claim, a landowner can obtain a surety bond, which is a contractual agreement that the bonding company will pay off all the valid claims that arise out of a construction job. Frequently, the landowner will insist that the general contractor provide a surety bond guaranteeing that all subcontractors, laborers, and suppliers will be paid if the general contractor fails to pay them. By this bond, the owner's property is protected from potential mechanic's liens. In a real sense, a bond acts as a substitute for the mechanic's-lien law in providing security that all those having valid claims will be paid. For instance, a subcontractor, laborer, or supplier can sue a general contractor on the surety bond filed instead of pursuing a mechanic's-lien claim. In return, a general contractor filing a surety bond has the right to attack any potential lienor's claim, just as the landowner would if no bond existed.

Cases on Mechanic's Liens

Gollehon, Schemmer & Associates, Inc., v. Fairway-Bettendorf Associates 268 N.W.2d 200 (Iowa 1978).

McCormick, J.

The question here is whether an architect is entitled to a mechanic's lien on real estate when he has provided services preparatory to development of the land which were not used because the project did not proceed beyond the planning stage. Plaintiff Gollehon, Schemmer & Associates, Inc., filed and sought to foreclose a lien for such services against an undeveloped 18.62

acre tract of land owned by defendant Fairway-Bettendorf Associates located in Bettendorf. Defendant Union National Bank held the first mortgage on the premises, which was subsequent in date to plaintiff's mechanic's lien. On defendant bank's motion for adjudication of law points, the trial court held plaintiff's lien was invalid and dismissed the action. We affirm.

Defendant Fairway-Bettendorf Associates employed plaintiff to provide architectural, engineering and planning services in preparation for the development of a multi-family dwelling project on the real estate involved.

Plaintiff complied with its employment contract. In doing so, its only work on the real estate consisted of surveying it, marking its boundaries with metal pins and lathes, marking the location of a pipeline easement in the same manner, and marking the location of a sanitary sewer easement with wooden hubs. The purpose of this surveying and marking was to assist in the preparation of maps and plans; it was not otherwise related to construction. Plaintiff produced plans and specifications for the proposed project, arranged for platting, secured municipal approval of platting, and prepared specifications to be used for subcontractor bidding.

The project was abandoned before bids were obtained. As a result, plaintiff's plans were never used, and no construction occurred.

The contract balance claimed by plaintiff is $14,229.50, with interest. Its mechanic's lien was filed October 17, 1974, and this foreclosure action was commenced in 1976.

. . . Plaintiff alleges it furnished labor for and upon the land and is thus entitled under the statute to a lien upon the land so "improved".

Defendant bank acknowledges plaintiff furnished labor for or upon the land but nevertheless contends it is not entitled to a mechanic's lien because its plans did not result in any improvement in the land. The dispute thus narrows to whether plaintiff's services improved the land as required . . . for a right of lien to arise.

. . . [We] are unable to find plaintiff's services constituted an improvement of the real estate even through liberal construction of the statute.

The theory under which mechanic's liens are justified is that the improvement constitutes visible notice of the furnishing of labor or material. In *Evans v. Tripp*, 35 Iowa 371, 373 (1872), this court said:

> The reason upon which the statute is based is quite as apparent as its language. It is this: The fact that the building or improvement is being made is notice to the world, open enough for all to have warning of the mechanics' and material men's rights. It is entirely competent for the legislature to so provide and to direct that all persons shall be chargeable with such notice for ninety days after the last item of labor or materials is furnished. . . .
>
> It is undisputed that plaintiff's services were preliminary to construction of any improvement on the land. Although we have no doubt these services were valuable and plaintiff is entitled to compensation for them, the fact remains they did not result in any actual or visible improvement in the real estate. In such a situation, although no two statutes are the same, most courts have held no right to lien exists. . . .

The rationale for allowing a lien for preparing plans which are actually used is that the plans become part of the labor expended for the improvement in the same way as the labor of a carpenter or bricklayer. When the improvement is begun the world is thereby put on notice of the rights of those who furnished labor or materials for it. When no improvement is undertaken, no such visible evidence exists. The reasoning which justifies conferring lien rights does not support recognizing a lien when no improvement has been commenced.

Plaintiff contends that, assuming this is true, the markers placed on the land during the course of surveying to assist in preparing maps and plans constituted the requisite evidence of improvement. While we agree these markers were visible evidence

of plaintiff's work, we do not think they improved the land within the meaning of the statute. They aided plaintiff in preparing plans; they were preliminary to rather than part of the contemplated improvement of the land.

Other jurisdictions which have confronted this issue under analogous statutes have reached the same conclusion. . . .

[The court concluded that plaintiff was not entitled to a lien; therefore, the trial court's judgment is]

Affirmed.

G. W. Bowen v. R. A. Collins
217 S.E.2d 193 (Ga. App. 1975).

Evans, J.

Bowen and Rogers, d/b/a Bowen-Rogers Hardware Company, were partners, and were engaged in the business of furnishing materials for construction of buildings. In this particular case they sued the contractor for a general judgment, which was rendered in plaintiffs' favor by default. The materialmen then brought a separate action against the owners of the property, Ronald A. and Carol C. Collins, as defendants, and sought a judgment in rem [on a lien] against the property of the owners.

The defendants contended the material furnished by plaintiffs did not go into construction of the building of defendants, and consequently plaintiffs were not entitled to a lien. *Held:*

1. Laws as to liens of mechanics and materialmen who supply labor or materials for the improvement of realty are in derogation of the common law and must be strictly construed; and one who claims such a lien must bring himself clearly within the law. . . .

2. The burden was on the plaintiffs to prove that the materials furnished actually went into construction of defendants' building, under a contract and the value of same. . . .

3. Since there was evidence here from which the jury could infer that much of the material charged against the defendant's job did not go into the construction of defendants' dwelling, the court did not err in charging the jury that to obtain a lien, the supplies must be furnished for the purpose of improving the owner's property and that they were in fact used in such improvements. . . . It was held that such improvements must be attached to and become incorporated in the realty.

4. Where a materialman furnishes and delivers material to the owner's premises in reliance on the owner's representation that the material is intended to be used for the improvement of the property, the owner is estopped as between the parties to contend that the material was not in fact so used. . . . But

there was no estoppel of the owner under the facts here, and the above statement of law does not apply.

5. Plaintiff proved the material was charged to the contractor but did not prove that all of same was delivered to defendant's job. Materials were supplied to several other houses in the immediate area, and some of the materials were suppos-

edly delivered to the job by the contractor's employees. Accordingly, the general grounds of the motion for new trial are not meritorious, and the evidence does not demand a finding that the material was delivered to defendant's home construction site and used to improve his dwelling. . . .

Affirmed.

Mitchell v. Flandro
506 P.2d 455 (Idaho 1973).

The plaintiff, a contractor, filed a lawsuit to foreclose a mechanic's lien. Although the architect signed a certificate of substantial completion on November 10, 1964, the contractor continued to do work until January 2, 1965. Thereafter, a claim of lien was filed on March 11, 1965. Relying on the architect's certificate as designating completion, the trial court held the claim of lien was not filed within the statutory time period. The contractor appealed.

Bakes, J.

. . . Of primary importance in this appeal is the district court's conclusion that respondent's lien was not timely filed as required in I.C. 45–507. At the time that respondent filed his lien, that section provided:

Every original contractor claiming the benefit of this chapter must, within ninety (90) days . . . after the completion of any building, improvement or structure, or after the completion of the alteration or repair thereof, or in case he cease to labor thereon before the completion thereof, then after he so ceases to labor or after he has ceased to labor thereon for any cause, or after he has ceased to furnish materials therefor . . . file for record with the county recorder for the county in which such property or some part thereof is situated, a

claim containing a statement of his demand, after deducting all just credits and offsets, with the name of the owner, or reputed owner, if known, and also the name of the person by whom he was employed or to whom he furnished the materials. . . . I.C. 45–507.

It is respondent's position that due to the fact that he allegedly performed work on the structure up until January 2, 1965, that the lien application filed March 11, 1965, was in fact filed within ninety days of the cessation of work under the contract and hence was timely filed. In finding that the lien was not timely filed, the trial court stated:

. . . as a matter of fact, that from the November [1964] date through the March

[1965] date that plaintiff did not prove services of such a nature as to expand the time for filing his lien and the court concludes, therefore, as a matter of law, that the lien was not timely filed. . . .

Since there is competent evidence in the record supporting the trial court's factual determination that no substantial work was proven done after November, 1964, we do not disturb it on appeal.

It is undisputed in the record that the certificate of "substantial completion" was submitted by respondent and approved by appellants' architect on November 10, 1964. According to the architect, the certificate issued when the construction was completed to the extent that appellants could assume occupancy. On issuance of the certificate, the respondent-builders were entitled to submit their final estimate for payment. From respondent Mitchell's own testimony it appears that the issuance of the certificate also marked the effective completion of construction under the contract.

It is established that "trivial" work done or materials furnished after the contract has been substantially completed will not extend the time in which a lien claim can be filed under I.C. 45–507. As well articulated in *Gem State Lumber Co.* v. *Whitty,* 37 Idaho 489, 217 P. 1027:

> While the time fixed in the contract for the completion of a building is not controlling against laborers or materialmen, it has a direct bearing upon the time when the building was to be completed under the contract, so that the time for filing liens for material and labor would begin to run. The statute provides that this time shall be computed from the date of the last item of material furnished, or from the last work performed. *The rule very generally prevails that such time begins to run from a substantial completion of the contract, and that new items thereafter added to the account will not extend the time in which to claim a lien or revive a lien already expired.* The more difficult question is to determine when under this doctrine the contract has been completed. By the weight of authority, this is to be ascertained by the conditions of the contract, the conduct of the parties with reference thereto, and the surrounding facts and circumstances. Ordinarily, *furnishing an article or performing a service trivial in character is not sufficient to extend the time for claiming a lien or to revive an expired lien, where the article is furnished or the service rendered after a substantial completion of the contract, and the article is not expressly required by the terms thereof.*

Since it is undisputed that the contract was substantially completed on November 10, 1964, and since the trial court found inadequate proof that any material or substantial work was performed or supplies furnished after that date which would extend the time for filing a lien, we conclude that the trial court was correct in ruling that the lien was not timely filed. . . .

Affirmed.

REVIEW QUESTIONS

1. Define the following terms:
   a. Lien
   b. Improvement
   c. Mechanic's lien
2. Oliver purchased a mobile home from the Masters Company, which agreed to deliver and set up the home on Oliver's property. During the construction

at Masters' factory, an employee performed electrical work on this home, for which he was not paid by Masters. Is this employee entitled to file a mechanic's lien against the mobile home once it is on Oliver's property? Explain.

3. Ramsey supplied materials and labor as a subcontractor in the construction of a condominium complex. Ramsey claimed a mechanic's lien against the project, which was owned by DiSabatino. Ramsey's lien, which was in the amount of $9,430, related to ten separate condominium units. The amount due for each unit was not separately indentified. DiSabatino attacked Ramsey's lien as invalid for failure to separate the costs for each unit. Was Ramsey required to specify the amount of the lien claimed applicable to each of the ten units? Why?

4. List the steps that must be followed in order to create and perfect a mechanic's lien.

5. In February 1978, Roger granted a mortgage to the Savings Bank in return for a construction loan. The Bank advanced funds in March 1978 to help Roger pay for the land being improved. During the summer of 1978, Gerrity supplied $7,849 worth of materials for which he was not paid. During October 1978, the Bank advanced additional funds to pay Roger's suppliers and laborers. In February 1979, Roger's mortgage was foreclosed and the property was sold for $19,000. Of these proceeds, the bank took all but $231 to satisfy Roger's debt to them. Gerrity had created and perfected a mechanic's lien and had obtained a judgment against Roger. Gerrity sues the Bank, claiming priority over the mortgage. Under what circumstances would the mechanic's lien have priority over a preexisting mortgage? Explain.

6. Explain the meaning and application of each of the following to mechanic's liens:
   a. Notice of nonresponsibility
   b. Preliminary notice of lien
   c. Claim of lien

7. Some states allow general contractors a longer time period to file a claim of lien than subcontractors, laborers, or suppliers are allowed. What is the justification for this difference?

8. Apex supplied materials to J & H Plumbing for several of J & H's jobs, including the Brookside Village complex. When J & H paid Apex, Apex failed to ascertain which of J & H's jobs the funds were for and credited the payments to jobs other than the Brookside Village complex. Apex claimed the materials used at Brookside had not been paid and filed a lien against the complex, after which it commenced an action to recover on the lien. Was the lien against the Brookside Village complex enforceable?

9. The property owner should always insist on receiving an affidavit from the general contractor stating that all subcontractors, laborers, or suppliers have been paid or otherwise have waived their rights to claim a mechanic's lien. Why? What is the effect of this affidavit?

10. CBC contracted with the owner of real estate to build a sewer plant. CBC engaged Yates Construction Company as a subcontractor. A dispute arose

between the owner and CBC, with the result that Yates was not paid by CBC. Yates recorded a mechanic's lien against the land. The owner then contracted with Shapiro as general contractor to complete the project. Shapiro filed a bond as surety with the appropriate court to release the property from all liens in conformance with a statute. Yates brought this action against Shapiro to recover on the bond. Shapiro defended on the ground that the lien was not valid. Could Shapiro assert defenses as a surety, even though he was not the owner of the land, on which the lien was filed?

16

Landlord-Tenant Relationships

1. Introduction

The landlord–tenant relationship is formed as a result of a contract called a lease. A lease must satisfy the essential contractual requirements that were discussed in Chapter 11, which include the offer, acceptance, consideration, lawful purpose, and competent parties. Although an oral lease is enforced at times, the statute of frauds in all states requires that leases be in writing if they establish a landlord–tenant relationship that will last beyond a minimum time period, such as one year, designated in the statute. Thus if a landlord and a tenant agree to create a relationship that will last for more than one year, their agreement must be in writing.

A *lease* simply transfers a possessory interest in real estate from the landlord to the tenant for the tenant's use. In order to be legally enforceable, this transfer must be supported by consideration. In most lease transactions, consideration is present because the tenant pays *rent* in return for the possession.

This chapter will examine some of the clauses commonly found in leases and the rights and duties of each party affected by them. In addition, various methods of terminating a lease without further liability will be considered, as well as the remedies available when the lease agreement is not fully performed. Throughout this discussion, it must be remembered that the landlord–tenant relationship may involve residential property, farmland, and commercial or industrial facilities. Although the lease agreement should be tailored to fit the needs of each particular situation, the basic principles covered in this chapter are applicable to all leases.

Creation of the Relationship

2. In General

The landlord–tenant relationship is created by a lease agreement between the parties, who in this relationship are the *landlord,* often called the *lessor,* and the *tenant,* who receives the right to possess the real estate in return for a rental payment. The tenant is granted these rights under a lease and therefore is sometimes referred to as the *lessee.* Although this chapter uses the more common terms of landlord and tenant, lessor and lessee are synonymous with them. Some of the common types of leases and clauses they contain are discussed in the next sections.

3. Types of Leases

In Chapter 2, Section 14, we introduced four types of leasehold interests, including the tenancy for stated period, the tenancy from period to period, the tenancy at will, and the tenancy at sufferance. A lease for a stated period occurs when a landlord and tenant enter into an agreement for a specified time. The stated period may be any length of time (years, months, or days) agreed upon.

The tenancy from period to period is created when the landlord and tenant agree to continue their relationship from year to year or month to month. For example, the agreement may establish an original term of one year, with the provision that the lease is to continue from year to year unless terminated by either party upon proper notice. The method of giving proper notice should be set forth in the lease agreement. This notice of termination will be discussed in Section 15 of this chapter.

If a lease term is not specified, the parties have entered into a tenancy at will. As the name implies, this lease lasts as long as both the tenant and landlord desire. A tenancy at will is sometimes treated as a lease from month to month. If a termination notice is required to end such tenancies, it is provided by state statutes. Although the tenancy at will may last more than one year, the original agreement does not have to be in writing under the Statute of Frauds, since the possibility of its ending within one year always exists.

Finally, a tenancy at sufferance occurs when a tenant refuses to leave the premises and return possession to the landlord at the termination of a lease. In this situation, the landlord must decide either to evict this holdover tenant or to negotiate a new lease agreement. The eviction process is discussed in Section 18 below.

In addition to these legal classifications, leases can be categorized on the basis of (1) whether the landlord–tenant relationship is established by a written or oral agreement, (2) the duration of the relationship, (3) the method of rental payment, and (4) the permitted use of the leased real estate. In general, it is better to have a written document carefully designed to establish the rights of the landlord and tenant. When the parties use a written lease, the statute of frauds will usually be satisfied. The other classifications depend upon various clauses that may be included in written leases. Before anyone signs a lease, the document should be read completely to make sure its meaning is fully understood. In this next section, some of the more common clauses found in leases are discussed. Included in this discussion are leases based on duration, rental payment, and use.

Typical Clauses in Leases

4. Introduction

A written lease should always identify the parties and contain an adequate description of the real property involved. Although this description should meet the formal requirements of a metes-and-bounds or a congressional-survey legal description, a reference to the street address has been held to be sufficient.

The lease should also contain a clause stating how long the landlord-tenant relationship will last. Indeed, this duration clause, in addition to indicating the type of tenancy provided for in the lease being signed—whether for a stated period, period to period, or at will—also may distinguish between a long-term and a short-term relationship. A lease that creates a landlord–tenant relationship for a stated period longer than one year commonly is called a *long-term* lease. Those that expressly last for less than one year or that can be terminated at either party's will are sometimes called *short-term* leases. Short-term leases may provide less stability, but they offer more flexibility than long-term leases.

In addition to the designation of the parties, the description of the real estate, and the duration of the lease, leases may contain provisions on the following: restrictions on use of the property, methods of rental payment, methods of renewal, responsibilities for maintenance and repairs, status of fixtures, rights to an option, and rights to assign or sublease.

5.   Restrictions on Use

A landlord may desire to limit the ways in which the tenant can use the real estate. As long as a restriction is reasonable, it will be enforceable. For example, a lease may limit the use to residential or to a specific commercial purpose, such as a grocery store. Other restrictions can be more specific, such as those stating that no animals or children are allowed within a residential apartment complex. Frequently, restrictive covenants or promises will be included in commercial leases to protect a party's interest. If a landlord who operates a grocery store leases part of its building space, it would be reasonable to prevent the tenant from starting a competing grocery business in the rented space. The scope of these covenants must be reasonable as to time period and territorial area of the restriction. If a restriction is unreasonable, it is an illegal restraint of trade and as such will not be enforced. Any party directly affected by the restriction may sue to enforce it, whether that person is the landlord, tenant, or someone else entitled to the restriction's benefits.

Case 16.1

Webster operated a "One Hour Martinizing" laundry establishment in a shopping center. Star Distributing Company operated a laundry business in the same shopping center. A restrictive covenant in Star's lease limited the use of its premises to coin-operated laundering and budget dry cleaning. Star began engaging in a practice known as "drop-off" laundry, an operation in which the customer drops the laundry off with an attendant. The attendants use the coin-operated machines, after which the laundry is dried and folded. Webster commenced this action to enjoin Star's "drop-off" laundry, asserting that the "drop-off" technique was beyond the scope of Star's restrictive covenant.

Issue: Should the "drop-off" practice be enjoined?

Decision: Yes. It violated the terms of Star's lease.

Reasons: Star argued that the restrictive covenant should not be enforced, as it was an illegal restraint of trade. However, this covenant was enforceable because it was reasonable as to territory and duration. It did not impose greater than necessary restrictions on Star, and it did not unduly prejudice the interests of the public. The remaining question was whether Star's "drop-off" laundering constituted more than a coin-operated laundry. While an attendant did operate the machine, the customer was charged an additional amount for the attendant's services. These services were clearly inconsistent with Star's "budget" type of operation.

Webster v. Star Distributing Co., 244 S.E.2d 826 (Ga. 1978).

What makes one restrictive covenant reasonable and another unreasonable may ultimately be based on the intent of the parties. A restriction on the use of land or space other than that being leased by the tenant may be enforced if reasonable. For example, a tenant operating a restaurant in a shopping center may insist that the landlord promise not to allow a similar restaurant in the same shopping center. This restriction on the landlord is binding as long as it is reasonable.

6. Rent

In consideration for possession and use of the real estate, a tenant pays an agreed-upon amount of rent periodically. When the tenant is not paying for electricity, gas, or other utilities, the rental payment is the gross amount that the landlord receives from the lease. If the tenant does pay for these utilities, insurance, repair costs, and other expenses, the rent received by the landlord is a net amount. This is the principal distinction between gross and net leases.

Instead of the rent being a fixed figure, it may be a percentage of a commercial tenant's sales or profits. This method of rental payment is found in a percentage lease. Rather than a fixed amount, the rent may be tied to some economic indicator, such as the consumer price index. This escalation-type rental payment is especially advantageous to the landlord during inflationary times. The tenant should insist on a de-escalation clause, so that the rent is reduced during deflationary periods. These percentage and escalation clauses concerning rental payment are more common in commercial than in residential leases.

Regardless of the method of payment, the tenant has the duty to pay rent on a regular basis (monthly, quarterly, yearly, etc.). What happens if a tenant fails to pay rent on the date it is due and pays one day or one week late? Whether a late rental payment results in a material breach of the lease depends on whether time is of the essence. The phrase "time is of the essence" often is included in form leases to make the time of payment a condition precedent to the landlord's duties to provide the space leased. A time-is-of-the-essence clause means that each deadline established in the lease is crucially important. If the phrase is in the lease and a rental payment is late, the landlord can cancel the lease. If time is *not* of the essence, a rental payment one day or one week late will not materially affect the landlord–tenant relationship.

In order to encourage the tenant to pay rent on time, the lease may contain a penalty clause. For example, if the tenant is more than ten days late paying rent, a 10 percent penalty may be required. Use of this type of penalty clause obviously means that a late rental payment is not a breach of the entire lease agreement justifying rescission.

7. Renewal Provisions

A lease may contain one of two distinct types of renewal clauses. If by its terms a lease is automatically renewed if neither party gives notice of termination, a *negative renewal clause* is involved. Courts generally will not interpret this clause as creating a perpetual lease.[1] A lease that provides for renewal only when the tenant gives notice to the landlord that renewal is desired contains a *positive renewal clause.* In accordance

[1]Lonergan v. Connecticut Food Store, Inc., page 433.

with this latter provision, if no notice of renewal is given properly, the landlord–tenant relationship terminates at the end of the original lease period.

Most leases have a specific time period within which notice to terminate (under a negative renewal clause) or notice to renew (under a positive renewal clause) must be given. Although the landlord and tenant always may agree to whatever time period they desire, one to two months prior to the expiration of the lease is very common.

8. Maintenance and Repairs

Whether the landlord or the tenant has primary responsibility for the maintenance and repairs of the improvements depends on the language and the nature of the lease. If the lease is silent about which party has this responsibility, the law implies a duty on the landlord to maintain the structural integrity of the building, while the tenant must make minor repairs to keep the improvements from deteriorating.

Unless clearly disclaimed, most states have held that the landlord implicitly warrants that the premises are habitable for the use contemplated by the tenant. The landlord's failure to maintain the improvements in a habitable condition allows the tenant to terminate the lease without liability. (See sections 13 and 15 below.)

What happens when an improvement is partially or totally destroyed? Generally neither the landlord nor the tenant must rebuild the structure. In essence, destruction of the improvement terminates the lease. Nevertheless, the question remains—Who had the risk of loss? In most situations, the risk of losing a building through unavoidable events falls on the landlord–owner. Indeed, in residential leases, the landlord maintains hazard insurance on the structure, and the tenants insure their personal household contents. In commercial leases which last for terms of several years, the parties may agree that the tenant has the risk of loss.

It is best for the parties to a lease to provide specifically for the responsibilities of each party. When a lease expressly provides for duties which are contrary to the general rules just stated, the lease will be enforced as written. In this next case a court was faced with such a conflict between the lease's terms and the generally implied responsibilities.

Case 16.2

Evco Corporation was the tenant of a building owned by Ross. The lease was for a period of five years, from April 1972 to April 1977, and it covered premises being operated as a restaurant and lounge. The lease provisions required the landlord (lessor) to "carry fire insurance upon the building structure for any damage thereto by fire." In addition, "the lessor shall be responsible for all major repairs that may become necessary to the building structure during the term of the lease and should same occur lessor shall make necessary repairs within a reasonable period of time." In April 1973 a fire of undisclosed nature substantially damaged the building. The damage was so severe that it amounted to the building's total destruction from a practical standpoint. The landlord refused to rebuild the structure after receiving proposals for more profitable uses of the premises. The tenant seeks specific performance of a duty on the part of the landlord to rebuild, as well as damages for delay covering the period of time from the occurrence of the fire. The landlord contends there is no duty to rebuild a totally destroyed structure.

Issue: Is the landlord obligated under the terms of the lease to rebuild a structure totally destroyed by fire?

Decision: Yes.

Reasons: Ordinarily, as between a landlord and tenant, a landlord has no obligation to make repairs upon leased premises—any such obligation rests upon their contract. The clause in this lease cannot be interpreted as anything less than a general covenant on the part of the landlord to repair so far as fire loss is concerned. Not only does the lease bind the landlord to make all major repairs, but there is a specific requirement for the landlord to maintain fire insurance upon the building "for any damage" resulting from fire. Loss in this case must fall upon the landlord. A breach of the covenants of the contract has occurred because of the landlord's failure to restore the premises.

Evco Corporation v. Ross, 528 S.W.2d 20 (Tenn. 1975).

9. Fixtures

Upon the termination of a lease, a dispute can arise over whether a fixture remains with the real estate or may be removed by the tenant. In Chapter 1 it was stated that once an item is found to be a fixture it usually is part of the real estate. Exceptions to this general rule include trade and agricultural fixtures, which may be removed by the tenant. Because of the potential confusion about whether personal property becomes a fixture and whether such an item belongs to the landlord or tenant, a lease should contain a clause specifying each parties' rights to these items. A clearly stated provision is the best indicator of the landlord's and tenant's intent, which is the crucial test in determining fixture status.

10. Options

Chapter 11 included a discussion of options. There it was stated that an option is simply an agreement to keep an offer open for a stated time period. A landlord may give a tenant an option to buy the leased real estate, or a tenant may give the landlord the option to sell. In either situation, the option may be made a part of the lease document. To be enforceable, an option to buy or sell real estate must be in writing and supported by consideration. Frequently, a tenant's consideration for an option to buy is included in the periodic rental payment. Option clauses must contain a previously agreed upon price. Furthermore, the parties must exercise their rights in specific compliance with the terms of the option. Normally a tenant exercises the option by notifying the landlord of his or her intention to buy the real estate.

Often the issue arises whether the rights under an option clause can be transferred to a third party who did not participate in the original lease negotiations. The answer to this issue depends on the intent of the parties, as discussed in the next section.

11. Assignment and Sublease

The typical lease of real estate involves two parties—the landlord and the tenant. Normally these original parties to the lease are the only ones who have a specific interest in it. However, additional parties who did not participate in the original negotiations can become involved in the transaction through an assignment or sublease.

The original parties to a lease can be analyzed as an obligor and an obligee. An obligor is the party who owes a duty of performance. An obligee is the party who expects the benefits of forthcoming performance. For example, in a lease, the tenant is both an obligor as to paying the rent and an obligee in expecting to receive possession of the property leased. In this example, the landlord also is an obligor (must transfer possession) and an obligee (will receive the rental payment). An obligor owes a *duty* to the obligee. An obligee is entitled to a *right* of expected performance.

An obligor may *delegate* a duty and an obligee may *assign* a right to a third party. Regardless of whether an obligor makes a delegation or an obligee makes an assignment, the original contracting party is called the *assignor* and the third party is called the *assignee.* The word *assignment* can be used in a general sense to cover both the delegation of duties and the assignment of rights.

When a tenant assigns the interest in a lease, a new relationship is established between the original landlord and the assignee. The original tenant (the assignor) remains liable to the landlord unless a novation or release is signed. An assignment of a contract may involve the delegation of a duty (to pay rent) or the assignment of a right (to possession) or both.

When a tenant subleases the lease interest, the original landlord–tenant relationship remains intact. In essence, the sublease creates an entirely new landlord–tenant relationship. The original tenant becomes a sublandlord (sublessor), and the new third party becomes a subtenant (sublessee). Under a sublease, the third party does not have a direct relationship with the original landlord. This fact is the major distinguishing characteristic between an assignment and a sublease.

Assignments and subleases by the original tenant generally are allowed if the lease does not prohibit such transactions. If the original landlord wishes to maintain some control over possible new relationships, the lease should contain a clause that requires the landlord's consent to any assignment or sublease. A clause that restricts only the tenant's right to assign a leased interest is not violated when the tenant subleases the premises without consent. When a lease contains this restrictive type of clause, the landlord cannot withhold consent to an assignment or sublease unless it is based on a good reason. In other words, a landlord must not arbitrarily refuse to approve an assignment or sublease.

A landlord's objection to an assignment or sublease is reasonable if the third party is not financially capable of fulfilling the original lease. The nature, character, or reputation of the proposed third party may be used as a factor in the landlord's approval or disapproval. Furthermore, the landlord generally has the right to insist that the use of the real estate remain the same after an assignment or sublease. If a landlord is justified in refusing to approve an assignment or sublease, the original tenant still is bound to make the rental payments. However, when approval of an assignment or sublease is unreasonably withheld, the tenant is excused from further performance of the lease. In essence, the landlord has breached the contract.

The following case highlights some of the general principles related to assignment or sublease by the tenant.

Case 16.3

Andy Griffith Products, Inc., leased certain premises from Jones and Graham for operation as a restaurant. The lease required the landlords to construct a suitable building and other improvements at their expense. The tenant was required to pay monthly rent as well as a percentage of average gross sales above a minimum sales amount. The lease permitted the tenant to sublease the premises "subject to the approval of the lessor, which approval shall not be unreasonably withheld." With the landlord's approval, the tenant subsequently subleased to codefendant Silver. Thereafter, Silver, the subtenant, decided to sublease the premises again. Silver found a new subtenant who was willing to assume responsibility for the lease. This prospective subtenant was in the electronic equipment sales and repair business. When the landlords refused to approve this second sublease, Silver abandoned the premises and stopped paying rent. The landlords filed this lawsuit to recover the monthly rental payments for the period the premises were vacated.

Issue: Was the refusal of the landlords to agree to a prospective sublease tenant an unreasonable breach of the lease contract?

Decision: No.

Reasons: Criteria for a reasonable refusal to sublet include: (1) financial responsibility of the proposed subtenant; (2) identity or business character of the subtenant; (3) legality of the proposed use; (4) nature of the occupancy. The landlords' refusal seems based on criteria 2 and 4 in that they preferred a restaurant in expectation of higher returns and in consideration that the nature of the building constructed was more suitable for a restaurant. The burden of proving the unreasonableness of the landlords' conduct rests upon the party challenging the conduct. Silver did not adequately show such proof of unreasonableness.

Jones v. Andy Griffith Products, Inc., 241 S.E.2d 140 (N.C. App. 1978).

Rights of Parties During Relationship

12. Introduction

The written lease, as a legal document, creates the landlord–tenant relationship. That document also may contain clauses that determine the rights and duties of the parties. Some of these common provisions have just been discussed. Of course, when the relationship will not necessarily last more than one year, there is no requirement for a written lease. Whether the landlord–tenant relationship is created by a written or oral agreement, there can be implied rights and obligations in addition to those stated. Implicitly, the tenant has the fundamental right to possession of habitable premises so that the use intended can be achieved. Very basically, the landlord has the right to receive the required rental payment and to regain possession upon the relationship's termination. In addition, each party has the right to terminate the relationship upon the occurrence of certain events. These matters and the interests that third parties have in lease agreements are discussed in the sections which follow.

13. Tenants' Rights

One way of studying a person's legal rights is to understand the duties of the other party to the legal relationship. Therefore, the tenant's rights are the landlord's duties. Specifically, from the basic nature of any landlord–tenant relationship it is obvious that the tenant is to take possession of real estate. Does this right of the tenant mean that the landlord has the duty to give an absolute or total right of possession to the tenant? Suppose that Lloyd owned a warehouse complex and leased units to individuals. Assume further that Harold Oliver, a current tenant, gave notice of termination effective June 30 and Lloyd leased that warehouse to Tom and Teresa beginning July 1. We have said that Tom and Teresa, as tenants, have right to possession as of July 1. What is Lloyd's liability to his new tenants if Harold Oliver holds over and does not vacate the warehouse? One theory is that the landlord, Lloyd, must make the property open for actual occupancy on the first day of the lease. If, after that day, someone encroaches on the premises, the tenant has the primary responsibility for removal of such interference.

A second theory requires the landlord to give the tenant only a superior legal right to possession. Under this logic, giving actual possession to the tenant is not necessary. The tenant's right to possession is satisfied if the tenant is given the right and power legally to remove any holdover tenant. The landlord's limited duty of giving legal, rather than actual, possession is the law in Georgia, Massachusetts, Mississippi, New York, Pennsylvania, and Vermont. Generally, this rule does not apply when there is an express agreement that the landlord will give actual possession to the tenant or when the land is occupied by the landlord.

A tenant who is in possession of the leased premises has the right to this possession exclusively and without interference of the landlord. A landlord usually cannot reenter the premises without the tenant's permission unless there is an emergency or a stated agreement to the contrary. A landlord who violates the tenant's right to exclusive possession is a trespasser who can be removed and is liable to the tenant. Of course, depending on the type of lease, a landlord may be required to maintain the common areas of several tenants free from possible hazards. In these situations, the landlord does have the right to come onto the premises to the extent necessary to meet these obligations.

A current trend in the law is for courts to find generally that a tenant is protected by the landlord's implied warranty that the premises are suitable for the tenant's intended use. This is particularly true in residential leases; the landlord implicitly promises the improvements are habitable. One of the tenant's best remedies for the breach of this landlord's warranty is the right to terminate the lease without liability. (See Section 15 below.) Furthermore, a tenant can claim this breach as grounds for having the rent reduced or as a defense in a landlord's suit for rent.[2] In commercial leases, when the tenant has the opportunity to inspect the property, the right to hold the landlord liable for unsuitable or uninhabitable conditions is less apparent. A tenant's suit for damages likely will fail when both parties were unaware of existing defects.

Case 16.4

In 1959, Marie Ann Linn Realty Company leased a warehouse then under construction to Dealers Hobby Inc. for storage purposes. The lease was to run for fifteen years and contained a clause whereby the landlord agreed to maintain the roof and

[2]Timber Ridge Town House v. Dietz, page 435.

exterior structure, except as to damages caused by the tenant. In April 1973, a heavy rain caused a portion of the roof to collapse, damaging some of the tenant's stored property and preventing use of a portion of the building until repairs were made by the landlord. At this time, an inspection of the building by city officials disclosed that the building as constructed did not comply with the city building code, resulting in the issuance of an "official notice of unsafe building." This notice apparently was removed when the landlord completed the repairs. Neither party was aware of any defects in the structure prior to the collapse. This action was brought by the tenant to recover damages caused to its merchandise and inventory as well as incidental damages. The landlord paid these damages in full prior to this appeal. Additionally, the tenant sought to recover damages which represent the difference between the rental value of the premises as warranted in the lease and the fair rental value of the premises as found defectively constructed for the entire period of the lease prior to the collapse. These damages are the subject of this appeal.

Issue: Is the tenant entitled to compensation for rent paid on the building for the period when the structure did not meet requirements of an implied warranty of habitability?

Decision: No.

Reasons: In typical cases regarding an implied warranty of habitability, numerous building code violations may be alleged which make the premises unfit for occupancy. In the present case, neither party had any knowledge of defects in the structure prior to the collapse. The ultimate purpose of awarding damages is to place the injured party in such a position as though no wrong had been committed. No breach of the express agreement to repair occurred until the collapse. Prior to this time, the tenant had suffered no harm whatsoever. Actual losses from the incident constitute the full amount of recovery to which the tenant is entitled.

Dealers Hobby, Inc. v. Marie Ann Linn Realty Co., 255 N.W.2d 131 (Iowa 1977).

Other laws and court decisions have seemed to favor or establish rights of tenants, especially those in residential transactions. One area where this trend can be seen concerns rent controls. Due to the inflationary spiral of the late 1970s and early 1980s, many cities controlled the landlord's ability to increase rental payments. In other words, under rent controls a landlord is permitted to increase rents only by a stated percentage at stated intervals. In the short run, rent controls can be a real benefit to tenants. However, we now are beginning to see a side effect of rent controls that do not allow the landlords to make a sufficient return on their investment. Rent controls can discourage new construction and can lead to abandonment or decay of many rental properties. Indeed, the recent surge of converting apartment buildings to condominiums or cooperatives often has been influenced by the existence of rent controls.

Other tenant-oriented protections include the fact that a landlord must complete a judicial process in order to evict a tenant (see Section 18) and the fact that certain procedures must be followed before a tenant's security deposit can be retained by the landlord (See section 19). The Uniform Residential Landlord and Tenant Act, which is discussed in Section 20, also can be viewed as tenant-oriented legislation.

14.   *Landlords' Rights*

A landlord also has the legal right to performance of the tenant's duties. Fundamentally, landlords have the right to collect prompt payment of rent, to receive possession of the rented property upon termination of the lease, and to benefit from the tenant's performance of all the other lease provisions. Section 6 of this chapter discussed the tenant's potential liability when rent was not paid on time. Landlords also have the right to hold a tenant's personal property until past rent is paid. This is known as a distress for rent, and it arises when the landlord obtains a distress warrant.

If a landlord believes that a tenant is about to move out of the leased premises without paying rent, the landlord may ask a judge to issue a distress warrant. After being authorized, this distress warrant is served on or delivered to the tenant by a court official (sheriff, police, etc.). In effect, the warrant places a hold on the tenant's personal property. In other words, the court official will not allow the tenant to remove any personal property that is still on the landlord's property. The judge then conducts a hearing to determine whether any rent is owed by the tenant. If past rent is owed, the tenant must pay it before having access to his or her personal property. If the rent is not paid, the tenant's personal property can be sold pursuant to a court order, and the proceeds of the sale will be used to pay the landlord the rent owed. Usually the landlord must post a bond when seeking a distress warrant. This bond assures the tenant of a fund to recover from if rent is not due and the tenant is damaged by these proceedings.

When a tenant fails to vacate the leased property at the end of the landlord–tenant relationship, the tenant is said to be holding over. Because the landlord has the right to have possession returned, the landlord can pursue the legal action of eviction. This remedy for the tenant's refusal to perform an obligation is discussed fully in Section 18, below.

A landlord has the right to expect that the property will be returned in basically the same condition as when the lease began. Normal wear and tear usually is a general exception to this requirement. If the tenant does not return the property in the same general condition, the landlord has the right to recover for the damages done by the tenant, either through a lawsuit or, more frequently, from the security deposit paid by the tenant at the commencement of the relationship. (A complete discussion of security deposits can be found in Section 19 below.)

15.   Right of Termination

As is the case in any contractual agreement, parties to a lease always are the masters of their relationship. For example, the lease document may provide for termination at the end of a stated time period. If a landlord and tenant both desire to terminate their arrangement prior to the end of the stated period, there is nothing legally wrong with their mutual agreement to do so.

A written lease may indicate the rights of the landlord and tenant to terminate their relationship. A lease for a stated period or from period to period will provide that either renewal or termination of the lease will occur automatically. Indeed, rights of termination are often dictated by the type of lease (see Section 2) and by the renewal provisions contained in the lease (See section 7). A tenancy at will lasts as long as both parties desire. In order to terminate this type of lease, notice must be given in accordance with the applicable statute. Most states provide that notice must be given thirty days prior to the anticipated termination, but some states do not require any notice.

The landlord–tenant relationship is terminated automatically whenever the tenant becomes the owner of the leased property. Termination in this manner is called *merger,* becuase the tenant possesses the leasehold and the fee simple interests at the same time. When this merger of interests occurs there is no need to maintain the landlord–tenant relationship. The most common occurrence of termination through the doctrine of merger probably occurs when the tenant exercises an option to purchase which was included in the lease. The following case is an example of such an occurence.

Case 16.5

Amann as a tenant and Frederick as a landlord entered into a lease of farmland in April 1972. The lease provided for a five-year term and also recited a purchase option which Amann could exercise at any time. The contract was silent as to whether Amann was obligated to continue rental payments for the duration of the lease term in the event that the purchase option was exercised during the term. Amann exercised the option in December 1975 with more than a year still remaining in the original lease term. Frederick refused to convey the land unless Amann paid all of the remaining rentals. Amann then brought this action for specific performance of the purchase option by Frederick.

Issue: Must Amann pay rental for the whole term of the lease in order to obtain a conveyance from Frederick?

Decision: No. Notification to Frederick that Amann was exercising the option and tender of payment made Amann the owner of the leased premises.

Reasons: When the holder of an option to purchase exercises his option, he then becomes the owner of the real estate. As the owner of the real estate, he would be entitled to collect the rents on the property from the tenant. Thus if Amann still had an obligation to pay rent, it would be an obligation to pay rent to himself, which would be a superfluous action. In any event, a tenancy for years merges into the fee interest which Amann owned after exercising the option. Upon exercise by a tenant of an option to purchase, the landlord is not entitled to rent in the absence of an express stipulation in the lease stating otherwise.

Amann v. Frederick, 257 N.W.2d 436 (N.Dak. 1977).

In Section 13, it was mentioned that a tenant normally has the right to expect that the leased premises will be maintained so that a habitable condition exists. Indeed, the landlord's unexcused failure to keep the premises habitable will allow the tenant to terminate the lease prior to expiration of its term without liability. The theory is that the landlord has forced the tenant to vacate the property. Thus, tenants are permitted to terminate their relationship when they are *constructively* evicted by the landlord's inaction. Examples of factual situations that might justify termination based on constructive eviction include rain water coming into a basement apartment, natural gas leaking from space heaters, and air conditioning failing in an unventilated building. Of course, constructive eviction occurs only if the landlord refuses to repair the conditions that caused uninhabitability. The tenant must act promptly and vacate the premises when they become uninhabitable and the landlord refuses to correct the problem. When the tenant fails to act promptly and remains in possession, the right to terminate is waived.

Whether death or other legal incapacity of the landlord or tenant terminates their relationship depends on the parties' agreement. The more personal the relationship between the original landlord and tenant, the more likely they will be to agree that termination will occur automatically on either's incapacity. For example, a lease of an apartment for one year is much more personal to the tenant than is a lease of a commercial office for twenty-five years. If the lease is silent on automatic termination, even residential leases do not terminate on either party's incapacity. Usually a party's interest in a lease passes to a legal representative. For example, when a tenant dies, the estate representative receives the leasehold interest. If that lease contained a clause prohibiting assignments and subleases without the landlord's consent, this transfer is not prevented. Likewise, a transfer to the landlord's devisees does not terminate the tenant's right unless agreed otherwise.

16. Third Parties' Rights

The obligations that landlords and tenants owe to protect third parties who are on the leased property is not always clear. Indeed, states have differed in their court decisions and statutes as to the rights of third parties. In the past, the landlord was not generally held liable for injuries suffered by third parties. The modern trend is to require the landlord to inform tenants and third parties of latent or hidden defects that the landlord knows about. Some states even require the landlord to make reasonable inspections periodically to discover these hidden problems. However, a landlord is not obligated to remove all potential hazards in areas where tenants or third parties are not expected to go.[3]

The duty to inspect is particularly essential when the landlord knows that third-party guests will be present on a regular basis. For example, there is a greater duty on the landlord to maintain common areas (yards, sidewalds, parking lots, hallways, etc.) in a residential apartment complex or a commercial retail or office building than in a single-family residential house. The landlord who allows a stairway in a complex to remain unlighted has greater liability than a landlord who fails to keep a house porch lighted. The extent of the landlord's responsibility to keep the premises free from potential hazards is ultimately a question of fact to be determined by a jury. In other words, did the landlord know or should the landlord have known about an unreasonable risk that caused a third person to be injured?

A lease provision requiring the landlord to make repairs as needed expressly places this responsibility on the landlord. A landlord's failure to comply with that type of provision results in liability if a tenant or third party is injured because of the landlord's negligence.

In addition to their growing protection against possible injuries while on the premises, third parties may also have rights in the original lease agreement due to a valid assignment or sublease. (Review Section 11.)

Remedies for Breach

17. Introduction

Throughout this chapter, discussions of the landlord–tenant relationship have been based on the assumption that the parties to a lease have been justified in all actions. However, as with other contracts, parties may refuse to complete their required performance. When a tenant breaches a lease by vacating prior to a valid termination, the landlord has the remedy of filing a suit for damages. If a tenant refuses to vacate when the lease is terminated, the landlord may proceed with eviction proceedings.

[3]Amburgy v. Golden, page 437.

On the other hand, if the landlord has breached the lease in some way, the tenant also can sue for money damages. A common conflict between the landlord and tenant occurs when the landlord refuses to refund all or part of the security deposit upon the lease's termination. The rights and duties of all parties with respect to the security deposit are discussed below.

18. Landlords' Remedies

When a tenant fails to complete the required performance under a lease, an aggrieved landlord has several possible courses of action. First, the landlord can regain possession of the premises and excuse the tenant from further liability for rent. Second, the landlord can let the premises remain vacant and sue the tenant for rent as it becomes owing. Third, the landlord can search for a new tenant and sue the breaching tenant for the loss suffered by the landlord. For example, assume the original lease called for a rent of $400 a month for a twelve-month term. If the tenant left after only three months and if the landlord found a new tenant to pay $350 a month beginning one month after the breach, the landlord's damages will be $800 ($400 for the one-month gap plus $50 difference for each of the eight months) plus the cost of locating the new tenant.

The best of the three remedies above probably is the third one. By reasonably attempting to locate a new tenant, the landlord is satisfying his duty to mitigate or minimize the damages caused by the breach. There is no need to wait until the rent becomes due from month to month because of the anticipatory-breach theory. Once the tenant has given a clear and unequivocal indication that the lease is breached, the landlord has the right to accept that breach and to pursue a remedy for damages. Certainly when a tenant vacates the premises without leaving the impression of planning to return, an anticipatory breach occurs.

Case 16.6

Beginning April 1, 1959, F & H Warehouse Company agreed to lease a warehouse to the Lubbock Bag Company for twenty years. Through a series of mergers, St. Regis Paper Company became obligated as the tenant. This landlord–tenant relationship continued until July 1968, when St. Regis abandoned the warehouse. The landlord filed suit seeking as damages the rental payments from July 1968 through December 1968. The complaint later was amended to include as damages rent due through March 1970. On May 11, 1970, the warehouse involved in this lease was totally destroyed by a tornado. In February 1971 the landlord again amended the complaint and sought damages based on the theory of anticipatory breach.

Issue: If a tenant anticipatorily breached a lease and then the leased premises are destroyed, what damages may a landlord collect from the tenant?

Decision: The amount of rent owed over the remainder of the lease minus the amount that can be mitigated by the landlord.

Reasons: [The court first finds that the landlord had accepted the lease as repudiated prior to the destruction of the warehouse by the tornado.] Once a tenant has breached a lease and the landlord has treated the lease as breached, the unforeseen destruction of the premises will not benefit the tenant. In this case, under the lease terms, the rent owed by the original tenant over the lease period was $189,000. The jury determined that the landlord could mitigate these damages by approximately one-half this amount. The award of $95,000 in damages cannot be found to be unreasonable and is therefore affirmed. This award is based on the possibility that the landlord could always rebuild the destroyed warehouse. Even if the warehouse is not rebuilt, the jury award cannot be seen as a windfall to the landlord.

Farmers and Bankers Life Insurance Co. v. St. Regis Paper Co., 456 F.2d 347 (5th Cir. 1972).

In addition to seeking damages upon a tenant's premature departure, the landlord has the remedy of obtaining a distress warrant (see Section 14) as leverage for collecting overdue rent. Courts seldom will order equitable relief, like specific performance, in a breach-of-lease case. Most courts feel that a monetary award can put the landlord in a position very similar to that if the lease had not been breached at all; therefore, an equitable remedy is unnecessary.

Landlords often experience an occurrence opposite to the tenant's vacating too early—that is, the tenant holding over without paying rent or remaining past the time the lease was terminated properly. Upon this happening, a landlord can no longer physically remove the tenant against his or her will. In most states, in order to evict a holdover tenant, the landlord must follow eviction statutes designed to protect the interests of both the landlord and the tenant. A typical statute requires the landlord to demand possession in the first instance. Upon the tenant's refusal to vacate and return possession, the landlord can file suit to evict.

The landlord must file a sworn statement—an affidavit—explaining the facts leading to the current holdover situation. Next, this affidavit and a summons are delivered to the tenant, who then has a fairly short time period (seven days, for example) in which to respond. The tenant's failure to respond to the court's summons results in an eviction order. If the tenant does respond, a hearing is held, and the judge determines the rights of both parties. If there is a delay before a hearing or the judge's ruling, the tenant can remain in possession if all past rent is paid into the court. Failure by the tenant to keep current on the rental payments means the court will automatically rule in the landlord's favor.

A tenant may have a valid defense to the landlord's eviction proceedings. Such a defense may be that the landlord is attempting to terminate the lease prematurely. Another is that this eviction proceeding is in retaliation for the exercise of the tenant's rights. For example, a tenant might justifiably complain to a local official that the landlord's building is violating the housing code. Courts generally will protect this right by allowing the tenant to prove a defense of retaliatory eviction. In other words, landlords cannot seek judicial assistance to evict tenants who merely are exercising their rights. In addition, landlords generally cannot raise the rental payments or decrease services formerly given to the tenant in retaliation for the tenant's exercise of a legal right.

Upon a finding that the tenant is holding over improperly, the judge will order that the tenant be evicted. The landlord will then have the assistance of law-enforcement officials in removing the tenant. The landlord's use of these eviction proceedings does not impair the right to seek a monetary award of damages. Indeed, these two remedies usually are pursued simultaneously.

19. Tenants' Remedies

Like landlords, tenants have the remedy of seeking money damages when the landlord improperly terminates a lease or fails to comply with all the terms in the lease. Generally, courts are more hesitant to grant the equitable remedy of specific performance, since a leasehold interest is considered to be less unique than the actual sale of real estate. However, the equitable relief of rescission is available if a landlord had defrauded or made misrepresentations to a tenant.

Upon the termination of the landlord–tenant relationship, whether properly or improperly accomplished, there often is a dispute about each parties' right to a security deposit that may have been paid by the tenant at the creation of the relationship. Many states now have a statute that provides some guidance in this issue. Generally, the security deposit is considered as a fund from which the landlord can collect the costs of repairing damage done by the tenant. To be able to ascertain whether damages were caused by the present tenant, both parties should make a written list of any defects found on the premises at the commencement of the lease.

Upon termination of the relationship, the landlord must prepare a list of damages found beyond normal wear and tear. A cost estimate of repairing these damages must be presented to the tenant, who has an opportunity to get another estimate of the repair costs. In many states, a landlord is entitled to part or all of a tenant's security deposit only after following this process. All tenants would be wise to investigate their state law requirements concerning security deposits.

Some states require that landlords with multiple rental units keep all security deposits in an escrow account or, in lieu thereof, file a bond in a stated amount with the appropriate legal official. In the event that a tenant must sue to recover a security deposit improperly retained by the landlord, the court can order that the tenant's attorney's fees must be paid by the landlord. In addition, some statutes provide for payment of a penalty by any landlord who acted in bad faith in refusing to return the security deposit.

Case 16.7

When Jeff Jaeckle and four friends leased a house owned by Amanda Hogg, they each paid a security deposit of $100. After the lease was terminated properly, these tenants asked Ms. Hogg to return all the security-deposit money to Jeff Jaeckle. His correct forwarding address was left with the landlady. Ms. Hogg failed to send a list of damages with itemized repair costs within thirty days after the premises were vacated, as required by Texas law. She also refused to refund any of the security deposits. These former tenants filed suit seeking triple the original deposits ($1,500), $100 as a penalty, plus $900 for attorney's fees. The applicable law provided for these remedies if a landlord acts in bad faith with regard to returning a security deposit.

Issue: Did Amanda Hogg act in bad faith?

Decision: Yes. These former tenants were awarded $2,500.

Reasons: The requirement that a list of damages be sent within thirty days of the lease's termination cannot be disregarded. Even assuming Ms. Hogg orally informed these tenants of the damages found, she has not met her obligations. Since Ms. Hogg could not prove that she had furnished this written list of damages with reasonable repair costs itemized, she failed to carry her burden of proving statutory compliance. Bad faith, which is willful failure to perform a statutory obligation, results in an order that a full refund be paid along with the stated penalties.

Hogg v. Jaeckle, 561 S.W.2d 568 (Tex. App. Ct. 1978).

Recently some states have required landlords to pay interest on security deposits held during the lease term. This development is only beginning, and it will be interesting to see if this tenant protection spreads.

20. Uniform Residential Landlord and Tenant Act

In 1972, the National Conference of Commissioners on Uniform State Laws recommended for adoption by the various states the Uniform Residential Landlord and Tenant Act (URLTA). Because this proposed act has been adopted by at least sixteen states (including Alaska, Arizona, Connecticut, Florida, Hawaii, Iowa, Kansas, Kentucky, Michigan, Montana, Nebraska, New Mexico, Oregon, Tennessee, Virginia, and Washington), it is appropriate to discuss its general principles.

The URLTA is divided into five major articles. Basically they include general provisions and definitions that govern the landlord-tenant relationship, the landlords' obligations, the tenants' obligations, and the remedies available to each of these parties.

A. PURPOSE AND SCOPE

The stated purpose of the URLTA is to simplify, clarify, modernize, and revise laws concerning the rental of dwelling units and the landlord–tenant relationship. In addition, the URLTA encourages the maintenance and quality of housing and attempts to make laws in this area more uniform. The scope of the act is limited to rental agreements for a dwelling unit, which is defined as any structure or part of a structure that is used as a home, residence, or sleeping place by one person who maintains a household or by two or more persons who maintain a common household.

An implicit purpose of the URLTA is to place both the landlord and tenant in equal bargaining positions. At all times during their relationship, the landlord and tenant must act in good faith, which means honesty in fact. The act further prohibits the use of certain clauses in a lease agreement by which (1) the tenant waives any right under the act, (2) the tenant agrees to a confession of a judgment on any claim arising out of the rental agreement, (3) the tenant agrees to pay the landlord's attorney's fees, and (4) the tenant agrees to excuse or limit the landlord's liability for failure to abide by this or any other laws. The URLTA allows a tenant to recover actual damages plus three rental payments plus attorney's fees if a landlord does try to include these provisions.

B. OBLIGATIONS

The landlord cannot collect a security deposit that exceeds one month's rent. Before the landlord can withhold any of the deposit, written notice indicating why the deposit is not returned must be given to the tenant within a stated time period (for example, fourteen days) after termination and the tenant's demand of the deposit. If the deposit is wrongfully withheld, the tenant can collect twice the amount withheld plus attorney's fees.

The landlord subject to the URLTA has the duty to deliver possession of the premises at the commencement of the rental term. This provision adopts the majority theory discussed in Section 13, above. Furthermore, the landlord must maintain the premises in habitable condition. This includes maintenance of electrical, plumbing, heating, and similar facilities, as well as any appliances furnished to the tenant. The landlord also must provide receptacles for removal of trash, garbage, and other waste material. Although a landlord may sell or otherwise convey the premises during the lease term, this event does not relieve the landlord of liability with regard to the security deposit or any prepaid rent.

The tenants' basic obligations under the URLTA are to pay rent, to keep the dwelling area within their control safe and clean, and to allow the landlord to enter the premises on a reasonable basis. The landlord should be allowed to enter the area under the tenants' control to inspect it, to make needed repairs or improvements, to supply services that are necessary or agreed upon, or to show the premises to prospective buyers, tenants, workmen, and other necessary people. Other than on these events, the landlord may enter the leased premises only in case of an emergency.

C. REMEDIES

Under the terms of URLTA, if the landlord fails to deliver possession, the tenant can cancel the agreement or maintain an action for possession against the landlord or any other person wrongfully in possession of the premises. The tenant can terminate the rental agreement upon the landlord's material noncompliance of the obligations owed. This remedy is basically an adoption of the constructive-eviction concept discussed previously. If the tenant refuses to pay rent and if the landlord sues for possession, the tenant can counterclaim for damages based on the landlord's noncompliance of any obligation.

When a minor defect exists and the landlord does not remedy it after having been notified by the tenant, the tenant may make the repair or have it made. The model URLTA states this principle of self-help is applicable if the repair is less than $100 or equal to one-half the periodic rent, whichever is greater. The tenant can deduct this amount of the repair from the rent owed by giving the landlord a written itemized statement of expenses. When the defects are more substantial, such as the dwelling having been partially destroyed or damaged by a fire or other casualty, the tenant can elect to terminate the agreement. In the alternative, the tenant can elect to continue the relationship and reduce the rent to an amount proportional to the area still in use.

The URLTA provides that if the tenant fails to meet all obligations owed, the landlord can terminate the agreement within thirty days after written notice is given to the tenant. When the tenant fails to maintain the premises and the breach is minor, the landlord can have the defect repaired and bill the tenant for those costs. The landlord has a duty to mitigate damages by searching for a new tenant whenever the tenant leaves or abandons the premises prematurely. One remedy that most states have allowed the landlord, but which the URLTA has abolished, is the distress for rent. (See Section 14 for the previous discussion.) If the tenant wrongfully holds over after the rental agreement is terminated, the landlord has the right to bring an action for possession. When the tenant holds over willfully or in bad ·faith, the landlord is entitled to an amount which is not more than three months' rent or three times the landlord's actual damages, whichever is greater, plus reasonable attorney's fees.

The URLTA adopts the common-law defense of retaliatory eviction. In other words, the landlord cannot increase the rent, decrease services, or bring or threaten a lawsuit for possession if the tenant exercises a legal right. The act specifies the following legal rights of the tenant:

1. Complaining to a governmental agency about possible building code violations;
2. Complaining to the landlord about lack of proper maintenance; and
3. Organizing or joining a tenants' union or similar organization.

Because of the need to modernize and to increase the uniformity of laws with widespread application, such as landlord–tenant laws, the URLTA likely will be adopted by more and more states in the future. The acceptance of this proposed act and similar ones affecting real estate transactions will determine whether there will be a stronger effort to make more areas of the law uniform among the states.

Cases on the Landlord–Tenant Relationship

Lonergan v. Connecticut Food Store, Inc.
357 A.2d 910 (Conn. 1975).

Evelyn P. Lonergan is the owner of a building consisting of two separate units rented as retail stores. In April 1962, she entered into a lease for a reasonable period of time of approximately five years. The written lease contained the following provision for renewal: "Upon the expiration of the term of this Lease, the same, including this clause, shall automatically be extended for a period of one year and thence from year to year, unless the Lessee shall give notice to the Lessor of termination at least sixty (60) days before the end of the original term or any extension thereof."

The landlord claims that the lease did not create a right to perpetual renewal in the tenant even though it has indicated no willingness to vacate voluntarily. The trial court ruled in the landlord's favor and the tenant appeals.

Longo, J.:

Although this is the first occasion this court has had to rule on the issue, it is well settled in most other jurisdictions that, absent statutory provision to the contrary, the right to perpetual renewal of a lease is not forbidden by the law, either upon the ground that it creates a perpetuity or a restraint on alienation or upon any other ground, and such provisions, when properly entered into, will be enforced. . . .

Courts do not favor perpetual leases, however; thus a provision in a lease will not be construed as conferring a right to a perpetual renewal "unless the language is so plain as to admit of no doubt of the purpose to provide for perpetual renewal." . . . Furthermore, "[a] perpetuity will not be regarded as created from an ordinary covenant to renew." Rather, "[t]here must be some peculiar and plain language before it will be assumed that the parties intended to create it."

In this connection, we have stated that in determining the intention of the parties to a lease, "[t]he controlling factor is the intent expressed in the lease, not the intent which the parties may have had or which the court believes they ought to have had." . . . Rather, "the lease must be construed as a whole and in such a manner as to give effect to very provision, if reasonably possible." . . .

The language of the instant lease, insofar as it purports to create in the lessee and right of perpetual renewal, is far from clear. It states that, upon the expiration of the original five-year term, the lease, "including this clause, *shall automatically be extended* for a period of one year *and thence from year to year, unless the Lessee shall give notice* to the Lessor of termination at least sixty (60) days before the end of the original term or any extension thereof." (Emphasis added.) Nowhere in the provision appear any of the words customarily used to create a perpetual lease, such as "forever," "for all time," and "in perpetuity," words whose presence or absence in a lease is of considerable significance to a court in deciding whether a right of perpetual renewal was intended by the parties. . . . It is true that the words emphasized above presume to characterize the successive renewals of the lease as self-executing (i.e., "Automatic"). But such language is construed as creating a perpetual lease only when the renewal period to which it refers is for a specific term, usually as long as that provided in the original lease. In the instant lease, these words are used, in combination with language describing the renewal period as one "from year to year." Where words of perpetuity are absent from the lease, courts generally do not construe a clause which establishes a renewal period as one merely "from year to year" as expressing an intention of the parties to create a perpetual lease.

Moreover, . . . [no] other clause in the lease, provides for escalation of rent beyond the $175 per month agreed upon by the parties in paragraph 3. Of course, failure to include an escalation clause in not fatal; perpetual renewal upon the same terms as the original lease is an enforceable option. . . . But an agreement to that effect is of such critical importance to parties creating a perpetual lease that it is generally stipulated in the same provision as that which creates the right in the lessee to perpetual renewal. In the present lease, the lessor agreed . . . to repair the demised buildings and to repair and restore them in the event of partial or total destruction; . . . the lessor agreed to pay all taxes, charges and assessments, including charges relating to the use of water. The absence of an escalation clause to provide a source of revenue from which the lessor might meet her continuing obligations under these two paragraphs strongly suggests that the creation of a right to perpetual renewal was not the intention expressed by the parties. . . .

A review of the lease in its entirety establishes that there are sufficient facts to support the court's conclusion that the instrument does not create a right in the lessee to renew the lease perpetually. . . .

Affirmed in part.

Timber Ridge Town House v. Dietz
338 A.2d 21 (N.J. 1975).

King, J.:

This is an action for summary dispossession alleging a default in rental payments for the month of October 1974. The monthly rental is $285 for this 3-bedroom, 2½-bath, 2-story garden apartment or townhouse in Lindenwold. Defendants withheld rent due for one month, depositing the funds in their attorney's escrow account. Thereafter the monthly rentals were deposited in escrow pending this court's decision. . . .

Defendants raise so-called habitability defenses and request an abatement of a portion of the rent. The questions are novel because the allegedly affected area is external to the actual leased premises. . . .

Timber Ridge was designed as a family community. . . . A brochure used in the rental of the properties was placed in evidence. Defendants leased the property in December 1973 in partial reliance upon the representations in the brochure. The brochure described the project as: "Quietly nestled in a gently rolling wooded glen . . . [offering] serene living in a beautiful country setting with on-site recreational facilities including a swimming pool and childrens' play area . . . and individual patio facing a spacious landscaped court yard." The written lease agreement executed on December 1, 1973 for a term of one year refers to the premises as "the apartment consisting of 5 rooms and baths."

Tenants here seek to extend the doctrine of implied warranty of habitability beyond the actual physical structure. . . . There is no doubt that the external conditions detract substantially from the tenants' living pleasure. Defendants' townhouse is immediately adjacent to the area where a large retaining wall is being constructed. Construction has been in progress for four months, and from the court's observation may continue for at least several more months. These defendant tenants are almost uniquely affected by the construction because of their proximity to the conditions. No other occupied unit is affected in such a severe manner. Their "individual patio facing a spacious landscaped court yard" is unusable, as it is surrounded and overflowed by mud and water. The mud flows over the walkway connecting defendants' main entranceway and the common parking area. The parking area itself, especially where defendants or their visitors would park their vehicles, is covered with mud. The "court yard" which these tenants could legitimately anticipate appreciating is nonexistent throughout the course of construction. The construction prevents use of the patio and affects ingress and egress, use of parking area and any outdoor recreational use of the area adjacent to the premises for either the two adult tenants or their three children. The subject premises is the highest price townhouse or apartment available in this municipality (oriented to multi-family dwellings). Tenants had a reasonable expectancy of a decent exterior environment from the sales promotion, the initial condition of the premises, and the higher price of the apartment compared to others in the community, whether the expectancy be characterized as one of amenity or necessity. They are deprived of a substantial attribute of the premises through no fault of their own and they have no control over any possible remedy to the situation. Plaintiff landlord and developer was required to install the new concrete retaining wall by the municipality after defendants took possession. The initial wooden railroad tie wall had become unsafe.

The landlord argues that the implied warranty of habitability should not be extended beyond the scope of the presently controlling cases so as to encompass conditions exterior to the premises. The evolution of the doctrine to date has not explicitly included exterior conditions within its scope. . . .

. . . [T]he covenant on the part of a tenant to pay rent, and the covenant—whether express or implied—on the part of the landlord to maintain the demised premises in a habitable condition are for all purposes mutually dependent. Accordingly in an action by a landlord for unpaid rent a tenant may plead, by way of defense and setoff, a breach by the landlord of his continuing obligation to maintain an adequate standard of habitability.

In deciding what kind of defect will be deemed to constitute a breach of the warranty of habitability, the court is guided by the factors . . . as follows:

1. Has there been a violation of any applicable housing code or building or santitary regulations?
2. Is the nature of the deficiency or defect such as to affect a vital facility?
3. What is its potential or actual effect upon safety and sanitation?
4. For what length of time has it persisted?
5. What is the age of the structure?
6. What is the amount of the rent?
7. Can the tenant be said to have waived the defect or be estopped to complain?
8. Was the tenant in any way responsible for the defective condition?

Here, no housing code violation is present, but the work on the retaining wall, causing the unsavory condition, was required by the borough engineer as a public safety measure. The defect affects all outside use of the premises. In the context of the promotional effort and type of townhouse development promised, the court feels a vital facility is affected. There is a possible effect on sanitation and safety. The defect has persisted now for a period of four to five months and is not transitory. The structure and the project are virtually new. Defendants were original occupants and had a reasonable right to expect first quality facilities. The rental was the highest in the municipality. Defendant tenants cannot in any sense be charged with waiver or estoppel and are in no way responsible for the defective condition. All of these factors support their position.

The court has considered the intention of the parties to this agreement as indicated by the representations of Timber Ridge to defendants, and defendants' reasonable expectations with respect to those represen-tations, the location and type of residential environment of Timber Ridge and the high rental fee for the premises. It is the finding of the court that an implied covenant arose between the parties, whether it is character-ized as an implied warranty of habitability or an implied covenant to provide certain amenities. Further, the court finds that the implied covenant or warranty has been breached. An abatement of rent in the amount of 15% a month will be allowed from the date the rent was initially withheld and the summary dispossession action commenced.

So ordered.

Amburgy v. Golden
557 P.2d 9 (Wash. App. 1976).

Farris, J.:

This action was initiated by Samuel and Sharon Amburgy to recover for inju-ries to her resulting from a fall over a 2-foot retaining wall in an apartment complex owned by Dan Golden and Max Kessler. The trial court granted Golden and Kes-sler's motion for a directed verdict at the close of the Amburgys' case. The Ambur-gys appeal.

Sharon Amburgy was injured when she stepped off the edge of a retaining wall while walking after dark between her broth-er-in-law's apartment and a neighboring apartment; she was not following a pre-pared pathway. The record fails to establish that anyone else ever took the route that she chose or that the owner knew or had reason to know that anyone would choose it. The trial court granted the defendants' motion for a directed verdict at the close of the Amburgys' case on two grounds: (1) knowledge of a tenant is imputed to a social guest who stands in the same legal relation to the landlord as the tenant and (2) the landlord has no affirmative duty to illuminate areas that are not "common areas."

Landlords owe their tenants' guests no greater standard of care than is owed to the tenants. They do not guarantee safety, but they have an affirmative duty to exercise reasonable care to inspect, repair and maintain common areas "in a reasonably safe condition for the tenant's use." Before this duty is found to exist, however, it must be shown that the alleged common area (1) is an area upon which the tenant or guest may be reasonably expected to go and is being put to its intended use. . . .

We find as a matter of law that the case presented by the Amburgys, given all rea-sonable inferences, would not sustain a jury verdict in their favor. They have failed to present evidence which would support a finding that the defendants breached a duty to them.

Further, the retaining wall here is not a "latent defect," a circumstance which, if it existed, would, together with other circumstances, create an issue of liability. Nor does maintence of the wall constitute an act of wanton misconduct, an occurrence which would establish liability.

Affirmed.

REVIEW QUESTIONS

1. Define the following terms:
   a. Lease
   b. Lessor
   c. Lessee
2. List and explain at least three different ways to classify types of leases.
3. Snyder leased commercial space in a shopping center from Sheehy. The lease provided that Sheehy would restrict the use of other premises in the shopping center for the sale or consumption of goods. The lease recited that "the restriction as to restaurants shall only apply to the type of restaurant operated by Snyder on the premises." In accordance with the lease agreement, Snyder installed a restaurant facility in its drugstore. The restaurant offered a four-page menu with food cooked to order and served on the premises by waitresses. Sheehy subsequently entered into negotiations to lease shopping-center space to a McDonald's restaurant. Snyder instituted this action to enjoin Sheehy from planning and constructing the McDonald's on the ground that McDonald's was the same type of restaurant as the one situated within Snyder's premises. Should the construction of a McDonald's be enjoined?
4. Central Motor Sales rented a garage from Holt continuously for approximately twenty-four years, during which it installed several heavy-duty hoists. Prior to the lease expiration, Central decided to change business locations and found a prospective successor tenant, American. Central tentatively agreed to sell American the hoist equipment for $4,000. Holt refused to agree to the sublease agreement, instead leasing the garage premises directly to the successor American. After moving, Central billed American for the hoist equipment. American then asserted the equipment had been included in the lease agreement with Holt. Central sued Holt for conversion, asserting the hoists were "trade fixtures" which belonged to Central and which could be removed or sold to a successive tenant. Is Central correct? Why?
5. Lancaster owned an apartment building and leased an apartment to Terry. While Terry was gone, Lancaster entered the apartment and found some illegal drugs. When Terry returned, Lancaster began eviction proceedings. Terry also sued, claiming Lancaster had trespassed. Who should win? Why?
6. Cascade leased land from Martin for a period of twenty-five years. This lease authorized Cascade to assign the lease or sublease without Martin's prior approval. Cascade did sublease the land to Interstate 8th Company, which subsequently subleased the land to Interstate 25 Investment Company. Inter-

state 25 paid rent for four years and then defaulted. Martin sued Interstate 8th Company for nonpayment of rent. Interstate 8th Company contended it cannot be sued because it has no direct contractual relationship with Martin. Is Interstate 8th correct? Explain.

7. Southland leased commercial property from McIntosh for a period of twenty-one years. The lease contained provisions which permitted Southland to sublease at any time, but assignments were restricted subject to McIntosh's written consent. The lease stated further: "Should the lessee either sublet the premises or assign this lease, in whole or in part, it shall nevertheless remain liable to lessor for full payments of the rent and performance of all terms." Southland assigned the lease with the written consent of McIntosh. Thereafter, the assignee defaulted. McIntosh sued Southland to recover the unpaid rent. Southland contends that McIntosh released it from any obligation by consenting to the original assignment. Did Southland remain liable even after an assignment was made with McIntosh's consent? Why?

8. In 1901, Sarah Cranston leased a parcel of land to the William Low Estate for a period of ninety years. The Estate built a five-story commercial office building on this land, which was located in an urban business district. The lease provided that during the last year of its term, the landlord would purchase the building for its fair market value unless the lease was terminated sooner. As suburban shopping areas began to appear, the demand for central business district office space declined. In 1975, Sarah Cranston's heirs (the current owners of the land) agreed with the Estate that the land and improvements should be sold. Upon this sale, would the Estate be entitled to share of the sales proceeds?

9. Explain what is meant by a distress for rent. How is this legal concept applicable to a landlord–tenant relationship?

10. Goodman owned the Plaza West Apartments. Rose entered into a one-year apartment lease beginning on November 1, 1975. Rose died on December 29, 1975, and Jardine was appointed executor of her estate. No rental payments were made from January to November 1976, and Goodman filed suit against the estate to recover the rent. Was Goodman entitled to rent after the death of this tenant?

Index

L

S

About the Authors

ROBERT N. CORLEY is the Distinguished Professor of Legal Studies in the Department of Real Estate and Legal Studies at the University of Georgia. He is the author of the *Principles of Business Law*, Eleventh Edition, *Fundamentals of Business Law*, Third Edition, and *The Legal Environment of Business*, Fifth Edition, texts used by hundreds of colleges and universities across the nation. Professor Corley received his J.D. from the University of Illinois and has been a member of the Illinois Bar since 1956. Currently he is a national officer of the American Business Law Association.

PETER J. SHEDD is an Assistant Professor in the Department of Real Estate and Legal Studies at the University of Georgia. He received his J.D. from the University of Georgia School of Law. Professor Shedd has published numerous articles, most of which concentrate on real estate law topics. He was a contributing author for the text *Real Estate Principles* by Charles F. Floyd, published by Random House. In 1980, Professor Shedd received the American Business Law Association Faculty Award of Excellence. In addition to that organization, he is a member of the American Bar Association and the State Bar of Georgia.

CHARLES F. FLOYD is Professor and Chairman of the Department of Real Estate and Legal Studies at the University of Georgia. He received his Ph.D. in Economics from the University of North Carolina at Chapel Hill. Professor Floyd has authored approximately forty articles in the fields of real estate, transportation and land-use planning, and regional development and has co-authored books on highway beautification and Georgia regional economics with Peter J. Shedd. He is a member of the American Institute of Certified Planners, as well as other academic and professional organizations, and serves on the National Advisory Committee on Outdoor Advertising and Motorist Information.